# THE
# SMALL
# GARDEN

# THE
# SMALL
# GARDEN

## JOHN BROOKES

## MARSHALL CAVENDISH

This edition produced in 1997 for Borders Group Inc, USA  by
Marshall Cavendish Books, London
(a division of Marshall Cavendish Partworks, Ltd)

ISBN  1–85435–885–5


Printed and bound in Dubai, UAE

Landscape architects and professional garden designers were responsible for many of the individual gardens featured on pages 110–175, as follows:

David E. Arbegast and Mai K. Arbegast: pages 162–163
John Brookes: pages 110–111, 138–139, 141–143
Roberto Coelho Cardozo, Inst.Arch. (Brazil): l.a.: pages 167–169
Wolfgang R. Mueller and Gregor Schmitz: pages 156–157
Ian Mylles: pages 116, 150–151
Åge Nicolaisen, Park Director B.S.: page 122
Han Njio: pages 154–155
Frank Pettersson: 160–161
John Roberts, Dip. Hort.: page 146
Takashi Sawano: pages 124–125
Malcolm Scott: pages 112–113
Victor A. Shanley: page 164
Victor A. Shanley of Clifton Nurseries, London: pages 140, 165
Geoffrey Smith, AIPRA, FILA: pages 128–129, 132–135
David Stevens (for *Homes and Gardens*): pages 117–119
Tuinarchitektenburo Mien Ruys, Hans Veldhoen,
Arend Jan van der Horst bv: pages 130–131, 170–172
Valerie Winter, MSIAD: page 166

The following gardens were designed by the owners themselves:

E. Beedham: pages 152–153
Eva Dickson: pages 114–115
James Gardner: pages 144–145
Dmitri Kasterine: pages 158–159
John Lapberry: page 123
Lee von Hasseln: pages 136–137
Keith Winnett: pages 126–127
W. L. Yuille, ARIBA: pages 147–149

(and the gardens on pages 120–121 and 173–175)

# contents

## Successful small gardens

## Designing with plants

## Living in the garden

# your design

## all things considered

*Before starting to plan your own garden in detail, it is worth looking first at the treatment of small gardens throughout history and then at distinctive contemporary styles and uses. Practical considerations of soil and climate will also have to be made before you can design a garden tailored to your personal requirements.*

# History of the small garden

Where space is restricted, the design of that space becomes all-important. A brief look at the garden in history still has a relevance for the owners of small gardens today, even though the terms of reference were often quite different. Many of the elements which make up the design of today's small garden have historical antecedents, while the number of old gardens which actually remain indicates that they have stood the test of time visually and as places for use.

In its earliest form the garden was basically an enclosure, made of thorn or scrub, to keep out marauding animals and keep in domestic ones. The enclosures later took the form of a mud wall, and were a defence against other humans as much as animals or were intended to shield off the heat of the sun. When nomadic communities settled, the enclosures became places for growing both food and plants. This creation of a small private sanctuary characterized early enclosed gardens all over the world, though their function of course varied according to climate and way of life.

### Early formal gardens
The earliest recorded gardens, seen in Egypt about 3000 BC, were surrounded by a mud wall to absorb some of the sun's heat. The house was also within this square or rectangular enclosure. The formal layout of early gardens was necessitated by the need for irrigation channels to provide water in a hot, dry climate. These divided the garden into geometric areas and, in the grander gardens, the irrigation channels became formal pools with fish and there were arbours to sit under, overhung with vines, and shade-giving palms. The Egyptians grew onions, which were their staple diet, and other vegetables and herbs for their medicinal value.

This basically formal style of garden characterized the whole Islamic world during the next few thousand years. The enclosed paradise gardens of Persia were often walled and the walls hung with grape vines and climbers. Fruit trees were cultivated, including peach, apple, cherry, banana, date, fig and olive. The Persians also grew flowers such as poppies, lilies, chrysanthemums, narcissi and roses in formal beds between the stylized cruciform shape of the water canals. The idea of a flowering paradise within a formal setting is captured in Persian writings, painted miniatures and woven into carpet patterns.

The Indian and later the Moorish garden evolved from the Persian *glorieta*. Water was the essential thread of continuity, weaving through and linking different planted areas, while creating a cooling effect. The Moorish influence stretched along the whole of north Africa, into Sicily and southern Italy and thence to the Sierra Nevada in southern Spain. The style and form of the garden remained much the same, enclosed by buildings and high walls to provide shade and privacy. They were designed for outdoor living while remaining within the confines of the house.

The Moorish garden in Spain generally consisted of several courtyards, known as patios, with water as the connecting link.

This fresco, found on the tomb of Nebamun in Thebes, dates from about 1400 BC. It shows the garden of a private estate with an ornamental fish pond in the centre. Fruit trees and vines are growing with palm trees to give shade from the intense heat of the sun

Some of the best water gardens were created in northern India, to provide a sublime setting for the outdoor life of the emperor and his court. This Persian miniature shows Babur, founder of the Mogul dynasty, directing the layout of the Bagh-i-Vafa, the Garden of Fidelity. It captures perfectly the intimate atmosphere and the gaiety of court life. The irrigation channels create a symmetrical design by dividing the site into four, while the abundance of nature is seen in the orange and pomegranate trees surrounding the reservoir

Many patios contained a long canal with a central fountain and there were ornate pillars and tiled walls and floors. Cypress or orange trees were planted in sunken beds and usually lined the walls to give extra shade, while aromatic plants grown in pots along the edge of the water scented the air.

From Spain, where even the grand palace gardens were divided into small walled enclosures, the paradise garden tradition can be traced to South America. From there it spread to the idyllic climate of California, where it was eventually metamorphosed into today's patio garden, with the element of water often present in the blue waters of the swimming pool.

### Greeks and Romans

The Greeks discovered the delights of Persian culture, including their paradise gardens, when they were waging war in Asia during the third century BC. They were more interested in public life out of doors but wrote on the subject of gardens and gardening. During the first century BC we also hear of influential Greeks having vegetables planted in their gardens, to furnish their tables. Homer wrote of Alcinous' large walled garden which grew vegetables, including beans, with an orchard of apple, pear and fig trees. Olive trees and a vineyard were also mentioned.

The Romans put into practice what the Greeks wrote but the Roman garden was brought into the centre of the house, becoming an even more important part of domestic life. We know of the ground pattern of early Roman town houses from excavations at Pompeii and villas elsewhere,

and of their garden design from the letters of Pliny the younger. The central courtyard within a colonnaded peristyle (known as an *atrium*) became a major feature of the house and was, in effect, the main living area; it still survives today in the cathedral court and cloister. The garden layouts were much on the Greek pattern, architectural and formal and made up of flower beds and paths, pergolas and statuary with fountains and pools for irrigation. Flowers such as the violet, poppy, iris, lily and pansy were popular and, in particular, the rose. Climbing plants were trained up the supporting columns of covered walks and pergolas.

The Romans carried vegetable growing much further in their country homes because it was the main form of sustenance for rich and poor alike. Salad crops were grown and cabbage was said to be the favourite vegetable. Cato also wrote of turnips, beans, garlic, asparagus and radishes and later writers added carrots, onions, peas, lettuce, chicory, parsley, fennel, parsnips and melons. When the Romans went as conquerors to Europe, they introduced various plants, vegetables and fruit to different countries, together with their knowledge of agriculture and horticulture.

### From the Dark Ages to the Middle Ages

Very little development in gardens took place in Europe for several centuries following the end of the Roman Empire. It is thought that knowledge of horticulture virtually died out and only those plants which managed to naturalize themselves

survived. However it is known that leeks, cabbages and dried beans and peas formed some sort of subsistence diet throughout this time.

Enclosed gardens gradually reappeared on a small scale at the end of the Dark Ages, within the confines of monasteries and fortified buildings. The monasteries were laid out on a Roman court and cloister plan and inside the court monks cultivated medicinal plants, herbs and some vegetables. The beds were divided by straight paths and there was sometimes a fish pond too. Within castle walls the ladies also began to grow herbs for medicinal and culinary use, with the occasional raised bed for flowers where space allowed. A garden plan survives from the ninth century for the monastery of St Gall in Switzerland, showing a cloister garden of flower beds, a herb garden containing sixteen raised rectangular beds and a vegetable garden consisting of eighteen raised beds.

Much more information exists about European than about British medieval gardens and it is generally assumed that English monastic and private gardens were less advanced, remaining essentially utilitarian until the early sixteenth century.

As times became more peaceful throughout Europe the defence walls were lowered, the garden area grew larger and a simple formal design developed. Illustrations in herbals and books of poetry such as the *Romance of the Rose* show walled and trellised gardens connected by arched doorways and adorned with fountains, close-clipped hedges, mulberry bushes and turf-topped seats. The English term 'knot

In the Generalife, the white-walled summer palace of the rulers of Granada, Spain, the *Patio de la Riadh* (Courtyard of the Pool) reflects the true spirit of the Arab garden. Its curving jets of water fall into the flower-edged central canal and the floor is tiled, matching the walls of the tiled palace itself

The Moorish tradition is still very much alive in this Californian water garden. Brick paving has replaced the tiled floor and the fountain is less spectacular but the design is still formal and symmetrical and the high walls give the garden a private, enclosed feeling

garden' refers to the style of flower beds which now evolved. They were small, usually raised, and laid out in geometric patterns, edged with dwarf clipped shrubs such as box or thrift or with a herb like rosemary. The most intricate designs were simply filled with gravel or coloured earth while more open beds contained flowering plants such as lilies, gilleyflowers, lavender, primroses, marigolds and roses. There were also orchards and vegetable gardens and among the fruit and vegetables mentioned were cherries, apples, pears, wild strawberries, vines, onions, peas, garlic, leeks, lettuces, turnips, radish and spinach.

### Italian and French Renaissance
The Italian Renaissance saw a dramatic development in the whole concept of gardens. In the early fifteenth century, as trade started to flourish again, merchants in the hot city of Florence began to build villas or farms on the surrounding vineyard hills where it was cooler. The earliest Renaissance gardens were at first in the formal, enclosed tradition but gradually a view was allowed into the garden through a hole in the wall. As a natural view became more important the enclosures were swept away and the hillside gardens were allowed to stride down their sites through olive groves and vineyards.

During the sixteenth century the initiative passed to Rome, where the architect Bramante designed a papal garden within the Vatican. This was the forerunner of the High Renaissance style, with a magnificent arrangement of steps and terraces, which became a prototype for everything which followed. From then on gardens became even more ostentatious in design, with

terraces at different levels retained by walls and interconnected by grand staircases. Water again became a major feature, as it was in Islamic gardens. It was pressurized and used spectacularly, progressing down an incline or displayed in an elaborate fountain. While these Renaissance gardens were still places for cool retreat, with shade and water of great importance, they were also showplaces where the site and its vegetation were deliberately manipulated. The Italians were really the first to make decorative use of plants, with hedges, for example, used to link the house and garden structurally.

The Renaissance movement originating in Italy spread northwards, together with increased knowledge about plants and their cultivation. In France the small formal gardens within the walls of moated châteaux moved outside, becoming much grander in scope. Unlike the Italian hillside gardens, the French ones were flat and straight, most of them situated in the flat marshy areas to the south and west of Paris. The style was still very geometric, as the original pattern of formal beds within a grid system of paths was simply repeated in order to enlarge the garden.

In the seventeenth century André le Nôtre changed French garden planning significantly. With the opening of the château garden at Vaux-le-Vicomte in 1661 he established a style which was to influence the whole of Europe for a century. His gardens were still basically formal and geometric in character but they became much more elaborate and interesting with long magnificent vistas, pools or rectangular canals and grand parterres. Parterres were both larger in scale and more intricate in

detail than earlier knot gardens. Another distinctive characteristic was the hedge-lined avenues which fanned out through the surrounding forest known as *pattes d'oie* (goose feet). Le Nôtre was appointed royal gardener to Louis XIV and the garden at Versailles is probably his best known creation. In concept it was a vast outdoor drawing room, intended for the entertainment of a court of thousands.

Though most of Le Nôtre's gardens were unashamedly for show they were still not places for colour or floral display; canalized and playing water, clipped and trained vegetation, statuary and the elaborate parterres provided the visual interest, along with the people walking about in them. This stylized layout, originally designed for large châteaux, was adapted to the quite humble manor house. Like the grand Italian gardens, as they became out of scale with the use of the individual, a smaller secret garden had to be created within them for family use.

At this stage garden design was fairly international in character and more or less uniform throughout Europe. The Germans imitated the Italian Renaissance style but readily switched to the grand geometric French style when it became dominant. The main historical contribution of Germany has been a numerical one—in the sixteenth century there were more gardens in Germany than in any other country in Europe—and a certain exaggeration of the elements in any style they adopted. The French formal style of gardening also flourished in the sandy soil of Holland, on a smaller and less sophisticated scale but with more emphasis on hedges, fantastic topiary and decorative planting. Their box-edged formal beds were filled with tulips in the spring, brought back from the Middle East. The Dutch were responsible, through their trading and through their rise as a colonial power, for the introduction of much imported plant material—from China, America, South Africa and many other countries. They introduced the lilac, the pelargonium and the chrysanthemum into Europe and popularized tulips and many other bulbs.

In the same way that English medieval gardens remained pale counterparts of the elegant and colourful enclosures found in Europe, the gardens of English royalty and aristocracy developed on the lines of Italian and French Renaissance layouts during the sixteenth and seventeenth centuries. They were, however, less rigorously formal, since the English climate is more conducive to mixed planting. There was also a developing interest in horticulture and a new emphasis on flowers grown for their appearance rather than for culinary and medicinal use.

One of the first gardens in the grand formal style was at Hampton Court Palace,

The house at Pompeii looks inwards on to a colonnaded peristyle or cloister with the peaceful courtyard garden in the centre. The walls of the cloister are painted with outdoor scenes which compensate for the lack of a view and make the area an outside living room for all activities

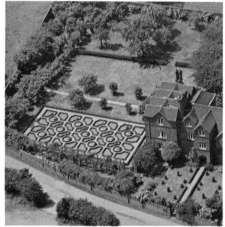

The English knot garden reconstructed at Moseley Old Hall is based on the original seventeenth-century design. Dwarf box hedges form the traditional geometric beds, with a standard 'mophead' *Buxus* in the centre of each part of the repeated pattern. Three colours of gravel are used to form the decorative infill for the beds

The reconstructed château garden at Villandry, France, shows the simple geometric features of medieval monastic gardens becoming grander and more elaborate. The symbolic garden, with its intricate parterres of clipped box hedges, represents different kinds of love while the *potager* or vegetable garden is designed for colour and beauty as well as food production, with its box enclosures round every patch of vegetables

The Italian Renaissance produced some spectacular gardens. At the Villa d'Este at Tivoli, water provides the great display, cascading down terraces carved out of the hillsides and creating this dramatic waterfall. Terraces are edged with balustrading and the theatrical setting is perfectly complemented by statuary, which was left over from ancient Roman sites and readily available in medieval Italian states

later emulated by all the Tudor nobility. The flower beds were laid out in a knot garden pattern and other characteristics included mazes, labyrinths, gazebos or pavilions, topiary, sundials, trellis and arbours. Vegetable gardens were usually walled and separate from the main garden. After 1660 the influence of Le Nôtre made itself felt briefly: grand parterres replaced simple knots and vast lakes and canals replaced the gentle fountain, while broad beech-lined avenues stretched out to the horizon. Though the English could not match the Italians or French as designers, nor the Dutch as growers, the closely-cut lawn was one feature of English gardens which attracted international admiration.

The seventeenth century was a time for pioneers on the English gardening scene. The first gardening text books appeared, the interest in horticulture increased and a great search for new plants began. The earliest botanic gardens were opened and there was an increasing use of orangeries and conservatories to protect tender plants. Men like London and Wise set up the first commercial nurseries and began selling plants throughout the land.

### The English landscape movement

During the eighteenth century a revolution took place in England, influenced by writers, landscape painters and philosophers, all of whom began to react against the artificiality of formal gardens. Literary men such as Addison, Steele and Pope theorized about the curved line and the irregularity of nature, and Jean-Jacques Rousseau's idea of the romantic natural garden also tied in with the new movement.

Formal gardens were entirely swept away by the designers of the landscape school and superb parkland layouts created in their place. Far from the mastery of nature, this was an attempt to improve and idealize her and for the next hundred years anything small was considered unworthy. In the hands of first William Kent, who pioneered the movement, followed by 'Capability' Brown and Humphrey Repton, contours were altered, hills built and valleys excavated; straight paths and avenues were abandoned and straight canals turned into serpentined lakes. Nature was triumphant—though in fact the freedom and naturalness were very carefully contrived. The sense of vast space could be very deceptive as landowners planted trees at the boundaries to obscure where an estate ended. There were no walls or hedges but instead the device of the ha-ha, a sunken ditch, was invented to keep animals out.

The style of this new movement spread all over Europe. In Germany, as in England, the earlier grand formal gardens were actually destroyed to make way for the new landscaped parks. The French, however, instead of destroying their formal heritage, simply set a pastoral landscape alongside or within the formal garden.

### Towards the twentieth century

While Europe was following the fashionable style of the English landscape garden, the quite different Victorian age of gardening

began in England. There was a general return to a classical and geometric layout but it was distinguished by cluttered ornamentation and over-patterned, brightly coloured flower beds. The villa garden really came into its own in the second half of the nineteenth century with the rapid growth of urban, industrial civilization. An emergent middle class began to move out into the suburbs or even the country, which meant that many more people had gardens of their own and an interest in gardening greatly increased.

Gardening publications and an unsurpassed interest in plants were the greatest influences on the design of the first suburban gardens. The books and magazines of John Loudon and his wife Jane first brought ideas on gardening to the middle classes, in particular *The Gardener's Magazine* which first appeared in 1826 and their book, *The Suburban Gardener and Villa Companion*, published in 1838. The era of plant-breeding had begun in Europe— a 'tulipmania' was dominant in Holland and in England the Royal Horticultural Society had been founded in 1804. The

many new plant discoveries at this time included conifers, anemones, winter jasmine, forsythia, primulas, rhododendrons and azaleas. The most significant aspect of this era of gardening is that it established the prime importance of plants in the creation of a garden.

The English garden as we know it today owes most to two Victorians, William Robinson and Gertrude Jekyll, and the influence of their ideas. William Robinson wrote a book, *The Wild Garden*, which called for natural gardens planted with shrubs and trees from other countries and then left to themselves. He was greatly influenced by having seen plants growing naturally in alpine meadows on his travels abroad. Gertrude Jekyll planted gardens as well as writing on the subject. She had a strong sense of colour, planting flowers and foliage for particular colour effect, but called attention also to leaf shapes and texture, especially of grey-leaved plants.

Many of the gardens planted by Gertrude Jekyll were for large country houses (often designed by the architect Edwin Lutyens) and were tended by gardeners. But the

The placing and sensitive juxtaposition of the plants in Gertrude Jekyll's herbaceous border are brought to life by her intuitive feeling for colour and texture. Woodland and water provide an appropriate 'natural' setting

The idealized re-creation of a natural landscape, seen here at Stourhead, England, made garden design a definite art form. The absence of straight lines, hedges and walls was in direct contrast to the formality of earlier gardens. Though hills and lakes were man-made the overall effect was reminiscent of a vast pastoral landscape

Unlike the vast geometric designs of Europe, Japanese gardens have always been asymmetric and on a more human scale. Every natural element is selected and placed with great restraint, as in this sand and moss garden at the Tofukuji Temple, Kyoto

writings of Miss Jekyll and William Robinson also coincided with the restoration and rehabilitation of long-neglected smaller country houses, farmhouses and cottages and their ideas appealed equally to these self-sufficient gardeners. Gertrude Jekyll invented the herbaceous border, planted with roses, shrubs and hardy plants, which has an element of romanticism always associated with the traditional English cottage garden.

Gertrude Jekyll even had advice for the owners of terraced town houses with only a dingy yard at basement level. She advocated that even the most modest scheme should contain at least one distinctive ornament, a fountain or a raised bed, as a focal point of interest. She suggested vines, Virginia creeper and a few ferns as the plants most likely to survive but it was generally considered at the time that soot and dirt made town gardening impossible.

The twentieth century has seen large gardens become an economic impossibility and small ones multiply. Garden cities have been conceived and built, each house having its own individual garden. No one

style has emerged as representative of the age but influences from different countries and different movements can quite easily be traced.

The garden is again part of the living unit, as it had been in ancient Roman times, rather than merely a showcase. At the same time economic pressure has revived the interest in cultivating vegetables and herbs that was shown in the medieval gardens. Perhaps the most significant change is that increased leisure time for everybody has at last made the garden a hobby or interest, to be enjoyed by many people, and no longer the prerogative of the rich and privileged.

### Japanese gardens

An assessment of the garden in history, however brief, cannot ignore the pervasive influence of oriental garden design. Gardening was a craft in China in ancient times and it crossed the sea to Japan in the seventh century AD to develop into a distinctive style of its own, which continues basically unchanged to this day. Japanese gardens today are small and surrounded by high

walls, as privacy is greatly prized; they create a landscape to be viewed from the house rather than a living area in itself. The aim is a sense of harmony with nature, to create a mood of rest and peace, and this is achieved not by imitating but by re-creating nature on a different scale.

The charm of Japanese gardens lies in their overall shape and design and in individual shapes and textures. There is a strict control over the diverse elements in the garden and the importance of each item in relation to the whole. The essential elements of Japanese design are stone and rocks, earth, sand and water, each used with a precise consideration of scale and balance. There is a restrained and very selective use of plants and blossoming fruit trees. Originally each element had a mystical significance though now the aesthetic effect is equally if not more important. In a country where space is strictly limited, the Japanese designers exploit the beauty and dramatic significance of every resource. Their lessons are particularly significant for present-day small gardens everywhere.

# Getting the style right

A garden should work as an extension of the house both practically and visually. While the form which a garden takes evolves primarily from its function, the style must above all be in sympathy with its location. Very occasionally a contrast in style can work by shock tactics, but in the main this is not a good idea.

The first problem is to recognize your style. For those who live in an old period house there is no difficulty, but for the vast majority who live in modern suburban houses it is more tricky. If your plot has any long-established features, such as a group of old trees, it may be a good idea to retain these and let them to a certain extent influence the style of your garden. The biggest problem arises with a badly neglected plot or where the site of the garden is little more than a barren heap of builder's rubble.

As a starting point, give some thought to building materials, then to the interior style of the house itself. All materials, to a degree, dictate how they should be used. In planning your garden try above all to avoid mixing materials and styles as it is rarely successful. Plants too have very definite characteristics and the selection of them will certainly influence the overall look of the garden. But the choice of materials must come first when establishing the layout and basic style.

With a small garden, be aware of the limitations of your plot. The challenge is to achieve the desired effect within narrow boundaries, always bearing in mind that a visual link between the house and the garden is of great importance.

### Choosing your materials

The character of any particular region, town or village will have developed partly from the materials available at any one time and the way in which it was possible to put these together. The village is in this sense organic, in that it springs from the ground of which it was made and therefore has an inherent fitness.

Look at the older buildings in your area which will probably be in the local material (the parish church is often a good guide to materials and how they were used, both inside and out). The local material is usually the cheapest and, if not available new, can often be bought second-hand. Many areas have no local rock, in which case the construction traditionally would be in wood or where clay was available in brick, though today more and more houses are built of concrete. Introducing an alien material into an area may also affect the scale of your design. The scale and shapes of a garden pattern link the garden to the house and surroundings as much as the materials used.

### Relating the outside to the inside

Now consider the interior of your house; it will, of course, be dictated by family use as well as aesthetic considerations. It is equally important that the style of the garden is in keeping with the inside if the house and garden are to be seen as a whole. Not only does the house lead out to the garden and thus form a unit in the physical sense but the garden can usually be seen from the

windows of the house and should harmonize with the interior as much as possible.

In this context it is often easier to define style in a negative way: concrete slabs, for instance, lack the subtlety and texture needed for paving a cottage garden, and asbestos pots would be out of character in the garden of a traditional brick house. In very broad terms, the rustic effect of country-style furnishings would call for a garden with a sweep of lawn and planting in herbaceous borders while a sophisticated modern interior will be complemented by a more streamlined type of garden with a stronger use of plant materials, concrete and cobble. Traditionalists will want a gentle, harmonious layout, with perhaps stone, soft curves and a glint of water. Many other

types of house, such as the summer house retreat, the seaside villa and the town house all have particular characteristics which call for a particular style of garden.

Once the fundamental style of your garden has emerged, from a consideration of building materials and the interior look of your house, from then on each individual's garden is unique. Its character grows partly out of practical solutions to practical problems and relates also to the specific functions the garden is expected to perform. At a later stage planting will of course flesh out the bones of your garden and give it finally a very particular feel. The constraints of existing features, local climate and soil will also have to be considered; they are dealt with in subsequent chapters.

A meadow garden, though seemingly easy to create, will only work in a rural situation. The totally natural effect, achieved simply by allowing wild flowers to seed themselves and grass to grow long, makes an appropriate setting for a simple country house. Brick is one of the most suitable materials for a rural setting, lending itself to gentle curves

The design of a modern house will be echoed in the use of severe paving materials and bold clumps of plants within a basic geometric layout. Discreet touches such as texturing the paving slabs and using gravel and natural stone as secondary materials will relieve the austerity of unadorned concrete. Planting can soften the harsh lines of a house by framing it and climbing up the walls

In a roof or balcony garden it is particularly important that the materials used link it with the house of which it forms an extension. Quarry tiles, being light, are suitable for inside and outside flooring; their rich tones also tie in with the tiles on surrounding roofs. Simple containers filled with flowering plants add enough colour to make such a tiny space a visual pleasure

Stark contrasts and vivid colours are best suited to gardens in a hot climate, especially those in a seaside setting. White walls and flowers in brilliant hues could look harsh in dull weather but they are brought to life when seen against a blue sky and under very bright sunlight

The influence of Japanese design is unmistakable. It owes its uniqueness to the careful choice of materials and plants and the shape and placing of each element. The unity and scale of the design allows materials to be combined in a seemingly natural way without creating any lack of harmony

The use of indigenous materials, where they are readily available, will link house and garden together and blend them perfectly with their surroundings. Stone is particularly versatile: it can be used in rough-hewn blocks for walls or laid flat in a crazy pattern; gravel, formed from stone chippings, will also harmonize well with it

18

The way in which elements of a design are used dictates the style of garden as much as the choice of them. A flat, rectangular expanse of water complements a very modern, streamlined house while a deep natural pond overhung with abundant planting is much more suited to a rural setting

Where a garden is looked down upon, as in a town basement, lush planting might well become the most significant influence in its style. Flowers overhanging their beds, in containers and covering the walls create a lively, colourful scene

Wood is an ideal material for blending a house into a natural setting, especially one surrounded by trees. Where wood is used in the house construction it becomes an even more appropriate medium

A front garden has to welcome visitors so its style is important. While bushy growth gives privacy to this garden, planting is kept low to one side for easy access and an unobstructed view

Where a garden seems a part of the house visually, its style should match that of the inside. A rectangular garden design will echo the uncluttered lines of a streamlined interior

Where appropriate, a traditional style can be the most successful. In an old cottage garden, every bit of space would be used for growing, with flowers intermingling with vegetables and spilling over walls and path

# Designed to meet your needs

A historical survey shows that the form of the garden was to a large extent dictated by its function. The function, in turn, was affected by many things, including climate and lifestyle. From the Renaissance onwards most gardens were large and designed mainly for show and for tranquil pursuits such as the gentle stroll; they were invariably tended by gardeners. At the other extreme there was also the tradition of the cottager's garden, used for growing vegetables and for keeping a pig and a few chickens.

Today the situation is very different: the twentieth century has brought increased leisure, while gardens have become smaller and available to many more people. The interest in gardening continues to grow but is, nevertheless, only one of many demands on our leisure time. It is therefore important that a garden is well designed from the outset, with the owner's requirements taken into consideration, so that it can be safely left to mature in the way it was planned without needing constant attention.

Having reached certain conclusions about the overall style of your garden, the first stage in planning it out is to consider how you will use it. The restricted space of today's small gardens should not be considered as a handicap; it is simply another factor which makes the initial planning all-important.

The illustrations show how the same garden area, 9 m long by 7·5 m wide (30 ft by 25 ft), can be planned to suit the varying requirements of seven different people or families. The plans not only demonstrate the enormous range of needs and activities which can be catered for within such a limited space, they also show how a design based on individual needs will transform the same basic plot into a unique, well planned garden.

## Planning for changing needs

The demands of a single family can vary enormously over a number of years. Where they are likely to be in the same home for some time it is important that the garden plan is flexible enough to reflect these changing needs. A young couple might use the garden mainly for sunbathing or entertaining and would want a simple layout which is easy to look after. The arrival of children would impose many new demands, from pram-standing space to soft play areas and tricycle runs. With a growing family a bigger area of the garden might be devoted to vegetables, with a large terrace space for outdoor activities and family meals.

As children leave home the garden area should become quieter and parents should have more time to spend in it. They may concentrate more on the plants themselves, possibly with special interests developing such as roses or a greenhouse. However, what can be looked after with ease at fifty becomes something of a chore at seventy.

When an elaborate layout becomes too complicated for eventual maintenance, it will be necessary to reduce the need for intensive gardening, preferably in a way which retains the original effect.

In the family life cycle of a garden its use can grow and expand and then slowly reduce its scope again. The demands on it may vary from, at one extreme, providing a tranquil retreat after a noisy day working in town to creating the need for physical exercise in otherwise sedentary lives.

However it is laid out and whatever the individual requirements it meets, a garden should always serve as an extension of the house. It should be seen as an outside room or rooms where suitable activities can take place—from shelling peas to tinkering with a motor cycle. During warm summer months the garden may well be in almost constant use, not only for sunbathing but also for family barbecues and outdoor entertaining.

The garden may also at any time need to provide a place for a car, possibly a caravan or even a boat. It might have to include an oil storage tank, dustbin enclosure, compost heap or rubbish dump and must work efficiently for deliveries and collections. In addition its frontage must enhance the house and be welcoming for guests. Making such a number of demands on a small area of land calls for very careful planning if it is to fulfil all its roles successfully.

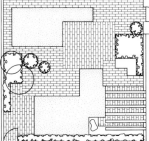

This courtyard garden, planned for people with limited leisure time, is a haven of peace and privacy. Being enclosed and secluded, it is ideal for sunbathing as it traps the sun. The brick paved areas which take up most of the space are set at slightly different levels to add interest. The entertaining area, with built-in seats and barbecue, is screened from the house by a bed of evergreen shrubs; the overhead pergola makes it a pleasant and romantic corner for eating or sitting out on summer evenings

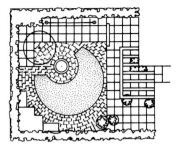

A garden for children should be designed to convert easily to a decorative layout at a later date. The circular lawn gives a soft area to play on and the brick paving around it makes a circuit for tricycles and wheeled toys. The small bed in the corner is for children's use and the raised sandpit cuts down the sand thrown about. A wide terrace adjoins the house for outdoor family meals and the pergola built out to hide the garage wall provides a shady standing space for a pram and for children's bicycles

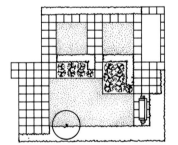

This garden is designed for a retired couple or indeed anyone who enjoys gardening and has the time to devote to it. The greenhouse and vegetable patches are sited so as not to dominate the area but they must be accessible from the house by means of a hard path; fruit trees are trained along the boundary fence. Mixed and colourful planting includes flowers grown specially for cutting and some beds devoted to roses. The seat is placed to get the benefit of the flowering plants—their perfume and their beauty

23

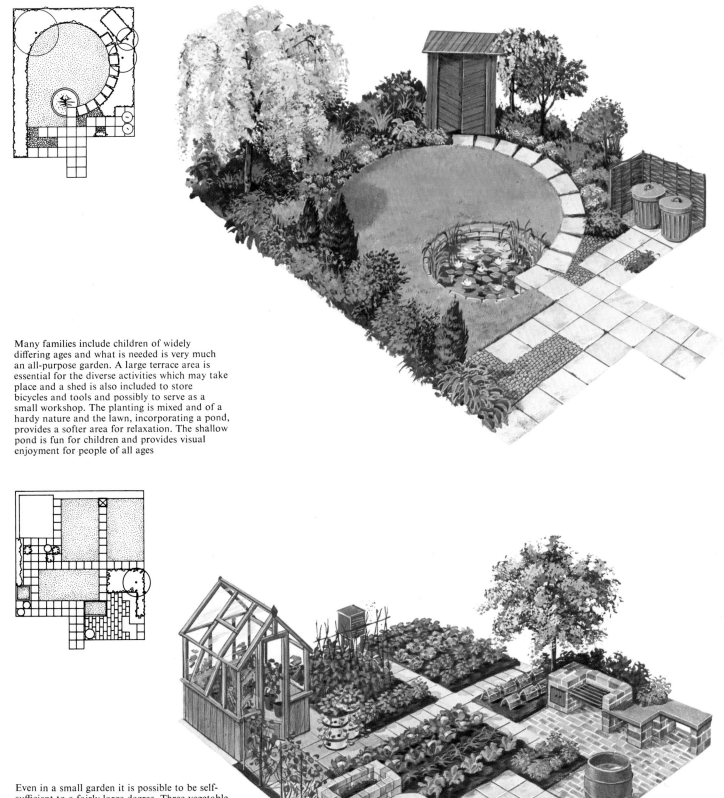

Many families include children of widely
differing ages and what is needed is very much
an all-purpose garden. A large terrace area is
essential for the diverse activities which may take
place and a shed is also included to store
bicycles and tools and possibly to serve as a
small workshop. The planting is mixed and of a
hardy nature and the lawn, incorporating a pond,
provides a softer area for relaxation. The shallow
pond is fun for children and provides visual
enjoyment for people of all ages

Even in a small garden it is possible to be self-
sufficient to a fairly large degree. Three vegetable
areas, approximately 2·5 m by 4 m (about 7 ft
by 12 ft) allow for the correct rotation of crops;
they are linked by hard paving which also leads
to the greenhouse. Space is used to the full with
a small beehive at the end of the garden, strawberries growing in pots and fruit trees against
the boundary fence. The compost and rubbish
area is tucked away in a corner and adjacent to
the house is a small terrace and a herb bed

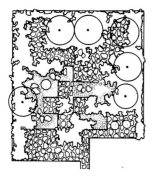

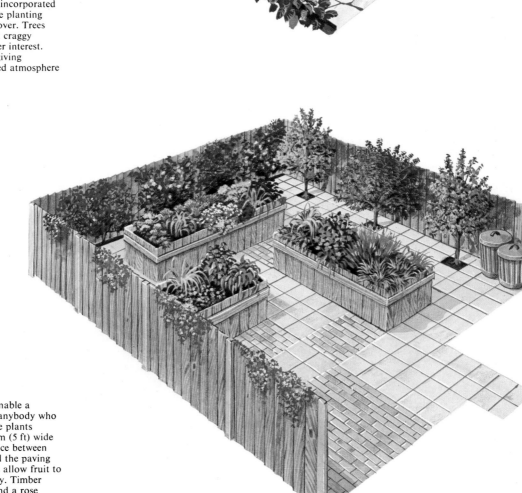

This garden is designed for the horticulturist with an overriding interest in plants. It has been given a definite character by the inclusion of boulders and a low birdbath to create the detailed Japanese effect. Areas of gravel are incorporated in the main paving, and much of the planting includes low-maintenance ground cover. Trees too are Japanese in feel, including a craggy pine whose twisted shape adds winter interest. The fence is shrouded with plants, giving the whole garden a pleasant, enclosed atmosphere

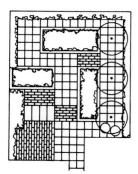

Beds are raised by timber walls to enable a disabled person in a wheelchair, or anybody who finds it difficult to bend, to reach the plants easily. They are not more than 1·5 m (5 ft) wide so that all sides can be reached. Space between the beds allows manoeuvrability and the paving is smooth and level. Bush fruit trees allow fruit to be picked and the trees pruned easily. Timber fencing, clad with climbing plants and a rose hedge, echoes the walls of the beds, giving a unified feel to the garden

# Knowing your soil

Soil is the medium in which most plants grow. From the gardener's point of view, its most important characteristics are its depth, its texture and its chemical composition. It is essential to find out all you can about the type of soil you have, but the way in which you adapt and improve it is of even greater significance in determining what plants will grow successfully.

### Depth of the soil

The topsoil is the essential layer for plant growth. Its texture and composition generally depend upon the parent rock from which it has very gradually been formed, by the interaction of water, climate and vegetation. Weathering agents such as frost, rain and sun break the rock down over thousands of years to form the basic mineral structure of the soil. Plants grow on the rock debris and myriads of micro-organisms work on the dead roots and fallen leaves to decay them, producing the essential organic constituent of the topsoil, known as humus.

In some parts of the world however the soil bears no relation to the rock beneath it because it has been carried to its place by a natural force: the material pushed along by a glacier, for example, forms a type of soil known as boulder clay, and the silt washed down by rivers builds up into alluvial soils.

The depth of topsoil varies. A site recently left by a builder may have no topsoil at all (or it may be covered by the subsoil layer), while in parts of the Mississippi Basin the rich alluvial deposits are 6 m (about 20 ft) deep. The average garden has between 300 mm and 600 mm (1 ft and 2 ft) of topsoil, but a depth of as little as 150 mm (6 in) is sufficient for growing a large number of plants.

You can test the depth of topsoil by the use of a soil auger, a tool like a giant corkscrew, which will bring up a sample of the soil profile, the several layers from which it is formed. A simpler test is to dig a hole with steep sides and so make the soil profile visible in that way. The hole will also show you how quickly the top- or subsoil drains after rain.

For the revitalization of an old garden, many writers suggest removal of the soured topsoil and its replacement with new, but this is both difficult to obtain and expensive. (On the basis of the calculation that it takes 25 mm—1 in—of topsoil a thousand years to develop, it is, of course, cheap.) When buying topsoil, it is important to establish its source and to be sure that it is 'vegetable' topsoil, with organic content, and free of disease and weeds. Beware especially of the roots of weeds such as couch grass.

A period of deep cultivation and the addition of plenty of organic material will increase the amount of topsoil already in a garden by encouraging bacteria to work within the top layers of subsoil.

Between topsoil and parent bed rock there may be many layers of stone and gravel, but the layer immediately beneath the topsoil is generally the subsoil. Its depth varies according to the hardness of the underlying rock and the amount of erosion it has suffered. The colour and texture of subsoil are usually different from those of the topsoil because it is in a transitional stage, without humus or organic material. For this reason, it is not a growing medium.

### Soil texture

The texture of soil depends upon the size of the particles which make it up. All soils contain sand and clay in varying ratios but they are classified according to the dominant constituent, most readily identified by its particle size. The particle size is crucial because it controls the amounts of air and water which reach the roots of plants.

Plants must have air to breathe and water to enable them to absorb their food in soluble form.

Clay soil chiefly consists of extremely fine particles. When these become wet, their composition causes them to swell and to stick together, so that they block air from the plants' roots and make it hard for them to take in food in solution. Clay soil is heavy, difficult to work and cold, as a result of being frequently waterlogged and badly aired. When it does dry out, it tends to crack and there is a danger of plant roots being damaged.

Clay soils are naturally rich in plant nutrients but these are not always available because air and water are blocked from the roots. The addition of humus-forming materials is essential to plant life and if this is done on a regular basis it can transform a heavy clay into a fertile and workable soil.

The addition of strawy stable manure, compost or peat gives clay soil a better texture, making it warmer, more aerated and less waterlogged. Lime will also help to break up clay and reduce its acidity but it should be used only after careful thought as many plants, such as rhododendrons and azaleas, will not tolerate it. It is very difficult to rid a soil of lime once it has been added. Never add lime and manure at the same time, as they interact chemically.

Sandy soil is composed mainly of large gritty particles which do not cling together. As a result, water is absorbed easily but drains away fast, taking essential nutrients with it and leaving plants undernourished and dry. Sandy soils soon become acid and generally need frequent but small applications of lime.

One advantage of sandy soil is that it is warm, because of the easy flow of air between the large particles. The fact that it warms up quickly in spring makes it a suitable soil for early vegetable crops. In addition it is easy to dig and also to cultivate

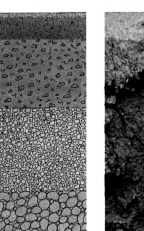

Between topsoil and rock are definite layers of subsoil, gravel and stones

A compacted clay soil cracks when it dries out. It may need artificial drainage

Sandy soil has a loose texture but water and nutrients drain through quickly

Loam has a balanced proportion of sand, clay and humus, ideal for growing plants

The limestone content of chalky soils makes them very alkaline and the topsoil thin

This chalky soil has a stony loam surface, with lumps of flint and limestone below

as organic matter is broken down fairly rapidly. Frequent watering and the addition of bulky organic material such as manure should greatly improve a sandy soil.

Strictly speaking, most garden soils are loam of one type or another. What gardeners commonly refer to as loam is the ideal growing soil, an optimum balance of sand, clay and humus. In reality the perfect loam rarely exists; most types of loam are either sandy or clayey. However the best loam is a rich, dark brown soil, made up of between 50 and 60 per cent sand particles to about 30 per cent of clay. Its other constituent, humus, is the valuable organic compound formed by decayed vegetable and animal material. When broken down completely, it forms a blackish, powdery substance. In general, the darker soils are the richer ones, as they contain more organic matter. They tend to be warmer too, as they absorb more heat from the sun's rays. This makes them early soils; they become workable before other soils in the spring.

### Chemical composition
Since parent rocks differ in mineral content, so too will the soil above them. Soil's mineral (inorganic) constituents are as important to plant growth as its texture and its organic content. Sodium, potassium, phosphorus, nitrogen, magnesium, iron and calcium are among the inorganic substances essential to plants. Some of them, such as iron, rarely need replacement; others have to be replenished by fertilizers.

A chalky soil is one which contains a high level of calcium. It is formed through the breaking down of calcium carbonate (limestone rock) by the action of the weather. Chalky soil contains white particles (called caliche) and sometimes pieces of flint. The topsoil is usually thin, allowing water to drain through and warming up quickly in spring. It is a very alkaline soil and heavy dressings of organic matter will be needed to counteract the excess lime as well as retain moisture.

Peaty soils are derived almost entirely from plants. They contain less than 50 per cent minerals and their high organic content makes them almost black in colour. Peat soils are usually wet and badly aerated and extremely acid, but the addition of lime will help to improve both conditions.

The pH scale is a scale of value for the degree of acidity or alkalinity of a soil. Soils below 7 are regarded as being acid, those above 7 as alkaline. A pH value of 7 indicates a neutral soil and an ideal garden reading is 6·5. Below 6 on the scale the extreme acidity of the soil makes it suitable only for acid-loving plants such as heathers and rhododendrons. A reading above 8 means that the soil is so alkaline that it will support few plants, due to essential foods being 'locked up' in the soil. However certain plants, such as carnations, sweet peas and onions, do prefer alkaline conditions.

One way to discover a great deal about soil—its type and fertility—is to observe the plants that grow in it naturally, including the weeds. There are also various home kits which test the acidity or alkalinity of your soil. Some register the pH value as a colour variation. It is advisable to take samples from various parts of the garden, as the level of acidity may vary from one area to another.

The level of acidity or alkalinity can be controlled by adding lime, peat and various chemicals such as sulphate of ammonia to the soil. Lime helps reduce the acid level of a peaty or sandy soil while peat and sulphur make a chalky soil less alkaline.

### Cultivating the soil
One of the best ways to improve your soil is to dig it, using a good spade or a fork for heavy clay soils. Digging will aerate the soil, kill the weeds and break up some of the subsoil so that the layer of topsoil is gradually increased. It should be done once a year, and autumn or early winter is the best time. This is particularly important with heavy clay soils, so that winter frosts will break up the compacted lumps and prepare the ground for planting in spring.

Digging should be done in small spadefuls at a time otherwise the task can be backbreaking. The roots of persistent weeds, such as couch grass, bindweed, dock, thistles or nettles, should be removed and later burned. When turning over a large area the best method is to dig in trenches, working with the last trench in front of you.

Digging to the depth of a spade is usually sufficient but with a very heavy clay soil, or for a large vegetable patch, it may be necessary to turn over the soil to two spade-depths, known as double digging. Apart from the extra effort involved, double digging is also more complicated because it goes down to the second layer, the subsoil. It is important to keep the two layers separate, so the topsoil should be lifted out of the trench and kept aside while the subsoil is broken up and turned over. Add any organic materials at this stage, forking them in well with the subsoil.

### Manure, compost and fertilizers
The addition of sufficient organic material, in the form of animal manure or vegetable compost, should cure the deficiencies of an infertile soil. In its decayed form it is known as humus and one way in which humus aids fertility is by storing nitrogen. The bacteria in the soil convert nitrogen into ammonia and this essential nutrient is released to the plant roots in the form of nitrates. Humus also absorbs and holds water so that the plant roots have time to take it up.

The texture of any type of soil will be improved as the strands of decaying vegetation will break up a sticky clay soil but bind together the large particles of sandy soil. The spaces between the crumbs of soil are sufficient for the retention of moisture but they allow any excess water to drain away. The good soil structure and aeration created assist root development.

A mixture of horse manure and straw is regarded as the best soil conditioner, as it is particularly rich in nitrogen, phosphorus and potassium and also contains good organic material. The nutrients are not in a form which can be immediately absorbed by plants but as the organic

Keep the spade upright when digging as it is less of a strain on your back. Make the trench 300 mm (1 ft) wide and dig to the approximate depth of a spade, about 250 mm (10 in)

Use a rake to spread the manure or compost evenly in the bottom of the trench. Farmyard manure will improve the soil's texture and increase its fertility by encouraging bacteria

Fill up the first trench with soil excavated from the second one, turning the soil right over in order to break it up and bury the weeds. The last trench will be filled with soil from the first one

# Establishing good drainage

material begins to decay they are converted by bacteria into chemical salts. They will eventually be taken up by the plant roots in the form of nitrates, phosphates and potash at a slow, steady rate over a long period. If the ground is planted, stack fresh farmyard manure for a while before using it as the ammonia may burn the plants.

Garden compost, formed from rotted down vegetable waste, is an excellent substitute as it returns to the soil all the materials taken out during plant growth and helps to improve the soil structure. It is a simple and economical matter to make a compost heap in the garden but careful thought should be given to the siting of it. Though it is preferable to place it out of full

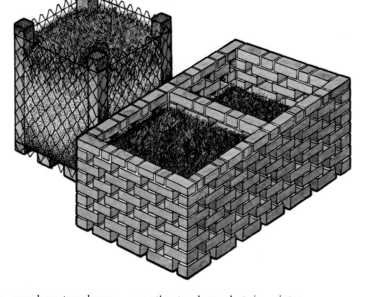

A simple container will ensure that your compost is kept in a tidy heap. The open wire structure and the honeycomb pattern of bricks allow air to pass through, which is essential if the bacteria are to do their work of breaking down the waste material. A slatted wooden structure would be equally effective. If you have space, a double compost bin allows one heap to decompose thoroughly while another is being started

view, it should not be anywhere too damp or shady or the waste matter will not rot down correctly.

Many waste materials can go on to the compost heap, from kitchen waste such as lettuce leaves and vegetable peelings to grass cuttings, dead leaves and straw—but diseased plant roots, perennial weeds or woody stems should always be burnt. The successful decomposition of this waste material depends on air, water and the action of bacteria. The bacteria depend on nitrogen for food and the rate of decay can be accelerated by sprinkling the heap with a nitrogenous fertilizer such as sulphate of ammonia or by spreading a layer of farmyard manure over it.

Each 300 mm (1 ft) layer of waste should be trodden or pressed down firmly to get rid of air pockets, and then watered. The compacted mass can be covered with a layer of soil, about 25 mm (1 in) thick, and then the farmyard manure or sulphate of ammonia if you are using it. Alternate layers can be covered with hydrated lime (unless your soil is naturally limy) instead. When the heap is the height you require, cover it with one more layer of soil and give it a watering.

Decomposition will be speeded up if the heap is turned about every six weeks,

moving waste matter from the outside into the centre and watering any dry patches. In the absence of rain, water should be sprinkled on the heap periodically—about every two weeks during a dry summer. Too much rain, however, will wash away the nutrients in the compost; during a period of heavy rainfall, a temporary cover could be placed on top.

Compost can be regarded as sufficiently decayed when the individual components can no longer be distinguished. It should be a crumbly, manure-like mass, dark in colour; if the texture is slimy the heap has not been made up correctly. In warm weather, and given the right conditions, the waste will take only about two to three months to decay but in winter you can expect it to take about four to six months.

Artificial or inorganic fertilizers are concentrated chemical salts from natural underground deposits. They are available in liquid or powder form and supply essential foods direct to the plants, acting quickly when applied to moist soils; it is important to use the exact quantity stated and to distribute it as evenly as possible, as overdoses can be harmful. Fertilizers are available containing individual chemicals or you can buy a general one which combines the three main nutrients: nitrogen (N), phosphorus (P) and potassium (K).

While the application of artificial fertilizers helps to stimulate plant growth it does nothing to improve the physical qualities of the soil. In fact over-application of these materials can cause soil deterioration by destroying bacteria. Soil texture can be improved by the addition of sterilized peat (moist, decomposing plant matter) but this has no mineral or food content at all.

The fertility of a soil is an extremely complex balance between its physiology, its humus content and its mineral content (shown by its pH value). Once a gardener understands how each factor in the balance works, he has control over his plot, over what will grow and where.

A well drained soil is essential not only for successful plant growth but also where paths and walls are to be built. It is therefore important to consider the drainage of your whole plot, not simply with regard to the growing areas.

Few plants like a lot of water around their roots and in a soil which is constantly wet the plant roots will remain near the surface or will start to rot. Wet soils are also cold, which retards plant growth. When drainage is inadequate, not only is air blocked from the plant roots but the general lack of air in the soil means that bacteria cannot live and the bacteria are a vital part of healthy soil.

It is in particular heavy clay soils which suffer from poor natural drainage; sandy or stony soils usually drain quite freely. However, where the topsoil is a stiff loam the subsoil may well be clayey and non-porous, preventing water from draining away completely.

The simplest way of testing your natural drainage is to dig a hole about 600 mm (2 ft) deep and watch what happens after heavy rain—or simply fill it with water. If the drainage is good, the water should disappear in 24 hours; if it is still there after 48 hours the drainage definitely needs improving. However, before spending money on expensive pipe drainage bear in mind that too efficient a system will impoverish your soil as the plant nutrients will be leached out very easily. Try one of several natural corrective methods first.

It is important for a gardener to know about the water table. This is the line under the topsoil or subsoil, depending on the depth of these layers, to which water standing in the earth's crust rises. It is not a horizontal line but conforms roughly to the contours of the ground.

The water table generally rises and falls following wet and dry periods. If it stands at about 900 mm (3 ft) below ground level it can be an asset, since water will be available to the deeper plant roots. However extreme fluctuations in the water table are a great danger: if it rises in winter the roots of plants are killed through saturation and if it falls in the summer the plants suffer from drought. On low-lying ground if there is perpetual standing water (usually in winter), this might mean that the water table has risen above ground level and no drainage system will relieve it.

### Simple remedies for poor drainage

Any measures taken to improve the texture and fertility of the soil will help to overcome drainage problems. Digging will aerate a clay soil, and mixing in bulky organic matter (such as peat, compost, strawy manure or dead bracken) well below the surface will improve its texture. The addition of inorganic materials such as gritty sand, weathered ashes or gypsum (calcium sulphate) will also make a clay soil more open in texture. As a rough guide, allow a bucketful of organic matter and two of inorganic for each square metre or square yard of ground.

Lime will make a clay soil more porous by breaking it up into crumb-like particles;

it also encourages earthworms, which help to aerate the soil and thus improve the drainage. Hydrated lime should be spread on top of the broken surface of the soil, not dug in but simply mixed into the top 75 mm to 100 mm (3 in to 4 in) of topsoil at the rate of about 225 g to a square metre (8 oz to 1 sq ft), preferably just before the winter.

Drainage may be impaired because the lower soil layers have consolidated into a hard 'pan' about 450 mm (18 in) below the surface. This might have been caused by continual treading or by heavy construction machinery. Double digging the whole plot may be the most effective remedy.

On new sites in particular it is common for the heavy machinery used during construction to have compacted the ground surface or a particular area of it, making it impossible for water to run through. This may be only a temporary state of affairs, so try to alleviate the situation first by spiking the ground with a fork. Alternatively, use a 'tyning fork' which goes in more deeply and takes out pieces of earth like an apple corer; then brush fine gravel into the holes.

If you have taken over a new site and some form of drainage is definitely needed, this will at least provide an excellent opportunity to get rid of any builder's rubble which you have inherited. Broken bricks or lumps of concrete should be used in the bottom of drainage pits or trenches.

### Three drainage systems

A soakaway is the simplest form of drainage for an isolated patch which stays wet after heavy rain. It is also useful to take the overflow and occasional outlet from a small garden pond.

Dig a hole about 1 m (3 ft) square and at least 1 m (3 ft) deep; it should be sufficiently deep to penetrate the impervious subsoil into something more porous below. Fill the hole first with brick or other large, hard rubble to a depth of about 600 mm (2 ft), then with about 100 mm (4 in) of gravel or ash. Finally fill with excavated topsoil up to ground level. The gravel layer is essential to prevent the coarse rubble becoming blocked with silt and soil leaching through from the soil replaced on top. During very wet weather surplus water will collect in this hole and slowly percolate from it into the lower strata. A soakaway should always be sited well away from the house, as it may weaken the surrounding soil.

A rubble drain is a short-term drainage run, which may be all that is required on a new site to relieve temporary lying water. Dig a trench 300 mm to 450 mm (1 ft to 1 ft 6 in) deep, depending on the depth of cultivated soil (since water collects on the comparatively solid pan of undisturbed ground that lies immediately beneath). Fill the hole at least half full with coarse rubble then with a layer of ash or gravel and finally topsoil.

This channel should obviously run to some form of outlet such as a soakaway—on no account allow your excess water to drain on to neighbours' property. The disadvantage of a rubble drain is that it becomes blocked comparatively quickly as soil leaches through from above.

Very bad drainage conditions may be indicated by permanent standing water but check first that this is not just a high water table. If you conclude that the drainage is totally inadequate you will need to lay a system of underground pipes running to a soakaway, placed preferably at the lowest point in your garden.

Earthenware or plastic pipes can be used, laid either in a run or, for greatest efficiency, in a herringbone system. Plastic drains are now available in long runs, perforated at regular intervals to take surplus water. They have an advantage over earthenware ones in being flexible; they can be made to curve round a tree root.

The pipes should be laid in trenches with the gradient of the side pipes in the herringbone pattern not greater than one in 250, with the main rib at a similar gradient to the soakaway. On a steeper slope there is too little time for the water to soak in. The depth and proximity of the pipes in the herringbone system will depend on the soil type and the depth of cultivation; the table is intended as a guide.

| Soil type | Spacing | De... |
|---|---|---|
| Clay | 4 to 7m (12 to 21ft) | 600 ... |
| Loam | 8 to 12m (24 to 36ft) | |
| Sand | 12 to 22m (36 to 66... | |

The trench... excavated... base ro... will e... som... of... holes ... pipes butt tog... the joint with a piece of ... broken tile or small piece of tough plastic sheeting to prevent soil leaching through from above.

Cover the pipes with coarse rubble, then protect this layer with upturned sods of turf if you have had to dig these up. Alternatively, use gravel or sand to prevent clogging. Fill up the trench with topsoil to just above ground level, to allow for sinking.

Construct the soakaway by the same method suggested for draining an isolated wet patch. However, as it is draining a much larger area, it should be deeper.

The main drains in a herringbone system will be about 100 mm (4 in) diameter with smaller side drains of 75 mm (3 in), laid at an angle of 45°–60°. Cover the joint with a piece of slate or tile to stop silting. Fill the trench with coarse rubble to a depth of about 250 mm (10 in), then a layer of turf or gravel to prevent clogging, and finally replace the topsoil. The main pipe should drain into a soakaway at least 1·2 m (4 ft) deep, filled with 900 mm (3 ft) of coarse aggregate then a layer of gravel or ash, joining it about 300 mm (1 ft) below the top of the aggregate

# Overall climate patterns

The weather will be a major influence on the design and planting of your garden. If you live in an area where the proportion of cold, wet days is high, you should site your vegetable patch near the house, or at least make sure there is a dry path to it so that it will be easy to pick a winter cabbage. While in a hot climate a patio should be sited to catch a cooling breeze, in more exposed areas it should offer shelter from the wind. Design can be as basic as this.

Before ordering new plants or making changes in the layout of your garden consider the fundamental climatic conditions of your region, any significant local differences, and finally your garden's own microclimate: that is, the small variations within the overall climate particular to your own garden, caused by the shade or protection given by a neighbouring building or

a group of trees, for example. Temperature, rainfall, the hours of daylight, solar radiation (the amount and intensity of sunlight) and frost frequency and severity are all important variables in the overall climate. Certain factors are of particular importance to the gardener. The lateness of late frost, for example, affects early planting, early sowing, fruit tree blossom, potatoes and the safe point at which to bed out dahlias and geraniums. At the other end of the season, it is a good thing to know when to take in plants which are not frost hardy.

The maps shown here cannot indicate the details of local variations, though these can be significant. The effect of local altitude, for instance, can mean that a garden in a sheltered valley above a frost pocket will enjoy one or two weeks more growth than a nearby garden up in the hills. Large towns

are another source of local climatic variation. As a result of the extra heat released in the urban environment, a town can be almost frost-free compared to the surrounding countryside. In addition, rainfall may be considerably reduced in a town, because buildings intercept much of the normal rainfall, causing 'rain shadows'. Industrial pollution is a particular hazard of the urban climate. The smothering dust may interfere with the breathing process of a plant, and not many varieties can withstand this pollution. In a garden near the coast a salt-laden wind, which can blow up to 8 km (5 miles) inland, scorches many plants and turns their leaves brown. Wind breaks may help but special plant selection will usually be necessary, since some species such as broom (*Cytisus*) are better adapted to these coastal conditions.

Europe is divided into climatic zones as defined by the average annual minimum temperature for each area. Average rainfall (in inches a year) is indicated by the lines on the map. The same information is given on the opposite page for the United States.

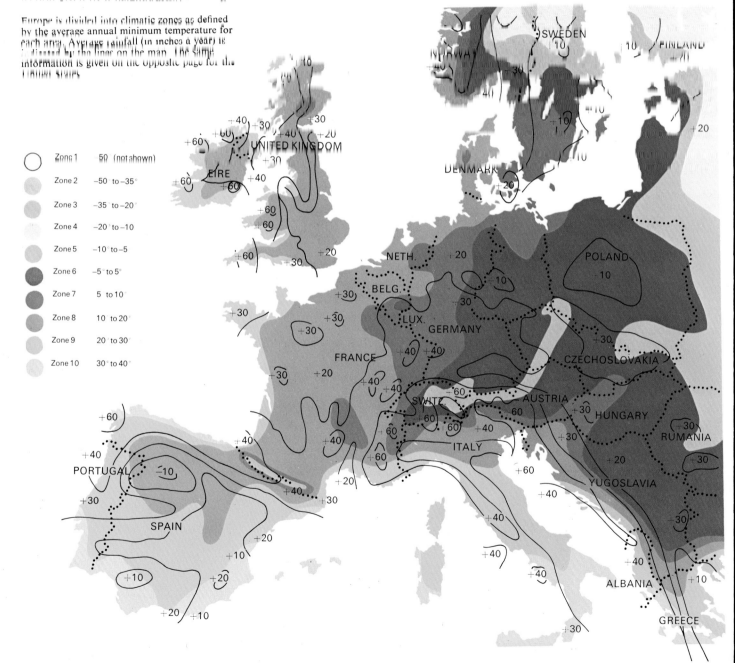

| | Zone 1 | 50 (not shown) |
| --- | --- | --- |
| | Zone 2 | −50° to −35° |
| | Zone 3 | −35° to −20° |
| | Zone 4 | −20° to −10° |
| | Zone 5 | −10° to −5° |
| | Zone 6 | −5° to 5° |
| | Zone 7 | 5° to 10° |
| | Zone 8 | 10° to 20° |
| | Zone 9 | 20° to 30° |
| | Zone 10 | 30° to 40° |

Based on Arnold Arboretum hardiness zones

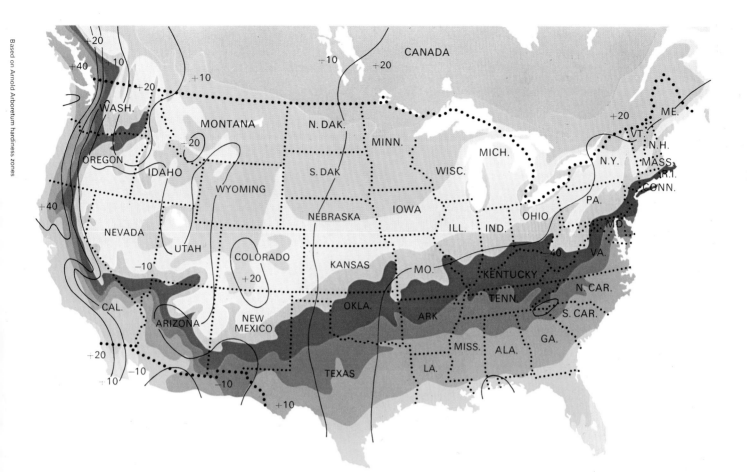

Solar radiation (the amount and intensity of sunlight) affects the growth and general health of plants. The amount of solar radiation received in different areas of Europe and the United States is shown during April and October, two important months in the gardener's calendar

April

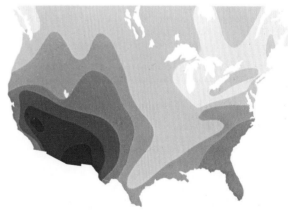

October

Radiation, measured in gram calories per square centimetre

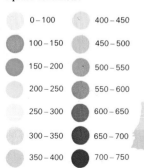

| | |
|---|---|
| 0 – 100 | 400 – 450 |
| 100 – 150 | 450 – 500 |
| 150 – 200 | 500 – 550 |
| 200 – 250 | 550 – 600 |
| 250 – 300 | 600 – 650 |
| 300 – 350 | 650 – 700 |
| 350 – 400 | 700 – 750 |

# Making the most of your microclimate

Even in the smallest garden a wide range of microclimatic conditions exists. These can be used to control the amount of sunlight, water and wind coming into contact with plants, which determines their health. For instance, the way plants are grouped creates a microclimate, since the proximity of one plant may reduce the water, sun and wind received by its neighbour.

Plants need light to achieve growth, through the process of photosynthesis. You can take advantage of the microclimate in various ways to increase the amount of sunlight available to a plant. A slope, for example, may catch more of the sun's rays than flat ground and the water of a small pond will reflect light, aiding the growth of nearby plants. However, some plants require less sun and more shade than others and too much solar heat results in excessive water loss. Shade-loving plants tend to be the ones with relatively large leaves, since these become hotter than small leaves when exposed to sunlight.

While plants and soil absorb heat from the sun during the day, at night they give off heat into the atmosphere. On cloudy nights, heat radiated from the ground is partly reflected back again, so that temperatures do not fall too rapidly. On clear winter nights, however, nearly all the heat is lost to space and the ground temperature falls rapidly until it is lower than that of the air. The soil then takes heat from the air at ground level, resulting in freezing. The incidence of frost will be less under overhanging trees and covering the ground with materials such as straw or sacking will also help to reduce night-time heat loss. A free flow of air, ensuring that cooled air gets whipped away by the wind before its temperature drops too far, prevents the formation of frost pockets.

Although sufficient wind is therefore desirable to prevent frost developing, high wind speeds can result in the atmosphere trying to make more water evaporate from the leaves than can be supplied from the roots. This is known as water stress and it stunts the growth of plants. Of course, too much wind can also have a more directly disastrous effect by uprooting plants.

The most common problem in the countryside is the direct force of the wind, whereas in town it is more often draught, or wind coming in sudden gusts which has been re-routed round buildings, that damages plants. Balcony and roof gardens may be particularly exposed to the wind. Wind breaks can be made from a variety of materials, including plants which do not themselves mind high wind speeds. Solid barriers create areas of turbulence so an open-work fence, a broken wall, a group of plants or another form of partial wind break may be the better solution.

A rough guide to the selection of suitable plants can be gained from observing what grows in similar conditions in the wild. In exposed places in Europe one often finds silver birch (*Betula pendula*), mountain ash (*Sorbus aucuparia*), pines (shrubby varieties are good on a roof), heathers and gorse. The trouble with any kind of wind break is that, although it lessens the wind pressure in one place, it may increase it elsewhere.

A well planned garden should make the most of variations in the microclimate. The plants behind the pond and under the tree—Himalayan poppies (*Meconopsis betonicifolia*), rhubarb, hostas and primula—all like shade and moisture; the fruit trees are trained up against the wall, since brick stores and re-radiates solar heat long after the sun has gone off the garden; and the vegetables are planted on a south-facing slope to catch the full benefit of the sun's rays.

The sun's rays are important because they provide the source of energy used in the process of photosynthesis, shown here for the tomato plant. Solar energy, which is assimilated by the green parts of the plant, causes carbon dioxide (taken in from the atmosphere) to be decomposed into carbon monoxide and oxygen; they then combine with water brought up from the soil to make the starch which the plant needs in order to grow. Oxygen and water vapour are given

A wind break can only re-direct the force of the wind and it may create as many problems as it solves. When the wind hits a solid barrier, such as a wall or group of closely planted trees with dense foliage, areas of turbulence are created on both sides of the wind break

With a semi-solid barrier, consisting of an open slatted fence or lightly foliaged trees, the wind is only partly blocked so that the wind speed is reduced without creating turbulence, and an area of shelter is provided on both sides of the barrier

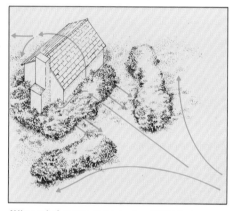

The way in which buildings channel the wind can damage nearby plants. If the airflow is at an angle to the building, there is a steady build-up of velocity along the wall. Air moving along the face of the building is forced to travel at increasing speed since it is trapped between the wall and the next gust of air pushing from behind

When wind comes at an angle of 90°, air is pushed upwards, downwards and round the sides of a building. As a result, fast-moving air blows out from the building at ground level and a barrier of wind-resistant plants close to the building may be necessary to provide protection for more delicate plants

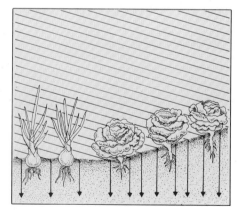

off into the air and the starch is converted into soluble sugar to be transported either directly to the growing regions or down to the roots where it is stored for future use

Radiation frost occurs when the soil loses so much heat at night that its temperature falls to below that of the air. On a clear winter night all the heat given off from the ground is lost to space. Clouds and overhanging trees help the soil to retain its heat, making it less likely that frost will form

The solar energy received by a south-facing slope can be considerably greater than that received by an adjacent flat surface. With the winter sun at 15°, a south-facing piece of land at an angle of 15° to the horizontal will receive twice as much solar energy as a similar area on the flat

| | |
|---|---|
| → Water | → Oxygen |
| → Sunlight | → Water vapour |
| → Carbon dioxide | → Sugar and starch |

# The advantages of your site

One of the first things to consider when planning out your garden is simply what you already have: the advantages and disadvantages of your existing site. You may have a view: perhaps not a panorama but just a peep of a church spire or even a fine tree in the next door garden, to which you can orientate your garden layout. Check the view by holding a couple of books 300 mm (1 ft) apart and then pan round the site, isolating bits of the view through them. By careful planting, the eye can be led towards the view.

Your garden may, on the other hand, look out on to eyesores which you want to block from sight. The immediate instinct may be to put up a barrier on the site boundary, but foreground planting can often be more effective and, being closer to the eye, will screen a wider area. The right design can hold the eye within the garden making a total barrier unnecessary because eyesores will simply be ignored in favour of the greater visual attraction.

The problem may be less what you see as you look out, as who sees you when they look in. One way to ensure privacy is to make a pergola to sit under, or even string wires across the width of the garden to create a real outside room. Attractive plants, such as vines or clematis, can be grown over wire or a pergola. Planting will also muffle the sound of noisy neighbours.

If your site contains an old outbuilding or shed, do not demolish it until you have made certain that it cannot be used in any way. With the roof reinforced it is sometimes possible to remove some of the walls to create a sort of loggia. If the building has a chimney, you can retain this to use for a barbecue. Or you could keep only the main ceiling braces to serve as a frame for climbing plants. The same idea can also be used with an old greenhouse or conservatory from which glass has gone.

### Making the most of trees

Your existing features may well include mature shrubs and trees. Once again do not get rid of them until you have fully explored their potential. Many old shrubs can be rejuvenated by simply cutting them down and letting them send out new shoots from the base; however, with fast growing shrubs such as broom and buddleia, it is probably easier to take them out and buy replacements. You may find that certain shrubs have been forced to grow in strange shapes and are worth preserving as a sculptural feature of the garden.

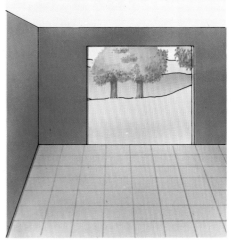

Although a panoramic view is a great asset, the site from which you enjoy it is often exposed and windswept. As well as offering shelter, planting in the foreground (right) may improve such a view by breaking it up into a series of images. A wall with a window in it (far right) performs a similar function and literally frames the view

The overall design and the use of plants can either lead the eye out or focus it within the garden. The garden illustrated above adjoins an equally attractive garden. So the curved bed (in the right foreground of the picture) has been kept deliberately low to allow a view through to the neighbouring garden and the trees beyond. By contrast, the design shown on the right holds the eye within the garden, with the pool and fountain creating an internal point of interest

Seedling shrubs and trees are often found in existing areas of planting, and these can be lifted in the autumn or spring and re-used in the new scheme. Conifers and evergreens transplant best in the spring. Seedling elms and sycamores should be cut out ruthlessly because, while they may look fine in themselves, they will ultimately start seeding and will prove a nuisance in the long run.

Before designing a garden round an existing old tree check its health. If it is only just surviving, it is best to be ruthless at the outset; an unhealthy old tree which is left may endanger both house and garden when it finally has to come down. If you retain the tree, cut out any weak limbs and paint over the scars; check the upper branches for rot as this often develops at junctions where water can stand, and top brace any particularly large limbs (you may need the expertise of a tree surgeon for this).

It can be a difficult task to remove an old tree trunk below ground level. A dead tree stump can always be made into an attractive feature of your garden, as a base for climbing plants to grow over, as a centre for children's play or as part of a bench seat. If you do have to remove a stump, try to get it right out below ground level. You may be able to do the job by burning or by rotting with acid, but it might be necessary to employ a tree surgeon who will use a power-driven drill.

Your plot may contain other unattractive but unavoidable features, such as an old oil tank or a manhole cover in the middle of the garden. With careful planning, using plants as a screen or to distract the eye, any eyesores can be made less obtrusive.

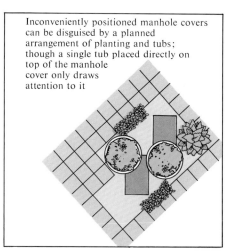

Inconveniently positioned manhole covers can be disguised by a planned arrangement of planting and tubs; though a single tub placed directly on top of the manhole cover only draws attention to it

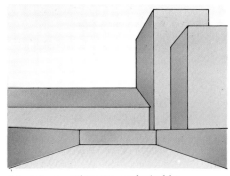

Many town gardens are overlooked by unattractive neighbouring buildings. These can be blocked from sight, at least from the sitting area, by careful planting of trees (right) and by a pergola (far right). One's instinct is to think of screening on the boundary, but the closer the screen is to the eye the wider the area it hides

Trees are probably the most common existing features and they can often be incorporated into the new design. In this attractive town garden (left) a raised patio has been built up round the existing tree

A dead tree is often difficult to remove. But it is sometimes possible to make it into a positive feature of the garden, for instance by using it as a base for growing plants such as ivy

# Measuring the size and slope of your plot

Some idea of the type of garden you want may already be beginning to form in your mind. Before you start to translate your thoughts on to paper, make a rough but accurate survey of the garden. If you have ever consulted an architect to extend your house you may already have a plan available, or a small site plan may be attached to the deeds of the house; any architectural drawing shop will enlarge this to scale for a small fee. But if you do not have a plan, the procedure for measuring up the garden is fairly straightforward.

First measure up the house and mark in the dimensions on a rough drawing of the shape of the house. From the rough drawing and the measurements, plot an accurately scaled plan of the house on to a large sheet of paper, using squared graph paper if you find it a help. Pick a scale which allows you to get the whole layout on one manageable sheet of paper. For the larger small garden, a scale of 1 :100, giving you 10 mm to a metre ($\frac{1}{8}$ in to 1 ft) will be about right. For a smaller garden, a scale of 1 : 50, giving 20 mm to a metre ($\frac{1}{4}$ in to 1 ft) should be possible. Then measure and mark in the site boundaries, followed by any existing features such as trees or manhole covers.

If the garden is on a slope, or if you plan to do any earth shaping or to build any structures, you will need to measure the changes of level. The simplest method is known as boning; to work out a contour map of the site is more complicated.

The first stage in drawing up an accurate map of your site involves marking in your house and any other large buildings, such as the garage shown on the left of this plan. Put in all the ground floor windows and doors. You can usually assume that the angles will be at 90°, though if your measurements fail to meet, check the angles again. Now start to indicate the site boundaries. If the site is regularly shaped, you should be able to get the boundaries right by simply extending lines at 90° from the house

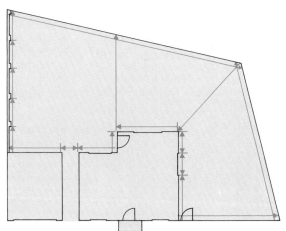

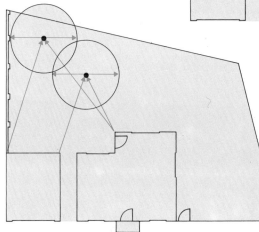

Triangulation is a simple method of plotting accurately the position of various elements in your garden. To establish the distance of a tree from the house or boundary, for example, measure the distance from two separate points on the house or boundary. To mark in the position of the tree on your map, use a pair of compasses to draw arcs from the two points, with radii corresponding to the two measured distances reduced to scale. Measure the overhang of any tree, as this will affect what grows underneath it

A contour is simply a map line joining points of the same height. To draw a complete contour map of your garden, you need a hand sighting instrument, which consists of a telescope and a level bubble, and a calibrated rod, which is a tall post marked out like a ruler. Peg out the ground at regular intervals indicated by a grid (A); set up the calibrated rod vertically in the ground some distance from a peg and move the sighting instrument up and down the rod, until you get a horizontal sight line to the base of the peg; the distance from the sighting instrument to the ground gives you the level of the peg (B)

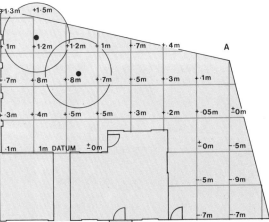

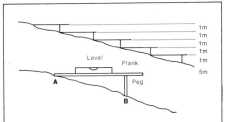

To measure a gradient by boning, rest a plank on a peg and a spirit level on the plank. Move the plank until the spirit level shows it to be dead horizontal. The height of the peg then indicates the difference in level between points A and B. By repeating the procedure, you can establish the gradient of the whole slope

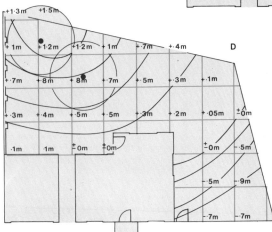

Repeat the method shown in B for another peg (C). Once you have marked in all the relative heights on your grid you can begin to infer the contours (A and D). So long as there is an equal difference in height between each contour, you can read a contour map at a glance (the closer together the lines, the steeper the slope). But the grid may not give you enough information to plot all the lines. In D, with a 0·3 m difference between contours, there are some areas, such as in between the 0 and −0·5 m points on the grid, where the location of the contour line is doubtful. Additional measurements, using the boning system, may therefore be necessary

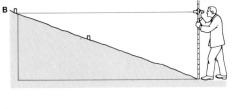

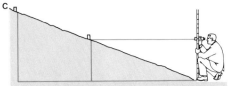

# Your basic plan

Once you have measured your site and noted on your plan the relationship of house to garden and the garden's existing features such as good or bad views, changes of level and trees, it is then time to start planning the overall design.

Think about what you want your garden to contain and roughly the amount of space you want to allocate to the major elements; then begin to mark in their approximate position on your plan. Consider how large a terrace you need, how much of the garden, if any, you are prepared to devote to growing vegetables and herbs, how much lawn you want in relation to flower beds, and where you will site any necessary services. If you have a front and a back garden, what goes in which area? Do you have any special requirements, such as a play area or a sand pit, a pond, rockery or a rose bed?

While you map out these areas, you should bear in mind several general considerations in addition to the obvious ones of convenience and appearance. Privacy, which involves sound as well as sight, is important. Shelter from the wind, for people and plants, also needs to be considered. The depth of soil in different areas of the garden can affect the siting of plants and the position of the sun, which determines which part of the garden will be in sunlight at different times of day, is crucial. A terrace for sitting out on, a greenhouse, most vegetables and many flowers demand sunny positions. So if your garden is shady or space is limited, work out your priorities with such limitations in mind.

As your plan develops from a tentative outline to the more definite and detailed stage, you will need to consider the character of the pattern which will result from your decisions about what goes where. Try to achieve convenient positioning within a general pattern that looks right.

### The overall pattern
The totally symmetric formal layout, with one side mirroring the other, is probably only suited to a site adjoining a period house which is itself strictly symmetric. However, an informal layout which is nonetheless almost symmetric may look effective alongside a modern house. An informal asymmetric design allows for greater juxtaposition of units within a garden site but balance is still important when you want to achieve a harmonious casual look.

The affinity of a garden to its site arises as much from a correct sense of proportion as from the use of sympathetic materials. A grid system mapped in on your plan can help you to achieve this proportionate balance (see the plans on pages 40–41). A major determinant of proportion will often be your house; its walls, subdivisions or other details of its elevation may be used to form the basis of a grid to lay underneath your plan.

Not all gardens relate primarily to a house or other building, in which case you can pick up the frequency of wall buttresses, fence verticals or anything else which is visually important and recurs regularly, and then transpose these on to your plan.

Often the most convenient place for the terrace is right outside the house. This terrace makes a visual link between indoors and outdoors, leading the eye out to a view of the garden

In certain situations you can turn the grid, possibly at a 45° angle to the house or boundary. This oblique layout can work quite well provided that adjustments are made where any pattern created meets the garden boundaries.

You can see patterns to adapt for the small garden all around you: in the regular shapes of materials such as tweeds or tartans, the arrangement of pictures on the wall, and most of all the free shapes of nature. For instance, the flowing line of a river can be transposed on a small scale if it works within the gridded layout.

### Siting the terrace
The terrace will be the centre of the garden in terms of activity. How much space you give to it will obviously depend on the size and shape of your garden, the size of your family and your particular requirements. For sitting space, however, an absolute minimum width of two metres (a little over 6 ft) is necessary. Especially in summer, the terrace may be in constant use for sitting,

eating out, sunbathing, children's play, preparing food and doing any number of odd tasks. The diversity of activities which it is likely to sustain often calls for a sunny, sheltered place which is not overlooked.

A terrace with easy access from the kitchen is highly practical—for carrying food in and out, cutting up vegetables, changing muddy boots and bringing in coal and wood. Grass running up to the windows may have an eighteenth-century feel about it, but in wet weather it is impractical as it will probably mean mud gets carried into the house. A terrace right outside the house will probably be the most convenient, though houses with their garden side facing north may need a terrace away from the house to catch the sun, in which case a sound, connecting hard surface will be necessary.

Other factors to think about when planning the terrace include the position of a barbecue if you want one, just where you sit to eat out, and whether the furniture will be built-in or free-standing.

### How much food to grow

The next priority is to decide how much space—if any—you want to devote to food growing, and to work out exactly where to site the vegetable plot and herb garden, if you want these areas.

It is arguable that the actual saving through growing your own vegetables in a small garden is marginal. Perversely, the saving may be greater in the countryside, since the distributive system favours large areas of population and often results in cheaper and more plentiful vegetables in towns. Naturally, the more vegetables you grow, the more economic the proposition becomes. To give some indication of the amount of space which vegetables take up: an area of 84 sq m (300 sq ft) would provide a family of four with sufficient lettuces, runner beans, peas, carrots and turnips in summer, and with leeks, cabbages and sprouts in winter. But of course great pleasure can be obtained from growing your own produce, even if you do not have enough space to make the enterprise really economic, and the fresh taste of home-grown vegetables is reward in itself.

The type of vegetables you grow will dictate the size of the plot, and this will determine how near the house it can be. Potatoes, most root crops and fruit and vegetables which need forcing, such as rhubarb and chicory, all take a lot of space. Green vegetables, such as broccoli and spinach—which is useful since the 'perpetual' variety goes on and on—are often well worth growing. For a busy family with little spare time, it is perhaps best to concentrate on salad crops. There are many varieties of lettuce worth growing and a few outdoor tomato plants in a sheltered place can be rewarding. Fruit bushes can be trained along a fence or grown against a wall, where they will benefit from the heat retained and gently released by the wall.

Many vegetables can be incorporated decoratively in the garden plan. Red cabbages look striking, runner beans can be grown up a fence, and artichoke plants are visually interesting and can be used to screen a compost heap, while marrows and courgettes are most attractive hanging over

There can be no hard and fast rules about bed width. But the mixed border shown here allows sufficient room for a variety of plants which will flower at different times, without being too wide to work

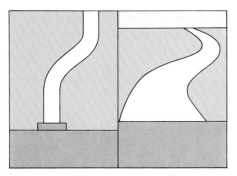

Any curve you may conceive on paper will foreshorten in reality, as the eye runs from directly above it to being at the side. To explore and check this, put your eye down to paper level to get the feel of what the design will actually look like on the ground. The path's curve will always seem more extreme in three-dimensional reality than when drawn on paper

## Allocating space for your vegetables

| CROP | DISTANCE BETWEEN ROWS | DISTANCE BETWEEN PLANTS | EXPECTED YIELD PER 9 METRE (30ft) ROW |
|---|---|---|---|
| Maincrop potatoes | 60 cm (24 in) | 38 cm (15 in) | 20-30 kg (45-65 lb) |
| Broccoli | 23 cm (9 in) | 61 cm (24 in) | 27 kg (60 lb) |
| Spinach | 30 cm (12 in) | 8 cm (3 in) | 7-14 kg (15-30 lb) |
| Carrots | 30 cm (12 in) | 8-16 cm (3-6 in) | 11 kg (25 lb) |
| Lettuces | 30 cm (12 in) | 30 cm (12 in) | 30 heads of lettuce |
| French beans | 60 cm (24 in) | 23 cm (9 in) | 9 kg (20 lb) |
| Onions | 30 cm (12 in) | 16 cm (6 in) | 10 kg (24 lb) |
| Summer radishes | 16 cm (6 in) | 2-5 cm (1-2 in) | 5 kg (12 lb) |

Vegetables can be as decorative as flowering plants and look particularly effective when combined with them (left). The shape and colour of the French beans and broccoli complement and contrast with each other

Neat beds of herbs can be an attractive feature of the garden. These beds, clearly defined by simple planks of wood, are stepped up on a slight slope to give a small-scale terraced effect, which makes them easy to cultivate

a wall from the edge of a raised bed. Raised beds look effective and can be worked into a terrace if space is limited; they are excellent for old people since they are far easier to work.

Most vegetables need a good depth of topsoil which is rich in humus and all need a certain amount of space. They should be grown in some sort of rotation. A vegetable plot need not be screened, as is often suggested, for rows of neat vegetables can be attractive. Admittedly there are times in winter when they look straggly—but a run of box edging should solve the problem.

Herb growing is becoming more popular, since not only are herbs used in most forms of cooking, but their medicinal properties are also being rediscovered. They grow in interesting shapes and the form, texture and colour of their leaves make them attractive plants. Many herbs, such as rosemary, purple sage, santolina, rue and golden balm, can be included in the mixed border as decorative additions or a herb garden can be sited on its own. But clearly it is sensible that herbs should be as close to the kitchen as possible. As many of them originate in scrub or downland, they can exist in fairly shallow poor soil.

### Lawn, ground cover and planted areas

Many small gardens include a fairly central lawn groundwork which sets off colourful flower beds. But where space is really limited a small area of grass will not be worthwhile—either visually or practically; a reasonable area of lawn in a simple shape looks uncluttered and is easier to maintain. Lawn running right up to the flower beds is attractive, though maintenance is easier when a line of paving runs along the edge, so that mowing stops about 400 mm (1 ft 3 in) short of the border. Convenience of mowing should be taken into account when planning areas of grass. Allow room to turn the mowing machine and, if you plan a grass slope, bear in mind the maximum gradient of 1 : 1 or 45° for cutting with a hand mower and 1 : 1½ or 33° for a smaller power-driven machine.

Ground cover such as heather or ivy is an alternative soft ground surfacing, especially over areas which are too small or steep for lawn but where you want to keep maintenance to a minimum. The use of ground cover need not be restricted to filling in spaces between beds or within beds. It can be employed to create bold areas of pattern, possibly combined with paving stones.

At this stage in your planning there is no need to decide on the exact varieties of trees, shrubs and plants. However, since all planting is important in drawing and directing the eye, you should be thinking in terms of the approximate height and density of plant varieties; these should be selected for their overall impact in the design as much as for their purely horticultural interest.

The width of beds and borders will obviously depend on the space you have, but bear in mind two general points. If beds or borders greatly exceed about two metres (a little over 6 ft) in width, it may

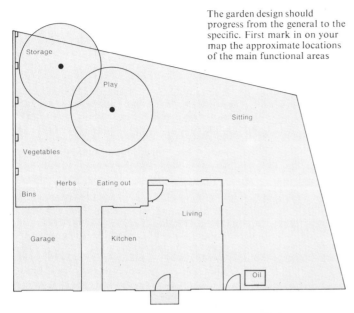

The garden design should progress from the general to the specific. First mark in on your map the approximate locations of the main functional areas

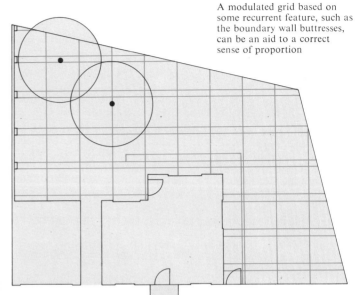

A modulated grid based on some recurrent feature, such as the boundary wall buttresses, can be an aid to a correct sense of proportion

prove difficult to hoe between the plants without trampling all over the bed. On the other hand, beds must be sufficiently wide to allow for an effective arrangement of plants. For example, if you want a herbaceous border which maintains a colour display for most of the year, you need enough space to arrange plants so that when one group stops flowering another takes its place.

### Siting awkward structures

If you are starting from scratch you should plan the location of items such as the greenhouse, tool shed, oil tank, coal or log storage, compost and rubbish bins, so that some sort of amalgamation is achieved, rather than an ever increasing number of small structures dotted around the site.

A greenhouse naturally needs full sun, good access to it and preferably a hard surface area around it, as it soon becomes another centre of activity within the garden. If you can combine it with or site it next to the tool shed, or any other necessary small structure, so much the better. When wrongly sited, greenhouses can dominate the whole garden and, despite recent attempts to improve their appearance, they are seldom handsome structures. If the greenhouse cannot be a lean-to or an extension of the house, try to site the free-standing building, running east to west, to one side of the main view.

If you have an oil tank, it should have easy access for the feed pipe which should not have to trail all over the garden. Coal or log storage and rubbish bins should be readily accessible from the house, preferably under some sort of covered way. The compost bin should be screened. If all the vegetable waste is to go on to it it should not be too far away, but neither should it be too close since rotting vegetables smell.

A space for any large vehicles to be parked, such as a boat or a caravan as well as a car, should be allowed for at this initial planning stage.

A well-designed structure to enclose and screen the compost heap should harmonize with the

### The front garden

This is your face to the world. It should welcome your guests and provide safe and easy access to the door in all weather. Good lighting and a clearly visible house number are essential. The front garden will probably need to house several of the service items and you may want a parking space for one or more cars. If possible, allow enough room not only to get out of the car without landing in a rose bed, but also to wash the car down; do not forget provision for a water point and for drainage. If there is not room to turn the car round, you will need to leave clear lines of vision for reversing out.

The front garden is liable to look somewhat unattractive unless well planned. Its

natural environment; it can even be a positively handsome feature of the garden

layout often develops piecemeal, the builder putting in the minimum amount of hard surfacing and successive owners adding bits and pieces, with the result that too many materials are used and untidy little strips of planting and grass are left over. If parking space is a necessity, you may have to treat the space more as service area than as garden and to use entirely hard surfacing or gravel, unless you have enough spare space for a broad sweep of grass. If you do use exclusively hard surfacing, you can always add groups of pots for spring bulbs and annual colour. Loose gravel with some plants in it looks attractive and can help give security by deterring the intruder who tries to crunch his way through.

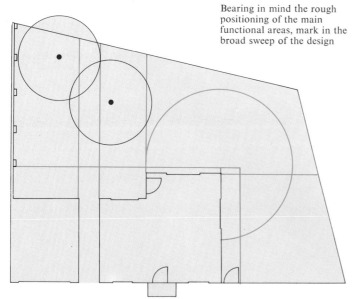

Bearing in mind the rough positioning of the main functional areas, mark in the broad sweep of the design

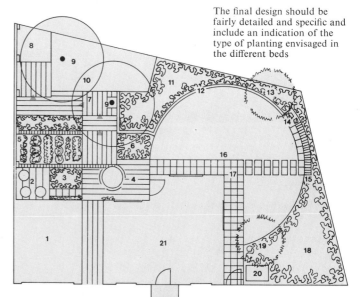

The final design should be fairly detailed and specific and include an indication of the type of planting envisaged in the different beds

1 *Garage*
2 *Dustbins*
3 *Herbs*
4 *Eating area*
5 *Vegetables*
6 *Colourful flower beds*
7 *Stepped terrace*
8 *Compost bin or shed*
9 *Existing trees*
10 *Play area under trees*
11 *Mixed border*
12 *Brick retaining wall*
13 *Flowering tree*
14 *Statuary*
15 *Built-in brick seat*
16 *Lawn*
17 *Paving*
18 *Bank planted with shrubs*
19 *Tree hiding oil tank*
20 *Oil tank*
21 *House*

The urban front garden often has to provide parking space. While it is difficult totally to hide parked cars, sensible planting can offer partial screening

Privacy, including protection from the dirt and noise of passing traffic, can be a problem where the house adjoins a busy street. Conifer or privet hedges certainly offer privacy but provide little visual excitement, and an attractive tree can be the simplest solution. With a large tree, lack of light may be a problem, but certain trees, the robinia or birch for example, have a fine foliage and are good in this kind of situation. Light foliage trees do not usually have too deep and extensive a rooting system so there should be little danger to house foundations. The head of the tree will need thinning out occasionally and watch out that it does not get too big.

It is often difficult to make anything of a narrow area at the side of the house. If the area is dark, colour washing can help, and you may want to reduce the feeling of being in a canyon by enclosing the space with overhead beams linking the house to boundary or garage wall.

### Making sure the design is practical
The most striking patterns will mean nothing if they cannot be translated into reality. Obviously it is no good planning to use a material which is unavailable and, in general, only materials available through a local garden centre or building contractor are suggested.

Other practical limitations may crop up. Certain paving materials may well prove impossible for particular jobs. For instance, squared paving slabs may be excellent for filling in your gridded module but it can be difficult to break them to form a curve. If you want to make a feature of an existing stream or pond, make sure the water runs all the year so that you are not left with a dry mud waste in the summer.

Having made sure that the conception is practical, and having checked that everything you want is on the plan, roughly peg out your design using string, canes, pegs and lengths of hose or rope. To delineate any curves, use a string running from the central radius point. Fake up the design as realistically as possible and live with it for some time before you start to do any work.

# shaping
## the
# garden
## the basic framework

When the contours and layout of the garden have been plotted on a flat plan, you can begin to translate the shapes into walls, steps and paved areas which will form the basic skeleton of the garden. The variety of available materials presents a further range of design possibilities, involving colour and texture as well as linear design.

# WALLS AND ENCLOSURES

Enclosures round the home and garden were originally built as a defence against enemies, animals and the savage disorder of nature outside. These pressing reasons for protection have largely disappeared: our motives for enclosing the garden are now more mundane—to protect against wind and weather, to shut out excessive noise and ugly views, to avoid being overlooked and to keep children and animals inside a safe area. Inside the garden, walls are built to screen off one part of the garden from another: the vegetables from the flower garden, for instance, or the washing-line and dustbins from the rest.

It is true, nevertheless, that we still feel an instinctive need to build a fence to define our own territory, which acts only as a marker to make the extent of our property clear to the world at large. For this purpose, no massive wall or close-boarded fence is needed; a low railing or even a line of stones can be sufficient. Keep the enclosure on a scale which is fitting to the size and nature of the garden.

### *Suiting the enclosure to the site*
Consider first the purpose which you want your wall or fence to serve. Imagine how it will look when finished, both in relation to your house and garden and to the neighbourhood as a whole. You may wish to shroud the wall in creepers and plants to produce a soft outline or to leave it bare and create a stark, angular effect, perhaps to harmonize with a modern house. However, if the effect you want is at odds with the overall look of the neighbourhood, you may in some places be infringing the law, or simply antagonizing the neighbours by creating an eyesore. A dry stone wall which is charming in the country looks ridiculous in suburbia; similarly a heavy concrete wall around a country garden can spoil a beautiful view completely. Another common error is to choose a poor substitute because it is cheaper than the right material; for instance the facsimiles of natural stone in concrete block will never look authentic when laid alongside the real thing. One mistake can dominate a considerable area and sometimes destroy the natural harmony of the landscape.

It is wise, therefore, at least for the external wall, to choose a material in common use in your area and preferably one which forms some element of the fabric of the house or garden paving, in order to create a unified effect. In this way, your fence will be a pleasure to yourself and your neighbours; they might even be persuaded to share the cost of a party wall.

Apart from these aesthetic considerations, take into account the practical aspects: the cost of the material, its durability and the probable maintenance that it will need. Any project which requires professional skills will, of course, be costly due to labour charges, but you may well be able to build your own fence for next to nothing using odd 'junk' materials such as old telegraph poles, field stones or driftwood. The cost of materials and their availability obviously depend on the area in which you live, but it is generally true that natural stone and brick, though far more durable, will involve a greater initial outlay than timber and are more difficult and laborious to deal with. Wooden fences, on the other hand, require annual care to prevent them rotting and warping, and one must be prepared to replace timbers quite frequently.

# Walls of natural stone

It is perhaps more important with natural stone than with anything else to build in the traditional local manner, since there are so many different types of stone, each with its own characteristic texture and appearance. Each of these is associated with a particular building style, and it is rash to try to force it into new and incongruous settings. For this reason, natural stone is not often used in urban areas, except where it is traditional; however, in the country it is an immensely attractive material, since it forms a sympathetic background to plants and weathers well.

Natural stone walls may be of hard or soft stone; granite, slate and flint for example, are hard stones, and soft stones include sandstone and limestone. If you have a variety of materials available, remember that soft stones, particularly sandstone,

Front cross-section of a random dry stone wall. Note the 'tie-stones' running across the width of the wall to bind it together and the chippings used to fill in the gaps between large boulders

are easier to work with. Reconstituted stone may also be used for walling, and has great advantages since it is lighter, often cheaper, cut to regular sizes and sometimes even more durable. However, as has been said, it should be used with restraint and sensitivity to the atmosphere of the setting. The cost of natural stone depends entirely on local conditions; it may be by far the most expensive of all walling materials or you may occasionally be able to pick it up free from the fields.

Most stone is available as rough-cut rubble (as it is left over from quarrying, in various sizes and shapes), as squared rubble (shaped into more regular blocks) and as ashlar—smoothly finished and squared blocks. Quarry-finished stone comes in a variety of hammered, smoothed and textured surfaces. The rough-cut rubble is laid in a random fashion, while the more regular blocks are arranged in 'courses', that is in orderly, level lines as bricks are laid. Stone can be laid without mortar (dry walling), or with mortar. Lay all stone with its natural grain horizontal or else it will split under the weight of the wall. In any case it is probably not a good idea to attempt to build any kind of stone wall above 900 mm (3 ft) high without professional help or advice.

## Working with stone

Working with stone involves much heavy, slow work, sorting the stones into different sizes, planning the construction of the wall so that it is stable, and finally doing a lot of heavy lifting. Do not strain your back; a helper is useful in carrying the heavy stones

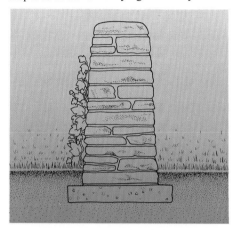

Front cross-section of a mortared rough-cut rubble wall laid random. The coping stone protects the mortar and the concrete base from waterlogging and freezing

to the top of the wall or you can use two logs as a ramp. The technique of dry walling, in particular, is a complex one, usually regarded as a job for the expert craftsman, so it is not wise to attempt it unless you are prepared to spend a great deal of time and effort.

Though the construction may look childishly simple, a matter merely of balancing one stone on top of another, to build a stable dry wall is a skill which can only be learnt with practice. There is no substitute for watching an expert at the craft or, better still, working with him. When you first start you will undoubtedly work very hard with very little result but progress will become faster if you persevere.

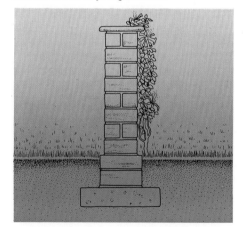

Front cross-section of a coursed ashlar block wall. These smooth quarried blocks are an expensive form of natural stone, but their regular look is often successfully imitated by artificial stone

Starting a dry wall is easy: dig a trench which should be shallow (about the depth of four of the stones in the wall) and almost twice the width of the top of the wall. Pour a layer of gravel and small stones into the trench to form a smooth bed for the first layer of stone and to improve drainage.

Mortared walls, whether random or coursed, should be built on concrete foundations laid *in situ* approximately 300 mm (1 ft) deep and twice the width of the wall, or larger if the soil underneath is loosely packed (see Mixing concrete, page 58). The top surface of the base must lie below ground frost level – 450 mm (1 ft 6 in) is deep enough. Alternatively, stone footings of a similar size can be used. The first stones are then set in mortar straight on this base (see Laying foundations for paving, page 65).

Mortared random walls are considerably more stable than dry stone walling, though they should be built with the same care and attention to detail. A stone which is slightly wobbly in a dry stone wall, and which might eventually work itself loose, will stay firm if it is mortared in place. For this reason a mortared wall has a longer life than a dry stone wall while the visual effect may be very similar; if you wipe the mortared joints out carefully, you will achieve an overall

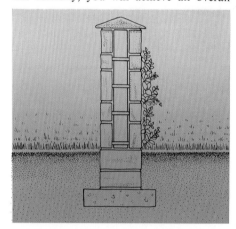

Front cross-section of an ashlar veneer wall with a concrete block core. The wall is reinforced by metal ties laid through the mortar joints and by the concrete blocks which are used as a base

look very close to that of dry walling.

Always use plenty of mortar and lay one stone at a time. Lay down a horizontal bed of mortar, place the stone on it, and trowel in more mortar until all the cavities are full. Cover the stone at both ends to form a joint with the next stone to be laid. Since stability is not such a problem, quite small stones, such as flint, can be used to construct solid walls, using plenty of mortar and with brick or stone piers at intervals to make it really sturdy. However, with mortared walls of random rubble, tie-stones and battering are still a good idea to improve stability.

In a coursed rubble wall, the occasional very regular course of similar sized stones acts as a firm bond, and adds variety to the pattern. Remember when laying courses to avoid continuous vertical joints and to vary the size of the stones, laying two small stones over one large one. The regular ashlar blocks can be laid almost as formally as brick, in alternate courses. Reconstituted stone is very often found in this style, perhaps with an artificial 'rough cast' surface on one side only which means that it has to be built as a cavity wall.

Another way to form a strong and probably cheaper wall is to use ashlar or coursed squared rubble as a veneer on a core of concrete blocks. A brick backing can also be used though it is more expensive. This method is often seen with sandstone blocks veneered over concrete or breeze blocks. You can also veneer random patterned stone over concrete; this is far cheaper than using natural stone all through the wall. However, the stones have to be fitted together with extreme care to fill in gaps, and to avoid an artificial 'stuck-on' look.

It is important for mortared walls to have a watertight coping in order to prevent the mortar becoming soaked and cracking in frosty weather. A variety of materials may be used: the same stone or another one (slate is particularly suitable), brick or concrete.

One advantage of building in stone is that though the initial cost is high and the work is not easy, the finished product needs little or no maintenance for years and should become increasingly attractive to look at, especially if grown over with plants. Mortared walls may need a little pointing and repairing occasionally, in which case brush out the old loose mortar and decaying stone, and fill the cracks with a suitable mortar mix (see Mortar for building walls, page 50). If dry stone walls collapse, they are, of course, simply rebuilt as before.

The joints of a coursed dry wall will gradually fill with soil, lichens and stone chips, forming a rooting place for creeping plants. The horizontal cracks in stone occur naturally

Round boulders and flat slabs must be skilfully balanced together to build a dry stone wall. Regular flat stones along the top form a level surface to support the flower boxes

Stone can be used in many decorative ways. This wall, known as a 'Cornish hedge', has an inner core of soil and rubble. Slabs are arranged in flat courses then built up in a herringbone pattern

Each stone block in this dry wall, laid with a concrete foundation, has been separately shaped, and tiny chips have been used to fill in the hairline gaps between the blocks

The front joints of this mortared wall have been raked and brushed to give it the appearance of a dry stone wall, while mortar behind gives it the strength to act as a retaining wall

Reconstituted stone looks convincing and effective when it is not used adjacent to natural stone. Stone slabs, also reconstituted, provide a coping for the gate posts at the end of the wall

Variations in colour, texture and shape of reconstituted stone blocks will add authenticity. This wall, laid in a varied but repeating pattern of blocks, has the occasional regular course

Flints are often used as a strong decorative surface on a mortared rubble core. In this mortared wall cut and uncut flints are used for their remarkable contrasts of colour and texture

Weathering, lichen and the rambling clematis give a varied surface to this heavily mortared rubble wall. The clematis has been trained along thin wire to allow easy pruning

## BUILDING A RANDOM WALL

To achieve maximum stability in a rough-cut stone wall laid in a random fashion, build up the wall on the foundations, using the larger stones for the lower layers and the smaller ones towards the top. You can set up a taut line of cord along the side of the foundation trench, to keep the wall straight from end to end. Raise the cord as you build, as a guide to help you keep the top fairly level, though of course with random rubble no surface will be flat. The characteristic irregularity of these walls is part of their beauty.

Arrange large 'tie-stones', laid across the width of the wall, at regular intervals; these run from one side of the wall to the other to form a strong link, bonding the smaller stones in the wall together. One tie-stone in every square metre (10 sq ft) of walling is about right. These tie-stones are also used to form a level top or coping along the top of the wall; a coping acts as waterproofing in mortared walls, but in dry stone walling it protects the stone from being dislodged by passersby and

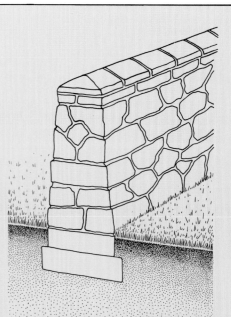

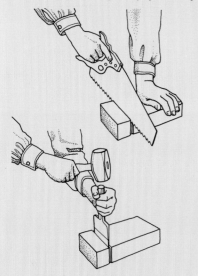

It is difficult to cut hard stone to shape, but soft and medium density stone can be shaped for easier handling. To cut a stone block, make a groove using a hammer and chisel or an old saw. Set the stone on a firm surface, place a cold chisel in the groove and split the stone with a few sharp blows from a mallet on the chisel handle

animals. It may be difficult to find enough large slabs to do the job.

Again to improve stability, the wall should be 'battered', that is, built with an inward slope of 25 mm in every 600 mm (1 in in every 2 ft) of height, so that the base of the wall is wider than the top. Most battered stone walls are very wide in proportion to their height and the battering angle can be greater than this. A 900 mm (3 ft) wall is usually at least 450 mm (1 ft 6 in) wide at the base, using a double thickness of stone, though of course this measurement depends on the size of the stones.

In a random dry stone and a mortared rubble wall place the stones with their most attractive face exposed, varying the sizes and shapes to give the wall an interesting appearance. If you have plenty of stone you can build a double thickness wall, of two layers of stone tilted slightly down into the centre of the wall, with the gap between filled with chippings; this wall will be very wide and thus more stable. With wet walls, use plenty of mortar to ensure that the coping is secure and watertight

A 'batter board', three struts nailed together at the angle of slope, is used to form the tilt of the wall; use a spirit level to check that the outside edge of the board is kept perpendicular

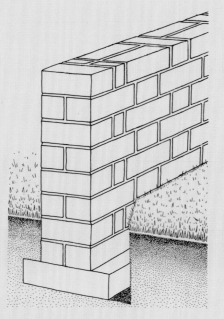

In the ashlar block wall neat joints, carefully brushed out, are barely visible if the stones are smoothly cut. Note the solid coping which is waterproof and also suitably emphatic for a formal wall

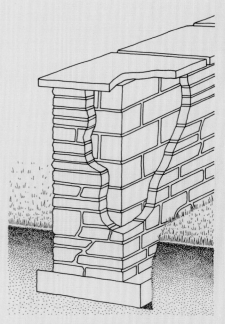

Coursed rubble veneer is mortared on to an inner wall of concrete block which forms a strong backing. For a retaining wall with a single visible face, only one layer of veneer need be used

# The versatility of brick

Brick walling is a popular choice for gardens because it is versatile and blends well with other materials. There is a special challenge in designing and building a brick wall which will harmonize with the style of your garden. Whereas most natural stone has an established style and character which it will impose on any setting, brick is more flexible in its appearance and can be used in relaxed and formal gardens, in rural or urban settings.

Well-weathered old bricks, grown over with plants, create the mellow effect of a traditional or natural garden while new slate-grey or white-painted bricks can look stark and formal, perhaps emphasizing the architectural lines of a modern house or patio. Where a house is brick-built, its virtue as a walling material is in unifying the whole space and creating a tailored effect which is restful to the eye. As a background for plants, brick is ideal, both visually and for practical reasons: the brick soaks up the sun's heat and gently radiates it out over a long period, which is especially beneficial for ripening fruit.

Bricks are usually more readily available than natural stone, with more choice of colours; depending on the composition of the clay and the method of their firing, bricks can be red, yellow, blue, black, grey or mixed colour tones. Different textures, sizes and shapes are also available. The normal appearance of brick can be further altered by colouring the mortar, by combining brick with other materials such as slate or flint within the wall or by topping a low brick wall with wooden fencing.

Unless you have a cheap source of bricks, a brick wall will probably be as expensive as one in natural stone and twice the price of a concrete block wall. The cost is usually increased because walls over 900 mm (3 ft) in height should be reinforced or of double thickness, that is 225 mm (or 9 in in Imperial sizes), to ensure stability. Stability is as important with brick walling as it is with natural stone; it is better to reinforce too much than too little. As with stone walls, too, it may be advisable to seek professional advice or help for walls over 900 mm (3 ft) high. It is possible to build a low wall which is only 112·5 mm (or 4½ in) thick, without reinforcements, but if it is situated near a sturdy brick structure—another wall or a house—it may well look flimsy or mean. Higher narrow walls may be built if they are staggered; the bonded corners strengthen the wall. A serpentine wall, curved in semi-circles, is also self-stabilizing and can be extremely graceful in the appropriate setting. However, this space-consuming design is not recommended for a small garden.

## Reinforcing a brick wall

Apart from these exceptional cases, the single-thickness wall of 112·5 mm (4½ in) has to be reinforced if it is over 900 mm (3 ft) high. Between 900 mm (3 ft) and 1.3 m (4 ft 6 in) high, walls can be either double or single thickness with reinforcements. Over 1.3 m (4 ft 6 in), walls should be double thickness and will need additional strength if they are over 1·8 m (6 ft) high or very long. There are two ways to reinforce and walls which are long and high or subject to special stress—strong winds, for example—may need a combination of the two.

The first, most commonly used with single thickness walls, is to build vertical brick 'piers' into the wall at approximately 3·6 m (12 ft) intervals and at either end, and also where they will support gates. The piers should be twice as thick as the wall and bonded into its main fabric right down

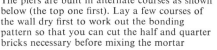
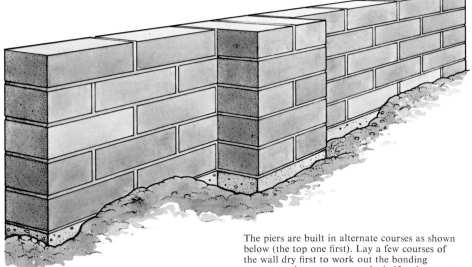

A single thickness wall requires reinforcing piers about every 3·6 m (12 ft) of length. They are bonded into the wall down to the foundations which should be of concrete laid *in situ* and as wide as the piers themselves

to the foundations. Alternatively, the wall should be strengthened with steel reinforcing rods. Sometimes, the rods are rooted in the concrete foundation before the wall is built and then held in the vertical position by specially designed hollow bricks. It is far more common, however, to have a double thickness wall and to build the two layers of the wall about 15 mm (½ in) apart, fill the cavity with a watery mortar known as 'grout', and fix the rods inside the wall. For extra strength, the rods are planted vertically in the foundation first and the two faces of brick are built up round them. The cavity is filled with grout to hold brick and steel together.

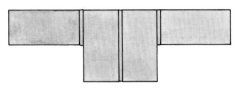

The piers are built in alternate courses as shown below (the top one first). Lay a few courses of the wall dry first to work out the bonding pattern so that you can cut the half and quarter bricks necessary before mixing the mortar

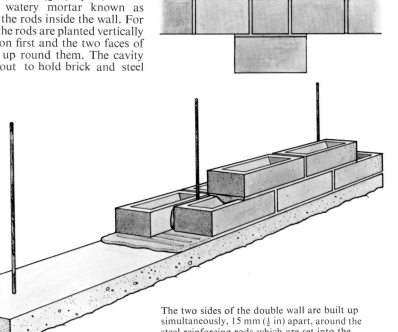

The two sides of the double wall are built up simultaneously, 15 mm (½ in) apart, around the steel reinforcing rods which are set into the concrete foundation. Metal wall ties or header bricks are laid transversely to join the two skins

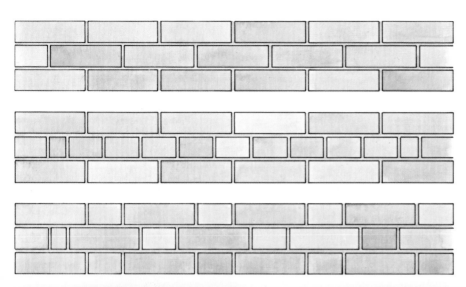

**Stretcher bond**
The most regular pattern of bonding, in which all the bricks are laid with their long face visible, is always used for single thickness walls. Though strong, its regularity could make it look monotonous over a large area

**English bond**
Courses of 'headers' and 'stretchers' are alternated for variety and extra strength; staggered joints are achieved by inserting part bricks head on, known as 'closers'

**Flemish bond**
Headers and stretchers are alternated in each course, again with closers to stagger the joints. Flemish bond is less strong than English bond but more decorative

*Bonding the bricks*
Walls can be built using a variety of different 'bonding' patterns. Bonding is the regular arrangement of the bricks, which can be decorative as well as of structural importance: by staggering the vertical joints in the wall, it distributes the downward pressure of the wall's weight all along its length. All single thickness walls must be built in 'stretcher' bond—totally regular alternate courses. In double thickness walls, this is varied by more complex bonding which involves courses of 'headers'—bricks laid across the width of the wall with their short face visible, which also act as a kind of reinforcement. To form an idea of how your wall will look, try out different bonding techniques with dry bricks.

Non-load-bearing walls can be built

Using a single material for walls, paving and a raised seat conveys the sense of a unified planned space, while different bonding patterns and the natural variety of brick colours prevent monotony; brick forms a natural background for climbing plants such as ivy

Facing bricks, those intended to be visible in the finished wall, are made in a wide range of shades and textures; changing the colour of the mortar further extends the number of possible effects

unbonded to create special effects, for example the basketweave pattern. Such designs need horizontal reinforcing rods or reinforcing mesh 25 mm (1 in) narrower than the wall, laid along the mortar joints, one layer in every 600 mm (2 ft) of wall. The courses of bricks below ground level in unbonded walls should be bonded to improve stability.

The basketweave design forms an unbonded wall with continuous vertical joints, which are strengthened by wire mesh placed along the horizontal mortar joints. Piers of bonded bricks or concrete blocks also provide support, as do the courses of stretcher bond below ground level

A double row of slates or tiles beneath a coping of headers will form a decorative damp-proofing course, blending with richly coloured old bricks

To add more variety to the standard wall, an interesting idea is to fill the cavity in a double wall with soil and plant it with creepers to form a kind of coping of plants. A few unmortared joints ('weep holes') at the base of the wall will be necessary for drainage. When there is no need for the wall to act as a windbreak, a cheaper and often very attractive screen is formed by a 'honeycomb' wall which is composed of a kind of extended stretcher bond, but leaving gaps between each brick.

### Finishing off the wall
Though bricks can be cut in half with a bolster and hammer or an old saw, you can buy bats (bricks cut in half across the width) or closers (cut in half longitudinally) from a brick merchant. These may be needed to complete courses or form corners. Headers, special brick copings, shaped concrete blocks, paving slabs and stone can all be used for coping the wall; avoid using a heavy-looking concrete coping on a low brick wall. Mortar all joints carefully to increase water-tightness.

Damp-proofing brick walls is important where the weather gets cold, as water seeping into the mortar may freeze and crack the masonry. A length of bituminous felt is laid between two courses of the wall about 150 mm (6 in) above ground level, extending beyond the joint to overhang the wall surface. Do not trim the felt back as it will provide a ledge for water to run off and prevent the brick from becoming stained. The edge should not be covered with mortar as this would allow water to seep into the mortar and make the damp-proofing ineffective. Damp-proofing material can also be laid in mortar directly under the coping; two layers of slate will look decorative and do the job well. Where the weather is not extreme, damp-proofing is not essential for garden walling; however, it would prevent the white stains of efflorescence creeping up the wall.

## MORTAR FOR BUILDING WALLS
The three constituents of mortar—sand, cement and lime—perform different functions: cement is the bonding material, lime makes the mixture plastic and easy to work and the sand, which has to be clean and pure, prevents shrinkage and cracking in the dry mortar. A mortar which contains a high proportion of cement is therefore stronger but less easy to work than a mix with a high lime content. A commercially produced plasticizer can be added in place of lime to make the mix more workable and frost-resistant. You should also use clean water which is as free as possible from excess alkalis, or any organic substance which might disturb the mortar mix.

Different materials, of course, have different requirements. Stone needs very strong binding mortar, of 1 part cement, $\frac{1}{2}$ part fireclay (here replacing lime which may stain the stone) and 3 parts sand. Concrete blocks generally require a weaker mortar, with more lime in it; most manufacturers recommend a specific mix for their product. Bricks are usually suited by a mix of 1 part cement, $1/1\frac{1}{2}$ parts lime and 5/6 of sand, though there are variations on this.

Apart from its binding action, well-laid mortar also waterproofs the wall, smooths over irregularities and faults in the walling material and can become a decorative feature if used thoughtfully.

### Mixing mortar
Until you are confident in your work, mix mortar in small batches, since it becomes too dry to use after an hour. It is also a good idea to mix a test batch to see what consistency is suitable for the job. Remember that wastage is about 15 per cent: allow for this in calculating the amount of mortar you will need.

Using a board to mix on, combine the dry ingredients thoroughly, make a well in the pile and stir in the water, as in mixing concrete (shown on page 59). Add the water gradually; the mortar should be wet enough to slide off the trowel but not runny.

### Laying bricks
About four hours before use, wet clay bricks with a hose; they should be damp but not waterlogged. Before mixing the mortar, try out a line of unmortared bricks on the concrete base to check the fit and the line, leaving a 25 mm ($\frac{1}{2}$ in) gap for the mortar joint between each. The first layer of bricks should lie below ground level.

Spread the mortar on the base and furrow it with a trowel, pressing it out towards the edges at the same time

Though they are less private, pierced walls provide a lighter touch in a small garden. Here the joints in a honeycomb wall are highlighted to add further interest. The coping of stretcher bond finishes the wall cleanly

### Finishing and cleaning the wall

Keep the finished wall wet, using a fine spray, for some days; two to three weeks later, when it has thoroughly dried out, any white stains of efflorescence can be cleaned off with a stiff brush dipped in a solution of muriatic acid. This substance is very potent; use nine parts of water to one of acid and keep it off the skin. After cleaning, wash the wall with plenty of water.

Finish off the vertical and then the horizontal joints while the mortar is still wet. A concave joint can be achieved by smoothing down the mortar with a length of dowel or piping

Spread one end of the brick with mortar and place it in position, tapping it into place with the handle of the trowel. Scrape off the excess mortar and use it to spread on the next brick. Check continually that the bricks are level, lengthwise and widthwise, using a spirit level. The vertical level should be tested continually

After one course of bricks has been laid on the foundation, build up the wall from the corners, bonding the corner bricks into each other in a step fashion to make strong joints. If you are laying a damp-proof course, it should be about 150 mm (6 in) above ground level, between two layers of mortar. When the corners are complete, run a line of taut cord or strong thread from corner to corner, fixed by nails into the mortar joints, to set the level for each course of bricks. Move the string up as you complete each course

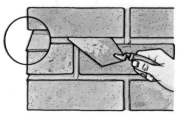

The commonly used 'weathering' joint is made with the trowel and forms a strong waterproof bond

Brick blends well with most other materials. A coping of large concrete slabs gives a crisp line to the brick wall, while the plants in a garden setting soften its outline

Curved brickwork can be very graceful, especially where it emphasizes natural ground contours

A white-painted brick wall is in keeping with a modern setting and brings light into a dark garden

# Wooden fences and structures

Wood is probably the most versatile and often the cheapest and easiest material to use if you are building your own garden enclosure. Whereas high walls in brick, stone or concrete may require professional help, any gardener can easily build a high solid fence in wood to block out unsightly views (but always check your local building regulations before erecting a high boundary fence). A low post-and-rail fence will mark a boundary or protect a lawn from passersby just as effectively as a solid but probably more expensive and time-consuming wall. Wooden fencing can be anything from the purely decorative, as in the Japanese style where the fence is as delicate as the plants which surround it, to the entirely utilitarian ranch-style fencing (though this is probably too heavy to enclose a small garden).

Timber, especially softwood, requires more preparation and upkeep than the solid walling materials. The best but often most expensive solution is to buy timber already pressure treated with preservative, or to use naturally hard-wearing wood such as jarrah, ironbark or stringybark. Some timber also needs special treatment against insects, so it is best to enquire when buying it what kind of treatment is suitable. Softwood requires several coats of preservative or, better still, several days' soaking in a cask of creosote or whatever preparation is being used. The preservatives used on timber fencing may well be toxic to plants; the commonly used creosote can burn creepers after it has been freshly applied, though it can of course safely be used to preserve the buried parts of posts. Painting the fence will also preserve it; remember to apply the paint only after cutting and shaping the wood; every bit of the exposed wood should be covered. Frequent applications of preservative or paint are worthwhile since they prolong the life of the fence.

### Preparing the site

Before starting to build the fence, measure the site and plot the line you want the fence to follow, with a length of cord fixed a little above ground level. Where a fence is designed to block out a view, test that it will serve this purpose by rigging up a line with sheets on at the intended height of the fence. Mark out the main fence posts, which should be 2 m to 3 m (6 ft to 9 ft) apart, depending on the weight of the intended fence and the probable amount of wind pressure. You may find that there is some block, such as a lump of stone or rock, which stops you fixing a post where you have planned it, so check that the ground is workable before you start cutting the timber. If there is a short length at the end of the fence, you can either re-space all the posts to balance this out or else put in a short piece of whatever kind of fencing you are using. This is easy to do if you are making the fence yourself but can be difficult with pre-fabricated panels; it may be better to extend or shorten the fence.

The most commonly encountered problem with erecting a fence is that the ground is uneven and sloping. With the open forms of fencing, such as picket fencing or the post-and-rail fence, it is very easy to cut the posts to the right length so that the fencing follows the ground contours, a method more commonly seen round farms and paddocks than in towns. With solid panelled fencing it is easier to build in steps, keeping the tops of the panels horizontal and building up or cutting down at ground level where necessary. To follow a very uneven or curving line, the most suitable form of fencing is the palisade; you can make a decorative feature of its irregular height. The main thing is to remember that the fence posts must always be vertical—use a plumb-line or spirit level to check this.

### Building the fence

The main posts of all solid wooden fences above 900 mm (3 ft) high require deep concrete foundations; though laying these is laborious, without them there is a risk of wind pressure uprooting the posts. The concrete foundations should be 750 mm (2 ft 6 in) deep for a 1.8 m (6 ft) high fence and 450 mm (1 ft 6 in) for lower ones. Dig a 300 mm sq (1 ft sq) hole with a post-hole borer, about 100 mm (4 in) longer than the required foundation depth, and fill the extra space with gravel or small stones to improve drainage, as the concrete will secure the wooden posts but not prevent them rotting if underground drainage is bad. Bevel—that is, cut a sloping edge to—the top of the fence posts to help rainwater run off and prevent damp. Alternatively wooden or metal caps can be fitted as waterproofing.

The method of measuring and setting up the main fence posts is common to all different types of fencing, close-boarded and open. By fixing rails horizontally between the posts, you form the simple post-and-rail which can stand as it is or act as a base either for boarded fencing or for pickets and palisades. The number and shape of the rails varies according to the height and purpose of the fence. Rails at the top and bottom of boarded fences are usually rectangular to support the boards; the edge should be bevelled, especially if the rails act as a coping. Triangular rails are designed to shed the maximum possible amount of water. Always use galvanized metal nails with timber to prevent rust stains. The joints in the rails should be staggered so as not to fall all on one post.

### Different kinds of fence

The most common fences are built of standard sized boards and rails in one of a small range of traditional designs, built up round the basic post-and-rail frame—the picket, the feather-boarded, the louvred and so on. However, there is great room for innovation, perhaps blending conventional looks with new ones, or following the old designs in unusual materials such as railways sleepers, or old beams.

The most solid types of fence, which also offer the most privacy, are the close-boarded—whether the boards are laid flush, feather-boarded, or double-sided (called 'board on board'). The boards in all these can be laid either vertically or horizontally and variety obtained by alternating vertical and horizontal sections or running a single timber along the top of the solid panels,

53

perhaps to grow a creeper along. Other possible materials for solid fencing vary considerably with the area in which you live, but treated plywood is available everywhere and is especially good for a painted fence. Spaced board on board and louvred fences offer less privacy but have possibly a more decorative surface, more welcoming in a small garden than a solid expanse of close-boarded fencing; they also have the considerable advantage of looking the same on both sides. Consider how the other side of your fence will look to the passerby or, more important, to your neighbour; some fences can look very unwelcoming on the 'wrong side'. The more open-work fences give greater opportunity for air to circulate and provide a frame for climbing plants.

Woven fences are a good background for plants too and can be bought in pre-fabricated panels, or you can design your own.

The basic design is the same in all woven fences, but the finished look can vary enormously, depending on the width of the slats, the width of the spaces, and the method of finishing. For a simple fence, nail all the ends of the slats to the post and weave in the spacers from the top. Many areas have a traditional style of woven fencing using the cheapest local material, such as reeds or bamboo or saplings, woven or wired up for extra strength into panels. These materials have the great advantage of blending into the local atmosphere, but remember that they often lack strength.

Picket fences may be used to enclose lawns and gardens which face on to the street; they are an elegant version of a post-and-rail fence with spaced pointed palings nailed to it. The pickets can be varied in size and spacing and, more important, in the shape of the top. Pickets are traditionally painted white or black.

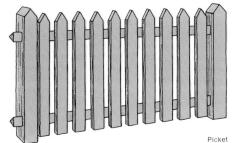

Picket

Palisade

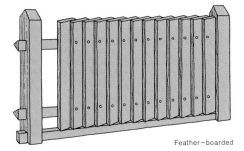

Post-and-rail

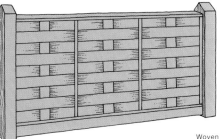

Woven

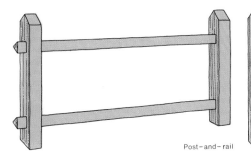

Feather-boarded

Board on board

A low, sturdy palisade fence also acts as a retaining wall round a planted bed. The logs are bevelled to let water run off, and should be painted with preservative on the inner surface to prevent rot

Close-boarded

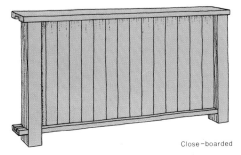

Louvred

A high fence need not look heavy if a light material like this reed panelling is used. The individually constructed panels are slightly stepped to mount a gentle slope

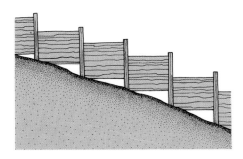

The 'stepped' design is the most suitable method for erecting close-boarded, louvred or solid panelled fences on a slope. The triangular gaps can be filled with earth or panels cut to fit

Palisade, picket or post-and-rail fencing can follow the contours of the slope more closely. Remember that, however uneven in length they may be, all posts must be vertical

The bamboo fence is designed not for strength but as a decorative part of a Japanese garden, adding to the contrasts of texture and colour. The flimsy bamboo is wired together and anchored in the ground by stronger posts

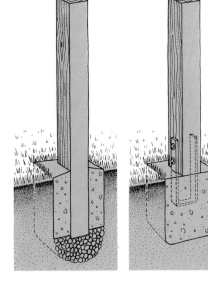

Posts for fences or any wooden structure can be set either in a poured concrete foundation drained by a pocket of gravel, or attached to a rustless metal bracket fixed in the same kind of concrete block

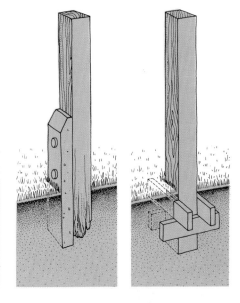

To avoid having to replace a rotting timber entirely, cut away the perished section and bolt the stump to a concrete brace. Where damp is not a problem, posts can be anchored with wooden cleats nailed across the base

Plants thrive on both sides of a spaced board on board fence, through which light and air can circulate freely. A well-finished framework of solid planks like this should last indefinitely

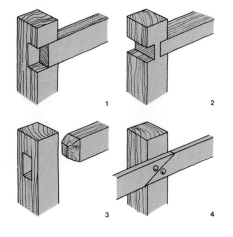

A range of simple post-and-rail joints. The end-housed rails (2) are most suitable for 'board on board', double-sided or louvred fences. The rails in (3) are cut to shape with a small axe. Remember to cover all the wood with preservative before the joints are nailed together with rustless nails

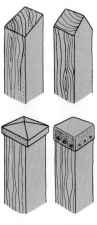

The tops of wooden fence posts can be bevelled, with either a single or double slope, to run the water off. Another method is to fit a wooden or metal cap which will protect the cut grain of the wood from exposure to damp. The flat metal cap is made of rustless zinc

PVC posts and caps are durable, can be cut to any length and need no maintenance though the initial cost is high

A wooden fence can be constructed very cheaply if you are able to gather the wood yourself. Here a simple but efficient technique is used to bind irregular sized rough strips of timber together with strong twine

Wide-spaced horizontal timbers, with plants growing up, makes a fence look delicate. Staggering the joints in the slats will spread the strain along the length of the fence

The texture of wood brings beauty to a fairly plain, solid enclosure. In this feather-boarded fence it is seen in the rough edges of the slats, the pattern of the knots and the uneven weathering of the timber

## BUILDING A WOODEN PERGOLA

A pergola is a delicate and useful addition to the garden, whether it is used to display a flowering climber or to provide shade at the side of the house over a patio. It can be a focal point of the overall design of the garden, or blend discreetly with the background. The variety offered by simple wooden structures is very large; you can choose between trellis or closely placed rafters grown over with plants, or an open top which will frame the sky and trees overhead. If you are planning to grow plants over the pergola, remember to keep the design simple so that the fully grown plants will be shown to their best advantage. The bare wood may seem stark at first, but have faith in nature—the plants will spread over it quickly.

The pergola may be built against a house wall or can be free-standing in a circular or square shape, or rectangular to form a walkway. The posts supporting the wooden beams and rafters can be wooden, metal or built of brick, stone or concrete. The wood used in the pergola's construction can be any type of strong beam; in places a 'rustic look' is appropriate, using unstripped poles.

The initial stages of building are similar to those in fencing; the same sturdy concrete foundations are necessary, as is the wood-preserving treatment. If the frame is supported by a house wall, it is a good idea to slope the beams, in case you ever want to roof the structure. Remember that the frame should be strong enough to hold a man, or stronger in areas with heavy snow.

This simple pergola, supported on two sides by the house wall and an adjoining honeycomb wall, can be built of fairly delicate timbers; free-standing structures should be sturdier

Round a balcony or a roof garden a screen is needed which effectively blocks out rooftops and television aerials without imposing a rigid sense of enclosure. This elegant wooden construction is somewhat complex, with its concealed uprights and alternating pattern which suggests a woven fence

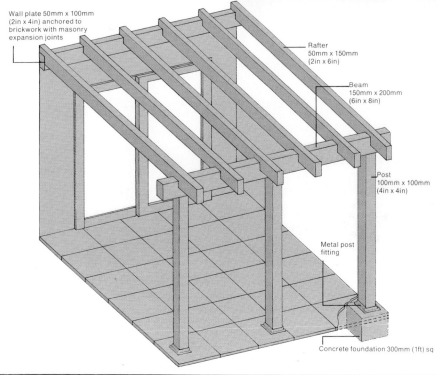

Wall plate 50mm x 100mm (2in x 4in) anchored to brickwork with masonry expansion joints

Rafter 50mm x 150mm (2in x 6in)

Beam 150mm x 200mm (6in x 8in)

Post 100mm x 100mm (4in x 4in)

Metal post fitting

Concrete foundation 300mm (1ft) sq

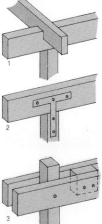

The simple notched joint (1) can be strengthened by a T-shaped brace (2) to reduce side sway on the posts. A double beam bolted through the post and a spacer block (3) adds interest to the overhead view

# Concrete: an underestimated material

Treated with delicacy and imagination, concrete is a versatile and satisfying material for the garden. Walls built of concrete are particularly appropriate for the small gardens of modern houses as they blend with the clean lines of modern design. Concrete also mellows well and forms a successful background for plants as it has a fairly bland and undemanding surface which highlights the outline of foliage against it.

On a small scale, concrete is also a rewarding medium to work with and has definite practical advantages such as its durability. It can be laid in the form of pre-cast blocks, either solid blocks or perforated with various designs (known as screen blocks), or as wet concrete laid *in situ*. All these forms are relatively cheap and, once a concrete wall is in position, it needs very little maintenance.

Concrete manufacturers are now making every effort to break away from the conventional utilitarian look of the material and exploit its lighter and more welcoming aspects, which make it suitable for the domestic situation. The range of textures and colours which are available or can be created with concrete, is continually expanding. The tinted shades weather particularly well into mellow colours, while white concrete may become slightly dirty with age. Concrete facsimiles of natural stone are a poor substitute for the real thing, however, and are best avoided. It is important to be aware of problems of scale, too; effects of pattern and colour which look right on the wall of a civic centre will be overwhelming in a small garden. The best results will be obtained if the design is simple and the material used sensitively.

## In situ *concrete*

High concrete walls built *in situ* are probably too heavy and massive in most small gardens but there are situations which demand a particularly strong structure—to retain a steep bank for instance. A fairly common use for concrete is to build smooth curved walls, but the formwork for these has to be very secure and they are often a job for professional builders—as are high walls, where the calculations of stress and weight involved become extremely complex. Concrete structures such as low walls, kerbings or planting boxes should, however, be well within the scope of most gardeners. Concrete *in situ* is very strong so a wall 150 mm to 200 mm (6 in to 8 in) thick will probably be adequate, unless you want the low wall to form a seat or give some particularly chunky effect. If a bench wall is required, set bolts in the concrete while it is still wet to secure the wooden top. Adjust the depth so that the bolts can hold the seat boards but will not protrude above them.

## *Building a concrete block wall*

The most usual type of solid structure wall is that constructed in pre-cast lightweight concrete blocks. They are now available with much finer surfaces, in varying colours and aggregate finishes to match natural stone types; they can also be rendered or painted with either concrete paint or ordinary paint.

Alternatively, screen blocks perforated with a variety of geometric and traditional patterns can be used to form a screen. The originals of these are the decorative screens of hot Middle Eastern or southern European countries which were constructed in

## CASTING CONCRETE *IN SITU*

The three components of concrete are cement, water and a mixture of fine aggregate (sand) and coarse aggregate (crushed stone or gravel). The coarse aggregate provides the strength in concrete, making it a bulky material stronger than mortar. The mixture of water and cement forms the bonding element. A low water content will strengthen the finished structure too, as evaporation creates tiny weaknesses.

The mix of concrete required varies according to the type of work you are doing. If you are using ready-mixed concrete, the supplier will probably advise you on a suitable mix. If you are mixing it at home, a combination of 1 part cement, $2\frac{1}{2}$ parts of sand and 4 parts coarse gravel aggregate is right for most heavy-duty work—foundations, walls and drives. For paths and thin strips of concrete, the best proportions are 1 part cement, 2 parts of sand and 3 parts of finer aggregate. For paving less than 50 mm (2 in) thick and bedding mortar for slabs and step treads, a mix of 1 part cement and 3 parts of coarse sand is suitable.

Mortared walls more than 300 mm (1 ft) high all need concrete foundations laid *in situ*. They should be laid below ground frost level—450 mm (1 ft 6 in) deep is adequate; it the area is particularly prone to frost, special anti-freeze can be added to the concrete mix. The base should usually be about 300 mm (1 ft) thick, twice the width of the wall

Foundations for walls on a slope should be laid in a stepped trench. For block or brick walls, the depth of the step should equal the size of the block unit. With low walls of concrete laid *in situ* foundation and wall can be laid as one, but with high heavy walls a separate grooved foundation will provide extra stability and will also accommodate expansion of the walling material in extreme temperatures

A concrete block wall has a bland and unobtrusive surface; the visual interest here has been created by placing several blocks crosswise

and extend a little way beyond the length of the wall at either end. If the ground is sloping, the foundation can be laid in steps, each step being the same height, or a multiple of the height, of the brick or block in use. Remember to make provision for any drainage holes or reinforcing rods which may be necessary. Place the rods about 25 mm (1 in) above the bottom of the concrete.

## Formwork

Formwork is necessary to mould *in situ* concrete walls and paving and it is imperative that this should be strong enough to hold the weight of the wet concrete. Straight, strong knotless timber

should be used; plywood is suitable and will give a smooth surface if this is desired. Wood with deep graining is sometimes used to produce an interesting pattern on the surface. Corrugated iron or asbestos might also be used in this way.

Before the concrete is laid, the forms should be soaked to swell and seal the wood, and then oiled on the inside with a thin oil. Making the formwork carefully is vital to the success of the wall, but it is far more taxing than the actual laying of the concrete.

## Pouring the concrete

It is important to work quickly with wet concrete; it should all be poured

within an hour of mixing. If you must leave the work, cover it in damp sacking but do not leave it for more than 30 minutes. In formwork, pour the concrete in layers of 150 mm to 200 mm (6 in to 8 in), prodding each layer into place and smoothing it with a shovel. On the top layer, press out air bubbles with a wooden board and then a trowel.

It is important to cure, that is, dry out the concrete slowly in order to increase its strength. Leave the forms in place for at least four days or longer in cold weather, and keep the top of the wall moist. If you want to give it a special finish and have to remove the forms, then keep the wall wet all over with damp sacking for a week. Concrete can be given a variety of treatments to alter its finished appearance. To get a smooth surface, ram a flat-bladed shovel between the form and the freshly-poured concrete to force the chips of aggregate into the centre of the wall. It is a common practice to leave the aggregate exposed, especially as a non-slip surface for paving. Rock salt crystals scattered over damp concrete will leave a pitted surface. Alternatively, a multitude of patterns can be brushed, stamped or scraped on to the wet surface. When the concrete is set it can be finished with a masonry sealer. Concrete paint is also available, as are colour pigments composed of metallic oxides which are added to the dry cement before mixing.

Formwork for concrete should be sturdily built. The walls of the form can be reinforced with 50 mm by 100 mm (2 in by 4 in) vertical braces and horizontal timbers of the same size at ground level. The supporting struts, of 50 mm by 100 mm (2 in by 4 in), are attached to stakes driven into the ground. Wire ties and wooden spreader blocks are used to keep the sides of the form apart. The blocks are removed during pouring, using the wooden handles for easy removal, but the wire ties remain; they are clipped back flush with the wall when the concrete dries and the formwork is removed

On a plastic sheet or board, mix the dry ingredients together evenly, cement and sand first and then the aggregate. Make a well in the middle of the heap and add water sparingly. Turn the pile carefully, drawing the dry material to the centre and making the whole mix evenly moist. It should be stiff enough to retain the mark of the shovel but not crumbly

The rough texture of this concrete wall cast *in situ* is starkly impressive, relieved only by its curved outline

clay or stone to provide a measure of privacy but allow air circulation. Concrete of course is much heavier to look at but the simple designs can be very effective when contrasted with the large leaves of creepers. A combination of solid and perforated blocks, or solid blocks laid in honeycomb fashion, can also lighten the heaviness of a solid wall. Remember, however, that a screen will not afford total privacy and may be more appropriate used within the garden than as a boundary wall.

The length of the wall should be a multiple of the size of block you are using, so that the first layer fits the foundation exactly. Concrete blocks cannot be cut to fit and half-blocks have to be bought specially; calculate the number you will need if you are laying the wall in alternate courses. Similarly, if you use coloured or treated blocks, buy all you need at the same time, for the colour shade may vary slightly in the next batch. Concrete blocks are laid coursed in the same way as brick, with a solid concrete foundation, steel reinforcements and a damp-proof course if necessary. Unlike brick, however, blocks can be laid with continuous vertical joints, with constant reinforcement of steel rods. Stone facsimile blocks, which have only one finished 'rock-face' surface, should be laid as the facing to a cavity wall.

Hollow block walls are reinforced with vertical steel rods which are rooted in the foundation; they run up through the reinforcing cells and are solidly grouted into place. Perforated walls need horizontal reinforcement (rods or wire mesh) along their length, and piers at approximately 2 m (6 ft to 7 ft) intervals. The piers are columns, either of brick or concrete blocks, or of special pier blocks which are grooved to hold the adjacent screen blocks. Consult the local building regulations to see what kind of reinforcing is necessary in your area. When you are spreading blocks with mortar you may have some trouble with the mortar falling into the reinforcing cells; in this case use a piece of wood to cover up the cavities, mortar the course of blocks along their edges and then remove the wood. In every other way laying concrete blocks is exactly similar to bricklaying (explained on page 51).

Concrete beams are sometimes seen enclosing farmyards in a fencing system which uses the beams horizontally, sliding into grooved verticals, like an enlarged lapped timber fence. This scheme is probably too heavy for a small garden, but vertical concrete beams let into the ground like a mammoth picket fence can have a surprisingly elegant and light appearance. Another unexpected source of cheap and fairly informal walling is slabs of broken concrete picked up from demolition sites. If the pieces are much the same size, they can be laid in the same way as a random dry stone wall with plants in the crevices. The wall should be very stable if it is battered and well balanced.

Screen blocks, originating in the Middle East, show a more delicate use of concrete. A pierced screen wall, supported by special piers (known as 'pilasters'), has reinforcing mesh through the mortar joints

The clear lines of a high wall of concrete laid *in situ* harmonize with a modern housing style to produce a quiet elegant effect (below left). The large expanse of wall area is relieved by the slightly roughened and grooved surface caused by the pressure of the formwork during casting. Plants are clearly outlined against the uncluttered background (below)

# More ideas for garden enclosures and screens

When planning the garden enclosure, you certainly need not restrict yourself to the traditional categories of walls and fencing. There is a host of other materials, many of which are not conventionally associated with a garden setting, which may be very successful in harmonizing with the individual style of a particular garden. The internal screen, especially, provides an opportunity for experimentation with modern materials—glass and plastic, for example—as well as for reviving the traditional garden screen of trellis work. Small gardens are particularly versatile in this way as you can use bold ideas over a small area which might become monotonous on a large site.

### Metal fencing

The two most common types of metal fencing are probably unsuitable in small gardens though for different reasons. The metal version of post-and-rail fencing is long-lasting and elegant to look at when painted, but around a small garden it offers too little definite line and may well look flimsy. Another common style, wrought iron work, is strictly limited to a particular kind of garden, usually urban and formal, though used in this setting it is unsurpassed. In other places it looks fussy and incongruous, and this is unfortunately emphasized by the crudeness of some modern ironwork designs. All ironwork needs a coat of red lead primer and two coats of exterior gloss paint to seal it against rust, and frequent repainting is necessary.

### Glass screens

Where strong winds disturb warm weather, for instance by the sea, clear glass screens will act as a wind break without blocking the view. Large sheets of 10 mm ($\frac{3}{8}$ in) thick safety or wired glass are advisable especially with children around; they may also be required by building regulations. Safety glass is expensive and the fitting is a professional job. The wooden or aluminium frame should be well stabilized particularly where the wind is strong. If the glass is framed only on three sides, the fourth edge should be ground off until it is smooth.

### Screens within the garden

There are situations inside the garden where a visual block is required, something less massive than a fence or a wall, which will hold the eye and be decorative in itself. One frequent use of the screen is to divide the leisure parts of the garden from the working parts like the compost heap and the dustbins. A screen will make a garden pleasant to sit in by creating areas of shade, a valuable luxury in hot countries. Planted screens can provide good protection against strong sunlight, only letting patches of green light and shadow filter through to the ground in front to form a cool retreat.

Some striking effects can be achieved with screens of rather 'unnatural' materials. Sheets of corrugated asbestos framed and painted, or coloured sheets of rigid plastic can be used. Bamboo canes, or metal or plastic pipes set into the ground like a

A glass panel will frame a view while protecting the garden from strong winds. Set the edges of the frame either well below or above the natural eye level to avoid a constant line disturbing your field of vision

Traditional wrought iron demands a particularly apt setting, usually in the garden of an old town house or, as here, round a balcony. Modern wrought iron is somewhat crude and flimsy in comparison with the sturdy and elaborate nineteenth-century original

palisade fence look surprisingly effective in some garden settings. By using plants to break up the straight lines of structures, an even wider range of effects can be gained. You can weave patterns, of nylon rope or taut wire covered in plastic, inside a frame and train plants up this.

When planning the kind of screen you want, consider whether or not plants will be grown along it, what kind they will be, and how long they will take to grow. Some screens are marked by a light pattern of creepers, while others are enveloped by an enormous wistaria or vine. This luxuriant growth will probably die down and have to be pruned in winter, however; make allowance for this when planning the appearance of the supporting framework. If you intend eventually to grow a thick hedge, you may only need a temporary screen, of light woven rush for instance, until the plants are fully grown.

Most screens, especially those grown over with plants or which are very delicate, require some kind of upkeep occasionally: timber needs repainting and coating with preservative, metal may rust and wires need replacing and tightening. With some structures, or against brick walls, it is probably more convenient to train the plants over a wire mesh held by screws a little distance from the surface. This not only allows you to remove the plant while you paint the timber, but also gives the plant more room to breathe and to grow.

## Wooden trellis

Wooden structures are probably the most common and convenient support for plants. The traditional trellis work of fine diamonds or squares has a very delicate air, complemented by plants such as rambling roses or clematis; or you can construct a plainer and sturdier framework. Trellis is easy to build so you can simply follow your own design, whether you are planning to heighten an existing fence, make a screen, form an entrance, or build a lightweight garden building. It is particularly suitable for roof gardens, or any site with a small ground area, because it exploits the available height. A rich variety of flowers, vegetables and creepers can flourish on very little ground space if they are grown up against trellis; moreover, when the plants die down in winter, the lattice pattern is by no means ugly and can be a decoration to the garden in its own right.

Pre-fabricated trellis is very convenient but it is ultimately more expensive and time-consuming than home-built trellis as the lath is often flimsy and will not last. Twining plants will weaken it considerably and they will be disturbed each time the trellis is replaced. It is worthwhile therefore to build your own frame, tailor-made to the shape of the site. Vary the width of the lattice to fit the plants: delicate plants cannot be trained over widely spaced laths without looking dwarfed and having to be constantly tied with twine.

A visual barrier is often desirable for shelter and privacy. Here a planted vertical screen shades the house entrance and separates it from the back garden in an imaginative way

Wooden frames provide a place for climbing plants and vines, even vegetables; their design can be varied according to the character and size of the plant. A massive creeper here rests on a suitably solid, wide-spaced structure

Iron need not always be moulded into impressive bulky forms, perhaps too heavy for a small garden, but can take delicate curving shapes as in this screen which complements a background of foliage. Ironwork should be painted frequently to keep it smart and protect it against rust

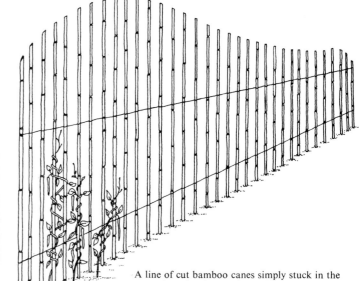

A line of cut bamboo canes simply stuck in the ground can be given a decorative curved outline. It will give sufficient support for light climbing plants and you may want to combine an evergreen creeper with an annual climber to produce constant foliage

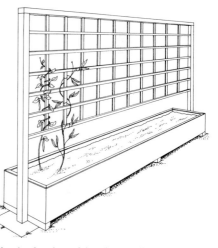

A planting box is useful under a trellis grid. The method of erecting a free-standing trellis is similar to building a fence and the timber requires the same preserving treatment. The laths should be glued together and then nailed with flat-headed short nails. Use a piece of wood as a template to ensure regular spacing

Plants themselves form a temporary screen, serving to separate two areas of the garden as here. Ranks of sweet peas add variety to the flat lines of the vegetable area; the screen could be of runner beans, thus becoming productive as well as attractive

Traditional diamond pattern trellis looks effective against a brick wall when painted white. Fixing it a little distance away gives more room for growth and an evergreen creeper such as ivy will be decorative throughout the year

# GARDEN PAVING

Paths and patios are the framework of the garden, linking
different parts of it together both physically and aesthetically
and providing firm surfaces to walk on, which dry out quickly
after rain. There are far more interesting ways of using paving
than to create paths running from one part of the garden to
another, cutting the area into strips. This places undue emphasis
on the path as a main feature, whereas it is one element of the
total composition, made up also of plants, grass and possibly
water. Using a greater area of paving, to include a terrace and
perhaps a play space, integrates the path more successfully into
the overall scheme, while it still provides accessibility.

### Choosing your material
A wide variety of paving materials is available, and your
choice should be based on a combination of aesthetic, practical
and economic considerations. The end result should be suited to
its purpose, pleasing to the eye and priced within the budget of
the buyer. Other factors are the time needed to complete the
work and, if it is to be a do-it-yourself project, the skill
and effort required.

It is inevitable that some of these considerations will conflict. For
instance, although concrete is a cheap, long-lasting material which
is relatively simple to lay, it is often thought to be unacceptable
for aesthetic reasons. Broken pieces of any material tend to be
cheaper than regular shapes, but to lay crazy paving without an
uneven and messy end result is no easy task. Ceramic tiles,
slate and marble can look magnificent in the right setting, but
they are expensive and may chip or crack if subjected to frost
or constant wear. Paving in mixed materials, such as combinations
of wood and brick or stone slabs and cobble, can be effective.
However, this type of treatment requires careful planning and
skilful design if it is to read as a unified visual concept.

Where possible use a material which is employed in
your house, making the garden an architectural as well as
a physical extension of the building. Stone, brick,
concrete and wood are the materials of which most houses are
built and all can be used successfully in the right situation;
their particular suitability is discussed in the following
pages. Where it is not possible to adopt the house material for
your main paving—for example, brick may be too expensive or
large slabs of stone unsuitable for curved paths—try to use
it as an edging to lawn or beds, or in combination with another
paving material.

The smaller the unit of paving, the more visually suitable it
is likely to be for the garden setting. The smallest units are often,
however, the most expensive and they can take a long time to
lay. The size of a unit of paving making up the surface often
sets the pace at which one travels over it and this should also
be considered when choosing your material. A thick layer of gravel,
for instance, can actually hold up the pedestrian as he crunches
his way through it. The effect of a single material in this
respect can also vary according to how it is laid. Thus cobbles,
when laid flat, lose some of their quality but the surface created
is relatively smooth; when laid loose or set high like eggs in a
crate, their surface is broken and forbidding and they can be
uncomfortable to walk on.

# Laying foundations for paving

Whatever the type of paving and wherever it is, it will sometimes get wet, so you must allow for drainage. Paving should always be laid to slope gently away from the house so that the water falls either into surrounding beds or grass, or into a gulley connecting with a soakaway or the surface drainage system from the house. The channels to gulleys can always be used as an element of the layout. A cross gradient of 25 mm in 2 m (1 in in 6 ft 6 in) should give sufficient slope.

If your house has a damp-proof course, make sure that the level of paving is well below it (at least 150 mm or 6 in) at the

Although there is some danger of movement or settlement, the simplest way to lay paving slabs is to bed them in sand spread on top of earth which has been consolidated with a roller

point at which it meets the house. In some countries this is a legal requirement, but in any case it is a sensible precaution to prevent damp from entering the house walls. If the house leads directly on to the outside paved area, possibly through sliding doors, and it is essential to have a continuous level, a step can be built, leading down from the indoor floor height to the lower paving level. There should be a gap of at least 25 mm (1 in) between the step and the wall of the house in order to catch rain. If the gap is any narrower it is likely to block with leaves, dirt and snow in winter.

All paving should be laid properly on a firm base to provide a stable, level bed. This is particularly important either on an access path to your front door which is in constant use or on a terrace, especially one which is used by the young or elderly. In some situations and for certain materials a sand base will be adequate; paving slabs can simply be laid on the base or 'spot bedded', using a few spots of mortar. However, a good foundation usually necessitates a base of hardcore (broken bricks or stone), ashes or coarse gravel, not less than 75 mm (3 in) thick and well consolidated by rolling.

Before considering each of the paving materials in detail, instructions are given on how to lay on a sand base and on hardcore and mortar, showing methods which will be suitable for most types of paving.

## SPECIALIST TOOLS FOR PAVING

If you intend to do your own paving work, it may be necessary to get hold of a few specialist tools. Some of these—the spirit level (1), for example—will probably be essential for several jobs, and therefore well worth buying. Others, such as the bull float (7), can usually be hired. Tools such as the wooden float (6) and screed (8) can easily be home made.

1 Long spirit level to check horizontal planes
2 Carpenter's square to check right angles
3 Pointed trowel for jobs involving mortar
4 Tamper to pack soil or hardcore
5 Steel float to finish concrete surfaces
6 Wooden float to spread concrete
7 Bull float to spread large areas of concrete
8 Screed for levelling large areas of mortar
9 Mason's hammer to chip away rough edges
10 Chisel to cut and dress brick and stone
11 Jointer to finish off mortar pointing

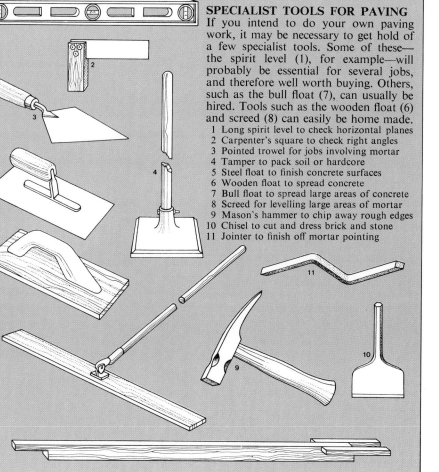

If subject to heavy loads or constant use, paving slabs should be bedded in mortar. After levelling the ground, use a tamper to consolidate a layer of hardcore (brick rubble or broken concrete)

Use a section of a plank to spread a layer of ash, lean-mix concrete (1 part cement to 3 parts sand) or similar fine material over the hardcore, as this will bind it together

Trowel the mortar over the area of the first slab. Make sure that it is spread to the correct height, with the necessary slope for drainage, by checking it against a string guideline

Pieces of wood can be temporarily inserted between the slabs to ensure even spacing. Tap the slabs into position, using a spirit level to check the desired fall

# Traditional paving in natural stone

There is a special technique for laying old stone slabs (left). Small square keystones are laid first, followed by the larger slabs which then radiate round them

Natural stone comes in many different shades, which can create very different moods. The austere colour and regular pattern of these slabs (below) give a clean architectural effect

Uneven chunks of natural stone, left over from quarrying, can be laid in a random pattern (above); they look right in an informal garden setting

Massive, irregularly shaped pieces of stone are used almost sculpturally within an asymmetric but exactly balanced Japanese design (below)

Natural stone slabs or flags can be found in almost every shade from creamy yellow to grey and they make a superb paving material, especially suitable for a rural or old urban setting.

Newly quarried stone is prohibitively expensive, especially when it has been cut to be laid coursed like old stone slabs. However, local stone slabs were used for paving the streets in many countries until comparatively recently and it is still possible to buy these second-hand. Not only are the old slabs cheaper, but they have a beautiful mellow appearance, weathered and worn. Though they do not have the standard thickness of new stone, they do come in regular shapes, either square or rectangular. Some of the slabs are in fact fairly massive, but these would be out of scale with new properties and too heavy for roof gardens.

It is important to work with the natural shape and size of the slabs; cutting is difficult and should be avoided if possible. Where you do not have enough stone to cover a desired area, old stone slabs can be used successfully in conjunction with bricks, cobbles or granite setts—any smaller element in fact.

For normal garden use, natural stone slabs can simply be bedded in sand as their own weight is heavy enough to stabilize them. A firm, well-drained foundation is essential, otherwise the slabs will settle unevenly. If the soil drains slowly, make a base of 25 mm to 50 mm (1 in to 2 in) of gravel, then fill the area with 50 mm to 100 mm (2 in to 4 in) of sand. Lay the slabs in position and check the level but remember to allow for the variations in thickness of old slabs.

Make sure they are well bedded by moving them around with both hands until they seem firm or tamping them down lightly with a hammer on a wooden block. Leave the joints open or brush sand and gravel in between them; alternatively, use topsoil and small plants to fill the joints.

### Slate and marble

Slate and marble are both luxury paving materials and tend to be expensive for areas other than those in which they are quarried or cut. Used in the right way, both are extremely attractive, hard-wearing and easily cleaned. They can be supplied thin, which makes them suitable for roof garden work or for flooring a conservatory which adjoins a living room in the same material.

Slate is a restrained and dignified paving material. One of its distinctive features is the texture of its cut surface (above), but its matt grey tone gives a slightly sombre appearance when it is used over a large area. However, slate mixes well with other materials and provides a good background for the brighter and richer colours of nature (left)

Cutting and laying pieces of stone in a crazy paving pattern is a difficult, precision job; when done with care the result can be particularly striking

Slate, being slightly more textured and having more subtle colouring, lends itself better to use with plants. Marble looks its best under sunlight but can be garish if used without care and restraint.

### Crazy or random paving

Most of the large elements of paving look best when laid in a regular pattern. One reason for this is that the outline of the terrace or path is usually straight so regular shapes fit into this and the overall design much better. But materials such as concrete slabs, old stone slabs or marble are all cheaper when broken and they can then be laid in a random pattern known as crazy paving. When badly laid, with large joints between the elements and poorly pointed, crazy paving lives up to its name, invariably being uneven into the bargain. It can look effective, however, when large irregular areas are laid to fit together like a jig-saw. Such laying requires great care and precision. The important thing is to edge the paved area with the bigger pieces of stone, as small ones break away more easily. It is a good idea to arrange the stones into a pleasing pattern before they are fixed in place, avoiding continuous joint lines.

# Paving the garden in patterns of brick

Brick is perhaps the most versatile paving medium for garden use. It is available in a great range of strong and subtle colours which do not fade, it is the right sort of scale for a small garden and it matches the material of which many houses are still built. Being made up of small units, brick can be used to make gradual changes of direction or level: to form footholds on a slope, for example, each brick can be laid slightly tilted. Brick also mixes well with most other materials; it can be used effectively for demarcation and pattern to retain concrete laid *in situ*.

The inadequate weather-resistance of normal walling bricks was formerly a drawback. They were often too soft to withstand the water in them which froze in winter and so started to break up the composition of the brick. The alternative was to use a harder surfaced engineering brick which was either too dark and sombre in colour or too bright a red. However, the recent widespread availability of the brick pavior has made brick far more feasible for domestic use.

Paviors come in varying shades and can be made either in the normal brick clay or, more recently, in concrete. Their great virtue is that they are thin, from 25 mm to 50 mm (1 in to 2 in) compared to the 65 mm (2½ in) thickness of ordinary bricks; this makes them comparatively light and therefore ideal for roof or patio work. Old bricks can usually still be obtained and they have a more mellow appearance—but check on the bricks' hardness, and be prepared to pay more since the price includes cleaning them.

### Laying the bricks

Bricks used for paving do not have to be bonded tightly as in a wall, as they are subject to less stress—they can therefore be laid in a great variety of attractive patterns. Certain patterns, such as herringbone, have directional characteristics that can be used to emphasize features of the garden plan. Building bricks can be laid flat, with the recessed area in the middle of the brick, known as the frog, face down (bedding

If bricks are laid slightly tilted, as in this herringbone path, the uneven surface ensures a firm foothold even in wet weather

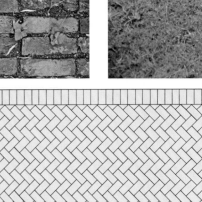

The varied colours and mellow tones of old bricks successfully blend with ground cover such as ivy. Planting which is allowed to grow over the paving softens its edges

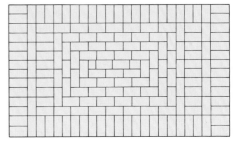

Stretcher bond, stretcher faces

Whole and half bricks, bedding faces

Herringbone with edging, bedding faces

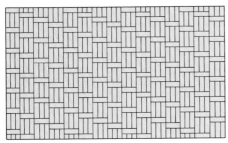

Stretcher faces

Whole and half bricks, bedding faces

Repeating unit pattern, bedding faces

An expanse of brick paving laid in a herringbone pattern gives a visual sense of unity. Laid on a mortar bed, bricks form a firm, level base

Depending on how they are laid, bricks can give a strong sense of visual direction. Here the eye is led along the side of the house by the brick path

Bricks combine effectively with most other paving materials. Here an area of stretcher bond brick paving is separated from the adjoining gravel by an edging of bricks laid on their bedding faces, giving a crisp finish

Right-angle herringbone with edgings

Stretcher faces

Bedding faces

Bedding faces

Stretcher faces, bordering herringbone

Stretcher faces

face). This uses less bricks than laying them more traditionally 'on edge', that is with the narrow side upwards (stretcher face). Certain patterns need to be seen over a large area to be effective while others, such as basket-weave, stretcher bond and herringbone, can be equally successful in a narrow path.

They can be laid directly on a 20 mm to 40 mm ($\frac{3}{4}$ in to $1\frac{1}{2}$ in) bed of sand after excavating to the required depth and first placing a 70 mm ($2\frac{3}{4}$ in) layer of consolidated hardcore or ash. For a firmer base they can be bedded in a mortar mix.

Where bricks are simply laid on sand, an edging will help to keep them permanently in place. A single or double course of bricks set on end and bedded in mortar makes a very attractive edging. Alternatively the outside edge of the path or terrace can simply be laid on a concrete or mortar base with mortar joints between the bricks. A timber edging can also be effective in the right setting but choose treated or durable wood which will not rot in contact with the ground —railway sleepers are one suggestion.

Mowing is easier if the lawn is separated from the beds by a border of paving; a line of bricks does this simple job well

A strip of wood which is durable in the ground forms a good edging for brick paving (below and right); the timber should be held in place by pegs below the surface. If the paving does not need to withstand heavy loads, the bricks can be laid directly on a bed of sand

The basketweave pattern (above) offers visual variety without being too complicated or difficult to lay. It is particularly suitable for narrow paths and smaller areas of paving

A row of upright bricks laid in a 'soldier' course is an effective alternative to wooden edging. If the bricks do have to support heavy loads, there should be at least 70 mm ($2\frac{3}{4}$ in) of concrete beneath the bed of sand

## Pointing

Good paving, like good walling, can be utterly ruined by the manner in which it is pointed. Paving can be flush jointed, that is without pointing between the elements, or with a little sand brushed in between them. This way weeds are encouraged to grow between units, which may or may not be desirable. Most paving looks best with the joints slightly brushed out or recessed so that each element stands out quite clearly.

The joints can be filled with mortar by using a trowel, or wet mortar mix, known as grout, can be poured between narrow joints. Both methods can be messy and one needs a good eye and a steady hand. Care should always be taken to keep paving clean while working since it is difficult to get dried mortar off a porous surface. Probably the cleanest way is to prepare a dry sand and cement mix; brush it in between the joints and lightly water it. If the paving is laid on a porous base, just leave the brushed-in mix and water will creep in, moisten and set the mix on its own.

Brick is an extremely versatile medium. It can blend with almost any atmosphere, depending on the overall style of the garden. Laid in a slightly random fashion, with grass allowed to grow between the bricks, the effect can be gentle and rustic

Bricks can be pointed by brushing dry mortar into the joints with a stiff brush

An alternative method of pointing bricks is to pack wet mortar into the joints with a trowel

Use a piece of wood to compress the dry mortar; finally wet the mortar with a fine spray

Both dry and wet mortar pointing can be finished off by running a wooden dowel along the joints

Contrasting with the informal, rustic use of brick, in this controlled, rectangular garden design precision-laid brick paviors contribute to the clean, architectural lines of the layout

# Concrete paving for strength and durability

For a large area of paving which has to be hard surfaced consider the use of concrete laid *in situ*, that is on the spot. It is permanent, needs no maintenance and can be moulded to suit any shapes or levels. Since concrete expands and contracts with changes in temperature it should only be laid in areas of not more than three metres (about three yards) square. If the area to be paved is larger than this it will have to be broken up into a pattern or reinforced.

When paving a small garden, *in situ* concrete is probably best laid in squares placed next to each other with only a slight gap between, possibly filled with sand. If each square is allowed to dry before the next one is laid, filling in the joints should not be necessary. Concrete can be textured in different ways to produce interesting patterns: drawing a stiff broom across it when it is nearly set, for example, creates a ribbed texture and brushing concrete before it is fully dry exposes the gravel aggregate in its composition, making a pebbly finish. If you are employing someone else to do this job, have a sample prepared on the ground or in an old seed box as a guide. A sophisticated way of using *in situ* concrete is to lay it in a pattern with brick, granite setts or even with concrete slabs in a contrasting colour.

Laying your own concrete is a comparatively cheap way to surface an area but the work is heavy and messy. It must be carefully planned and requires more than one pair of hands. The first thing to do is to calculate the volume of concrete needed, which is indicated by the chart; then decide on the correct mix for the job (see page 58). For a small area you can buy bags of dry-mixed concrete, so that all you have to do is add water. Otherwise you can order the ingredients and mix them yourself, either with a shovel or with a small hired concrete mixer. For major jobs—if you are using more than about 3 cu m (4 cu yd) of concrete—the most practical method is the ready-mix truck that delivers the concrete and pours it by chute directly to where it will be used. If you use ready-mixed concrete, have the site fully prepared, with all the wooden formwork ready, when the lorry arrives. When it is not possible to pour directly into the formwork, you can transport the concrete by wheelbarrow. But you will need help, since the concrete must be laid within two hours of delivery and 1 cu m (1·3 cu yd) takes about 40 barrow-loads.

*In situ* concrete requires a firm, level surface. If the soil is fairly firm and you want a surface level with the surrounding ground, all you need to do is dig down to the same depth as the concrete area—100 mm (4 in) for a drive, 50 mm (2 in) for a path. With loose soil, put down a layer of rubble first and compact it with a roller; paths need 25 mm to 50 mm (1 in to 2 in) of rubble, while drives need 75 mm (3 in). When laying concrete on a cracked base, first break this up and compact the rubble, as a new layer laid on top of an old base will often crack or scale.

Concrete slabs with the aggregate exposed, in this instance laid in combination with brick, give a rough pebbly surface

Concrete need not look stark and formal. The different textures and shapes of these paving sections, along with the plants allowed to grow in between them, contribute to the relaxed atmosphere of this garden

Interlocking concrete blocks come in many interesting shapes and sizes (left). They fit tightly together to give a firm surface and can be laid relatively quickly and easily

Use this table (right) as a guide for working out how much concrete to order. Working in metric, read across from the area scale to the thickness line and then down to the total quantity scale; for Imperial measurements, read from the right

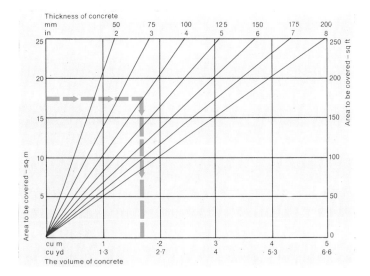

## LAYING CONCRETE *IN SITU*

In setting out the formwork for *in situ* concrete, prepare a base at least 100 mm (4 in) wider than the proposed size of the finished area of paving. Build a strong formwork from 25 mm by 75 mm (1in by 3in) timber, with pegs at 1 m (3 ft) intervals. Check the formwork with a spirit level, allowing a drainage slope of 6 mm in 300 mm ($\frac{1}{4}$ in in 1 ft). A 20 mm ($\frac{3}{4}$ in) thick block of wood placed under the batten supporting the spirit level will give the correct slope for a path 1 m (3 ft) wide

Pour the concrete into the formwork, getting it as near as possible to its final position so as to minimize further handling. Use a rake or shovel to spread the mix evenly, leaving about 25 mm (1 in) above the formwork to allow for compaction

Compact and level the concrete with a heavy plank. Lift the plank a little and then drop it, moving it along half the thickness of the plank each time; repeat this process and finally remove excess concrete by sliding the plank from side to side with a sawing action

When the surface water has evaporated, finish the concrete with a wooden float. Move the float in sweeping arcs to bring the fine particles to the surface

If you want a rough, non-slip texture, drag a broom across the surface of the concrete. The stiffer the bristles, the rougher the final texture will be

The aggregate in the concrete can be exposed to give a pebbly surface. When the concrete begins to harden, hose it gently and brush away the top layer of cement. Cover newly laid concrete with damp sacking, waterproof building paper or polythene sheets. After about four days in warm weather—and up to ten in winter—the concrete should have set sufficiently to take light weights, but keep heavy loads off for another four to ten days

### Concrete slabs

The pre-cast slab is by far the most commonly used paving material, though it is more expensive than concrete laid *in situ*. Used sensitively over a limited area, without too much pattern and with little colour, it is an excellent material, being hard-wearing and easy to clean. Concrete slabs also mellow fairly quickly and their colours even fade; this is often a blessing, for the over-patterned terrace is as demanding to walk on as the over-patterned carpet inside. Check the colour of any slab you want, seeing it both wet and dry.

Paving slabs now come in most sizes and shapes—squares, rectangles, circles and even pre-arranged crazy paving—and many textures are also available. Patterns can then be made up as desired but remember that a paving pattern is only part of a larger design and it should not be allowed to disrupt the whole, so keep it simple.

Depending on the wear which the path or terrace will take, slabs can be laid either in sand or in mortar (see page 65). Another method, when laying them in sand, is to use four or five evenly spaced spots of mortar for each slab. They should always be laid to fall away from any structure, allowing the surface water to run off. Make sure you lay the slab the right way, with the coarse textured side upwards. If the paving abuts the lawn, set the slab 10 mm ($\frac{1}{2}$ in) below the grass to allow for mowing.

Interlocking paving blocks, used for road construction in some countries for years, have recently been adapted for home landscaping. They are ideal for use in the garden, on a terrace or a drive. They are made of higher quality concrete and can be laid flush in an interlocking pattern without mortared joints. Their virtue is that they can take considerable weight and do not creep laterally, as most smaller paving materials tend to do with weight upon them. Concrete blocks are available in various colours and are textured like brick, patterns varying according to manufacturer.

### Kerbing paved areas

A kerb may not be necessary, if the paving itself holds back the earth sufficiently. A kind of mini retaining barrier is needed only where there is an abrupt change of level between path and bed and where you cannot simply excavate earth from below the paving and throw the soil back into the bed.

If possible, make a kerb out of the same material as the paving. Builders, left to their own devices, have a tendency to kerb the edge of any paving with a heavy piece of concrete whether it complements the paving material or not. The advantage of concrete kerbs is that they are available in fairly long runs. They can work well if the path is paved with concrete slabs, for instance, or where concrete forms part of the paving pattern. A concrete kerb looks better placed so that the square edge of the kerb is upright, with the rounded edge in the ground. Additional foundation should be placed underneath a kerb, or the kerb itself set higher than the main paving so that it effectively retains it (the smaller the paving unit the more essential this is).

Concrete slabs can be laid on a concrete base as stepping stones across a shallow pool. Made of brilliant white concrete, these slabs stand out in dramatic contrast to the dark expanse of water

An interesting pattern of paving can be created by the restrained use of different coloured concrete slabs

Manufacturers now make concrete slabs which imitate most natural paving materials. The result can be unsatisfactory, but these imitation stone slabs are difficult to distinguish from the real thing

Individual white concrete paving slabs, carefully placed, contribute dramatically to a striking abstract pattern (left) in this Japanese-influenced corner of a garden

To create an informal atmosphere, a path laid with concrete slabs can be softened by allowing plants in the bordering flower beds (above) to spill out on to it. For a neater and more clear-cut appearance, the path can be separated from the beds by a line of concrete kerbing (right)

75

# Tiles: an elegant form of paving

Tiles make a distinctive, rather formal paving material, particularly appropriate for linking indoors and outdoors. A tiled floor would be suitable for a patio leading off a sitting room and separated only by a glass door, for example, or to link a conservatory with a hall. The thinner tiles are also excellent for roofs and balconies, being comparatively light and easy to lay.

On the whole, when we talk of tiles as a garden paving medium we mean quarry tiles, which are made of clay and fired to a very high temperature. Glazed ceramic tiles are softer and chip with constant wear, but they can look superb in the right setting, such as a courtyard, balcony or roof garden in a sunny climate. Asbestos tiles are another possibility though, having no finish, they tend to look functional. They can be sealed (which also darkens the colour) or even painted, using special paint from a builder's merchant. They come in two main sizes—230 mm (about 9 in) or 300 mm (about 12 in) square—and their main virtue is that they are relatively cheap; they are also easier to cut than quarry tiles.

The chief advantages of quarry tiles are that they are very hard-wearing and virtually maintenance-free. It is a good idea to use them for barbecue and outdoor eating areas because they do not absorb stains, do not burn and they clean very easily. While they have an elegant appearance, the earthy brown and red shades in which they are made blend well with the natural colours found in a garden and do not fade. Quarry tiles are, however, rather expensive to buy and they are not easy to lay. They also tend to be slippery when wet and, being slightly porous, they are by no means frost-proof.

It is difficult to cut quarry tiles and calculations should, where possible, be based on numbers of whole tiles. They come in a variety of sizes and shapes (square, rectangular, hexagonal or lozenge-shaped) and the thickness varies from 12 mm ($\frac{1}{2}$ in) to 30 mm ($1\frac{1}{2}$ in), increasing as the size goes up. Tiles 12mm or 15mm ($\frac{1}{2}$in or $\frac{3}{4}$ in) thick are machine-made and more tightly compressed than those between 20 mm and 30 mm (1 in to $1\frac{1}{2}$ in) thick, which are hand-made and have a rougher, more absorbent surface. The hand-made ones also vary slightly in size and shape and need wider joints to allow for these irregularities.

If the paved surface is to be hard-wearing and permanent, quarry tiles are best laid on a concrete base and bedded in a 1 : 3 cement-sand mortar mix. Thicker hand-made tiles should be soaked for several hours first, to prevent them taking up moisture from the mortar. Allow twenty-four hours for the mortar bed to harden. If the tiles are laid close together the joints can be filled by spreading thin mortar with a squeegee; if they are widely spaced, use a pointing trowel to fill gaps.

Make sure that any wet mortar spilled on the tiles is wiped off with a clean, damp cloth immediately; dry mortar is much more difficult to get off a porous surface (though it can be done with wire wool or with a muriatic acid solution—but follow the manufacturer's instructions).

Patterned ceramic tiles are used widely in the countries bordering the Mediterranean. They are especially suited to roof, balcony or courtyard gardens. If the tiles are over-patterned or too colourful, they may detract from the overall garden design; the simple black and white pattern makes this courtyard paving successful

Quarry tiles come in many shapes and sizes. These small hexagonal tiles have the same mellow red colour as old bricks and form a contrasting but compatible background to the foliage of a garden

# LAYING QUARRY TILES

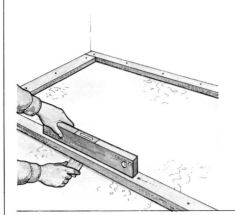

Cut two pieces of wood the length of a row of six tiles and their joints; these will then act as gauge rods and the position of the tiles should be marked on them. Lay battens either side of the first area to be tiled and check their height with a spirit level, using wedges of wood to get them even and nailing them temporarily with masonry nails

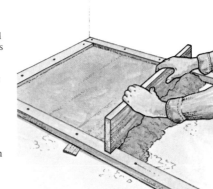

Make a dragging board slightly longer than the gauge rods, and cut notches 9 mm (⅜in) shallower than the thickness of the tiles, so that the board fits between the battens. Use the dragging board to spread mortar over the first area to be tiled

If the tiles are being laid against a wall, the batten next to the wall should be laid within the length of the gauge rods so that, having spread the rest of the mortar, you can remove this batten and fill the gap by trowel. Dust the mortar with dry cement before laying the tiles

Lay the first area of tiles between the wall and the outside batten, using the gauge rods to space them correctly. Then tamp the tiles down with a wooden block to get them secure and level with the batten

The tiles may get slightly displaced by the tamping down, so run a trowel along the joints afterwards to straighten them. Move the gauge rods and battens along and repeat the laying process for another area. Dust the edge of the already laid mortar with dry cement before spreading the next area

Twenty-four hours after the whole tiled area has been laid, mortar the joints with a pointing trowel and finish them off with a rounded stick. Use a wet cloth to wipe off surplus mortar and, after this has dried, wash the tiles finally with soapless detergent

Quarry tiles can be laid inside and out and are particularly effective to link the two areas (right)

# The natural beauty of wood

Timber is perhaps the most natural-looking paving medium, especially pleasing in a rural setting or where the house is constructed entirely or partly of wood. Its use unfortunately is limited to areas without much rainfall; it is ideally suited to countries with an extreme climate, where the summers are hot and dry and the ground covered with snow for long periods in winter. Where the climate is damp, wood soon becomes mossy and too slippery to be used for a main path; regular wire brushing would be needed to keep the surface rough.

It is important to select durable, un-warped wood which is strong enough to withstand the wear and the loads it will have to take. Rough-textured wood is preferable for appearance and for safety but it should also be as splinter-free as possible. The next step is to treat it with preservative. Timber can never make permanent paving but treating it against rot and against insect-attack will extend its life by many years. A way of preventing moisture seeping up from the ground is to put a polythene sheet down underneath a bed of sand, with holes punched every square 300 mm (1 ft) for drainage. As a further precaution against the dangers of woodworm, make certain that wood laid in the ground does not touch the house walls.

Some trees produce more durable wood than others, for example redwood, cedar and cypress. Ordinary construction timber like deal needs to be pressure treated if it is to come into contact with the soil as painting on a preservative, or even soaking with one, rarely penetrates far enough.

### Laying wooden paving

Wood presents several interesting possibilities for use in paving and the beauty of it is that it is easy to lay. An attractive and very simple idea is to use round or oval heavy logs, sawn in discs about 75 mm (3 in) thick, from the trunk of a tree. The discs will vary in diameter from about 300 mm to 1 m (1 ft to 3 ft). Allow them to dry first, then treat them with a wood preservative, as the end grain soaks up moisture from the ground

Using a paving material which echoes that of the house construction can be most successful. The pergola, raised beds and terrace paving in this garden are all of wood, which makes for a well integrated and harmonious design

Old railway sleepers are one of the most durable kinds of wooden paving and they can form a powerful design element. Their rough texture and solid bulk add to the natural woodland atmosphere evoked in the corner of this country garden

Heavy planks of durable wood or old railway sleepers can be laid close together directly on the ground or on a sand base to form an effective and solid area of paving

Timber discs, cut from a tree trunk, can be laid as individual 'stepping stones' in an area of lawn or ground cover or, as in this path, laid close together to form a continuous paved surface

A simple deck built below ground level will have its surface flush with the ground. The wooden slats can be widely spaced, like duckboarding, to allow plants to grow up between them

very quickly. The soil should be dug out to the same depth as the log, loosened at the bottom, and each disc simply dropped into place; alternatively they can be placed in a 50 mm (2 in) bed of sand. The spaces in between can either be planted with grass or ground cover, or they can be filled with a small-scale paving material such as gravel, pebbles or chips of wood or bark.

Another way to use logs is to cut them in cross-section lengthways and lay them across the path in the same way as railway sleepers. An attractive effect can be achieved when logs or sleepers are used in conjunction with other materials. Old railway sleepers are particularly versatile in this way—they harmonize with almost any other paving material and have the added advantage of being very durable. They are effective as 'demarcation' lines to divide up large areas of paving materials such as concrete. Sleepers with good square edges can be laid either close together or some distance apart with grass between them. Lay them directly on the ground or on a

sand base, or you can dig down far enough to have them level with the ground.

Wooden blocks, cut from a square section of timber, can be arranged in the same variety of patterns as brick; lay them in sand or on a 1 : 3 cement-sand mortar base. Laid on sand they should be fitted tightly against each other to prevent wobbling; in addition they can be nailed together to stop them lifting and warping.

Another method of paving with wood is to make what is really a low level deck below ground level, so that the resulting surface is flush with the ground. For instance, you can dig out an area 150 mm (6 in) deep, lay wooden support beams measuring 100 mm by 100 mm (4 in by 4 in) in the excavated area, and then nail a surface of planks measuring 50 mm by 100 mm (2 in by 4 in) across these. The planks can either be laid close together, allowing just enough of a gap for drainage, or be more widely spaced. The pieces can be pre-assembled as grids and placed in position. Make certain water can drain away from underneath.

## BUILDING A WOODEN DECK

An above ground deck provides an interesting change of level in a garden; it is also a good way to create an outdoor sitting area which extends an indoor room, avoiding changing the level between inside and out. Used in a raised deck, the wood is not in contact with the ground and is therefore far less likely to rot; being surrounded by air, it also dries out much more quickly after rain.

There is no reason why anyone should not be able to construct a low deck, though a deck raised more than 1 m (3 ft) above the ground is probably a job for a carpenter or at least a highly skilled amateur. The first thing in either case is to check the building regulations, as there could be some restriction on siting decks or it may be necessary to obtain planning permission.

The size of the timber used for the posts, bearers and joists depends on the spacing between the posts. For the decking boards, used planed timber with slightly bevelled edges, 25 mm by 50 mm, 75 mm or 100 mm (1 in by 2 in, 3 in or 4 in). To get the correct height of the posts use a long, straight plank and a spirit level. The table gives details of bearer and joist size, relative to their spacing.

| | Hardwoods | | Durable softwoods | |
|---|---|---|---|---|
| | Max. spacing | Max. span | Max. spacing | Max. span |
| **Bearers** | | | | |
| mm | m | m | m | m |
| 100 × 75 | 1·8 | 1·6 | 1·8 | 1·3 |
| 125 × 75 | 1·8 | 2·0 | 1·8 | 1·7 |
| | 2·4 | 1·7 | 2·4 | 1·3 |
| 150 × 75 | 1·8 | 2·4 | 2·0 | 1·8 |
| | 2·4 | 2·1 | 2·4 | 1·6 |
| **Joists** | | | | |
| mm | mm | m | mm | m |
| 100 × 50 | 450–530 | 1·9 | 450–530 | 1·6 |
| 125 × 50 | 450–530 | 2·5 | 450–530 | 2·2 |

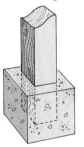

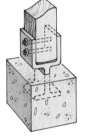

Supporting posts of timber which is durable in the ground, such as redwood or cedar, can, if treated, be set directly in a concrete base

Special metal fittings can be made to support posts of non-durable timber, such as many pines, and keep them above the ground

Non-durable timber posts can alternatively be fitted over a steel dowel set in the concrete base, with a damp-proof course below the wood

To get the deck square with the wall, use the 3-4-5 method. Measure from where the corner of the deck will be (A), to a point (B) 3 units of length (300 mm or 3 ft, for example) along the wall. Attach strings at both points: where these meet at C, so that A-C measures 4 and B-C measures 5, the angle at A will be 90°

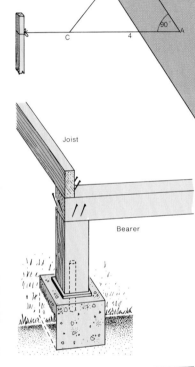

After cutting the posts to the precise height (use a long plank and a spirit level to check this), skew-nail the bearers to the top of the posts using galvanized nails. Then skew-nail the joists to the bearers at right angles to them. For extra strength, brace the joint with a metal bracket

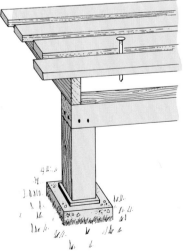

Nail the decking boards across the joists, checking carefully that the first board is square to the house and parallel to the bearers. Maintain even spacing, allowing a 3 mm ($\frac{1}{8}$ in) gap; use a nail to separate each board from the next. Leave all the boards slightly too long and cut them level once they are all fixed in place

# Paving on a small scale: granite setts, cobbles and gravel

The main characteristic of these smaller elements of paving is that they are all, in differing degrees, difficult to walk on. However, they all come into their own as attractive paving materials when used skilfully in combination with larger units of paving. They are also extremely flexible, in that they can be used to pave areas of intricate shape more easily than larger paving slabs.

### Granite setts

Quarried granite is available in the form of cubes or blocks of stone, of similar shape to bricks but in different sizes. They are known as 'setts' or 'Belgian blocks' and have a rather sombre, blue-grey colour. It is sometimes possible to obtain second-hand setts from a local council, as they were traditionally used, laid coursed like bricks, to surface industrial roads and provide a foothold for horses' hooves. In countries where they are no longer quarried they have to be imported from Portugal, which pushes up the price.

Despite their sombre colour, granite setts are richly textured and can be laid in beautiful radiating patterns to make a very special surface. They are not a good idea for a main path as they are somewhat uneven when laid. They are best used in combination with other materials, as an edging round a lawn or laid round the base of a tree or statue. Granite setts also make a pleasing and practical surface for a drive as their dark blue-grey colour and their uneven surface conceal oil marks.

Granite setts are laid in a similar way to bricks and can either be arranged coursed or on the square, with their end up. On a slope they can be deliberately laid at an angle, to provide a foothold.

### Cobbles and pebbles

Cobbles are small rounded stones, formed either through glacial action rolling and wearing stones down or by being constantly washed by water at the edge of a river or by the sea. When these rounded stones are flat they are known as pebbles, usually found at the water's edge. In many countries it has become illegal to take pebbles from a beach; however cobbles are now available in standard sizes and can even be bought in plastic bags from a local garden centre.

Small cobbles can effectively be used for paths but, unless they are set in mortar fairly deeply, they are not very comfortable to walk on. Their use on a large scale, especially when they are placed end up to look like eggs, is generally intended as some form of deterrent—to stop tradesmen taking a short cut to the front door, for example. The beauty of cobble stones is brought out by a contrast in textures and they look best between larger areas of paving—concrete, asphalt or stone slabs. Laid loose, they can also be a significant element in Japanese design, especially effective in conjunction with water or contrasted with strong, architectural plants such as bamboo.

When laying cobbles on a permanent bed, make sure they are placed close together with as little mortar as possible visible

Granite setts, like bricks, are an extremely versatile paving material. They can form part of a complex design which involves other small paving elements, such as cobbles and bricks (top). They can also make an attractive textured paved surface when laid on their own, particularly for an area which will not be walked on very much, such as underneath trees (left). A radiating circle of setts is tricky to lay but results in an interesting pattern (above)

between them. Cobbles and pebbles can either be laid in clay mud or set in mortar. For the former method, prepare a 50 mm (2 in) layer of gravel, topped with a 25 mm (1 in) layer of sand. Sieve dry clay soil until it forms a fine dust and pour this into the area where the cobbles are to go. Wet a section of the clay with a fine spray of water until it is the consistency of dough. Set the cobbles on end in the mud, initially a little higher than you want them; then press the stones down with a board to get them firm and level. Finally, loosen up the clay and soak the surface with water. This process will drive nearly all the air out of the clay so that, when dry, it will be almost impervious to water.

For greater permanence, set cobbles or pebbles in at least a 12 mm ($\frac{1}{2}$ in) mortar mix of 1 part cement, 3 parts sand, on top of an area of concrete. If you need to pour a fresh area of concrete for the base, leave it to set for more than 24 hours before laying the mortar on top. Stones should be bedded in the mortar within two hours. If the area to be paved is large, set the stones in sections; this method also allows you to vary the pattern within sections.

Keep the cobbles in a bucket of water and set them when still wet; otherwise they will weaken the mortar by absorbing water out of it. The cobbles should generally be bedded to just past their middle at the point where their circumference begins to narrow; use a board laid across the area to get the stones level. Two or three hours after bedding the stones, pour a layer of grout between them and hose and brush away any excess mortar before it finally sets.

### Gravel

Gravel is made up of angular chippings from a parent block of stone. Both its colour and its texture make it a sympathetic material; though it forms a hard surface in one sense, gravel is somehow the intermediate stage between a paving and a ground covering or planting medium. Indeed one of its virtues is that, while its overall appearance is neat, an attractive natural effect can be obtained by growing plants through it.

Its versatility makes it particularly suitable for use in the small garden. In a town setting gravel can look sophisticated and effective: used in conjunction with bold leaf plants and ivies, for instance, it has a severity about it and is in fact used as a surround to many French châteaux, giving them their precise, uncluttered look. At the same time a gravel path is somehow reminiscent of old country gardens, evoking the smell of box and the scent of roses, while its crunch underfoot suggests carriage driveways.

The colours of gravel are as varied as the different rock types from which it is formed, so it is always possible to choose one which matches the material of your house. The almost pure white chips, which come from marble or are produced as an extract from lime workings, can be effectively used to help bring light down into a dark garden. Areas of different colour could be arranged in a chequer-board pattern, using strips of wood to divide the areas.

Laying stones loosely is probably the easiest way to cover an area of ground (above). The resulting surface may be difficult to walk on, but in the right setting it can be visually effective

An expanse of cobbles produces a richly textured pattern of light and shade (left)

Pebbles are an appropriate paving material round water in a garden (right). They form a flatter surface than cobbles, easier to walk on

While setting cobbles in mortar, push them in to just past their middle. You can vary the pattern by spreading the mortar and setting the stones in sections

When bedding the cobbles make sure that you maintain a level surface by checking against a straight plank which rests on the ground on either side of the area to be paved

fall of 1 in 30, otherwise areas of moisture form and patches of gravel will sink into them. You can adjust the feel of gravel according to how you lay it. The crunchy sort, which slows down movement, should be at least 40 mm ($\frac{1}{2}$ in) deep, laid over a thin layer of sand or small rubble on top of a 100 mm (4 in) layer of consolidated hardcore. Omit the hardcore at intervals where plants are to be grown through the gravel. Lay the gravel in two separate layers, using a rake to distribute it evenly. For faster movement, roll a 25 mm (1 in) layer of gravel into a similar layer of hoggin (a mixture of brick dust and clay), binding gravel or simply unwashed gravel. The clay contained in hoggin combines with moisture to bind and hold the upper layer.

To establish plants in gravel, scoop out the base material, replace it with soil and the plant, then surround the plant closely with gravel. Lady's mantle (*Alchemilla mollis*), sisyrinchium and limnanthes, the poached egg plant, are all highly suitable plants. In time the gravel will pick up a certain amount of dirt in which new seedlings will grow. Treating the gravel with a granular weed killer once a year should keep the weeds sufficiently at bay.

Gravel is a softer-looking paving material than most and forms a suitable background for plants grown through it

Though gravel is quite cheap and easy to lay, it has several disadvantages as a paving material. Most of these can be overcome, but it is important to be aware of them. First of all it does need constant maintenance. Regular rolling is necessary to remedy the effects of rain and traffic, both of which redistribute the gravel in an irregular way. Gravel is also difficult to walk on when first laid, before it is properly compacted. Unless it is used in combination with other paving, gravel is not a good idea for children —it is difficult to push a pram or ride a bicycle over it; wheelchairs pose a similar problem. The angular chippings of gravel make it rather painful to fall on and children also tend to throw it about. Probably the major disadvantage of gravel is that it gets everywhere. It is carried about on shoes, particularly in wet weather; where it is laid adjacent to the house a foot scraper is a good idea. If it is next to grass or flower beds some sort of edging, such as brick, cobble or wood, is advisable.

It is important to lay gravel well, with a

Gravel combines successfully with most other paving materials to create variety over a wide area of flat ground. The virtue of gravel is that it can be laid in precise shapes, right up against plants or other types of paving

# Mixing materials for successful paving

Concrete slabs, brick paviors and cobbles offer interesting contrasts of both colour and texture

An area of gravel, through which plants can be grown, harmonizes with brick of a similar shade

Stone slabs and bricks of approximately the same colour have weathered to a uniform tone

Brick paving can be broken up by demarcation lines of wood and slate laid 'on edge'

Individual large slabs act as flat stepping stones through an area of loosely laid gravel

Granite setts and concrete slabs contrast in scale and texture to produce a satisfying pattern

Cobbles create a radiating pattern round a tree; a double row of bricks edge the circumference

In this design, stone-facsimile concrete slabs are both softened and defined by a row of bricks

Timber rounds, a concrete strip and brick paviors form an unlikely but very effective combination

An island of cobbles and plants round a tree breaks up a regular, monotonous expanse of paving

Wooden railway sleepers mix naturally with stones and ground-covering plants

# Changing the level to add interest and drama

Though a change of level can at first seem to be an extra problem in a small garden, with imaginative treatment it may turn out to be an inestimable advantage. It may even be worth creating an artificial slope to add variety and drama to a flat garden.

A change of level will draw the eye down into the garden. Diagonal slopes, steep terraces, flights of steps and raised planting beds in the garden all provide focal points for the eye in the general view. This is a particular advantage in a small site or an awkwardly shaped one where the boundary walls can look very conspicuous. In a triangular-shaped site, for instance, terracing across the natural sight lines will divert the line of view from running straight out of the garden at the apex of the triangle. Land rising away from the house will foreshorten the view, leaving every feature visible from the house, while falling ground creates a sense of open-ended space.

Consider first whether you want to emphasize the natural lines of the garden or to create a controlled architectural design. Changes of level may be supported by walls and steps or may simply be mounds and banks whose outlines are not defined by masonry structures. There are many possible variations in atmosphere and style which may be achieved by these two methods.

## Ground shaping

Shaping the land into man-made but natural looking contours without walls or terracing is a small-scale imitation of the idealized pastoral landscapes created in eighteenth-century gardening. These large engineering projects, in which lakes and valleys were excavated and the position of each tree planned according to its probable appearance in a century's time, aimed to improve on nature. Despite the difference in scale the ground shaping techniques employed in private gardens have the same general purpose—to disguise the bad points in a view and emphasize the harmony of rising and falling land. There is also a Japanese tradition in which mounds, emphasized by an arrangement of stones or raked sand patterns on their surface, are planned to imitate natural landscapes in an idealized and abstract form. This style of design, which pays great attention to the line of the ground and the texture of rocks and trees, is well suited to a small garden.

Generally speaking, however, slopes and heights designed to look natural require more space than is available in the small garden. It is easy to forget that a gently sloping mound which is comfortable to walk on and allows the lawn mower to run along it will occupy a wide ground area. A slope should lie at an angle of not more than 30°. A bank steeper than this is liable to erosion by surface and underground water movements. If the back of the mound is concealed by a screen of plants then the back slope can be more abrupt, perhaps supported by a hidden retaining wall. You may need to obtain more topsoil to cover mounds and slopes; at least a 50 mm (2 in) covering is needed for laying turf and 230 mm (9 in) for planting shrubs. Trees should be planted in a hole at least 1 m (3 ft) deep and wide.

Different garden styles can be separated and emphasized by changes of level. The raised areas in this site become progressively wilder, leading to the woods above. The fan-shaped timber steps are welded into the slope by planting and the bank itself retained by a sturdy wall of seasoned timber

A long shallow flight of steps, even in a strong material like concrete, provides a gentle curving line in the garden design, here strengthened by the gradually sloping lawn beside it. Bushy foliage overhangs the steps and softens their outline

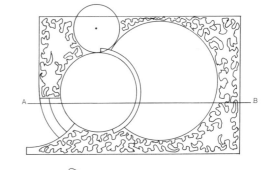

A change of level can
be dramatized by
skilful use of plants and
masonry. Shallow steps
with broad treads
invite leisurely walking
and interest is added
by a change of
direction, marked by
widening the second
step into a platform

An explicit contrast
of ground covering
materials can effectively
delineate falling
ground. A neat
timber retaining wall
here divides a 'moat'
paved in pebbles from
the raised lawn

Mounds can be used in a skilful way to disguise piles of rubble which are disfiguring the view. Again be imaginative about this and use plants to weld the bank into its background. Some building rubble will drain too fast to allow plants to grow so you may have to combine the rubble with good soil. All banks tend to drain faster than level land so provide a drain and/or a soakaway at the bottom of the slope.

When you are planning your design, consider the existing contours of your garden. It is not a good idea to attempt great changes in the ground levels, but merely to accentuate or soften what is there already, using the cut-and-fill method (shown right).

### Retaining walls

A retaining wall, one which prevents the earth behind it from spilling out of a banked shape, can be on any scale. Retaining walls over 1.2m (4 ft) high, however, often have to be built according to local safety regulations and professional building standards, so they are not an easy project for the home gardener. Expert advice will be helpful in building low walls too, as even they must withstand a heavy weight of earth behind them. Retaining walls can be very wide and

A slight change of level marked by shallow steps can easily be planned to create interest in a flat area. The cross-section along the line A to B shows the use of the cut-and-fill method of ground shaping to form a rise and dip in level land. The circular design is an elegant one

Ground level

The original ground profile has been altered, using the cut-and-fill method to form a gentle slope. A soakaway might be necessary at A to prevent soil erosion

low to act as seating round a raised planting bed in a level garden, or to form terracing along steeply sloping ground.

The earth moving and provision of proper drainage and reinforcement in a stable wall may be more time-consuming and laborious than you at first realize. If you want to make a planting bed part of your new scheme, remember to put aside the topsoil and the plants which you want to keep. The rest of the soil removed should be consolidated and levelled, on top of a layer of hardcore.

The most important problem with a retaining wall is arranging adequate drainage, so that the earth behind the wall does not become waterlogged and heavy, thus weakening the wall and eventually causing it to collapse, or freezing behind it and cracking the masonry. Even if you live in a dry area, you should always make provision for drainage, in case of freak rainstorms and sudden excesses of surface water.

For drainage at the back of the wall, pipes of porous unglazed terracotta or plastic can be laid horizontally in unmortared sections behind the wall. The water soaking into these is carried to a soakaway or suitable drainage point at the end of the wall. Front drainage is generally provided by 'weepholes'—small holes in the masonry at about 2 m (6 ft) intervals along the horizontal and at 450 mm (1 ft 6 in) levels up the wall, the first line running about 300 mm (1 ft) above ground level. Weepholes in a brick wall are created by leaving some vertical joints unmortared, but in other masonry walls pipes have to be laid to form the weepholes, running through the masonry from back to front at a slight tilt. If the soil is very impervious, a sloping gutter, covered with a grating to prevent blockages, will be necessary to carry the water away along the

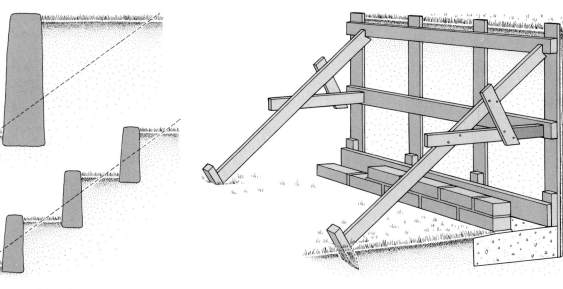

Except where a high retaining wall is absolutely necessary, for instance to retain a steep bank, a series of lower walls is stronger and more pleasing to look at. A gradually terraced slope will offer better opportunities for varied planting on the different levels and the individual walls are more secure since they are bearing less weight. Terracing also involves less shoring up of heavy earth loads

On a slope, the earth behind a wall will have to be held back while the foundations are laid and the wall is built. A system of timber struts and braces is used to shore up the vertical poling boards which are laid directly against the face of the soil. If you are building a high wall, or working in an area with loose soil, build the shuttering in stages as you excavate. Leave plenty of space between the back

of the intended wall and the face of the shuttering to allow easy movement when laying the foundation and building the wall. Once the foundation has been laid and the lower part of the wall is complete, drainage pipes can be laid behind it in pockets of gravel. Drainage pipes and guttering are essential with a very impervious soil. When the shuttering is removed the space behind the wall is filled with soil

Dry stone retaining walls are often laid at a considerable angle, sometimes seeming to lean into the slope rather than support it. Plants housed in the earth pockets between the stones and along the banks will prevent soil erosion by surface water movement

A tree or shrub in a central position is given extra emphasis by a masonry planting box, however low. This circular brick planter, capped with bricks laid to radiate outwards, harmonizes with the formal paving

Railway sleepers, telegraph poles and heavy duty timber designed for outdoor use make impressive retaining walls. The lapped corners and rough texture of these beams form a strong design element in a simple garden

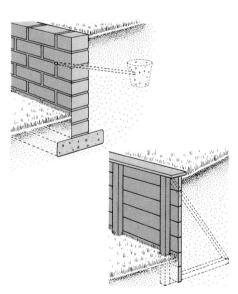

Repeating the building materials of the house in the garden is especially important where terracing lies close to the house. The creepers here could be allowed to shroud the walls completely or might be kept clipped for a more formal style

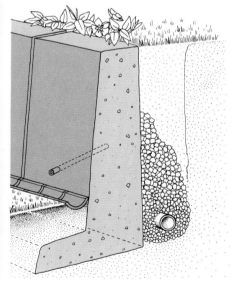

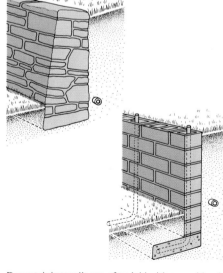

There should be a slight slope of not less than 1 in 40 on drainage pipes; they should also be surrounded by a pocket of gravel to quicken water movement. The front guttering carries off water seeping through the weepholes. Excessive surface water can be drained behind the wall by another gutter along the junction of bank and wall. Planting will improve drainage and prevent earth erosion

Dry retaining walls are often laid with a considerable battered angle (50 mm in 300 mm of height, or 2 in in 1 ft), with each stone tilted downwards into the bank to lodge it firmly (top). In a concrete retaining wall, a projected foot on the downhill side of the foundation acts as an extra brace against the weight of the bank. Reinforcing rods run continuously through foundation and wall (above)

A brick retaining wall (top) is reinforced by metal rods set through the face of the wall and back into the bank where they are linked to sections of poured concrete known as 'deadmen' which act as stabilizers. Naturally resistant hardwoods or chemically treated timber should be used for wooden walls. Each fence post should be braced with 100 mm by 100 mm (4 in by 4 in) timbers set into the bank (above)

front of the wall. Check occasionally that weepholes and gutters are not blocked by leaves and dirt.

In addition to back drainage and weepholes, brick walls can be fitted with a damp proofing course and will also benefit from a coat of waterproof paint on the inner wall surface to prevent damp rising.

Any of the usual walling materials, concrete, stone, brick and even wood, may be used for retaining walls. With a brick wall the basic unit—the single brick—is rather small so the wall can easily bulge out along lines of weakness. When using bricks, you will either have to build a cavity wall reinforced by steel rods (see Brick walls, page 48), or lay a brick veneer over a core of concrete.

All types of concrete will form strong retaining walls for relatively little work and at low cost. Pre-cast posts can be stacked in a dovetail fashion, so that strips of soil are left visible between each horizontal, into which you can introduce creeping plants to shroud the wall. Pre-cast concrete retaining walls in L-section are now available. Railway sleepers or preservative-treated timber beams can form a surprisingly sound low retaining wall, which is easy to build, or they can act as a veneer over concrete. Very low walls and raised planters are often devised out of short poles in pine, which is soft and would need treating, or some naturally resistant hardwood, set into the ground vertically like a miniature palisade fence.

### Building steps

The design of steps must depend on the type and amount of use the steps will receive; they may form the main access route between the house and the road or may be simply acting as an invitation to take a stroll to a little used part of the garden. A flight of steps with smooth wide treads can form comfortable garden seating, or act as staging for displaying potted plants. The intended use should determine the height of the risers. Very shallow steps will invite slow walking while higher risers encourage brisk, purposeful movement. Outdoor steps should always be shallower than indoor flights, however, and designed with deep, broad treads to provide a wide passageway in keeping with the larger scale of the garden. Steep, narrow steps should be avoided except where the garden design definitely requires them, as they are tiring to walk up and can be dangerous in wet weather.

It is vital to blend the steps with their surroundings visually, by choosing a material used elsewhere in the house or garden and by following an established contour in the garden; the lines of the risers could be continued by a retaining wall or planting bed for instance. The edging is also important; treads can be grown over with plants until they are almost invisible, or left clear and bare, drawing far more attention to the steps as an intended feature in the garden design. You might also want to use a contrasting edging material or a set of potted plants to accentuate the line of the steps. Treads which protrude from the line

Delicate edging plants can soften the look of rough concrete steps

Timber's versatility and ease of use make this adventurous design possible

Staggered brick courses form entrance steps which repeat the house material

Random cut slate paving is used with plants to form stepped levels

Low-growing planting enlivens plain steps and marks changes of level clearly

## BUILDING STEPS IN WOOD

Simple wooden steps can be constructed off site; the 'stringers'—supporting side pieces—are bolted on to the top board and strengthened by blocks screwed underneath (1). Metal holders set into the concrete foundations anchor the steps at the base (2). Treads can overhang risers and stringers (3) and can be set in the stringers using cleats (4), grooves (5) and notches (6)

## POURING CONCRETE STEPS

A small flight of concrete steps can be poured in one on a separate foundation. It will need strong formwork, with braces outside the forms at front and sides. Build the sides first, and then the formwork for the risers, starting with the top step. The depth of concrete in a continuous flight should be at least 100 mm (4 in) from the inner junction of the tread and riser. A beveled edge at the front of each step will stop them crumbling and prevent children cutting themselves on a sharp edge, while a bevel at the bottom of the riser will allow the float to pass over the whole surface of the tread during finishing (1). Reinforcement is supplied by steel rods set into the concrete across each step and by the concrete foundation (2). Roughened or corrugated treads and recessed risers prevent the steps from becoming slippery

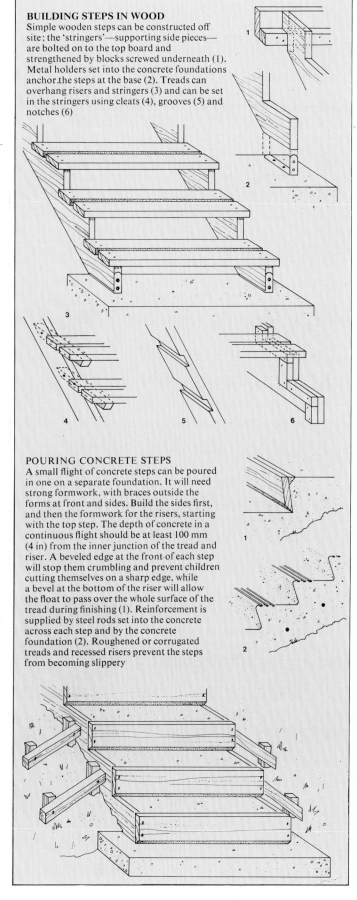

## BUILDING STEPS ON A LEVEL SITE

Lay a concrete foundation under the site of the steps, extending it slightly beyond the position of the first riser. When it is dry, lay a stretcher course of bricks bedded in mortar (1:3 cement-sand) to form the riser

Infill with hardcore behind this course to its own level and consolidate firmly to support the first tread. Then lay a bed of mortar over the bricks and hardcore to the approximate depth of the first tread

Lay the stone paving slabs on the mortar bed, making a mortar joint between each slab. The slabs are set to overhang slightly the line of stretcher bricks; this can be by as much as 50 mm (2 in) in some cases

Spreading another bed of mortar along the back of the tread, from the second riser by laying a stretcher course of bricks on the stone slab. Check the level of the bricks with a spirit level, ensuring a fall to drain off water

Lay the second tread as before, raising the level of hardcore behind the riser, tamping it down and setting the slabs on this. There should be a slight slope on the front or side of the tread to allow water to run off.

The finished steps are wide and shallow with an elegant curved step to finish them off. A low wall or sunken gutter might form the side edging of the steps, or they can be welded into their setting with plants

---

of slope will be more obtrusive than those set below it. Consider the plan of the stairway in relation to the whole garden; an incongruous set of badly planned steps can dominate the view in a small garden.

On a long gradual slope, a ramp or a stepped ramp may be more suitable than steps, especially where wheelchairs or tricycles are used. For a ramp, about 1 in 10 is the maximum gradient for comfortable walking, and the slope may be as gradual as 1 in 15 on a long ramp where space allows. Ramps should be paved in a non-slip material, for instance gravelled tarmac or concrete laid *in situ* and brushed to texture it. Stepped ramps, with low risers spaced the length of a few paces apart and long treads, though very elegant, are probably more suitable for larger gardens.

Steps are more economical than ramps in terms of space since they can ascend steeper slopes. When designing the steps the first problem is to set the proportion of riser height to tread depth. The maximum height for risers in the garden is about 175 mm (7 in) and they can be as shallow as 100 mm (4 in). The shallower the slope the shallower the risers should be. The tread depth should be in proportion to this measurement, and at least 300 mm ($11\frac{1}{4}$ in). The table gives some good tread/riser combinations.

| Tread | Riser |
|---|---|
| 300 mm ($11\frac{1}{2}$ in) | 175 mm (7 in) |
| 350 mm (1 ft $1\frac{1}{2}$ in) | 150 mm (6 in) |
| 400 mm (1 ft $3\frac{1}{2}$ in) | 140 mm ($5\frac{1}{2}$ in) |
| 450 mm (1 ft $5\frac{1}{2}$ in) | 115 mm ($4\frac{1}{2}$ in) |
| 500 mm (1 ft $7\frac{1}{2}$ in) | 100 mm (4 in) |

Steps should be wide: at least 1 m (3 ft) wide for one person, and 1.5m (5 ft) wide if two people are to walk abreast. A flight of more than ten steps should incorporate a flat, square landing half way up to make it look less steep and forbidding.

To determine the number of steps necessary, measure the angle and the vertical height of the slope, making a plan of the cross-section on squared paper. You can calculate the number of steps by dividing the height of each riser into the vertical height of the slope. To fit the risers exactly into the height, it may be necessary to lengthen the slope slightly, using the cut-and-fill method (shown on page 87).

Small details of design will make an appreciable difference to the look of the finished steps and also make them safer. Tread slabs which overhang the risers by up to 50 mm (2 in) create a line of shadow at the edge of each step, which is attractive and also acts as a safety feature by outlining the changes of level. All treads must be set at a slight angle falling about 6 mm ($\frac{1}{4}$ in) in 300 mm (1 ft) to the front or side, so that water will run off; in freezing conditions, badly drained steps are very dangerous. It is a good idea to choose a non-slip material which is textured or roughened in some way. Timber steps overgrown with moss can be particularly treacherous in wet weather, so take care to keep them clear. For steps which are sunk into the surrounding slope, a useful addition is a narrow channel at one or both edges of the flight which will act as a drainage and cleaning gutter.

## BUILDING STEPS INTO A SLOPE

In a loosely packed bank of earth you may have to dig out the whole area of the steps, but when working on firm ground you need only cut out the general shape of each step in the soil before you begin to build. Pack down the surrounding earth and add a layer of hardcore as reinforcement. A concrete foundation is always necessary under the site of the first riser, laid in a trench about 100 mm (4 in) deep and twice the width of the riser. The brick riser, made up here of two stretcher and one header course, is laid on a bed of mortar on the foundation. This riser and the layer of hardcore then forms a support for the first tread, which is also bedded in mortar. Subsequent treads and risers are laid in the same way (right). They might be of a variety of materials; bricks and stone slabs (above) have a neat appearance and are integrated with the adjoining brick retaining wall.

# extending the house into the garden

There is a seemingly universal desire for a living area in which the qualities of the house and the garden are combined. Sunrooms, pergolas and balconies are a transitional stage which can successfully bring plants closer to the house and create shelter and comfort for outdoor areas. Essential storage areas should also be integrated into the garden design to make them less obtrusive.

# Up on the roof

For those who live in city apartments, a roof garden, however small, can be an invaluable retreat, especially when it is well grown enough to screen off the city views around it. Some roof gardens, especially those cared for co-operatively by the inhabitants of a block of flats, may include lawns, trees, pools and fountains, with raised beds behind masonry retaining walls. However, large amounts of topsoil are needed for these grand gardens—trees will need a depth of at least 450 mm (1 ft 6 in) to prevent their being uprooted by wind. So unless you have a large area of roof which will bear the heavy weight of wet soil, masonry and flooring, the plants should be housed in lighter containers; the lighter they are the more you can have, so it is worth using asbestos, plastic and fibreglass pots. Check the weight loads which your roof can sustain with an expert and plan accordingly; you will probably need the landlord's or agent's permission, as well as the neighbour's agreement, before you start on the garden.

You should also make sure that both the water-proofing and drainage of the roof are adequate, to prevent water seeping through the ceiling below. A solid layer of asphalt is usually laid on a roof to waterproof it; on top of this a floor of light tiling (asbestos or quarry tiles, perhaps) or wooden decking can be laid with suitable gulleys or pipes for drainage. A combination of paving materials will provide variety in the roof surface which can sometimes look too flat and uniform.

Roof gardens are usually very exposed, bringing problems of excessive wind and sun. Plants are as much in danger as people, for cold winds can kill young shoots and damage even quite sturdy plants, while severe sun brings problems of watering. A screen or pergola is the best solution for both these hazards. Screens can be made of hardy planting, sheets of plastic or glass, or possibly bamboo or reed if the wind is not too strong. They should be securely anchored especially if the roof is several storeys high. Again you may need permission to put up a solid structure which impinges on a neighbour's view.

Since most roofs are entirely open to the sun, deep and thorough watering is essential in summer, especially for plants in containers; containers dry out faster than large beds. When laying the flooring it is often a good idea to install a fixed irrigation system and a water pump as water on the roof is indispensable and watering by hand is very laborious.

also find a small fountain a worthwhile … the sound and movement of playing … soothing in the summer. When you …, add liquid fertilizer to replace the ric… il which has leached away. A layer of br… r other drainage material will be necess… om of the containers. Cover this with hi… nting fibre or with a mixture of soil an… a very lightweight planting medium whi… o nutrients but makes less soil necessary… ontainers should be on blocks raised o… to prevent them rotting through the botto…

A combination … r flowering creepers with some hardy an… ide colour is ideal for the roof garden. E… ailable height by training plants or espa… the walls on a trellis, all securely fixed t… he wind.

Screens will give a roof garden privacy and shelter from the wind; here sheets of fluted plastic disguised by plants form an unobtrusive wind barrier

Trees can be rooted in large containers to form an effective screen on the roof. If they are evergreen they will add a touch of cheer during the winter months

Unattractive views are a hazard of any city roof garden but here they are screened by a woven fence. The roof garden itself, with its variety of potted and submerged greenery, is a quiet oasis, showing how well nature can be adapted above ground (left)

Flowering plants grown in containers will give vivid colour and variety to the smallest roof garden and any available height can be used to train up climbing plants

Where the roof is strong enough to support the weight of topsoil and underlying drainage (above), the sight of a lawn outside the living room in a modern apartment can be very striking

A roof which is not suitable for lounging on (left) can be planted with evergreen and shrubby plants which need little attention. The foliage and colour of the plants provide visual relief by breaking up the stark lines of flat masonry

# Balcony gardens

Balcony gardens in a sheltered position with a mild climate all year round can provide constant blossom and foliage to be enjoyed from inside the house or flat, even where the balcony ground area itself is too small for sitting out. Where the weather is less mild, half hardy flowering plants and bulbs can still be used to brighten up the balcony in summer and can be taken inside in the winter. Large balconies offer a wider range of possibilities; they can be treated either as a raised garden with climbing plants spreading over railings, walls and floor or as an extension of the internal room, with furniture of the same style and more restrained plants in containers. Unfortunately, in modern blocks, many balconies are designed on a uniform plan, often overshadowed by the floor above and overhanging the one below. This arrangement can present a problem for gardeners because of the lack of direct sunlight, and also because there is a likelihood of showering the neighbours when you water the plants. However the touch of individuality given by plants is valuable in counteracting this uniformity of design; a screen of creepers on a trellis will also provide a welcome measure of privacy.

The most common problem with balcony gardens, as with roof gardens, is their exposure to cold winds; to prevent this, some kind of screen on the windward side will be necessary. A glass screen, though expensive, can be a good idea as it will not block out any light from your garden or from your neighbour.

Slatted wooden verticals or bamboo screens can also be attractive, especially with creepers growing up them. Always ask the neighbours and, in municipal housing, the agent, before building any permanent structure on to the balcony, however.

Since a projecting balcony cannot support excessive weight, try to hang screens and plants in containers from the walls, and from overhead beams if these exist. Exploit the vertical space available as much as possible, training creepers upwards towards the light. This is particularly important where only a small area of the balcony is in full sunlight, and all the plants have to be positioned along the outside edge of the balcony. As with roof gardens, lightweight containers of asbestos or fibreglass are most suitable as they will not overload the balcony.

Watering the plants will probably be by means of a hose fed from the kitchen tap or a watering can, though a tap on the balcony itself would be invaluable. A convenient way to water several pots thoroughly is to lay a length of hose pipe along the line of containers, pierced at intervals to spread the water evenly. Self-watering pots can be obtained as well but these are heavier than the standard type. There will probably be adequate floor drainage but it is as well to check before you soak the balcony. You may want to pave larger balconies used for sitting out with lightweight tiles. Quarry or asbestos tiles, or wooden decking, are all more attractive than the usual asphalt or concrete floor surface.

Even where a balcony is small and shady, green creepers and other plants will soften the hard outlines of railings and obscure the city views. Asbestos tiles, being lightweight, are particularly suitable for balcony flooring

A tiled floor will drain and dry quickly after rain; quarry tiles are light and their colours blend particularly well with plants and terracotta pots

A display of flowers along the edge of a balcony will brighten up the outside of an apartment block as well as the inside. An adjustable awning pulls down to provide shade

A wide verandah with a solid roof (above) will screen people from strong sunlight while climbers growing in the full light along the edges provide further shade themselves. Cane or basketweave furniture has an informal look which is appropriate for outdoor use

A balcony built on to the street-facing side of the house (right) has been extended into a raised garden with fully grown trees, lush tropical shrubs and small plants in containers

A screen at the side of an exposed balcony will supply both privacy and shelter from the wind. Here woven bamboo forms a more sympathetic background for flowering plants than the concrete walls

# Rooms of glass

A sunroom can be any structure from an elegant conservatory to a small lean-to greenhouse attached to a house window. Its design will be determined by the climate and the intended use. Where a new room is built to adjoin the house, either as a separate room or as a living room extension, a major aim is usually to increase the light and sense of space indoors.

Some rooms are designed primarily for people, with plants as a decorative background, while others are seen first as a plant house, a purpose which can make them unsuitable for sitting in. The high humidity of a sunroom or conservatory containing tropical plants, for instance, makes them far too hot for all but the most cold-blooded people. The temperate conservatory, with rows of plants arranged on staging, is a far more agreeable place in which to sit, designed to display the less hardy plants which will not live outside.

A successful garden room can be a multi-purpose space—playroom, storage area, plant house or communal dining area out of the wind and sun. It will be very popular with the elderly, as it gives them a chance to sit and do some gardening in a sheltered site. Alternatively, you may want to provide a sheltered space which, though not versatile, makes a virtue of its contrast with the rest of the house in appearance and atmosphere. There are some traditional garden room styles – the elegance of the nineteenth-century conservatory, for example, or the luxurious marble and ironwork of Spanish colonial decoration.

### Adding on a sunroom

You may well want to introduce a sunroom when planning to open out a basement or make a ground floor extension, or even by slightly extending the back porch. A sheltered L-shaped corner of the house can be filled in with a lean-to glass room; it will be cheap to build because it uses two existing walls. This kind of extension, with access to the house through a living room, is clearly part of the house and is usually designed expressly to let more sun and light into the interior and give a clear view of the garden. However, you should also consider its outside appearance, matching the newly designed structure to the original building so that from outside they seem a single unit. Materials, shapes and proportions should be repeated where possible; the shape of the window frames is particularly important as they form the hard outlines round the view. Prefabricated structures are of course convenient, but their designs are often too flimsy to match most houses, looking incongruous and awkward in comparison. They may weather badly too.

If you design your own glass room you can decide exactly how much glass to use and where to place it to suit the site. The usual practice is for glass walls to face south in the northern hemisphere and vice versa, but you may well wish to alter this according to the individual circumstances. Though glazing lets in light and sun and allows a windless view, it can have adverse effects as well, making the room unbearably hot in summer and very cold in winter, even with double glazing, where seasonal changes are extreme. The room could be put to some other purpose in winter—a storage room for summer sports equipment and garden furniture perhaps.

If there is a choice of possible sites for the extension, consider the direction of cold winds, the shelter provided by trees and walls on the site, and the glare of the sun's rays at sunset. Adequate ventilation may also be a problem. An open wall can be screened with bamboo or reed blinds to allow some air circulation, or with mesh screening to protect a

With the right treatment, a conservatory can be as hospitable to people as to plants. Plants benefit from the maximum light allowed through the glass roof and windows (left). The quarry tile floor is both durable and elegant and the informal furniture in cane and bamboo, though not sturdy enough for use outdoors, is ideally suited to a conservatory; its soft lines and colours blend well with the delicate shapes of plants

In the right period setting, and with suitably extravagant planting, the grace and charm of the traditional English nineteenth-century garden room is undeniable; even a tiny conservatory creates a distinctive atmosphere

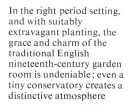

Strong, simple designs are usually most successful for house extensions; elaborate or flimsy structures may look out of proportion with the rest of the building. Transparent plastic roofing lets in the light; it is cheaper and less breakable than glass

A plant window is a simple lean-to structure which lets additional light into the house and provides a view of greenhouse foliage for those sitting inside. Blinds can be used in summer to break the direct rays of the sun

room from flying insects or dust. Glazing the roof will make the room far hotter in summer with the sun directly overhead, but will produce a more open-air feeling. If you simply want extra light to reach the interior of the house, a line of roof windows can be set along the junction of the house wall and the extension roof. Plants will benefit from this overhead light, especially creepers and vines.

The solid walls and floor of a sunroom should be built to retain heat. In colder climates it is worth insulating the room well as it will mean a saving on heating bills in the rest of the house. Floors can be set on thick concrete foundations, or underfloor heating could be laid, which prevents the room becoming bitterly cold and provides an even temperature for plants. Flooring materials should be hard-wearing and capable of withstanding damp, especially if there are many plants in the room which will all have to be watered. If the room adjoins an internal living room, it is a good idea to repeat the material already used inside as this makes both rooms look larger. Vinyl or unglazed quarry tiles are very suitable. Cork tiles look attractive too but they are less capable of withstanding damp conditions.

### Greenhouses

The greenhouse is intended for all sorts of plants at every stage of growth—a forcing house for cuttings, seedlings and delicate fruit and vegetables. Even the most modest greenhouse with a minimum of heating will widen your choice of plants and growing methods immensely. One simple idea to avoid complex heating arrangements is to build a pit greenhouse with a pitched roof which uses solar heating. The south-facing side of the roof is glazed while the opposite one is solid and painted black to retain the heat. The whole structure is buried about 1.2 m (4 ft) deep, since soil is an insulator, and has solid masonry walls which also retain heat.

If possible, plan the greenhouse to adjoin the house or site it in an inconspicuous position. Light, prefabricated structures with aluminium or wood frames are functional but they can look jarring or too dominant in a small garden and should be blended into their setting by screens of plants. Deciduous hedges and trees are often most suitable as they shade the greenhouse from excessive heat in summer and allow maximum light through when they are bare in winter.

Abundant use of plants, with exotic flowers and fast-growing creepers, can disguise the most massive supporting beams and plain high walls. Elegant furnishings here emphasize the richness of the foliage

Some sunrooms are more a part of the garden than the house, especially where one side is completely open. Loosely woven bamboo blinds allow the sun to filter through and cast gentle shade without too much loss of light

The light angular look of many greenhouses, the prefabricated aluminium ones in particular, is difficult to blend in with more solid buildings. Screens of planting can disguise this (right), though be careful not to block out the sunlight with overhanging trees. A hard-surfaced path leading to the greenhouse is essential in wet weather

A conservatory built against a brick wall which faces the sun is an ideal place for exotic plants and fruit trees to grow (left); the wall will retain the heat and slowly radiate it for the fruit to ripen

Slatted wooden stagings are necessary for standing plant containers on in the greenhouse so excess water can drip through on to the floor. Banked levels of staging are used for displaying plants, but a single shelf at a convenient working height is adequate elsewhere

# A ceiling of greenery

Pergolas mark the transitional point between a sunroom and an open garden, providing shelter and shade with a covering of outdoor plants. A pergola is probably the simplest and cheapest extension which you can build on to the house and incorporates many of the advantages of more complex structures; though its use may be limited by seasonal weather changes, yet the pleasure of eating or sitting outdoors under a green or flowering roof is hard to surpass.

A carefully sited pergola can link house, garden and any outbuildings in a visually satisfying unity which improves the appearance of the whole site. Where a house has a dull or irregular frontage, a pergola along the width of the house can disguise this deficiency. Similarly any oddly shaped spaces between the house walls and nearby garden buildings can be covered by a pergola so that the structures are brought into a harmonious relationship. A corner between two walls of the house, or a house wall and an adjoining garage wall, would be an excellent site.

It is useful to remember that an overhead frame tends to make the floor space beneath seem larger. If the terrace beneath the structure has the same paving material as the adjoining room inside the house, this will increase the sense of a unified space; in warm weather the difference between indoors and outdoors will almost seem to disappear. Flooring materials should always be durable, frost resistant and dry off quickly as the overhead plants will drip for a long time after rain or after top spraying.

A pergola in close proximity to the house will always look best if designed to echo not only the materials of the original building but the lines of its windows and door frames. The top line of the pergola should usually lie just above the window lintel. In some houses it may be possible to extend the floor beams of the house outwards to form the overheads. Take care, however, that the pergola will not provide too easy a route into the first floor windows for burglars and try to discourage children from using it as a climbing frame although, if strong enough, it can provide a support for a swing or hammock.

Generally speaking it is more effective to build a plain strong structure and let the plants growing over it supply the variation in pattern and colour, though a more ornate design, perhaps in trellis-work, may suit older houses. Avoid the common error of making the verticals too heavy for the horizontals; metal or timber supports are generally more suitable and easier to erect than massive brick or stone ones, though these may be in keeping with a country setting.

Pergolas supported by a house wall are obviously simpler to design than the free-standing kind, and possibly more versatile as they form the most convenient sitting and dining areas. Free-standing pergolas can be used as a kind of colonnade leading people through a green walkway towards some focal point, but the small garden may well not have enough space to provide the right view. You may find that a bare frame looks stark in winter; this can be avoided by combining deciduous and flowering annuals with evergreens or, on a new pergola, fast growing climbers with slower evergreen ones.

Hardy vines can provide the most attractive overhead shade, with their variegated foliage colours and even bunches of grapes in a warm climate

Building a pergola between two adjoining walls creates an intimate sitting area. This metal frame supports heavier beams of natural wood, emphasizing the overhead bulk of the pergola; large foliage plants harmonize with the strong lines of the design

A pergola offers a fine support for rambling roses; a trellis structure or delicately shaped frame is particularly in keeping with this traditional country-garden climber

Where the pergola adjoins the house directly, it is particularly important to maintain a continuous style in the shapes and materials of the new structure. This plain lean-to wooden frame is painted white to echo the distinctive window frames

A thick overhead screen of creepers will make a real outdoor room and create interesting patterns of light and shade. An evergreen climber might be used to shroud the bare metal framework in winter, unless extra light in the house is more important

Large spreading pergolas intended primarily to display plants can be erected over walkways. Flowering trees or climbers may have a short period of bloom but the effect created is splendid

105

# Storage and screening within the garden

Unless you plan for ample storage space in the garden it is all too easy for the surroundings of the house to look like a dumping ground for children's toys, tools and dustbins. Part of the problem is to provide a permanent screen for the ugly but necessary objects such as dustbins, the oil tank if you have one or perhaps the coal store or wood pile. This is particularly important in a small garden where the whole outlook can be ruined by an unsightly oil tank or large amounts of wood which have to be stored for winter use.

Easy access from the road and the house is vital for fuel stores; the compost heap and the dustbins also need to be within easy reach of the back door, but beware of placing them too near a window as the flies and the smell can be unpleasant in hot weather. It is usually more convenient and cheaper when building screening for these utilities to group them together, rather than trying to spread them all round the site in the hope that they will look less conspicuous. A wooden screen or a hedge can hide the dustbins and the fuel store housed in two adjoining cupboards of similar design, which will at least look uniform and neat. This kind of modest orderly scheme is generally more successful than attempts to transform the offending objects into 'features' in the garden: shrouding a coal store or an oil tank in rambling roses usually only succeeds in drawing more attention to its underlying plainness. The exception to this is a well stacked wood pile, which can look very homely and welcoming.

Another problem is to provide storage space for items which are only sporadically in use, yet should be within easy reach when needed. This category might include sports equipment, garden boots, outdoor furniture, a sled, skis or children's bicycles. It is convenient for all these to be stored near the house, protected from the rain and perhaps even under lock and key. This often means storing them in inadequate prefabricated sheds which are out of style and proportion with the rest of the house and may be too small to cover all needs—as, so often, is the back of the garage.

You can, however, design your own flexible scheme to make the best use of the space available; a home built lean-to shed or set of large cupboards designed to suit the site can cater for all your storage needs in one master plan. You can fill in nooks and crannies in the existing building — a corner between two walls, say, or an oddly shaped recess between house and garage—with a simple outhouse complete with racks and shelves for all tools and toys. In some houses a line of waist-high cupboards with a workbench top might be built along a side wall with a roof projecting from the eaves above to keep off rain. Such storage areas, which are integrated into the existing lines of the house, are less obtrusive than separate structures and often more convenient, being close to the sources of water and electricity in the house.

If your garden design incorporates built-in furniture, low seating units can serve as additional storage space if they have a simple hinged lid. This neat idea is particularly relevant for roofs, balconies and small courtyard gardens, where space is very restricted. Unless the seating itself is waterproof or is in a sheltered position, storage should be restricted to items such as plant pots or polythene bags of fertilizer which cannot be damaged by rain.

In a small garden, where the storage areas can never be far from the windows of the house (right), screens of planting can supply decorative and effective breaks in the view. Evergreen plants trained up a trellis here provide all-year-round screening for a plain wooden shed, while trees have been planted to cover the roof eventually

Dustbins or fuel stores which must be accessible from the street can be concealed in a simple unobtrusive storage unit which is easy to build; it can be disguised by climbing and trailing plants such as ivy or honeysuckle

The front view of the unit pictured on the left shows its neat design; the ground cover of pebbles repeated on top of the unit provides a strong colour contrast which diverts attention from the cupboard doors

Manholes and gratings in the garden can simply be concealed by a large plant container. The slatted wooden stand makes more of a feature of the flower box, but it can easily be removed for access to the manhole

Dustbins have to be within easy reach of the kitchen, but they should not be allowed to clutter up the back entrance of the house. A thick low hedge has been planted here to provide a convenient hiding place

The compost heap is best situated as far as possible from the house to avoid flies and the smell of rotting vegetation in hot weather. This curving palisade fence hides it effectively and blends into the garden site

An integrated storage unit for dustbins is best formed by repeating a finishing material used elsewhere, here vertical wooden slats

# successful
## small
# gardens

*All gardens are individual, both in the problems they face
and the way they are planned and planted. From rooftops
and balconies to a fully productive vegetable plot the
following pages illustrate the scope of design possibilities
for small gardens. The problems vary from awkward shapes,
such as a long, narrow strip, to a steep slope or a shady
position. The design themes are equally diverse: some
gardens make a central feature of water, others have a
Japanese flavour or make use of a single colour theme. The
character of the planting, using bright seasonal colours
or subdued evergreens, can also be compared and contrasted.
A garden planned on geometric lines can work as well as
a distinctly circular motif if it is right for the site. Each
of these gardens is unique because it is tailored to
suit the situation and the needs of a particular family.
Illustrated plans help to convey the layout and planting;
an explanation of the symbols used can be found on page 248*

# Old meets new for an easy-care garden

The walled garden to this eighteenth-century house is a section of a larger garden, split up when the original mansion was divided. The high south wall, covered with lattice work and well established ivy, was the original perimeter wall of the large garden. The new walls were built of brick, in keeping with this and the character of the house.

The owners, a young working couple with a small child, wanted a garden with a minimum of maintenance. A small area of old stone slabs was retained and brick paving laid to blend with it. Elsewhere, gravel was used to cover the ground, with the occasional plant grown in it to break up the surface. Brick stepping stones were laid across the gravel to the gate at the end.

The only major existing feature was a tall maple in the centre of the garden. This was retained and made a focal point by constructing a brick plinth round the base—for use either as seating or for potted plants. Being so near the house, all the lower branches of the maple had been removed over a period of years, so it formed a shady umbrella over much of the area. Lack of sunlight near the house prevented planting for colour. Specimens were chosen, therefore, for shape and form, using a large proportion of evergreens to provide a pleasant view in winter as the garden is the principal outlook from the house. Annuals and spring bulbs grouped in pots and tubs on the terrace provide seasonal colour.

The sunniest corner of the garden, furthest from the house, was chosen as the sitting, sunbathing and outdoor eating area. Here a wide brick bench seat was constructed with a raised sandpit at the end, big enough for a child to play in without sand being spread around too much.

A garden like this acquires atmosphere and character with age: as it mellows the paving mosses over and the climbers become rampant. When photographed it was only three years old and already the mellowing process had begun to make itself apparent; the ivies, clematis and other climbing plants had established themselves and started to cloak the walls, shrubs had become more bushy and self-seeded hollyhocks provided their own softening influence.

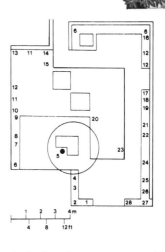

The garden is linked by a gate to the path outside and approached by brick stepping stones across an area of gravel. Planting round the sides of the garden leaves the middle area free and uncluttered, giving an impression of space. The boundary walls are softened by climbers and creepers which have been allowed to grow over them.

The mature tree in the middle of the garden, an *Acer negundo*, is surrounded by a brick plinth and this feature is echoed in the far sunny corner by a brick bench seat, terminating in a sandpit

| | |
|---|---|
| 1 *Daphne odora* 'Aureomarginata' | 14 *Choisya ternata* |
| 2 *Fatsia japonica* | 15 *Euonymus radicans* |
| 3 *Garrya elliptica* | 16 *Clematis montana* |
| 4 *Skimmia japonica* 'Rubella' | 17 *Rosmarinus officinalis* 'Miss Jessup's Upright' |
| 5 *Acer negundo* | 18 *Agapanthus* 'Headbourne Hybrid' |
| 6 *Hedera colchica dentata* 'Aureo-variegata' | 19 *Rosa* 'Mermaid' (climber) |
| 7 *Chaenomeles* 'Knap Hill Scarlet' | 20 *Kniphofia caulescens* |
| 8 *Anemone japonica* | 21 *Rosa* 'Iceberg' |
| 9 *Alchemilla mollis* | 22 *Kerria japonica* 'Tamariscifolia' |
| 10 *Arundinaria murielae* | 23 *Juniperus sabina* |
| 11 *Hedera canariensis* 'Gloire de Marengo' | 24 *Senecio laxifolius* |
| 12 *Jasminum nudiflorum* | 25 *Hydrangea petiolaris* |
| 13 *Acer negundo* 'Variegatum' | 26 *Hydrangea macrophylla* |
| | 27 *Macleaya cordata* |
| | 28 *Bergenia stracheyi* 'Silberlicht' |

The sandpit (above) is
raised and large enough to
allow a small child to sit in it,
which means that the hazard
of sand spreading outwards
is reduced. The ivy behind
is the golden variegated
*Hedera colchica dentata*
'Aureo-variegata', and
colourful flowering plants
such as nasturtiums are
bedded out each summer

Planting in the gravel,
against a wall which gets
little sunlight (left), includes
the graceful bamboo
*Arundinaria murielae*. Self-
seeded hollyhocks (*Althaea*)
provide splashes of colour

Evergreen planting in this
garden maintains interest
throughout the year (right).
The lush green leaves of
*Choisya ternata* make a
background to *Euonymus
radicans* and variegated ivy.
*Hedera canariensis* 'Gloire
de Marengo' shrouds the
wall behind

# Shapes which interlock

The random ground plan is made up of blue engineering bricks with areas of concrete, stone and slate (left). Such a strong layout reads clearly through the heavy planting

Different types of seat complete individual corners of this garden. The slatted bench (above) is tucked away in a shady corner, with the bower seat (below) in another

The layout of this very personal plantsman's garden shows how, with ingenuity, many different areas of interest can be incorporated in a small space, without the final result being confused; the various small incidents work together to create an overall conception.

The basic idea was to design a garden where the paving and planting form interlocking shapes. The conception is held together by a very strong, though random, ground plan. Bricks were chosen for the paving for their texture and subtle colour. The brickwork is enlivened by bands of polished slate running through it which looks particularly effective after rain; the owner feels it is important that gardens look interesting in wet weather too and do not rely on hot, sunny days for their effect.

On entering the garden through a conservatory, the pattern leads the eye from one group of plants to another, to end in a little vegetable area and storage shed, both of which are cleverly concealed behind planting. The layout of the garden, dividing the plot into interlocking shapes, creates areas of different character. Such corners—of, for example, sun, shade or seclusion—are emphasized not only by planting but by different types of seating, from a slate bench to an ornate wrought iron 'bower' seat. These form as much a part of their composed setting as the surrounding foliage.

The ground pattern is complemented by equally strong mixed planting chosen to give form and interest through the year. Several silver and grey plants are incorporated, for their soft, spreading leaves which overlap the paving. Considerable use has also been made of shrub roses, which are less formal than ordinary bush roses and vary widely in size and habit. Pots and urns are planted with annuals, to provide summer colour. The plants selected require little attention, apart from watering the pots in the summer and whatever pruning of shrubs is necessary to control the seemingly casual plant groups, so that they do not become imbalanced.

1 *Ruta graveolens* 'Jackman's Blue'
2 *Lonicera periclymenum* 'Serotina'
3 *Viburnum* x *juddii*
4 *Buddleia crispa*
5 *Rosa* 'Mme Edouard Herriot' (climber)
6 *Euonymus fortunei radicans* 'Variegatus'
7 *Hibiscus syriacus* 'Coelestis'
8 *Fuchsia magellanica gracilis*
9 *Cytisus battandieri*
10 *Rosa* 'Bloomfield abundance'
11 *Phlomis fruticosa*
12 *Buddleia colvilei*
13 *Senecio greyi*
14 *Rosa* 'Mme Isaac Pereire'
15 *Santolina chamaecyparissus*
16 *Rosa* 'Penelope'
17 *Syringa vulgaris*
18 *Helleborus argutifolius*
19 *Rosa gallica*
20 *Chaenomeles japonica*
21 *Paeonia officinalis*
22 *Artemisia abrotanum*
23 *Rhododendron luteum*
24 *Rhododendron specie*
25 *Iris sibirica*
26 *Rhododendron* x 'Cilpinense'
27 *Rosa* 'Honorine de Brabant'
28 *Sorbaria arborea*
29 *Cercis siliquastrum*
30 *Buxus sempervirens*
31 *Betula pendula*
32 *Rosa* 'Zephirine Drouhin' (climber)
33 *Cotoneaster dammeri*
34 Apple tree
35 *Anemone japonica*
36 *Ceanothus* 'Autumnal Blue'
37 Blackcurrant
38 Vegetables
39 *Dianthus*
40 Herbs
41 *Eucalyptus gunnii*
42 *Rosa* 'Fruhlingsgold'
43 *Spiraea* x *vanhouttei*
44 *Geranium ibericum*
45 Redcurrant
46 *Cistus* x *corbariensis*
47 *Rosa rugosa* 'Roseraie de l'Hay'
48 *Rhododendron griersonianum*
49 *Syringa microphylla*
50 *Hebe* 'Carl Teschner'
51 *Malus floribunda*
52 *Cotoneaster salicifolius floccosus*
53 *Lavandula angustifolia*
54 *Rosa* 'Peace'
55 *Rosa* 'Mme Pierre Oger'
56 *Hedera helix* 'Cristata' and *Vinca minor*
57 *Lonicera involucrata*
58 *Rosa* 'Nevada'
59 *Pieris taiwanensis*
60 *Hydrangea macrophylla*
61 *Hamamelis mollis*

Fronds of self-seeded ferns overhang the brick and stone paving (left). Moss allowed to grow between the bricks softens the paving and helps to create a natural effect

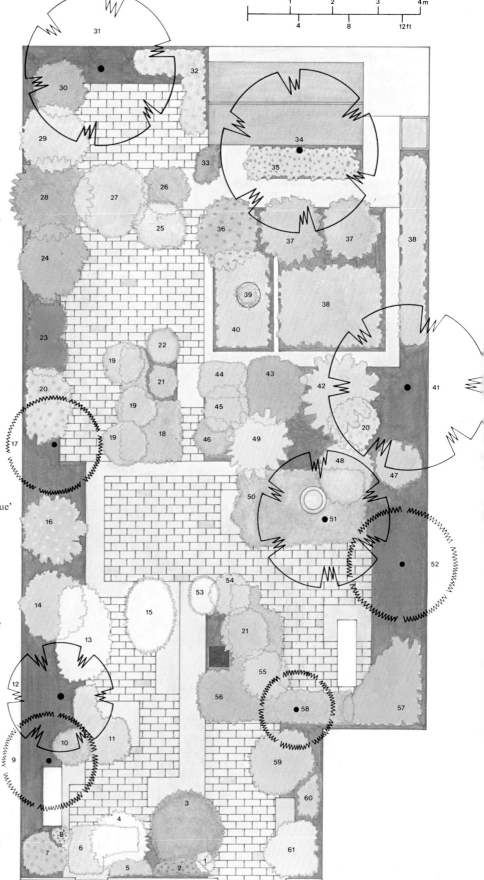

# An all-seasons garden

Ten years ago, when this family moved into their newly built house, the garden was a waste land of mud and builder's rubble. Although the task of creating a garden seemed daunting at the time, it proved to be an excellent opportunity to plan a garden which would suit their own needs exactly.

The rectangular plot was not large—only 16.5 m by 6 m (54 ft by 20 ft) and part of the area was taken up by the garage and by steps down to a cellar. One of the first structural things the family did was to lay a curved path to the front door, to soften the stark approach from the gate. Once the land was levelled and cultivated, grass was sown over most of it, creating a lawn which was suitable for the children to play on.

The main planting areas were situated round the sides so that the boundary walls and fence, and the garage wall, were partially screened by climbers such as clematis, roses and a vine, as well as by other plants: tomato plants, for example, are grown up against a concrete boundary wall, almost a metre (about three feet) high. Confining the planting to the edges also left an open area in the middle, which had the effect of making the garden look more spacious than it actually was.

Three trees were amongst the first subjects to be planted: an apple tree by the house, a weeping birch in the lawn and an American maple at the end of the garden. Several years later, these trees had grown sufficiently to give a very distinctive framework to the garden. The family had no previous knowledge of either gardening or plants but, over the intervening years, they learnt from experience when and for how long the various flowering plants bloomed. They also realized how important it was to have one species or another coming into flower or leaf all year round. Slowly, according to their means and new knowledge, they carefully planned for and acquired the right plants. The result, ten years later, is very much an all-seasons garden.

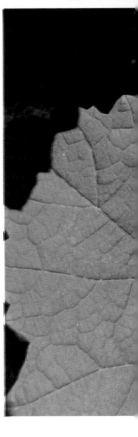

The brick wall of the garage and the clean lines of a modern house are softened by planting and by the curved path (above). The grape vine clings to the brick wall, with a climbing yellow rose and a blackberry bush beside it. Edging the path with touches of seasonal colours are wild strawberries and other flowering plants. A clematis blooms against the fence for several months during the summer and in the background are several evergreen shrubs

Yellow and white tulips, with crown imperials (*Fritillaria imperialis*), planted in the border by the house (left) herald the spring. The delicate beauty of the apple blossom adds another touch of colour

Even with snow on the ground, the evergreen shrubs maintain winter interest in the garden (right). The mahonia is a fine all-season plant: it is evergreen, with shiny dark green leaves, and bears mimosa-like yellow flowers in spring and misty-blue berries in autumn.
The tall slender birch tree breaks the severity of the winter sky

This small bunch of grapes (below left) is the first yield of the vine grown along the garage wall. The bricks absorb and radiate heat so that the grapes have a chance of ripening. They celebrate the height of summer in the garden and contribute a slightly exotic touch to its character

At the end of October a sternbergia shoots up its yellow cones from the ground (below right) as an announcement of autumn. The wild strawberries are a perpetual variety and bear fruit for quite some time: they will even withstand a few frosty nights of early winter

# A shady outdoor room

A family garden needs to be a place which can be used throughout the year, an aim which has been realized in this town garden by creating two adjoining living areas. The overall plan was designed to draw the eye away from the perimeter and create interest within the area. To this end old stone slabs were laid in a regular manner, radiating round small keystones. The existing central fig tree was retained as a major feature; though it casts a lot of shade this helps to create the feeling of a sheltered outside room. Large cobbles were laid round the bole to draw attention to the sculptural beauty of its multi-stem.

A kennel for the family bulldog was boldly sited in the centre of the garden adjacent to the tree. With clever screen planting this was used as a sort of 'room' divider, an effect further emphasized by the change of level at this point. The dog had a passion for eating anything planted, so beds were raised and retained by walling at different levels.

Planting along the far boundary was primarily for privacy, and throughout the garden species were chosen to cope with the almost constant shade as well as the rigours of family use. Shade-loving plants lack bright colour but are often strong in leaf character; used here in bold masses they complement, sculpturally, the strong ground plan of the garden. Tubs of bulbs in spring and annuals in summer provide seasonal colour. Despite the shade, climbing roses as well as clematis and honeysuckle have flourished.

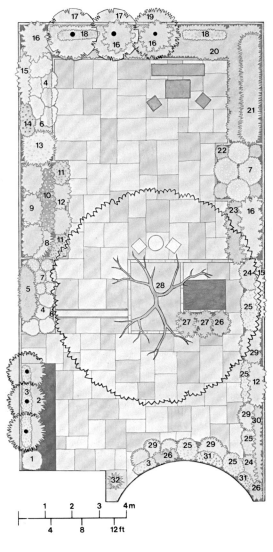

This green and leafy city garden is paved with beautifully laid old stone slabs which give it a distinct character. Half way down the level changes under a fine old fig tree (*Ficus carica*) which is surrounded by loose cobbles. The positioning of the dog kennel serves to emphasize the feeling of this being a 'two-room' garden. Planting of evergreen climbers along the back fence adds to its enclosed atmosphere

| | |
|---|---|
| 1 | *Artemisia absinthium* |
| 2 | *Magnolia grandiflora* |
| 3 | *Lonicera x tellmanniana* |
| 4 | *Berberis thunbergii* |
| 5 | *Clematis montana* |
| 6 | *Sedum maximum* |
| 7 | *Rosa* 'Iceberg' |
| 8 | *Ajuga reptans* |
| 9 | *Garrya elliptica* |
| 10 | *Macleaya cordata* |
| 11 | *Helianthemum* |
| 12 | *Acanthus mollis* |
| 13 | *Cytisus scoparius* |
| 14 | *Rosa* 'Z. Drouhin' |
| 15 | *Vitis coignetiae* |
| 16 | *Fuchsia magellanica* |
| 17 | *Robinia pseudoacacia* |
| 18 | *Lamium galeobdolon* |
| 19 | *Pyracantha angustifolia* |
| 20 | *Hosta sieboldiana* |
| 21 | *Galtonia candicans* |
| 22 | *Euphorbia robbiae* |
| 23 | *Helleborus argutifolius* |
| 24 | *Choisya ternata* |
| 25 | *Alchemilla mollis* |
| 26 | *Clematis armandii* |
| 27 | *Fatsia japonica* |
| 28 | *Ficus carica* |
| 29 | *Euphorbia wulfenii* |
| 30 | *Jasminum nudiflorum* |
| 31 | *Rosa* 'New dawn' |
| 32 | *Cordyline australis* |

# Oasis in the heart of a city

A small walled garden is a typical feature of many town houses. Where space is so restricted (in this case only 7 metres by 5.8 metres—or 23 ft by 19 ft) it is often best used as an extension for the activities of the house. It is therefore logical that the layout should be more that of an outside room than a garden as such, with plants used as furnishings to soften the layout. The design of this garden is simple, as the best ones should be, while the use of surface textures is subtle and imaginative. Every aspect has been considered: the materials of which the garden is built, how it is planted and the uses it can serve. The whole treatment transforms the walled space into a delightful and secluded courtyard; it is a lovely example of the type of integrated thinking that is the secret of good garden design.

Seen from the house, the garden has raised beds on either side constructed of old railway sleepers. The first area is paved with old stone slabs laid, as they should be, radiating round a smaller keystone. There is a slight change of level, leading up to a terrace paved with brick laid on edge, providing a natural link with the brick walls enclosing the garden. The same yellow brick is used to construct a built-in barbecue and, underneath, a cupboard for storing charcoal and

cooking implements. This area becomes the focal point of the garden; it is emphasized by a white-painted pergola structure overhead, which both gives privacy from above (often necessary in town), and provides shade in summer. A scaffolding pole is used for the vertical post and is set in concrete below the brick paving.

The pattern is continued with another raised bed at the back, extending into more seating along the left-hand wall. Raised beds in such a garden have a dual use, providing admirable casual seating when the need arises. While the surrounding brick walls give protection for tender plants, they are inevitably a somewhat dominant feature. To offset this, one wall is clad with vertical timber sleepers which offer a change of texture and tie in with the wooden raised beds on three sides of the garden.

A balancing feature to the living area of the garden is the simple pool in the foreground; it is painted black internally, giving a feeling of depth and mystery. The serenity of this garden derives from the very simple planting, where the leaf colours, textures and shapes contrast and blend with each other without being dominated by too much strong colour and while complementing the strong layout.

The living corner of the garden has a built-in brick bench seat topped with white-painted softwood. This runs into a barbecue grill with a cupboard underneath for storage. The wall is capped with brick on edge, and the same brick is used for both the structures and the paving. The white-painted wooden pergola overhead rests on a simple scaffolding pole support, painted black; it gives the living area a sense of seclusion and provides shade in the summer. The overhanging wistaria, with its graceful drooping flowers, further enhances this corner

117

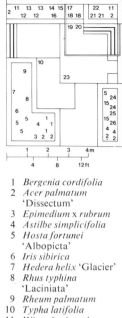

1  *Bergenia cordifolia*
2  *Acer palmatum*
   'Dissectum'
3  *Epimedium* x *rubrum*
4  *Astilbe simplicifolia*
5  *Hosta fortunei*
   'Albopicta'
6  *Iris sibirica*
7  *Hedera helix* 'Glacier'
8  *Rhus typhina*
   'Laciniata'
9  *Rheum palmatum*
10 *Typha latifolia*
11 *Wistaria sinensis*
12 *Mahonia japonica*
13 Mollis azalea
14 *Rhododendron ponticum*
15 *Potentilla fruticosa*
16 *Elaeagnus pungens*
   'Maculata'
17 *Lonicera japonica*
   'Halliana'
18 *Fatsia japonica*
19 *Hypericum patulum*
   'Hidcote'
20 *Verbascum bombyciferum*
21 *Senecio laxifolius*
22 *Helichrysum splendidum*
23 *Hosta* 'Thomas Hogg'
24 *Dracaena australis*
25 *Hosta sieboldiana*
26 *Kniphofia uvaria*

Old railway sleepers, treated with preservative, are used to construct the raised beds surrounding the garden (left). The yellow brick paving and old stone paving slabs have the pointing brushed back slightly to expose each element clearly. The edging is trim where the paving meets the small dramatic pool, while planting round the pool is simple and effective. There is a variegated hosta ('Thomas Hogg') in the tub, with the cut leaf sumach (*Rhus typhina* 'Laciniata') hanging over the water and a group of bullrushes in a tub submerged in the pool itself

From the house one looks straight out on to a raised bed of large-leaved, sculptural plants (right): hostas, astilbes and a large rhubarb plant (*Rheum*) underneath the cut leaf sumach tree. Low Japanese maples overhang the pool gracefully

# A rooftop garden

When the owners moved into this penthouse fourteen years ago, the flat roof was paved with asbestos tiles and screened off on two of its sides. It could not be described as a garden, however, as no planting at all had been undertaken; the built-in containers were full of pebbles.

The first thing they did was to screen off the third side of the garden to complete their privacy, leaving only one side open to an extensive south view. They then replaced the pebbles in the containers with earth and created a small pool with a fountain over a storm drain between the two large raised flower beds.

Climbing plants such as honeysuckle, wistaria and clematis were the first to be introduced, with roses and small trees. More wistaria was planted in two strawberry pots placed strategically beside the unscreened wall. This is now well established and has had a softening effect on the starkness of the concrete over which it is climbing.

The rest of the planting, which continued over a long period, was to a certain extent dictated by trial and error: some plants liked the open, rather dry situation, others did not. Some quite hardy species died suddenly after a seemingly good start, while other more delicate ones thrived. One of the notable successes is the oleander, which was grown from a cutting. This is kept outdoors all the year round and survives even in the cold weather. A pot-grown orange tree (*Citrus sinensis*) grown from a pip also spends all year on the roof: during the winter the pot is simply placed in a more sheltered spot.

Gradually the permanent raised beds were filled and the number of containers along the unscreened wall increased. Near the entrance into the garden is a charming collection of plants in smaller pots: colourful pelargoniums, white alyssum, thyme, mint and other culinary herbs are grouped together, interspersed with a daisy-like weed of the *Anthemis* family, an attractive wild flower which grows in several parts of the garden.

The aim was to create a green and peaceful retreat, high above the city, and as the shrubs and climbers mature this is increasingly the impression. As the garden faces due south it is often used for sunbathing during the summer. Lamps are fixed to the walls so it is possible to eat and entertain on the roof garden in the evening as well as during the day.

A plant trough and a collection of different sized terracotta pots (above) form an attractive group along the house wall. They contain white *Alyssum maritimum* some red geraniums, the wild, daisy-like *Anthemis* and several herbs

The view towards the penthouse (left) shows the asbestos paving which, being lightweight, is suitable for a large roof. Raised beds line the two walls with a variety of large plant containers along the open side. By keeping planting to the sides of the roof, the main weight is distributed at the strongest part of the structure

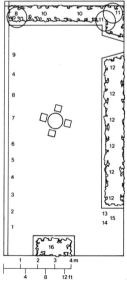

Plants housed in containers of different shapes and sizes give this roof garden its particular character. The strawberry pot (above) contains a large wistaria, but smaller plants spilling out of the sides provide additional interest. The greyish foliage of yellow alyssum contrasts well with the green sea pink (*Armeria maritima*) and in spring with the white flowers of candytuft (*Iberis sempervirens*)

One side of the roof is left unscreened (left) to take advantage of the splendid view over a park. Two container-grown wistarias twine up the central supports, framing the view. The variety of shrubs in pots along this side are mainly evergreen and provide year-round interest; they include *Aucuba japonica*, *Fatsia japonica* and yuccas

1  *Prunus laurocerasus*
2  *Cotoneaster franchetii*
3  *Helianthemum nummularium* and *Wistaria sinensis*
4  *Aucuba japonica*
5  *Mahonia japonica*
6  *Yucca flaccida*
7  *Armeria maritima*, *Alyssum argenteum*, *Iberis sempervirens* and *Wistaria sinensis*
8  *Fatsia japonica*
9  *Hosta fortunei*
10 Mixed border of *Rosa* 'Albertine' (climber), *Wistaria sinensis*, *Lonicera japonica halliana*, *Agapanthus caulescens* and *Senecio laxifolius*
11 *Hydrangea macrophylla*
12 Mixed border of *Clematis montana*, *Lonicera japonica halliana*, *Forsythia ovata*, *Hedera*, various roses
13 *Nerium oleander*
14 *Laurus nobilis*
15 *Citrus sinensis*
16 *Pelargonium*, *Alyssum maritimum* and herbs

121

# A town courtyard

In city centres, many people living in apartment blocks share a small overlooked courtyard as their only outdoor space. The walls of this one were of drab old brick and the flooring was solid concrete; with flair and imagination the area has been turned into a focal point, seen as one enters the building and from all the windows surrounding it.

The most striking feature of the courtyard is the spiral staircase, which acts as a sculptural piece. Beside it are two large and several seedling *Ailanthus glandulosa* (trees of heaven) casting their lovely leaf patterns against the white-painted rear wall. *Buxus sempervirens* (box) is massed in a bed against one yellow side wall and along the opposite one a long pool is fed by two sea-horse fountains. The whole pattern is drawn together by a surfacing of granite paving stones (or setts) which, being small, increase the feeling of intimacy. In the evening, low lighting within the planted areas casts a warm glow.

The planting in the courtyard is mostly evergreen, which gives it a green and pleasant appearance all year round. The change of seasons is indicated by the low rhododendrons under the *Ailanthus*, by bulbs planted with the *Buxus*, and by pots of flowering annuals for bright spots of summer colour.

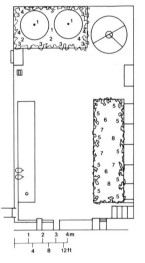

1 *Ailanthus glandulosa*
2 *Rhododendron catawbiense*
3 *Pachysandra terminalis*
4 *Tulipa*
5 *Buxus sempervirens*
6 *Crocus*
7 *Galanthus*
8 *Narcissus*

The focal point of this courtyard garden is the spiral staircase (right), dramatically painted white and red. Its circular shape is enhanced by an *Ailanthus glandulosa* planted at its foot. The 'tree of heaven', growing upwards, enhances the proportions of the courtyard area

An aerial view of the courtyard (left) shows the effective simplicity of its layout. The pool and regular shaped beds are sited along the edges, leaving a free view up the centre from the entrance. The high surrounding walls are painted, bringing light, colour and interest into what was a dark, unpromising yard

Small granite setts (right) give the area a feeling of intimacy. Their texture and the distinctive ground pattern they create is a contrast to the evergreen planting in the surrounding beds. Low hooded lights situated within the planted areas bring the whole courtyard to life at night

# Container-grown: a productive balcony

This laden balcony provides the answer for a couple of flat-dwelling gardeners who, a few years ago, moved here from a house. At first they feared they would miss their former garden but they soon turned the whole balcony into a miniature—but abundant—garden in itself.

In moving from a house to a small flat, the occupants found they had a good deal of surplus furniture. Instead of selling it or throwing away the unwanted pieces they converted them into troughs and plant stands. Nothing was wasted: the tops were removed from tables to make containers and a painted cupboard was converted into a storage place for gardening tools and plant stand. A place was found for everything: the space underneath the raised troughs by the balcony wall is used for storing sacks of mould and peat, screened from view by polythene sheeting.

Access to the balcony is from the living room and so cleverly has the tiny area been utilized that there is enough room for tables and chairs to be brought outside in summer for sunbathing and for meals. In spring the area is bright with tulips, daffodils and other bulbs. When these have finished flowering, they are replaced with an ingenious interplanting of flowers and vegetables, creating a unique and fascinating little garden which is both a pleasure to look at and a source of food. Tomato plants trained up in large pots along the edge of the balcony also act as an effective screen, with their dense foliage.

In autumn, when the crops have been harvested and the roses and chrysanthemums have finished flowering, the containers are left empty for two weeks as a form of sterilization. More peat and fertilizer is then added, as intensive cultivation and frequent watering impoverish the composted soil.

Every bit of available space has been exploited to the full on this cheerful summer balcony (above). Lettuces, tomatoes and spring onions co-exist with roses and colourful annuals, showing just how ornamental vegetables can be. Utilitarian sacks of mould and peat are tucked away behind plastic sheeting and tools are stored in the yellow cupboard

Viewed from the street, the lush growth of culinary and ornamental plants softens the austere lines of this city block of flats (left). A row of lettuces in pots is backed by strong, tall tomato plants, ensuring an abundant supply of salad crops throughout the season. Runner beans and onions are also grown, in boxes against the wall of the flat

# A Japanese balcony

A narrow balcony, scarcely wide enough to step out on to, is the only outdoor space offered by many city apartments. The treatment of this balcony, at once restful and dramatic, offers inspiration to those who feel that such a small area has no possibilities.

The Japanese buddhist statue was the starting point for the design: its owner decided that the statue would best be viewed on the narrow balcony and asked a Japanese designer to create an appropriate environment for it. The balcony, in its small way, is a true reflection of the principles of Japanese garden design, in which the garden is primarily a landscape to be viewed from the house. Every element is chosen and placed with care and restraint.

The whole balcony has been lined with black polythene (as for a pool lining) and large, smooth white pebbles cover the floor. Both statues (the Japanese figure and an abstract one which was made to complement it) are surrounded by round wooden posts of irregular sizes which sets them off admirably. The few plants are similarly enclosed.

Since the balcony is attached to the bedroom and the only furniture there is the bed itself, all attention is focused on the balcony. In the morning it is filled with sunshine and at night it is lit by a spotlight on the wall and by a light placed inside the abstract statue, and these create a restful glow.

The dwarf bamboo plant and abstract statue (left) form part of a balanced composition. They complement each other by contrast, one made by man, the other by nature, and are perfectly set off against the white, rounded screen and the large pebbles. The few plants on the balcony, including two weeping fruit trees, are Japanese in origin or character

Seen at close range, the buddhist statue (right) creates, from its graceful sculpting and positioning, a mood of calm and peace that has turned what might have been a very ordinary area and view into one of inspiration

The irregular wooden posts (left) are made of stripped Scots pine; they provide the only rich colour on this balcony and form an original surround for the plants and statuary. They are subtle in effect by being warm in both colour and texture and yet extremely simple, keeping the uncluttered but exotic mood of the Japanese garden

The two statues dominate the balcony (right), showing how effective statuary can be even in a small space such as this. The continuous lines of the screen run horizontally behind the curved stone of the statues. The screening blocks out the ugly view beyond the balcony and creates a simple background, against which the dramatic qualities of the design elements are brought out

# The oriental influence

To the European eye much of the attraction of the Japanese garden is the contrast between its restrained and conscious layout and its harmonious planting. The owners of this plot, who are not professional designers, have tried to re-create such an appeal and have produced a fascinating and very human sculptured garden.

The triangular-shaped site was inhospitable, lying below the house and having heavy clay soil. But by cultivation and the addition of much peat a great deal has been achieved, and the strength of the layout has been enhanced by the scale of the strongly architectural planting.

The garden is approached from the house through an extension; the terrace lies above the garden and is connected with the ground below by a series of stepped levels on which are grouped, in an abstract way, pots and tubs, stones and pebbles. Below the terrace is a rectangular pool with a bench seat from which to contemplate the water. Beyond this, as a sort of pivot to the garden, a small hexagonal greenhouse, sited like a tea-house, is bursting with well cared-for succulents and cacti. This greenhouse prevents the garden being overlooked by a neighbouring house. On the other side of the terrace is a free-shaped water garden; the two pools make another abstract set piece. To achieve the flowing lines of hard edged pools, the owners cast the paving slabs themselves. What could have been an arid waste of concrete has been softened with bold clumps of foliage planting.

The long border at the far end of the garden has been broken with interesting, incidental features so that the whole area is a place round which to progress gently. A shady corner, furnished with an L-shaped concrete bench seat, is made inviting by the interesting detail round it. Another area is covered by a simple pergola of white-painted timber horizontals set on vertical scaffolding. In summer and autumn the feathery, dark red foliage of a cut leaf sumach contrasts well with the rigidity of the overhead pergola, while in spring the blossom of a magnificent magnolia makes a spectacular display.

Planting throughout is for form and texture. Architectural plants were chosen to contrast with the paving and the sculpture in the garden; the variety of leaf shapes is enormous and much of the foliage is evergreen and will last throughout the year. Indeed a garden with such strong bones is bound to be as much pleasure in winter as in summer.

A rowan tree (*Sorbus aucuparia*) casts dappled shade over this intimate corner of the garden (left). The built-in bench seat makes it a pleasant site for summer meals. Tiles on the brick wall, random pots and boulders and pebbles under the tree are details which bring the area to life. In the foreground is a clipped box (*Buxus sempervirens*) in a large container

In spring the magnificent blooms of *Magnolia* x *soulangiana* (above) make a spectacular display under the pergola. This hybrid produces its pink-flushed flowers before the leaves

The water garden (right) is in a shady corner, so shade-loving plants such as ferns, hostas and alpines cover the rockery by the waterfall. The rounded, glossy leaves in the pond are of the water hyacinth (*Eichhornia speciosa*)

| | |
|---|---|
| 1 *Taxus baccata* 'Aurea' | 17 *Spiraea* x *arguta* |
| 2 Alpines | 18 *Hebe pinguifolia carnosula* |
| 3 *Hosta sieboldiana* | and *Cotoneaster dammeri* |
| 4 *Dryopteris filix-mas* | 19 *Rhus typhina* 'Laciniata' |
| 5 *Eichhornia speciosa* | 20 *Vitis vinifera* 'Purpurea' |
| 6 *Iris laevigata* 'Variegata' | 21 *Magnolia* x *soulangiana* |
| 7 *Viburnum tomentosum* | 22 *Cotinus coggygria* |
|   'Lanarth' | *purpureus* |
| 8 *Rhododendron* 'Gomer | 23 *Rhododendron loderi* |
|   Waterer' | 24 *Sorbus aucuparia* |
| 9 Mollis azalea | 25 *Rhododendron ponticum* |
| 10 *Crataegus laevigata* | 26 *Acer japonicum* 'Aureum' |
|   'Coccinea plena' | 27 *Chamaecyparis* |
| 11 *Juniperus* x *media* | *lawsoniana* 'Allumii' |
|   'Pfitzerana' | 28 *Bergenia cordifolia* |
| 12 *Prunus* 'Fudanzakura' | 29 *Acer palmatum* |
| 13 *Buxus sempervirens* | 'Dissectum' |
| 14 *Hydrangea paniculata* | |
|   'Grandiflora' | |
| 15 *Chamaecyparis* | |
|   *lawsoniana* 'Ellwoodii' | |
| 16 *Rhododendron obtusum* | |
|   'Amoenum' | |

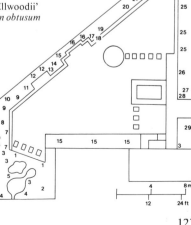

# Plan for a narrow site

A long narrow garden is a shape which can present great difficulties. This tiny rear garden is a good example of how strong ground planning with the right planting superimposed upon it can disguise the problems of such a site, and prevent the eye from simply running along its length.

The narrow space has been moulded to give the impression of separate 'rooms' within the area. Both layout and planting contribute to this feeling of an extension of the indoor living space. On entering the garden through a gate one is led across the first 'room' to a second one—the division accentuated by a slight change of level—and then on to the entrance of the house proper. The main view is framed by a white-painted timber pergola which leads into the brick-paved 'living area'. Pre-cast concrete slabs form the running surface of the layout, with brick paving in the static areas, and the surrounding brick walls are clad with creepers and climbing plants such as clematis, jasmine and wistaria.

Planting is used to define the rooms of the garden, and the strictness of clipped masses of yew and box is contrasted with full and flopping shrubby foliage. The choice of subjects is strong, with a preference for architectural shape and coloured foliage, which are attractive throughout the year. The owner has carefully considered the colour of flowers as well as leaves, however. The planting aims at two main colour areas which, of course, work best in the summer. He has planted mainly for a yellow effect near the gate, with a few blues and with matching foliage effects in the variegated honeysuckle and golden thyme. Softer pinks and whites, with a touch of crimson and blue, predominate in the main area near the house. Further splashes of colour are supplied by annuals—a pot of begonias, for example, and an urn filled with petunias.

The fullness of the planting masks the strict edge of the layout but, as the plan is a simple one, the combination of soft and hard materials is exactly right for the site.

A splash of annual colour is supplied (above) by an urn overflowing with bright petunias. These bold flowers look particularly well when seen against a dark leafy background, as against the formal box and *Mahonia japonica* in this corner of the garden

The main view up the garden (right) is confined by a pergola, made of timber horizontals with painted scaffolding verticals. The focal point is a brick-paved sitting area, with a dramatic clump of blue agapanthus beyond. The pergola, covered with white and red roses and white jasmine, is framed on all sides by glossy, dark green foliage

1  *Euphorbia robbiae*
2  *Wistaria sinensis*
3  *Agapanthus campanulatus*
4  *Arctostaphylos nevadensis*
5  *Ficus carica*
6  *Choisya ternata*
7  *Hebe* 'Simon Delaux'
8  *Indigofera gerardiana*
9  *Rosa* 'Cecile Brunner' (climber)
10  *Mahonia japonica*
11  *Taxus baccata*
12  *Hebe* 'Pagei'
13  *Pyracantha atalantioides* 'Aurea'
14  *Cotoneaster salicifolius*
15  *Rosa* 'Mermaid' (climber)

16  *Vitis coignetiae*
17  Herbs including golden thyme and variegated sage
18  *Lonicera japonica* 'Aureoreticulata'
19  *Rosmarinus officinalis*
20  *Hedera colchica*
21  *Ruta graveolens*
22  *Jasminum nudiflorum*
23  *Buxus sempervirens*
24  *Bergenia purpurascens*
25  *Helleborus argutifolius*
26  *Clematis macropetala*
27  *Polygonatum* x *hybridum*
28  *Helleborus orientalis*
29  *Vitis vinifera* 'Purpurea'
30  *Hypericum* 'Hidcote'
31  *Rosa* 'Wedding Day' (climber)

32  *Hydrangea villosa*
33  *Rosa* 'Fantin Latour' (grown as a climber)
34  *Jasminum officinale*
35  *Hydrangea petiolaris*
36  *Rosa* 'Etoile de Hollande' (climber)
37  *Hosta sieboldiana*
38  *Pieris formosa* 'Forrestii'
39  *Geranium renardii*
40  *Vinca minor*
41  *Weigela florida* 'Variegata'
42  *Viburnum davidii*
43  *Clematis cirrhosa balearica* and *Hedera canariensis* 'Gloire de Marengo'
44  *Akebia quinata*

The main feature of this plant group (top) is the yellow canary creeper (*Tropaeolum peregrinum*) grown in a pot. Its delicate, light green leaves contrast well with the leathery bergenia leaves and the dark green fingers of *Helleborus argutifolius* on either side

The plants in this garden are chosen for their shape and juxtaposed to bring out contrasting foliage. A good pale green/yellow leaf combination (above) shows up well against the blue engineering brick: from the left are a hosta, pieris with its bright green/gold bracts, *Geranium renardii* and a gold variegated weigela. Periwinkle covers the ground beneath them

# Dividing up a long plot

This long, narrow town garden was designed as four distinct sections, each with an individual atmosphere. Because of its shape, parts of the garden catch the sun at different times of day, bringing each area to life in turn. When one section is right for sunbathing another serves as a cool shady retreat. The garden contains a large number of different species, particularly in the densely planted central section. It is therefore, in a sense, a plantsman's garden; a place for looking at a collection of interesting plants. But the overall plan remains important, since it moulds the individual elements together to read as a visually satisfying whole.

The first section is a narrow passageway leading from the house. It is closely planted, mainly with ferns and other shade-loving plants and with climbers trained up a wooden trellis. The total effect is lush and green.

A path of random stepping stones then leads through into the second section, consisting of a terrace paved with granite setts which is ideal for open-air breakfasts in summer, since it is near the house and catches the morning sun. A timber screen helps to divide this patio and the beds which adjoin it from the wild middle area of the garden.

This third and largest section is a mass of shrubs, creating a forest-like pattern of deep shadows split by shafts of light. A brick path winds through to a paved clearing; an attractive feature which makes a virtue out of necessity, since it would have been difficult to grow plants directly under the large existing plane tree.

At the far end, the garden once more opens out into a terrace. This is the sunniest spot in the garden and is planted chiefly with roses in interlocking square beds enclosed by low box hedging. The formal design, echoing a medieval knot garden, contrasts effectively with the wild central section.

The roses, growing within interlocking, box-edged beds benefit from the sunniest position in a generally shady garden. The terrace of granite setts is enclosed on the site boundary by a wooden fence draped with climbers and is divided from the central wooded area by a border of herbs and herbaceous plants

1 *Rosa* 'Pink Perpetue'
2 *Rubus trilobus*
3 *Clematis* 'Ville de Lyon'
4 *Rosa* 'White Wings'
5 *Rosa* 'Caprice'
6 *Rosa* 'Michele Meilland'
7 *Rosa* 'Amite'
8 *Rosa* 'Papa Meilland'
9 *Gypsophila*
10 *Phlox* 'Lilac Time'
11 *Prunus triloba*
12 *Buxus sempervirens* 'Suffruticosa'
13 *Vitis vinifera* 'Riesling Sylvaner'
14 *Taxus baccata*
15 *Berberis thunbergii* 'Atropurpurea Nana'
16 *Dracocephalum sibiricum*
17 *Rosa* 'Claire Martin'
18 *Anaphalis triplinervis*
19 *Delphinium*
20 *Forsythia* x *intermedia* 'Lynwood'
21 *Eupatorium purpureum*
22 *Rudbeckia purpurea* 'The King'
23 *Avena sempervirens*
24 *Scutellaria indica*
25 *Chelone obliqua*
26 Pear tree
27 *Philadelphus coronarius*
28 *Geranium* 'Johnson's Blue'
29 *Aquilegia caerulea* 'Crimson Star'
30 *Cimicifuga simplex*
31 *Rhododendron obtusum*
32 *Cotoneaster melanocarpus*
33 *Pieris floribunda*
34 *Diervilla sessilifolia*
35 *Vinca minor*
36 *Ilex aquifolium*
37 *Juniperus communis* 'Hornibrookii'
38 *Viburnum opulus* 'Compactum'
39 *Deutzia* x *hybrida* 'Mont Rose'
40 *Chamaecyparis lawsoniana*
41 *Buddleia davidii* 'Royal Red'
42 *Buddleia farreri*
43 *Lavandula spica* 'Munstead'
44 *Hebe* 'Blauriesin'
45 *Thalictrum aquilegifolium*
46 *Hydrangea macrophylla* 'Blue Wave'
47 *Sambucus nigra*
48 *Weigela florida venusta*
49 *Viburnum* x *bodnantense* 'Dawn'

50 *Ligularia przewalskii*
51 *Heracleum mantegazzianum*
52 *Hosta sieboldiana* 'Elegans'
53 *Dicentra eximia* 'Alba'
54 *Astilbe* 'Spinell'
55 *Pachysandra terminalis*
56 *Primula pulverulenta*
57 *Bergenia*
58 *Kalmia latifolia*
59 *Rosa* 'China Town'
60 *Senecio clivorum* 'Desdemona'
61 *Clematis vitalba*
62 *Campanula lactiflora* 'Prichard's Variety'
63 *Verbascum nigrum*
64 *Phlox paniculata* 'Orange Perfection'
65 *Veronica teucrium*
66 *Clematis bonstedtii*
67 *Hosta albomarginata*
68 *Waldsteinia ternata*
69 *Viola odorata*
70 *Lamium galeobdolon*
71 *Polypodium vulgare*
72 *Doronicum pardalianches*
73 *Lonicera periclymenum* 'Serotina'
74 *Matteuccia struthiopteris*
75 *Acaena microphylla*
76 *Gaultheria procumbens*
77 *Epimedium rubrum*
78 *Clematis montana*
79 *Kirengeshoma palmata*
80 *Lonicera henryi*
81 *Parthenocissus quinquefolia*
82 *Athyrium filix-femina*
83 *Polygonum aubertii*
84 *Hydrangea involucrata*
85 *Aronia melanocarpa*
86 *Stephanandra incisa*
87 *Euonymus fortunei* 'Vegeta'
88 *Staphylea colchica*
89 *Prunus laurocerasus* 'Zabeliana'
90 *Aucuba japonica*
91 *Corylopsis pauciflora*
92 *Rhododendron ponticum*
93 *Symphoricarpus* x *doorenbosii* 'White Hedge'
94 *Sorbaria aitchisonii*
95 *Rosa* 'New Dawn'
96 *Clematis* 'Jackmanii Superba'
97 *Phlox paniculata* 'Rosa Spier'
98 *Phlox paniculata* 'Aida'
99 *Gillenia trifoliata*
100 *Saponaria ocymoides*
101 *Nepeta* x *faassenii*
102 *Rosa gallica* 'Versicolor'
103 *Potentilla nepalensis*
104 *Anemone vitifolia*
105 *Geranium psilostemon*
106 *Iberis sempervirens* 'Snowflake'
107 *Cornus kousa*
108 *Sedum cauticolum*
109 *Campanula portenschlagiana*
110 *Monarda*
111 *Aconitum* 'Spark's Variety'
112 *Symphytum peregrinum*
113 *Ajuga reptans*
114 *Crataegus* 'Punicea'
115 *Platanus* x *acerifolia*
116 *Anemone* 'De Caen'

The strong contrasts of light and shade, which are an important feature of the garden, are brought out clearly in this view of the central clearing under the plane tree (left). The brick paving is surrounded by a circular seat in the same material. *Anemone* 'De Caen' grows round the base of the tree trunk; the plant in the foreground is *Corylopsis pauciflora*, an attractive deciduous shrub which produces yellow flowers in spring

# In a secret garden

This was once two entirely separate plots—the larger a chicken run—divided by a wall. Part of the old wall has been retained and, with its archway and the rustic steps at the end, now provides both division and link between the two gardens. The areas each have their own individual character but are inter-dependent: together they make a fully satisfying whole.

The garden was created and realized entirely by the owner, a landscape architect. Over the years he has made certain modifications to suit the changing needs of his family: as his children grew older, for example, he was able to replace a very shady lawn with a delightful water garden, complete with fountain. The pool reflects the light, enlivening what was once a rather dark corner. 'Stepping stones' along one side of it give an illusion of floating on the water, like the water lilies nearby.

Brick walls surround the site on all sides. A large proportion of one boundary wall is made up of the back of a garage block and some old stables, now converted to more mundane use. To give greater height along two of the other boundary walls, brick pillars, supporting double wooden rails, were built. These match the brickwork of the wall and make an attractive framework for growing climbing roses and honeysuckle. The way in which the site is broken up means that from all parts of the garden one has very different views; a tantalizing vista down one side of the garden to the bench seat is glimpsed through the arch and from the fountain the eye is drawn to an overhung, wilder-looking corner.

The use of paving is a particularly interesting feature of the garden. Hard materials, which were obtained second-hand from the local council, have been combined to make distinctive, textured surfaces. Discarded granite setts, blue engineering bricks and patches of cobble are used with concrete slabs to make up the paths and paving throughout the two areas. Softened by lawn and by planting, the paving contributes much to the informality of the garden.

The atmosphere of the garden is that of a country retreat, remote from the pressures of the world: in fact, it is in the heart of a bustling town. It is completely self-contained and detached even from the house; the approach is along a walled passageway. The enclosed, private feel of the garden is emphasized by trees overhanging some of the walls from outside and by a big old pear tree inside the smaller plot. Cotoneasters trained as standard trees are used to

The view across the pool (left) down towards the house is framed by foliage—the glossy leaves of a *Fatsia japonica* in the foreground, and *Mahonia japonica* on the right. In the bed at the far side of the pool is a large clump of grey-leaved *Senecio laxifolius*.
The paving of brick and concrete slabs makes a crisp overhang to the pool. The slabs are continued along one side, on an unseen concrete base, to form 'stepping stones'

The charming water garden (above) replaced a rather shady lawn. A splashing fountain, and the light reflected on the water, bring life to a dark corner. The stone slabs down one side of the pool seem to float on its surface, like the lily pads. A waterfall from the smaller to the larger pool is formed by serrated tiles. This is a good example of the effective re-use of old materials

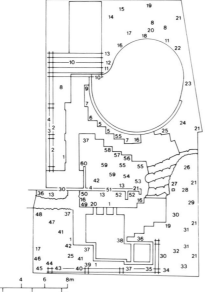

1 *Buxus sempervirens*
2 *Euphorbia wulfenii*
3 *Hydrangea petiolaris*
4 *Rosa* 'Albertine' (climber)
5 *Polygonum affine*
6 *Viburnum davidii*
7 *Iris sibirica* 'Perry's Blue'
8 *Elaeagnus* x *ebbingei*
9 *Alchemilla alpina*
10 *Vitis coignetiae*
11 *Stachys lanata* 'Silver carpet'
12 *Arundinaria nitida*
13 *Anemone japonica*
14 *Rhus typhina*
15 *Rosa primula*
16 *Pulmonaria saccharata*
17 *Hydrangea macrophylla* 'Blue Wave'
18 *Euphorbia robbiae*
19 *Cotoneaster* x *watereri*
20 *Hosta sieboldiana*
21 *Hedera helix*
22 *Mahonia aquifolium*
23 *Magnolia* x *soulangeana*
24 *Aralia spinosa*
25 *Hypericum* 'Hidcote'
26 *Viburnum* x *bodnantense*
27 *Epimedium pinnatum colchicum*
28 *Cornus alba* 'Spaethii'
29 *Sorbus aucuparia*
30 *Lamium maculatum*
31 *Mahonia* x 'Charity'
32 Pear tree
33 *Aucuba japonica* 'Variegata'
34 *Cotoneaster dielsianus*
35 *Lonicera* x *tellmanniana*
36 *Fatsia japonica*
37 *Senecio laxifolius*
38 *Nymphaea* 'Escarboucle'
39 *Rosa* 'Emily Grey' (climber)
40 *Cytisus scoparius*
41 *Geranium macrorrhizum*
42 *Iris pallida*
43 *Ceanothus thyrsiflorus*
44 *Rosa spinosissima*
45 *Macleaya cordata*
46 *Cobaea scandens*
47 *Helleborus orientalis*
48 *Bergenia stracheyi* 'Silberlicht'
49 *Forsythia* x *intermedia*
50 *Jasminum nudiflorum*
51 *Clematis armandii*
52 *Mahonia japonica*
53 *Hypericum elatum* 'Elstead'
54 *Abutilon vitifolium*
55 *Avena candida*
56 *Asperula odorata*
57 *Hebe divergens*
58 *Geranium pratense*
59 *Euphorbia characias*
60 *Euphorbia polychroma*

A cross axis of the garden along one side of the water 'room' is emphasized by an arch (right) with winter jasmine rambling over it. Leafy foreground planting for the shade—bergenia and spotted pulmonaria—is offset by cobbles

A vine-covered pergola built against a honeycomb brick wall (left) partially obscures a storage shed at the top of the garden. Lush planting round the edge of the lawn—including a *Rhus typhina*, bamboo and Japanese anemones—conceal it even further

form a cordon above one wall while various climbers and rampant ivy shroud others.

One difficulty which had to be faced was a light soil and the fact that roots from large walnut and ash trees in a neighbouring garden penetrate the subsoil. Both trees do not come into leaf until late spring but when this happens there is a noticeable check on general plant growth due to the trees taking the lion's share of the moisture. Plants have been chosen which will accept this situation with good grace but nevertheless in dry summer periods watering is essential to ensure survival of the lawn and a number of the herbaceous plants.

Low-growing ground cover, taller herbaceous plants and a wide variety of shrubs and trees make up the majority of the planting. Leaf shapes and colours are numerous and additional colour is provided by self-sown bluebells, poppies, foxgloves, forget-me-nots and honesty. This last plant serves a double purpose: in late spring it bears purple flowers and in autumn the silvery white seed pods provide indoor decoration.

In some parts of the garden plants spill over the edge of borders densely packed with shrubs and ground cover, such as lamb's tongue (*Stachys lanata*) and lungwort (*Pulmonaria*). The lawn, for instance, is surrounded for half of its circumference in this way. Much use has been made in other areas of formal box edging. In these beds, along the east wall and flanking the pool, additional colour as well as scent is provided by seasonal planting of wallflowers and cottage tulips in spring, and tobacco plant and pelargoniums in summer.

Winter is a serious test of a garden's visual character and the designer is frequently persuaded, where there is limited space, to concentrate his efforts on spring and summer planting when the garden will be more widely used. In this case, however, an effort has been made to provide a source of interest and pleasure to the eye at all seasons, and emphasis has been placed on the use of plant species that are in leaf during the winter, bear berries, or flower at this season. The effect is inevitably restrained by comparison with spring and summer but is nevertheless rewarding.

A close-up view of the 'stepping stones' (above) beside the pool. In winter the yellow racemes of *Mahonia japonica* provide this corner of the garden with a beautiful scent as well as colour

An imaginative feature of the garden is the use of hard materials for surfacing. On the left, blue engineering bricks are contrasted with concrete paving slabs, laid in a regular pattern

# A white theme for a wooded site

Designing a garden around a particular colour can be very effective and, used carefully, gives unity to the planting. A white theme, accentuated by the plants but given support by the materials used, dominates this garden by the sea. The small wooded site sweeps down from the road to the house, the other side of which faces the sea. The garden itself is enclosed by a stone wall. Although not very big, it has been divided into even smaller areas outside various rooms of the house; the dining area, master bathroom and kitchen each has its own terrace or patio.

The existing trees, oaks and pines, have been retained and other trees added—cypress along the driveway, plane trees on either side of the entrance and a Japanese black pine by the small pool in the corner. The number of trees makes the site fairly shaded. In addition to this the soil is acid, which is

another limiting factor; however, the rhododendrons and azaleas thrive in such a situation.

On a trellis by the long wall at the side of the house a white wistaria grows, the sweet-smelling flowers appearing in late spring and early summer. Much of the planting is of spring interest, but the bulbs are succeeded by annuals. All the flowering plants are white, however, as this is the owner's particular joy.

The paved areas are either of brick, to match the house, or of 100 mm (4 in) square cedar blocks. These are laid end-grain up on a sand base, making a textured, soft-looking terrace. The wooden blocks make ideal paving for gardens in a sunny climate, like this one, but they are not a suitable surfacing medium to use in a moist climate; the wood becomes mossy and slippery, and the lovely silver-grey of old cedar is lost—the wood simply looks black.

Cedar wood block paving, laid with its grain end up in a circular pattern, and retained by vertical cedar posts (above), makes an unusual surface for this charming small patio. The flowering tree is a crab apple (*Malus*), and ferns surround the patio's perimeter, softening its appearance

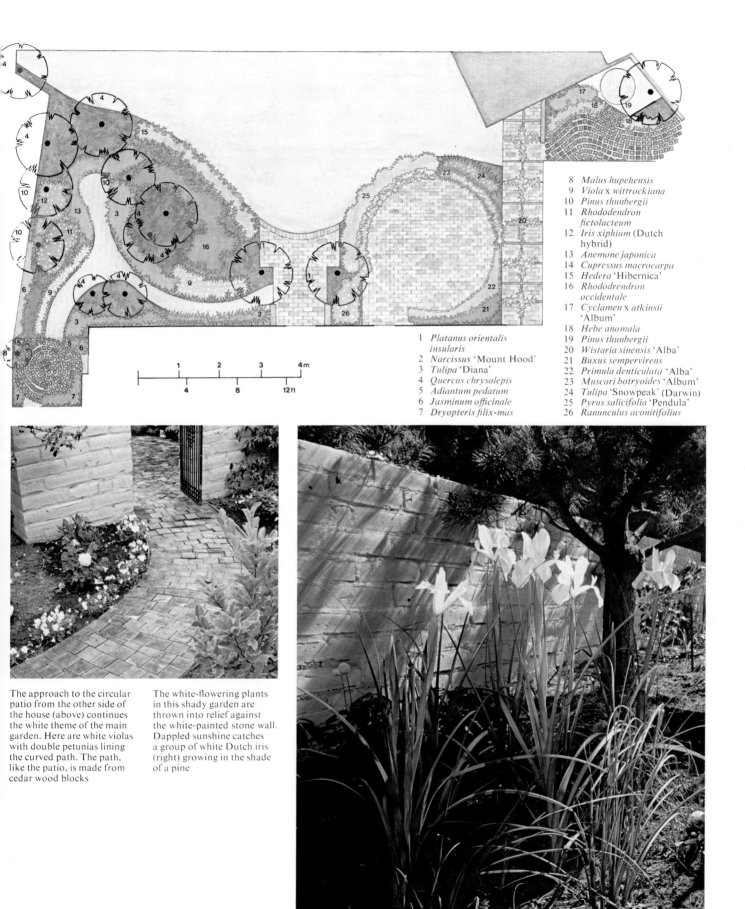

8 *Malus hupehensis*
9 *Viola* x *wittrockiana*
10 *Pinus thunbergii*
11 *Rhododendron fictolacteum*
12 *Iris xiphium* (Dutch hybrid)
13 *Anemone japonica*
14 *Cupressus macrocarpa*
15 *Hedera* 'Hibernica'
16 *Rhododrendron occidentale*
17 *Cyclamen* x *atkinsii* 'Album'
18 *Hebe anomala*
19 *Pinus thunbergii*
20 *Wistaria sinensis* 'Alba'
21 *Buxus sempervirens*
22 *Primula denticulata* 'Alba'
23 *Muscari botryoides* 'Album'
24 *Tulipa* 'Snowpeak' (Darwin)
25 *Pyrus salicifolia* 'Pendula'
26 *Ranunculus aconitifolius*

1 *Platanus orientalis insularis*
2 *Narcissus* 'Mount Hood'
3 *Tulipa* 'Diana'
4 *Quercus chrysolepis*
5 *Adiantum pedatum*
6 *Jasminum officinale*
7 *Dryopteris filix-mas*

The approach to the circular patio from the other side of the house (above) continues the white theme of the main garden. Here are white violas with double petunias lining the curved path. The path, like the patio, is made from cedar wood blocks

The white-flowering plants in this shady garden are thrown into relief against the white-painted stone wall. Dappled sunshine catches a group of white Dutch iris (right) growing in the shade of a pine

# Lush planting in a formal setting

The strictly formal layout of this garden is based on a design for a town garden by the eminent Edwardian architect, Sir Edwin Lutyens. The planting of the original was by Gertrude Jekyll, the influential garden innovator and writer. In this copy the planting is close to the designs of Miss Jekyll at the turn of the century, using a controlled range of colours and with a great emphasis on the shapes of plants and the textures of their foliage.

Planting screens the boundaries and focuses the eye on the feature at the end of the garden—a fine bench seat flanked by statuary—but it has considerable secondary interest of its own. Colours are principally cool—white, pale yellow and green—becoming stronger in the foreground. The beds are full and spill on to the gravel, making it look as though the plants had seeded themselves both in the border and out of it. It is often such incidents which make a garden look established, although it has to be admitted that this form of gardening calls for high maintenance and belonged to an age which expected a garden staff. Miss Jekyll changed her annuals two or three times a year, sinking subjects in pots as they came into flower.

As this garden was designed for an exhibition, all the plants had to be in their prime, and preferably in flower, for the duration of the show. This demand means that an exhibition planting layout cannot be valid for a real garden, as no consideration is given for interest at other times of the year. However, these plants could well form the basis of a design if other subjects were introduced to provide year-round interest in the garden. Gertrude Jekyll's books have now become standard works on the subject of planting design and would provide many ideas. A greater variety of shrubs, for example, could be substituted for the large quantity of *Rhododendron ponticum* used for infill at the back of the borders. Here it has been stripped of its flowers, so that all attention is focused on the composition in the foreground.

In a historical reconstruction the plants can only be as close as possible to the type then used, actual varieties having died out long since, in many cases. The central tree in this garden should in fact have been mulberry but it was impossible to find one grown in a container, so a weeping beech (*Fagus sylvatica* 'Pendula') was substituted.

The planting of this garden (above) complements, and leads the eye to, the classical statuary at the end. The flowering plants are chosen for their muted colours as well as their shapes: green-flowering euphorbias in the foreground, with *Alchemilla mollis* and Solomon's seal (*Polygonatum* x *hybridum*). The spiky perennial grass beyond (*Phalaris arundinacea* 'Picta') is a good neighbour for the verbascum, not yet in flower

Borders on either side of the garden (above right) spill out on to the paths, softening the formal lines of the layout. Some subjects give the appearance of having seeded themselves in the gravel, such as the grey-leaved dianthus and *Stachys lanata*. The large terracotta wine jar is seen as a sculptural piece, framed by the surrounding foliage

A detail of the planting (left) shows a green composition of verbascum, fatsia and *Alchemilla mollis*, highlighted by white-flowering hydrangeas

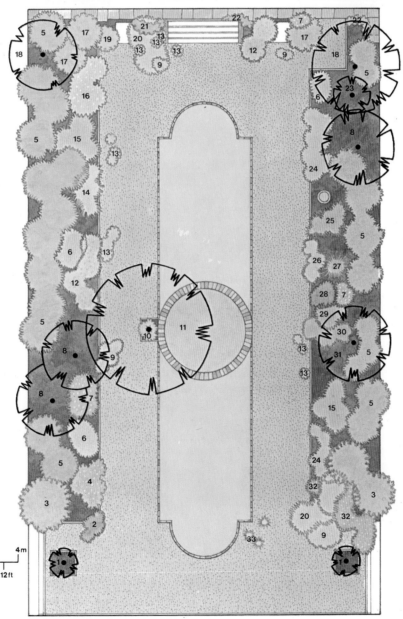

1 *Laurus nobilis*
2 *Ajuga reptans* 'Atropurpurea'
3 *Mahonia bealei*
4 *Geranium sylvaticum* 'Album'
5 *Rhododendron ponticum*
6 *Polygonatum* x *hybridum*
7 *Lilium regale*
8 *Acer japonicum*
9 *Stachys lanata* 'Silver carpet'
10 *Bergenia cordifolia*
11 *Fagus sylvatica* 'Pendula'
12 *Euphorbia wulfenii*
13 *Alchemilla mollis*
14 *Phalaris arundinacea* 'Picta'
15 *Verbascum hybridum*
16 *Hydrangea macrophylla* 'Madame Emile Mouillière'
17 *Fatsia japonica*
18 *Sorbus aucuparia*
19 *Passiflora caerulea*
20 *Yucca gloriosa*
21 x *Fatshedera lizei*
22 *Hedera canariensis* 'Gloire de Marengo'
23 *Taxus baccata* 'Fastigiata'
24 *Bergenia purpurascens*
25 *Iris germanica* 'Golden Alps'
26 *Dianthus* 'White ladies'
27 *Avena candida*
28 *Salvia officinalis* 'Purpurascens'
29 *Verbascum bombyciferum*
30 *Santolina chamaecyparissus*
31 *Rhus typhina* 'Laciniata'
32 *Anthemis cupaniana*
33 *Sisyrinchium striatum*

# Simple solutions for a low-maintenance garden

The keynote of this compact town garden is simplicity. Rather than imitating the complexities of a larger country garden, the design consists merely of a uniform expanse of paving surrounded by a few selected shrubs growing in narrow borders or tubs, with the whole patio enclosed by a wooden screen.

The paving of concrete slabs, heavily textured to look like stone, allows for two relatively spacious areas for sitting and eating out. The plants have been selected more for their architectural shape or for foliage effect than for flower colour. They act as a screen, with the taller shrubs and trees helping to hide the sitting areas from overlooking windows.

The fence of cedar verticals makes a warm, textured backdrop to the plants and, by clothing the three different existing materials—old wall, new wall and metal fence, gives an overall visual unity to the design. It is extended into the paving at various points, breaking the flat expanse along one wall and creating two wings which divide the garden into two separate outdoor rooms.

When designing with plants it is important to consider all the different angles from which they will be seen. The strong leaf forms of the shrubs (left), in particular the *Rhus typhina* and the *Fatsia japonicas*, show up well when seen from the upstairs windows. When viewed from the ground floor, the same group of plants effectively blocks off the car park beyond

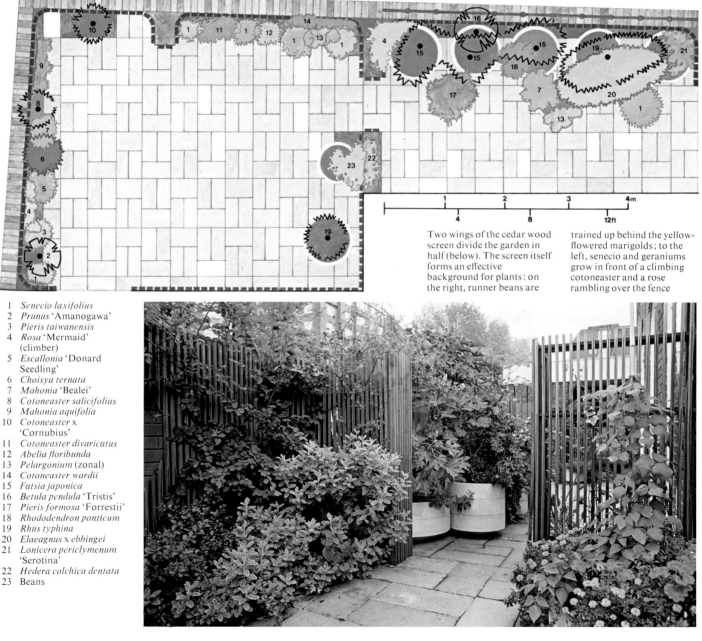

Two wings of the cedar wood screen divide the garden in half (below). The screen itself forms an effective background for plants: on the right, runner beans are trained up behind the yellow-flowered marigolds; to the left, senecio and geraniums grow in front of a climbing cotoneaster and a rose rambling over the fence

1 *Senecio laxifolius*
2 *Prunus* 'Amanogawa'
3 *Pieris taiwanensis*
4 *Rosa* 'Mermaid' (climber)
5 *Escallonia* 'Donard Seedling'
6 *Choisya ternata*
7 *Mahonia* 'Bealei'
8 *Cotoneaster salicifolius*
9 *Mahonia aquifolia*
10 *Cotoneaster* x 'Cornubius'
11 *Cotoneaster divaricatus*
12 *Abelia floribunda*
13 *Pelargonium* (zonal)
14 *Cotoneaster wardii*
15 *Fatsia japonica*
16 *Betula pendula* 'Tristis'
17 *Pieris formosa* 'Forrestii'
18 *Rhododendron ponticum*
19 *Rhus typhina*
20 *Elaeagnus* x *ebbingei*
21 *Lonicera periclymenum* 'Serotina'
22 *Hedera colchica dentata*
23 Beans

# Designed on two levels

The potential of this small, walled town garden was immediately obvious to the author, to whom it belongs. The garden appears to be a natural extension of the apartment as the main studio room leads straight out on to it, through glass doors, and the bedroom window also overlooks it. In addition, the aspect of the garden is due south so it gets the sun most of the day: not only is this important for the plants but the author wanted a place in which to sunbathe and to sit and write in the summer.

However, at first sight, not many people would have thought the plot ideal. The garden, enclosed by yellow coloured brick walls, was divided by a retaining wall about one and a half metres (five feet) high. Brick steps led up to the top level, with a drab concreted area on one side and a planting bed on the other; a concrete path curved its way from the bottom of the steps to another area of concrete by the house. The depressing outlook, common to many urban gardens, was only emphasized by the layout, whose effect was to lead the eye up and out of the site to the ugly backs of houses. A major requirement of the new design, therefore, was to keep the eye focused down on the garden so that one did not feel

The change of level brings a sense of drama to the garden (above) and draws attention away from the fact that it is overlooked. The photograph was taken about five months after the garden had been created and shows how quickly a sense of maturity can be achieved. Tall annual sunflowers help, of course, but among them is a planting of eucalyptus which will quickly screen the background houses with dense foliage

Before its alteration the lower part of this town garden (left) had curved beds and a curving concrete path leading to the steps, which in no way suited the geometric outline of the garden. The view was a depressing one of the backs of houses

constantly overlooked by the surrounding houses.

Structural changes were undertaken first. The existing concrete paving and curved path of the lower level were broken up and replaced by raised square beds which related to the angularity of the general layout. The raised beds used up the surplus earth excavated from the gravel area; their walls are built in the same golden brick as the boundary walls and are intended to provide an occasional sitting place. The top area of concrete proved too difficult to break up, even with a pneumatic drill, so only the occasional hole was made in which to plant.

The next move was to widen the bottom steps to make them appear more sculptural and to provide a useful standing place for pots. The lower level was laid with rounded, washed gravel, in shades of light and dark brown, providing casual paving through which plants could be grown. A slightly raised brick step was laid across the gravel, dividing the area and providing continuity with the material used elsewhere.

The strong use of brick throughout the garden called for bold planting. At the same time the fact that the garden is seen from the house at all times brought the need to create a·striking effect quickly. These major considerations led the author to choose plants which in some cases flagrantly contradict advice given to other people. However, the first priority was for privacy, even at the risk of having a jungle to be thinned out in a few years time. He rashly planted a weeping willow, with its roots retained, outside the bedroom window and another on the top level. Although this tree reaches enormous proportions quickly, it is very graceful at all times of the year and its strong vertical form makes it a very good background plant. In summer it will shade the window and provide an umbrella under which to sit. Three eucalyptus were planted at the top of the garden to make a quick screen for the houses beyond and a winter-flowering cherry tree was sited at the back of the lower right hand bed to give pleasure through the dark days.

In the front corner of this bed large-leaved plants were worked in to make as interesting a composition as possible with the 'Doves' sculpture: ornamental rhubarb and hostas in the foreground, with choisyas in the shade and a group of blue-flowering African lilies. The corner of the bed is punctuated with a ball of clipped box. In the longer bed on the left blue ceanothus are planted with the grey-leaved Californian poppy. These pick up the grey of the eucalyptus on the higher level. The smaller subjects at the front all have blue/grey foliage too: rue, stachys, dianthus and the grey grass *Avena*, contrasting with purple sage and black fennel.

To thicken up the beds in the first summer a host of annual white tobacco plants (*Nicotiana*) were planted, which make the garden magical at night with their deep sultry scent. Sunflowers were used to thicken up the eucalyptus planting at the top (as the photographs were taken in the first summer, much of the permanent planting is hidden by these quick-growing flowers). A large-leaved variegated ivy and winter jasmine are grown against the walls and a honeysuckle hides the pipes of the house.

The garden was only a few months old when it was photographed. The results show what can be achieved by a strong layout and by skilfully interplanting fast-growing subjects between the more permanent, slower-growing species. The author is aware that his garden is far too full to be viable in a few years' time; this is justified because, for him, half the joy of a garden is manipulating the plants in it. Though planting them is his favourite occupation, taking them out and thinning them follows a very close second.

In a small circular bed within the concrete of the upper level of the garden, decorative cabbages are growing. The grey-green colour of their leaves provides interest throughout the winter. The shallow pot contains basil and mint and a *Yucca gloriosa* grows in the large plant pot at the back

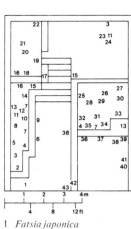

scale:
1 2 3 4m
4 8 12ft

1  *Fatsia japonica*
2  *Anemone japonica*
3  *Salix* x *chrysocoma*
4  *Buxus sempervirens*
5  *Lilium regale*
6  *Avena candida*
7  *Stachys lanata*
8  *Romneya coulteri*
9  *Sisyrinchium striatum*
10 *Beschorneria yuccoides*
11 *Yucca gloriosa*
12 *Rosmarinus officinalis*
13 *Hedera canariensis*
    'Gloire de Marengo'
14 *Pelargonium tomentosum*
15 *Euphorbia wulfenii*
16 *Ceanothus* 'A. T. Johnson'
17 *Yucca gloriosa* 'Variegata'
    and *Chlorophytum elatum*
    'Variegatum', outdoors
    for the summer
18 *Cotinus coggygria*
    'Notcutt's Variety'
19 *Buddleia davidii* 'White
    Cloud'
20 *Eucalyptus gunnii*
21 *Heracleum
    mantegazzianum*
22 *Parthenocissus
    tricuspidata* 'Veitchii'
23 Basil and mint
24 Cabbage
25 *Salvia officinalis*
    'Purpurascens'
26 *Hedera helix* 'Gold Heart'
27 *Prunus subhirtella*
    'Autumnalis'
28 *Cynara scolymus*
29 *Choisya ternata*
30 *Taxus baccata* 'Fastigiata'
31 *Agapanthus
    campanulatus*
32 *Pelargonium peltatum*
33 *Rheum palmatum*
34 *Hosta sieboldiana*
35 x *Fatshedera lizei*
36 *Alchemilla mollis*
37 *Helleborus argutifolius*
38 *Hosta* 'Thomas Hogg'
39 *Geranium pratense*
40 *Polygonatum* x *hybridum*
41 *Jasminum nudiflorum*
42 Avocado
43 *Lonicera* x *tellmanniana*

A sculpture called 'Doves' by Marie Gill (above) is a focal point of the garden. Being placed low, it helps to keep the eye within the first area. The smooth concrete shape of the birds is enhanced by the surrounding foliage: the large leaves of ornamental rhubarb ( *Rheum palmatum* ) and the rounded hosta leaves in the foreground

The weathered yellow brick of the steps is repeated in the paving, the retaining wall and the raised beds, making a well-integrated design. The plants are allowed to spill out, softening the edges and making the overall effect more casual; they are also grown in the gravel

1   *Sambucus nigra*
2   *Vinca minor*
3   *Hedera colchica dentata*
4   *Hedera helix*
5   *Aralia spinosa*
6   *Prunus laurocerasus*
7   *Acer palmatum*
    'Dissectum'
8   *Chamaecyparis pisifera*
9   *Saxifraga* x *urbicum*
10  *Endymion nonscriptus*
11  *Rubus tricolor*
12  *Acanthus mollis*
13  *Magnolia* x *soulangeana*
14  *Melastomataceae*
15  *Bergenia purpurascens*
16  *Fatsia japonica*
17  *Laburnum alpinum*
18  *Symphoricarpos albus*
19  *Kerria japonica*
    'Variegata'
20  *Iris xiphium*
21  White flag iris
22  *Ailanthus glandulosa*
23  *Cordyline australis*
24  *Camellia japonica*
25  *Ligustrum ovalifolium*
26  *Cotoneaster horizontalis*
27  *Thuja orientalis*

A rich collection of strong
foliage plants (above left)
frames the small terrace of
this paved garden. Simple
wooden furniture echoes the
white timber horizontal bar
fence behind

# A city jungle

An abundance of evergreen shrub planting, at different levels, using strong foliage forms gives an almost tropical feel to this city garden. Leaf and tree shapes, greens, greys and shadows provide the visual interest, rather than flower colour.

Around a central paved area, the planting was carefully planned to create an ordered jungle. A focal point is the tall clump of bamboo which flourishes next to the small pond. The shape of its foliage contrasts with a palm tree in a wooden tub and a sculptural group of spiky cordylines. In the central raised bed a vigorous juniper and two cotoneasters spill over the brickwork. Alongside the house, a weeping willow and a grey eucalyptus shade hostas and ferns beneath; the white weatherboard wall behind throws them all into sharp relief. The willow's curtain of delicate green stems encloses much of the paved area, creating a sheltered spot for sitting out in summer. The top end of the garden is shaded by an old elm under which bluebells, ivy and perwinkle make a thick carpet.

This leaf garden consists, therefore, of mostly common plants; they have been chosen and positioned with care and then allowed to develop naturally to achieve this jungly effect. Nevertheless, the garden looks somehow balanced and orderly, needing no more than two half days a year to maintain. The same ordered thinking has gone into the planting of the built-in window box on the sill of the house, but on a reduced scale the effect created is very different. Two bonsai cypress trees—one grey, one green—and a Japanese maple only 500 mm (20 in) high and twenty years old, contribute to this corner of subdued elegance.

As well as the white timber steps which lead down into the garden, there is also a rear approach to it through a hole-in-the-wall gate. Up a narrow passage and past an old cannon as a piece of sculpture, the visitor enters a green 'room' furnished with simple wooden chairs and a table. In the midst of so much greenery, this small garden is a perfect retreat from the rush of city life.

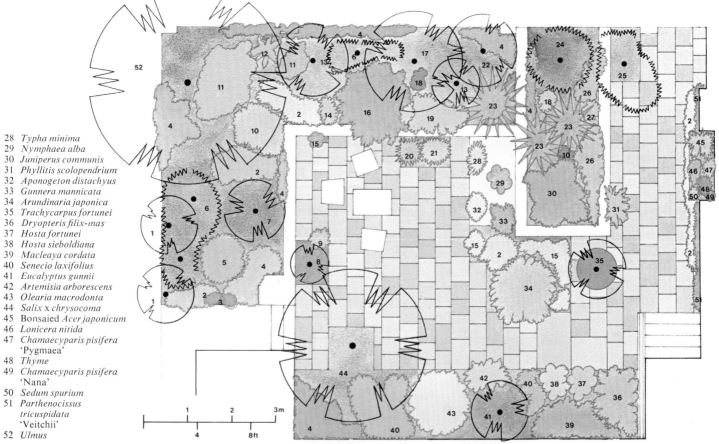

28  *Typha minima*
29  *Nymphaea alba*
30  *Juniperus communis*
31  *Phyllitis scolopendrium*
32  *Aponogeton distachyus*
33  *Gunnera mannicata*
34  *Arundinaria japonica*
35  *Trachycarpus fortunei*
36  *Dryopteris filix-mas*
37  *Hosta fortunei*
38  *Hosta sieboldiana*
39  *Macleaya cordata*
40  *Senecio laxifolius*
41  *Eucalyptus gunnii*
42  *Artemisia arborescens*
43  *Olearia macrodonta*
44  *Salix x chrysocoma*
45  Bonsaied *Acer japonicum*
46  *Lonicera nitida*
47  *Chamaecyparis pisifera*
    'Pygmaea'
48  *Thyme*
49  *Chamaecyparis pisifera*
    'Nana'
50  *Sedum spurium*
51  *Parthenocissus*
    *tricuspidata*
    'Veitchii'
52  *Ulmus*

The changing colours of
Virginia creeper surround
this elegant window garden
(above), whose daintiness
offsets the jungly effect of the
rest of the garden

Contrasting leaf shapes and
colours, ranging from
feathery silver to glossy dark
green, provide a wealth of
visual interest in this shaded
part of the garden leading to
the house

# A heather garden

All garden sites have their problems, but this front garden seemed particularly difficult at the outset. Roughly rectangular in shape, it was situated on a plateau which sloped steeply down to the existing drive and the access road. It also had an acid soil which limited the choice of plants to some extent.

The plan for the area was devised to eliminate the unmanageable slope by creating a series of levels, retained by dry stone walls cut into the banks. The walls were built at an angle, or batter, to make them more stable, with open joints to prevent the soil becoming waterlogged. The curving pattern of the levels was reinforced by planting two yew hedges, which also form a dark green formal backing to the looseness of the rest of the subjects chosen.

Planting was selected to provide interest and colour all the year round, and the choice of acid-tolerant plants such as rhododendrons, broom and a high proportion of heathers was ideal for the purpose. The *Erica carnea* varieties are in flower from January to April, the brooms, rhododendrons and daphnes from April to June; after June, the roses and the *cinerea* and *calluna* species of heather bloom until October, with a red-foliaged heather giving colour throughout the winter. Another factor which influenced the choice of subjects was ease of maintenance; by using heather and other low ground cover weeding is almost eliminated. Bulbs were also planted to grow through the ground cover, giving bold splashes of colour from January to June.

Mixed planting of heathers forms soft mounds of rich colour on the terraces of this front garden. Variation in height and foliage is introduced by the broom (*Genista lydia*) in the foreground and *Juniperus chinensis* in the middle. The pampas grass at the back, with its feathery white fronds, is planted in the neighbouring garden; there is no formal boundary and the adjoining lawns are allowed to run into each other, both parties benefiting from the increased sense of space

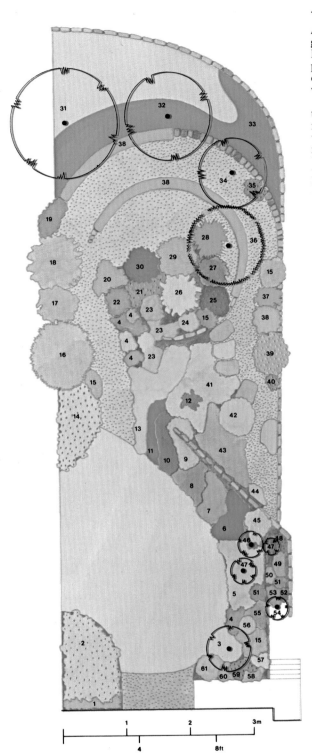

| | | | |
|---|---|---|---|
| 1 *Pyracantha coccinea* | 12 *Juniperus sabina tamariscifolia* | 24 *Rhododendron* 'Praecox' | 39 *Genista hispanica* | 49 *Calluna vulgaris* 'Foxii Nana' |
| 2 *Rosa* 'Anna Wheatcroft' | 13 *Calluna vulgaris* 'H. E. Beale' | 25 *Hebe* 'Autumn Glory' | 40 *Geranium subcaulescens* | 50 *Rhododendron impeditum* |
| 3 *Chamaecyparis lawsoniana* 'Stewartii' | 14 *Rosa* 'Evelyn Fison' | 26 *Cytisus praecox* | 41 *Calluna vulgaris* 'Mrs Ronald Gray' | 51 *Chamaecyparis obtusa* |
| 4 *Rhododendron japonicum* | 15 *Potentilla fruticosa* | 27 *Cotinus coggygria* | 42 *Juniperus chinensis* 'Pfitzerana Aurea' | 52 *Daphne collina* |
| 5 *Erica cinerea* 'Lavender Lady' | 16 *Cytisus scoparius* | 28 *Iris germanica* | 43 *Calluna vulgaris* 'Alba Plena' | 53 *Rhododendron* 'Elizabeth' |
| 6 *Erica carnea* 'King George' | 17 *Viburnum carlesii* | 29 *Senecio greyi* | 44 *Iris pumila* | 54 *Chamaecyparis lawsoniana* 'Columnaris' |
| 7 *Erica carnea* 'Springwood White' | 18 *Cytisus scoparius* | 30 *Rhododendron* 'Vanessa' | 45 *Genista lydia* | 55 *Dryas octopetala* |
| 8 *Erica cinerea* 'Rosea' | 19 *Hebe* 'Pagei' | 31 *Betula papyrifera* | 46 *Chamaecyparis pisifera* | 56 *Picea glauca* |
| 9 *Calluna vulgaris* 'Gold Haze' | 20 *Rhododendron fastigiatum* | 32 *Crataegus oxyacanthoides* | 47 *Chamaecyparis lawsoniana* 'Fletcheri' | 57 *Saponaria ocymoides* |
| 10 *Erica cinerea* 'C.D. Eason' | 21 *Fritillaria imperialis* | 33 *Polyanthus* | 48 *Lithospermum diffusum* 'Grace Ward' | 58 *Lonicera nitida* |
| 11 *Calluna vulgaris* 'Aliportii' | 22 *Erica* x *darleyensis* | 34 *Prunus cerasifera* 'Nigra' | | 59 *Skimmia japonica* |
| | 23 *Rhododendron* 'Blue Diamond' | 35 *Cotoneaster horizontalis* | | 60 *Primula juliae* 'Wanda' |
| | | 36 *Rhus typhina* | | 61 *Corylopsis pauciflora* |
| | | 37 *Pinus mugo pumilio* | | |
| | | 38 *Taxus baccata* 'Fastigiata' | | |

# A natural setting for a new house

The owner of this garden, himself an architect, was able to design the house and garden as one unit. The site, which had previously formed part of a larger walled garden, included prominent fruit trees, most of which were retained. With space limited, it was decided to let the garden dominate and make the house an unobtrusive single-storey building of dark brick covered with climbers.

One of the principles followed in planning the garden was to disguise the existence of boundaries, so the garden harmonized with the surrounding environment. This necessitated fairly dense planting, round the perimeter, of trees, shrubs and climbers; these, combined with overhanging trees from the adjoining garden, create the illusion of a clearing in a wood.

Another idea which informed the whole design was to create a succession of outside rooms—of separate, secluded areas which would offer anyone

walking round the garden a series of different and interesting views. A narrow passage runs out from the front door; a shady courtyard then opens out to one side, while the line of old stone paving—flanked by mahonias and bamboo—leads along the side of the house. Round the corner of the house a weeping cherry tree divides the path in two: to the right there is a patio, completely enclosed by plants, with a wooden table and benches for eating out; to the left the gap between tree and house opens out into a large expanse of lawn dominated by three old apple trees.

A line of shrub planting effectively screens this expanse of lawn from another enclosed area beyond, which itself winds back along the boundary eventually to join up with the enclosed eating area. A walk round the garden thus takes you through at least five separate outside rooms, creating the visual variety normally found only in much larger gardens.

An autumnal view of the garden shows the dark-bricked house situated unobtrusively among the mature apple trees. These three old trees dominate the lawn and give a distinct character to the whole garden. *Cotoneaster horizontalis, Hemerocallis fulva, Euonymus fortunei* and *Fatsia japonica* grow in their shade

147

Dense planting ensures a profusion of lush green foliage in much of the garden. The outside eating area (above) is glimpsed through the flowering currants, azaleas and cotoneasters which grow under the weeping cherry

The patio for eating out is almost entirely surrounded by plants (below), with only narrow openings to the house and garden beyond. As well as the overhanging cherry, plants include rhododendrons and rue

From the front door the eye is led along the side of the house by a narrow path of individual paving slabs (right). Strongly architectural plants have been chosen for this area, including a clump of bamboo at the end and mahonias and *Cotoneaster salicifolius floccosus* in the foreground. The climber against the house wall on the left is *Schizophragma hydrangeoides*

The shady courtyard next to the house (below) is dominated by the central apple tree, under which mahonias and variegated cornus grow. Pebbles set between the old stone slabs make an interesting paved surface and add to the slightly Japanese feel of this corner of the garden

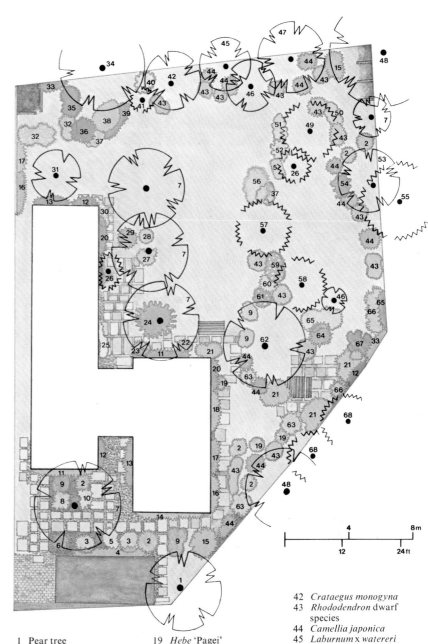

1 Pear tree
2 *Mahonia pinnata*
3 *Cotoneaster salicifolius floccosus*
4 *Wistaria sinensis*
5 *Iris pallida*
6 *Berberis buxifolia*
7 Apple tree
8 *Cornus alba* 'Westonbirt'
9 *Pieris formosa* 'Forrestii'
10 *Cornus alba* 'Elegantissima'
11 *Parthenocissus quinquefolia*
12 *Lonicera periclymenum*
13 *Jasminum nudiflorum*
14 *Schizophragma hydrangeoides*
15 *Arundinaria nitida*
16 *Rosa* 'Albéric Barbier' (climber)
17 *Rosa* 'May Queen' (climber)
18 *Rosa* 'Mme Plantier' (climber)

19 *Hebe* 'Pagei'
20 *Clematis montana*
21 *Ribes sanguineum*
22 *Dicentra formosa*
23 *Spiraea thunbergii*
24 *Cotoneaster horizontalis*
25 *Campanula lactiflora*
26 *Forsythia* x *intermedia*
27 *Hemerocallis fulva*
28 *Euonymus fortunei*
29 *Fatsia japonica*
30 *Lunaria rediviva*
31 *Prunus subhirtella* 'Autumnalis'
32 *Cytisus* x *praecox*
33 *Hedera helix*
34 *Fraxinus excelsior*
35 Gooseberry
36 *Osmanthus delavayi*
37 *Lavandula spica*
38 *Rosa rugosa* hybrids
39 *Rosa* dwarf varieties
40 *Eucalyptus gunnii*
41 *Corylus avellana* 'Contorta'

42 *Crataegus monogyna*
43 *Rhododendron* dwarf species
44 *Camellia japonica*
45 *Laburnum* x *watereri*
46 *Acer palmatum*
47 *Betula youngii*
48 *Taxus baccata*
49 *Hosta sieboldiana*
50 *Philadelphus* 'Belle Etoile'
51 *Phalaris arundinacea*
52 *Hydrangea macrophylla*
53 *Pseudotsuga menziesii*
54 *Leucothoe*
55 *Pyracantha*
56 *Senecio laxifolius*
57 *Magnolia fraseri*
58 *Buddleia davidii*
59 *Paeonia officinalis*
60 *Hosta undulata*
61 *Anemone* x *hybrida*
62 *Prunus* 'Kiku-shidare Sakura'
63 *Kerria japonica*
64 *Hypericum calycinum*
65 *Choisya ternata*
66 *Aristolochia*
67 *Chaenomeles japonica*
68 Rhubarb
69 *Syringa vulgaris*

149

# A circular theme

The main features of this town garden dictated that it should be laid out on strong lines. As the house is in a crescent road, the garden is wedge-shaped, being narrower towards the house; it is also at basement level, which means that the main living rooms look down upon it. Pattern was therefore of primary importance, both to overcome the odd shape and be arresting when seen from above. Furthermore, in an enclosed town garden without distant views the design should aim to keep the eye within it.

A simple layout composed of two intersecting circles solves all these problems, and planting has been chosen both to complement the design and to emphasize the length of the garden. The first circle is simply an area of lawn, while a round pool within the second, paved circle reinforces the circular theme. The mature trees at the end appear to frame this second circle, especially when seen from above; they also help to create the intimate feeling of an enclosed garden. Sunlight is filtered through the trees, casting pools of light on the garden. The trees also cast a lot of shade and planting at the far end of the garden consists mainly of foliage specimens which can cope with this.

Spaces have been left in the paving for shade-loving plants such as hostas and balsams which cluster attractively round the pool. In the summer the spaces are filled out with pink and white *Impatiens sultani* for a delicate touch of colour. The pool itself has a central fountain jet, which contrasts well with the vertical sprays of bamboo beyond. A step and gate behind the background planting leads to a hidden rubbish area, while lattice screens the end wall, which is lost in shade.

The paved circle forms a kind of terrace area and is used for sitting by the pool on hot days, when the shade of the trees is welcome. The main terrace, however, is adjacent to the house; this area of the garden receives more sun than any other part and, being next to the kitchen, is convenient for outdoor entertaining. The terrace is paved, like the surround to the lawn and the second circle itself, with slabs of reconstituted stone which mellow quite quickly to resemble natural stone. Planting against the house walls softens this area and links house and garden: a wistaria twines dramatically upwards, looking beautiful in summer when it is in flower, and smaller evergreen subjects maintain winter interest. Ivy and other evergreen climbers alleviate the possible austerity of the surrounding high brick walls, with jasmine, clematis and roses blooming at different times of year.

The back of the house has been improved by covering much of it with lattice, or *treillage*, creating a sort of verandah (left). The sunlight on this southern aspect filters gently through the lattice and the leaves of the wistaria, casting a cool green shade

From the first floor living rooms the circular design of the garden and its figure-of-eight outline (above), appears very striking. The view is dramatically framed by trees, particularly the large fig tree on the right with its distinctive leaves. The paved edging to the lawn links it with the second, paved circle and has a practical role in that it facilitates mowing

The reconstituted stone slabs are specially designed to surround the circular pond (right). Spaces have been left between the paving slabs to allow planting of hostas, ivy, *Lamium maculatum* and *Impatiens sultani*, which will survive in the shade of the overhanging trees

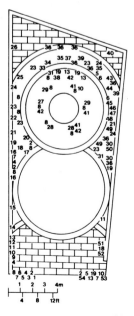

1 *Wistaria floribunda* 'Macrobotrys'
2 *Senecio laxifolius*
3 *Eucalyptus gunii*
4 *Chrysanthemum maximum*
5 *Fatsia japonica* 'Variegata'
6 Mollis azalea
7 *Cytisus scoparius* 'Cornish Cream'
8 *Hedera helix* 'Glacier'
9 *Ruta graveolens* 'Jackman's Blue'
10 *Ballota pseudo-dictamnus*
11 *Ficus carica*
12 *Rosa* 'Sympathy'
13 *Camellia* 'Mathotiana Alba'
14 *Passiflora caerulea*
15 *Clematis* 'Marie Boisselot'
16 *Hedera canariensis* 'Gloire de Marengo'

17 *Hebe leiophylla*
18 *Rosa* 'Iceberg'
19 *Euonymus japonicus* 'Albomarginatus'
20 *Rosa* 'Aloha'
21 *Jasminum officinale*
22 *Jasminum nudiflorum*
23 *Camellia* x *williamsii*
24 *Elaeagnus pungens* 'Maculata'
25 *Viburnum tinus*
26 *Acer pseudoplatanus*
27 *Artemisia stelleriana*
28 *Lamium maculatum*
29 *Hosta sieboldiana*
30 *Arundinaria murielae*
31 *Yucca flaccida* 'Ivory'
32 *Cotinus coggygria*
33 *Campanula stella*
34 *Prunus* 'Amanogawa'
35 *Rhododendron* 'Mount Everest'
36 *Dryopteris filix-mas*
37 *Cortaderia argentea* 'Pumila'

38 *Acanthus mollis*
39 *Arundinaria nitida*
40 *Aesculus hippocastanum*
41 *Phormium colensoi*
42 *Hosta albomarginata*
43 *Betula* 'Youngii'
44 *Mahonia bealei*
45 *Vinca minor*
46 *Cornus florida*
47 *Parthenocissus quinquefolia*
48 *Hydrangea macrophylla* 'Blue Wave'
49 *Aucuba japonica* 'Variegata'
50 *Juniperus communis* 'Repanda'
51 *Forsythia* x *intermedia* 'Lynwood'
52 *Hydrangea petiolaris*
53 *Parthenocissus tricuspidata* 'Veitchii'
54 *Clematis* 'Lady Northcliffe'

# Seasonal-colour garden

The small plot of this bungalow was laid out to give the owners maximum privacy, for initially the rear of the house was overlooked by an ugly coal store on the left, a large garage straight ahead and another house to the right. A high surrounding fence was erected and the planting designed to screen this in summer and winter: climbers at the back and evergreens in front with plants of small-scale interest in the borders.

The climbers were chosen for individual features such as highly scented flowers (honeysuckle and jasmine), berries (pyracantha), variegated leaves or spectacular flowers, like clematis. Other trees and shrubs used to soften the boundary have an interesting shape; the twigs of the contorted willow and hazel are particularly attractive against the sky in winter.

The owners of the garden are keen horticulturists and in the large mixed border groupings were made for contrast, so that the yellow-leaved robinia is juxtaposed with the purple-leaved *Cotinus coggygria* and the striped leaves of phalaris.

The garden was designed as a picture to be seen through the sliding glass doors of the living room. The view culminates in a standard apple tree, which incidentally screens the south-facing greenhouse, well placed behind the garage. A deciduous hedge of *Prunus cerasifera* 'Atropurpurea' also screens the greenhouse, letting light through in winter. A sheltered sitting area was created against the garage wall, furnished with a pond. The paving which connects the house and greenhouse also forms a terrace round the house and links all parts of the garden. This crazy paving has an informal character entirely suited to this green and intimate suburban garden.

Annual colour massed in pots (above) near the house includes blue asters and orange tagetes. The bright grey foliage of santolina and the silvery white seed pods of honesty in the foreground are thrown into relief against the varied foliage of the large mixed border which is beginning to take on autumn tints

An enormous variety of herbaceous plants are grown in the long mixed border, and each season the planting creates a different impression. In early summer delphiniums in mixed shades make a splendid display (above). This photograph was taken some time ago and, as often happens in a garden, some of the planting has since changed. This large herbaceous border is the garden's most eye-catching feature. In choosing the plants for it, one important consideration was scent; plants with aromatic leaves or fragrant flowers are placed towards the front. Certain plants, like atriplex and foxglove, have been allowed to seed themselves, making the planting lush and luxuriant and keeping down weeds

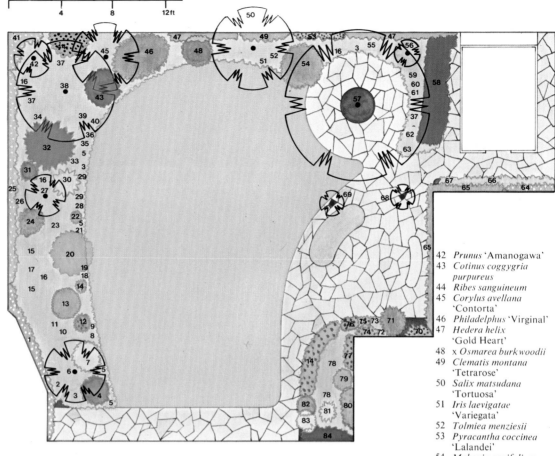

In high summer and again in autumn the brilliant blooms of this climbing form of the floribunda rose 'Masquerade' (right) clothe the garage wall. The flowers of this variety open yellow, turn pink and slowly fade to a deep red. As the roses do not all open at the same time, a triple-tone effect is created. Spaces are left in the paving for low-growing plants

1 Jasminum officinale
2 Miniature roses
3 Galanthus nivalis 'S. Arnott'
4 Euonymus japonicus 'Ovatus aureus'
5 Lamium maculatum 'Aureum'
6 Magnolia denudata
7 Atriplex halimus
8 Ajuga reptans 'Atropurpurea'
9 Convallaria majalis
10 Thalictrum dipterocarpum
11 Verbascum thapsiforme
12 Fuchsia 'Riccartonii'
13 Callistemon citrinus 'Splendens'
14 Lavandula spica 'Hidcote'
15 Delphinium
16 Narcissus 'Golden Harvest'
17 Physalis franchetii
18 Origanum vulgare 'Aureum'
19 Erica carnea 'Springwood'
20 Cornus alba 'Sibirica'
21 Sedum maximum 'Atropurpureum'
22 Ruta graveolens
23 Paeonia officinalis 'Rubra-plena'
24 Abutilon vitifolium
25 Lonicera japonica 'Halliana'
26 Lysimachia punctata
27 Ilex altaclarensis
28 Helichrysum serotinum
29 Melissa officinalis 'Aurea'
30 Artemisia abrotanum
31 Philadelphus microphyllus
32 Cytisus x praecox
33 Monarda didyma
34 Phlox paniculata
35 Lithospermum diffusum 'Heavenly Blue'
36 Coreopsis verticillata
37 Primula vulgaris
38 Robinia pseudoacacia 'Frisia'
39 Phalaris arundinacea 'Picta'
40 Rudbeckia fulgida 'Goldstrum'
41 Lonicera japonica 'Aureoreticulata'
42 Prunus 'Amanogawa'
43 Cotinus coggygria purpureus
44 Ribes sanguineum
45 Corylus avellana 'Contorta'
46 Philadelphus 'Virginal'
47 Hedera helix 'Gold Heart'
48 x Osmarea burkwoodii
49 Clematis montana 'Tetrarose'
50 Salix matsudana 'Tortuosa'
51 Iris laevigatae 'Variegata'
52 Tolmiea menziesii
53 Pyracantha coccinea 'Lalandei'
54 Mahonia aquifolium
55 Dicentra spectabilis
56 Laurus nobilis
57 Apple tree
58 Prunus cerasifera 'Atropurpurea'
59 Pulmonaria angustifolia
60 Pulmonaria saccharata
61 Pulmonaria officinalis
62 Aquilegia alpina
63 Campanula portenschlagiana
64 Clematis x 'Nelly Moser'
65 Rosa 'Masquerade' (climber)
66 Colchicum speciosum
67 Mint
68 Chamaecyparis lawsoniana 'Ellwoodii'
69 Chamaecyparis lawsoniana 'Minima Glauca'
70 Clematis x 'Mrs. N. Thompson'
71 Syringa microphylla
72 Lilium speciosum rubrum
73 Sempervivum tectorum calcareum
74 Lippia citriodora
75 Hebe pimeleoides 'Glaucocaerulea'
76 Fuchsia magellanica 'Gracilis'
77 Clematis 'Madame Grange'
78 Aquilegia vulgaris 'McKana hybrids'
79 Abutilon megapotamicum 'Variegatum'
80 Clematis x 'Hagley Hybrid'
81 Senecio leucostacys
82 Rosmarinus officinalis
83 Santolina chamaecyparissus
84 Hedera 'Hibernica'

# A wild garden in a controlled setting

The overall design of this garden is modern and mainly rectangular, consisting of a paved courtyard surrounded on two sides by borders and intermittently broken up by islands of planting. But the abundance of plants which have been encouraged to spill over in all directions, and the grass and weeds which have been allowed to appear through the paving, superimpose a complex pattern of lush green foliage on top of the simple layout. Nature has been allowed to take over where man left off. Such a garden of course has great advantages for anyone who cannot, or does not want to, devote much time to gardening; there is no lawn to mow and maintenance is kept to an absolute minimum.

Near the house the paving is of neat, regular quarry tiles. One corner is covered by a bamboo pergola which supports a vine, and a bench seat for sitting out in the evening sun is positioned against the wall. The major part of the garden is covered with granite setts, which have been laid on a consolidated ash base, enabling grass to grow up between the joints. Distributed within this courtyard, apparently at random but in fact with an eye for the creation of satisfying views within the garden, are about twelve islands of planting. Some of these contain a single medium-sized shrub, such as a forsythia or euonymus; others combine taller species with spreading areas of low ground cover—rhododendrons with heathers, for instance. The largest island includes one of the most distinctive features of the garden: the beautiful *Sophora japonica*, or Japanese pagoda tree, an ornamental species much used in the subtle garden design of its country of origin. Three old stone troughs provide sculptural interest and also serve as raised beds to be filled with colourful annuals.

At the far end of the garden is a small stone-paved terrace flanked by rhododendrons and pieris. This sunny, south-facing corner of the garden is ideal for sitting out. A wild-looking tamarix dominates the middle section at this far end of the site while the most jungly and overgrown area is the opposite corner, where a rich profusion of ferns grows happily in the shade of a stag's horn sumach tree (*Rhus typhina*).

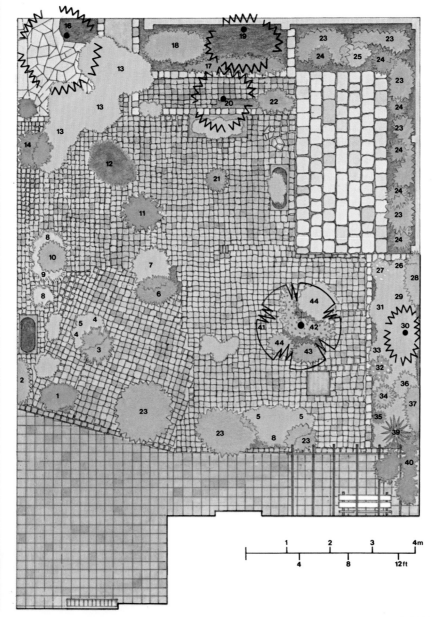

1 *Euonymus japonicus*
  'Microphyllus'
2 *Lonicera caprifolium*
3 *Spiraea* x *arguta*
4 *Sedum spurium*
5 *Erica carnea*
6 *Pyrethrum roseum*
7 *Hydrangea macrophylla*
8 *Sedum spectabile*
9 *Calluna vulgaris*
10 *Aucuba japonica*
   'Variegata'
11 *Chaenomeles japonica*
12 *Forsythia* x *intermedia*
13 *Polipodicae* (ferns)
14 *Rhus glabra*
15 *Buxus sempervirens*
16 *Rhus typhina*
17 *Iberis sempervirens*
18 *Euphorbia polychroma*
19 *Weigela* 'Bristol Baby'
20 *Tamarix tetrandra*
21 *Chamaecyparis*
   *lawsoniana* 'Ellwoodii'
22 *Thymus doerfleri*
23 Rhododendron hybrids
24 *Pieris japonica*
25 *Hebe* 'Pagei'
26 *Geranium endressii*
27 *Alyssum maritimum*
28 *Clematis montana*
29 *Helianthemum*
30 *Viburnum carlcephalum*
31 *Aubrieta deltoidea*
32 *Aster novi-belgii*
33 *Berberis buxifolia* 'Nana'
34 *Spiraea bumalda*
35 *Cotoneaster horizontalis*
36 *Poncirus trifoliata*
37 *Jasminum nudiflorum*
38 *Berberis candidula*
39 *Yucca filamentosa*
40 *Vitis alba*
41 *Sophora japonica*
42 *Lavandula spica*
43 *Thymus vulgaris*
44 *Gypsophila repens*

1       2       3       4m

4       8       12 ft

A general view of the garden (above left), looking out from the house towards the far wall, is dominated by the elegant Japanese pagoda tree. Tall neighbouring trees contribute to the intimate, enclosed atmosphere of the courtyard

Ferns and suckers from the overhanging *Rhus typhina* have been allowed to grow completely unchecked in this area of the garden (left). The crisp whitewashed walls surrounding the site contrast with the lush greens of the overgrown foliage

This attractive corner of the garden by the house (right) makes an ideal sun trap in the late afternoon. The red-pink flowers of *Spiraea bumalda* with the dramatic white spike of *Yucca filamentosa* provide contrast in this overall green garden

155

# On geometric lines

The exciting atmosphere of this enclosed garden is created by the sensitive combination of opposite elements. The severe shapes and discreet textures in the layout form both the background and a contrast to the abundant and beautiful planting. Concrete paving is the thread of continuity. The house opens on to a paved terrace which is the eating area and the eye is carried past the pond, under the pergola and down a path, edging the lawn, to the wall at the end. The view is punctuated by a concrete unit-formed bench seat at the end of the terrace, which forms a strong sculptural element in the setting and creates a visual divider between the two areas of garden. Being low, however, it is never too dominant and its strong, architectural outline links it with the concrete paving slabs and with the style of the house and the whole garden.

The geometric lines of the basic design are never allowed to dominate. They are relieved, for example, by the use of large cobbles round two sides of the pond and underneath the concrete seat. Elsewhere, clumps of plants break up the paving, as on the terrace, or low spreading heathers are allowed to cover it as they do round the step and the seating unit.

Water is a very important element in the paved terrace area which forms almost half the garden. It softens the use of concrete and this effect is enhanced by the water plants such as rushes and water lilies. The clump of bamboo and the overhanging rowan tree make attractive reflections on the face of the water, while the goldfish create small ripples of movement below the surface.

The profusion of plants against the restrained, textured concrete brings the whole garden to life, especially where they spill out from their beds on to the paving, almost as if they were trespassing. Bold masses of plants, chosen for their varying shades of colour and their leaf shapes, are juxtaposed, while the hard landscaping of the garden checks their advance.

The uncluttered lines of the terrace (above) make it a visual as well as a practical extension of the modern house. The clematis-covered pergola frames the entrance to the second and softer area of garden—the lawn. The textured concrete slabs are also used for the path bordering the lawn, linking the two areas

Though the pool (left) is a focal point and softens the paved area, the sharp overhang of the paving on two sides of it echoes the strong architectural character of this garden. The crisp line is broken only by the vertical clump of rush (*Botumus umbellatus*)

The simple, unit-formed seat (right) is one of the garden's most distinctive features. The area is nicely softened by the use of cobbles, and by low-growing planting of *Juniperus sabina* and the heathers which spread along the ground

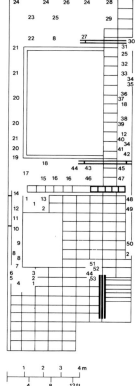

1 *Iris sibirica*
2 *Cotoneaster microphyllus*
3 *Taxus baccata* 'Fastigiata'
4 *Hydrangea petiolaris*
5 *Sorbus aucuparia*
6 *Caltha palustris*
7 *Clematis* x *jackmanii*
8 *Rhododendron forrestii*
    *repens*
9 *Rhododendron* 'Praecox'
10 *Clematis montana*
    'Rubens'
11 *Ligularia* x *hessei*
12 *Miscanthus sinensis*
13 *Hemerocallis citrina*
14 *Polygonum aubertii*
15 *Calluna vulgaris*
16 *Liatris callilesis* 'Kobold'
17 *Rhus typhina* 'Laciniata'

18 *Avena candida*
19 *Aster dumosus*
20 *Berberis aggregata*
21 *Pyracantha coccinea*
22 *Aruncus sylvester*
23 *Betula verrucosa*
24 *Hypericum calycinum*
25 *Pieris japonica*
26 *Cotoneaster salici folius*
27 *Lonicera henryi*
28 *Cornus mas*
29 *Pachysandra terminalis*
30 *Carex pendula*
31 *Lonicera* x *tellmanniana*
32 *Azalea pontica*
33 *Cotoneaster horizontalis*
34 *Achillea filipendulina*
35 *Rosa* 'Don Juan'
36 *Rosa* 'K. Davigneau'

37 *Oenothera missouriensis*
38 *Delphinium*
39 *Rudbeckia speciosa*
40 *Festuca glauca*
41 *Coreopsis verticillata*
42 *Chaenomeles lagenaria*
    'Crimson and gold'
43 *Clematis* x 'Nelly Moser'
44 *Helianthemum*
45 *Cotoneaster adpressus*
46 *Juniperus sabina*
    'Tamariscifolia'
47 *Pinus mugo pumilio*
48 *Sedum spurium*
49 *Aristolochia durior*
50 *Rosa* 'Amarillo'
51 *Arundinaria nitida*
52 *Cotoneaster dammeri*
53 *Veronica longifolia*

157

The steps (left) linking the paved terrace to the main part of the garden are built from reconstituted stone, and defined at either end by an urn of the same material. Bold planting makes a splendid background: the large-leaved *Hosta sieboldiana* with tall eulalia grass (*Miscanthus sinensis*) and, to the left, evergreen senecio. Massed pots of geraniums on the terrace are backed by lavender, with tall fronds of ferns and spires of acanthus growing against the rose-covered wooden fence and trellis

The intimacy and informality of the garden is carried through in the casual arrangement of seating on the lawn (above). The garden beyond fades into shadow, creating the impression that it runs on forever. The yellow rose 'Golden Showers' tumbles out of the trees while clematis smothers another shrub. This is exactly how rambling climbers ought to grow—in their natural way

# An evergreen retreat

This suburban garden in many ways goes back to the principles on which the early paradise gardens were created. It is a green retreat, affording shelter from the city—from people, noise and fumes. The garden is designed to be a private and enclosed space at all times and to act as an extra room to the house. Fortunately it contained several mature trees, which established a framework for the layout and without which the garden could not have achieved its leafy illusion of nature. One is never aware of the limitations of the site in terms of size or adjoining gardens; the surrounding fences are screened, not only by the shade of overhanging trees and shrubs but also with climbers, and the lawn in fact gives the sense of a forest clearing.

The garden is approached up a broad flight of steps leading from an L-shaped terrace surrounding the house. Planting in pots and two stone urns softens the steps. The lawn is roughly the shape of two interlocking circles and the lush, abundant planting round the edges intensifies the jungle feel of the garden. The edge of the lawn is in fact lined with bricks to retain the flower beds and make the grass easier to cut. Ferns and hostas thrive happily in the areas of shade.

When selecting his plants the owner deliberately chose strong-growing forms, in order that they might look after themselves. He now finds, however, that this idea has worked almost too well: the plants need constant cutting back, and in some cases digging up, if they are not to get out of control. Vines and roses ramble attractively through old fruit trees but these too need much attention to achieve successfully such an invitingly casual look. The use of evergreen and grey plants, as well as deciduous ones, ensures that the enclosed, intimate atmosphere of the garden is there all year round. Viewed from the house in the winter months, it still looks pleasantly green and is sufficiently sheltered to sit in even in the middle of winter.

From the shade of an overhanging apple tree (right) the eye is led to table and chairs in the curve of the lawn. The feel of a green jungle is created by the lush, slightly overgrown planting which seems almost to spill out over the lawn. Behind the seating are vines and a variegated cornus, while foreground planting includes flowering green euphorbias and various ferns at the base of the tree

# Designed for all-round interest

This house is set fairly and squarely within its small rectangular site. At the south end of the house the roof projects to provide a sunny, sheltered verandah as a progression from the sitting room. The living areas of the house are all on one floor so views from all the windows are important. Another strong consideration in the mind of the designer was that upkeep should be kept to a minimum: today most owners are their own gardeners and in many cases both husband and wife work, leaving only weekends free for garden maintenance. Trees and shrubs therefore predominate in the planting.

The boundary to the site is stepped back on its east side; planted with robinia trees, it provides a useful off-street, shaded parking area. From the car park one enters the garden up side steps and the designer has made what could have been a depressingly narrow approach into an attractive pathway, fully planted with a mixed loose hedge of cotoneaster, pyracantha, stranvaesia and mountain pine on the side opposite the house wall.

The path leads past the front door and on to a wide terrace area adjacent to the verandah. Below the terrace

on the west side of the house is a sheltered lawn area for sunbathing and children's play. It is divided from the terrace by a hedge of evergreen bamboo, which is decorative and graceful throughout the year. A distinctive feature of the garden is the low wooden fencing which retains the shrub borders and protects them against the rigours of children's games. This cleverly echoes the theme of the timber-floored verandah. Paving on the terrace and paths surrounding the house is principally of granite setts, their small scale giving a pleasant sense of intimacy.

Down the run of the west side of the house, and overlooked by the bedrooms and the living room, is a well-stocked herbaceous border. At the far end of this border is the working end of the garden, where storage sheds for fuel and dustbins are sited, as well as a small plot for growing soft fruit.

Many gardeners and designers despair at the odd bits of ground left at the sides of properties, thinking them bleak, unfriendly wind tunnels. This garden, which has several such small uncompromising areas, proves that they can be successfully incorporated in the general layout.

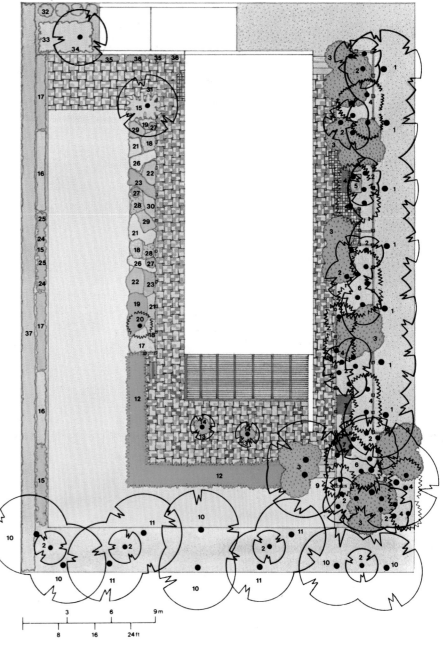

The verandah (left) under the roof overhang has a split bamboo screen which can be rolled down for added summer shade. The detail of the wooden decking is cleverly repeated in the low fence round the shrub bed. In the paved terrace area hornbeams are planted as a sculptural feature

Autumn and winter berries of *Cotoneaster salicifolius floccosus* (above) show up well against the narrow, polished evergreen leaves. The mature shrub has an attractive drooping outline

The garden is approached along a narrow passage at the side of the house (left) surfaced with random granite setts. Outside the front door the area widens to allow space for a bench seat and pots of annuals. The clump of bamboo (*Arundinaria murielae*) makes an attractive overhang

1 *Robinia pseudoacacia*
2 *Pinus mugo*
3 *Pyracantha coccinea*
4 *Cotoneaster salicifolius floccosus*
5 *Epimedium grandiflorum*
6 *Stranvaesia davidiana*
7 *Brunnera macrophylla*
8 *Pinus sylvestris*
9 *Rhus typhina*
10 *Pinus contorta*
11 *Pinus nigra*
12 *Arundinaria murielae*
13 *Carpinus betulus*
14 *Lavandula spica*
15 *Rubus tricolor*
16 *Hedera helix*
17 *Vinca minor*
18 *Achillea filipendulina*
19 *Pachysandra terminalis*

20 *Sorbaria arborea*
21 *Veronica incana*
22 *Delphinium*
23 *Heuchera sanguinea*
24 *Endymion hispanicus*
25 *Eranthis hyemalis*
26 *Stachys lanata*
27 *Paeonia lactiflora* 'Whitleyi Major'
28 *Potentilla atrosanguinea*
29 *Scabiosa caucasica*
30 *Salvia patens*
31 *Ailanthus glandulosa*
32 Blackcurrants
33 Strawberries
34 Apple tree
35 *Clematis* x 'The President'
36 *Rosa* 'Blaze'
37 Existing boundary hedge

161

# Terracing a steep site

One of the most difficult sites to deal with is that which slopes steeply upwards from the house. The garden appears to fall in on the building and the more that can be done to counteract this top-heavy feel, the better. In this layout the problem has been intelligently overcome by using a series of levels and terraces. The impression is therefore a lateral one, emphasizing the width of the garden and breaking the main view up the site. The use of terraces makes the garden's sense of enclosure pleasant rather than oppressive and within the area numerous corners have been carved out for sitting, sunbathing or eating.

The garden is approached from the first floor of the house over a timber bridge, spanning a basement area. From the landing level, steps lead up to a small lawn and down to a red brick paved terrace used for eating out. The tailored feel of the garden is emphasized by the extensive use of timber, for construction and for fencing, and by horizontal lines of boxwood hedges. The varying heights of the walls and hedges mask the steepness of the slope.

Planting is chosen to emphasize the sculptural nature of the layout and good use is made of bold clumps of phormium and agapanthus. Succulents grow in large masses in the beds on either side of the bridge and flowering annuals and perennials, such as primulas and pansies, add bright colour.

The garden is retained in shallow terraces (above) by timber walls. Their discipline is emphasized by hedge planting of box and rosemary, which contrasts with softer planting, for colour, of primulas in the foreground and pansies glimpsed behind

The view down to the brick-paved area surrounding the house (right) conveys the enclosed feeling of this multi-level garden. A graceful flowering cherry (*Prunus* 'Shirotae') in a timber-edged bed is under-planted with bright pansies. The lawn is made of gout weed (*Aegopodium podagraria*), a drought-resistant ground cover which can be mowed like grass

The warmest part of the garden (left) is planted with a selection of exotic succulents. They are set-off against the contrasting herbs: the curly, bright green leaves of parsley and behind them a hedge of flowering rosemary

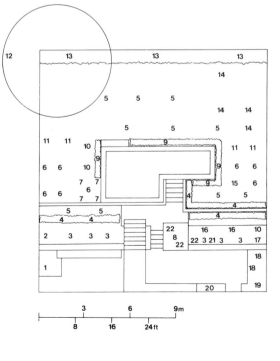

1 *Citrus sinensis*
2 *Phormium tenax*
3 Succulents
4 *Buxus sempervirens*
5 *Fragaria chiloensis*
6 *Raphiolepis* 'Coates' Crimson'
7 *Agapanthus campanulatus*
8 *Prunus* 'Shirotae'
9 *Erica* x *darleyensis*
10 *Viburnum* x *burkwoodii*
11 *Chaenomeles speciosa*
12 *Quercus agrifolia*
13 *Ligustrum japonicum*
14 *Arbutus unedo*
15 *Fagus sylvatica purpurea*
16 *Rosmarinus officinalis*
17 *Laurus nobilis*
18 *Primula malacoides*
19 *Betula papyrifera*
20 *Camellia japonica*
21 Parsley
22 *Viola* x *wittrockiana*

# Disguising an awkward shape

A collection of plants in pots makes an attractive corner where steps connect the lawn to the terrace. Plants include geranium, lemon-scented verbena and the palm-like *Cordyline australis*

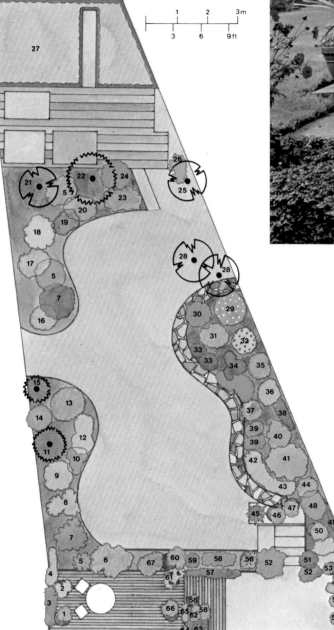

This awkward site, in the shape of an elongated triangle cut off at the point, presented considerable design difficulties. The solution devised to disguise the unsatisfactory overall shape involved dividing the garden into separate areas and positioning curved beds on the perimeter.

An existing change of level near the house has been made into a positive feature of the design. A giant wooden planting box, running across almost the whole frontage, forms a retaining wall which divides the higher-level lawn from a narrow patio directly outside the house; steps link the two levels. The patio itself consists of a paved area beneath the steps, scattered with pots containing herbs and other plants, and an attractive timber deck furnished with table and chairs for sitting and eating out. A trellis, draped with honeysuckle and wistaria, cuts across the deck to give a semi-enclosed feel to this outside dining room.

The main section of the garden consists of a large expanse of lawn flanked by curved borders, which are planted with shrubs at the back and annuals and perennials at the front. A line of paving runs along the edge of the largest of these borders, making the job of mowing the lawn easier.

At the narrowest point in the garden, furthest away from the house, is a thriving little vegetable patch. In front of this, wooden decking supports two small greenhouses and a tool shed. This service area is completely hidden from the rest of the garden by a dense screen of trees and shrubs, which includes roses, maples, hornbeam, broom, a crab apple and a stag's horn sumach.

| | | | |
|---|---|---|---|
| 1 *Spiraea* x *arguta* | 14 *Ribes aureum* | 26 Blackberry | 40 *Acanthus mollis* | 53 Mint |
| 2 *Azalea* 'Gog' | 15 *Syringa vulgaris* | 27 Vegetables | 41 *Rosa* 'Lord Penzance' | 54 Rhubarb |
| 3 *Hedera helix* | 16 *Lonicera* x *purpusii* | 28 *Betula pendula* | 42 *Papaver nudicaule* | 55 Herbs |
| 4 *Rosa* 'Mermaid' (climber) | 17 *Rosa* 'Fritz Nobis' | 29 *Rosa* 'Iceberg' | 43 *Crocosmia* x | 56 *Dahlia* |
| 5 *Rhododendron* 'Yellow | 18 *Elaeagnus pungens* | 30 *Cistus* x *purpureus* | *crocosmiflora* | 57 *Cotoneaster dammerii* |
| Hammer' | 'Maculata' | 31 *Hebe* 'Bowles' Hybrid' | 44 *Hosta sieboldiana* | 58 Spring bulbs |
| 6 *Cotoneaster conspicuus* | 19 *Acer palmatum* 'Dissectum | 32 *Malva alcea* | 45 *Cordyline australis* | 59 *Daboecia cantabrica* |
| 'Decorus' | Atropurpureum' | 33 *Rosa* 'Whisky Mac' | 46 *Geranium ibericum* | 60 *Syringa velutina* |
| 7 *Mahonia bealei* | 20 *Acer palmatum* 'Aureum' | 34 *Helleborus orientalis* | 47 *Lippia citriodora* | 61 *Arundinaria variegata* |
| 8 *Rhododendron* 'Elizabeth' | 21 *Carpinus betulus* | 35 *Rosa* 'Félicité et | 48 *Forsythia* x *intermedia* | 62 *Ceanothus azureus* |
| 9 *Erica arborea* | 'Pyramidalis' | Perpétue' | 49 *Rosa* 'Bantry Bay' | 63 *Mahonia* 'Undulata' |
| 10 *Primula juliae* 'Wanda' | 22 *Rhus typhina* | 36 *Rosa hugonis* | 50 *Rhamnus* 'Argenteo- | 64 *Wistaria floribunda* |
| 11 *Aralia chinensis* | 23 *Rosa* 'Penelope' | 37 *Fothergilla major* | variegata' | 65 *Lonicera japonica halliana* |
| 12 *Skimmia japonica* | 24 *Cytisus* x *praecox* | 38 *Clematis heracleifolia* | 51 *Agapanthus* | 66 *Prunus* 'Cistena' |
| 13 *Choisya ternata* | 25 *Malus* 'John Downie' | 39 *Senecio maritima* | 52 *Hedera helix* 'Glacier' | 67 *Daphne cneorum* |

# Strong curves round an L-shaped garden

A bold linear layout ties together the two parts of this L-shaped garden. The concrete-paved terrace curves right round the house before connecting with a rectangular lawn. Extending into a wide brick step and backed by bold shrub planting, the strong circular motif holds the eye within the layout and disguises the garden's awkward shape. The garden illustrates a successful compromise solution to the problem of the L-shaped plot—whether to deal with the two parts separately or as an overall design. Here the bold curve of the terrace dominates the garden; it ties the two parts together but allows each a character of its own.

The wide brick step round the paved area emphasizes its shape and provides a platform for large terracotta pots containing ivies and pelargoniums. The planting behind was influenced by a neighbouring weeping willow which overhangs much of the flower bed: senecio and rosemary with camellias and rhododendrons survive well, however.

The lawn area is rectangular, its shape emphasized by an ivy hedge on the boundary side and rose beds on the other. With its standard cherry, its lavender and hybrid tea roses, this part of the L is in direct contrast to the geometric motif dominating the rest.

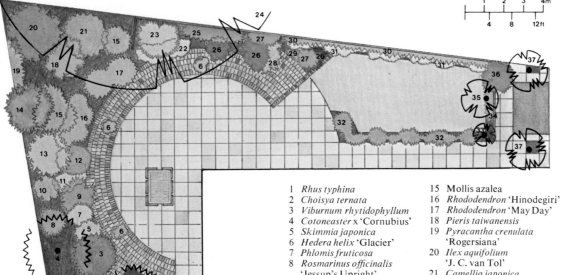

A wide brick step sweeps round to encompass this concrete-paved terrace, linking it with the regularly shaped piece of garden. Huge terracotta pots filled with ivies and pelargoniums stand on the first level of brickwork with a collection of smaller pots on the corner to provide seasonal colour—here, autumnal busy lizzies

1 *Rhus typhina*
2 *Choisya ternata*
3 *Viburnum rhytidophyllum*
4 *Cotoneaster* x 'Cornubius'
5 *Skimmia japonica*
6 *Hedera helix* 'Glacier'
7 *Phlomis fruticosa*
8 *Rosmarinus officinalis* 'Jessup's Upright'
9 *Kalmia latifolia*
10 Ghent azalea
11 *Hebe carnosula*
12 *Senecio laxifolius*
13 *Acer palmatum* 'Dissectum'
14 *Stranvaesia davidiana*

15 Mollis azalea
16 *Rhododendron* 'Hinodegiri'
17 *Rhododendron* 'May Day'
18 *Pieris taiwanensis*
19 *Pyracantha crenulata* 'Rogersiana'
20 *Ilex aquifolium* 'J. C. van Tol'
21 *Camellia japonica* 'Adolphe Audusson'
22 *Hydrangea macrophylla* 'Blue Wave'
23 *Forsythia suspensa*
24 *Salix* x *chrysocoma*
25 *Rosa* 'Mermaid' (climber)

26 *Juniperus chinensis* 'Pfitzerana Aurea'
27 *Garrya elliptica*
28 *Fuchsia magellanica* 'Riccartonii'
29 *Magnolia* x *soulangeana*
30 *Hedera helix* 'Hibernica'
31 *Lavandula spica*
32 Rose bed of hydrid teas, including 'Troika', 'King's Ransom', 'Spek's Yellow', 'Whisky Mac' and 'Wendy Cussons'
33 *Juniperus virginiana* 'Skyrocket'
34 *Rosa* 'Sander's White'
35 *Prunus* 'Kanzan'
36 *Cotoneaster wardii*
37 *Malus* 'John Downie'

# In the shade of willows

One problem with a new house and garden is to make them blend happily, and quickly, with their surroundings. This particular modern property was built on the edge of an ancient cemetery. Fast-growing weeping willow trees were planted first, which are in leaf for almost three-quarters of the year: these trees soon reconciled the horizontal lines of the new house and the 150-year-old cemetery wall.

The aim was to draw something of the overgrown mystery of the surrounding cemetery into the garden. Planting has been confined mainly to shade-loving shrubs and invasive ground cover. Emphasis has been laid on contrasting foliage rather than bright flower-colour, which is kept principally to white and blue.

Climbers like ivy, clematis, honeysuckle and vine cloak the walls.

The brick-paved courtyard, entered from the house through sliding glass doors, was laid over builders' debris. On fine days throughout the year family meals can be taken in this outside room. A number of stones found on the site have been utilized for seats and edging in various parts of the garden.

The area at the side of the house, once a tunnel leading to the cemetery chapel, was purchased a little after the rest of the site. It was filled in, grassed over and a fig tree planted in the corner. Later it is planned to add a small pool, mossy statuary, reeds and more ferns.

A patch of cobbles (below) and a small vegetable plot terminate the side bed of the courtyard. Vegetables such as cabbages, lettuces and fennel are grown as much for their decorative foliage as for eating. A horizontal laurel (*Prunus laurocerasus* 'Zabeliana') in a pot stands on an old stone slab, completing the composition

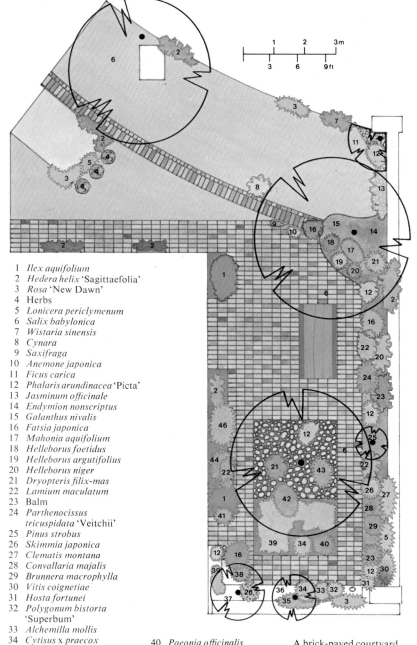

1  *Ilex aquifolium*
2  *Hedera helix* 'Sagittaefolia'
3  *Rosa* 'New Dawn'
4  Herbs
5  *Lonicera periclymenum*
6  *Salix babylonica*
7  *Wistaria sinensis*
8  *Cynara*
9  *Saxifraga*
10  *Anemone japonica*
11  *Ficus carica*
12  *Phalaris arundinacea* 'Picta'
13  *Jasminum officinale*
14  *Endymion nonscriptus*
15  *Galanthus nivalis*
16  *Fatsia japonica*
17  *Mahonia aquifolium*
18  *Helleborus foetidus*
19  *Helleborus argutifolius*
20  *Helleborus niger*
21  *Dryopteris filix-mas*
22  *Lamium maculatum*
23  Balm
24  *Parthenocissus tricuspidata* 'Veitchii'
25  *Pinus strobus*
26  *Skimmia japonica*
27  *Clematis montana*
28  *Convallaria majalis*
29  *Brunnera macrophylla*
30  *Vitis coignetiae*
31  *Hosta fortunei*
32  *Polygonum bistorta* 'Superbum'
33  *Alchemilla mollis*
34  *Cytisus* x *praecox*
35  *Rosa* 'Albertine' (climber)
36  *Laburnum* x *watereri* 'Vossii'
37  *Prunus avium*
38  *Prunus laurocerasus* 'Zabeliana'
39  Vegetables
40  *Paeonia officinalis*
41  *Doronicum plantagineum*
42  *Arundinaria japonica*
43  *Viburnum tinus*
44  *Choisya ternata*
45  *Pulmonaria officinalis*
46  *Prunus laurocerasus*

A brick-paved courtyard (right) leads from the house, forming an outside room under the fronds of a weeping willow. Bamboo and ferns grow in the shade of the tree

# An original design for family use

The strength of this town garden lies in its unconventional layout, designed to overcome the regularity of the usual rectangular plot. The garden is the work and inspiration of a Brazilian designer, who created it for a young couple with a small child. Before they had a child the couple were more mobile and the garden was of secondary use. With a baby, they found they were able to go out less and their immediate surroundings became more important to them. Their enrichment now had to be found within the home—and, moreover, they needed more space for the child to play in. The designer was entirely in sympathy with their needs and the garden he has produced is essentially an outdoor room. For adults it is a place in which to relax, for children an exciting play area.

For the basic structure of the garden, old materials have been used which were left over after a house conversion. Old bricks and seasoned wood have a particular sympathy about them, which the designer wanted to exploit. The wall of wood at the end of the garden, for example, made use of old floor joists of varying length. The brick paving, in areas of contrasting pattern, is laid on sand and earth rather than on concrete, so that the finish was not too crisp; if weeds come through, they are either left or hand-

picked. Two of the containers in the garden are old chimney pots which came from the house; filled with bright flowers, these help to furnish the area. Another focal point is a hammock, brought back from Brazil; special supporting posts have been worked into the design, and are sunk into the ground in the sunniest part of the garden. Other incidents within the garden, such as the logs and the sandpit tyre, have been collected in a random way, and all serve a useful or a decorative purpose.

The designer was principally asked to provide the bones of the garden, a framework within which the owners could indulge their own ideas. Although he suggested some of the main planting—for example, the trees and shrubs placed strategically to mask views outside the area—there was no real planting plan, as the lady of the house preferred to buy plants on impulse. She chooses plants for their scent or flowers, in addition to plants which produce food; thus there are tomatoes growing by the wooden stakes, a marrow on the rockery and a plum tree.

Though this is not really a strong garden in the horticultural sense, its layout and its personal details make it unique. Its quality lies in its individuality, a garden tailored to particular requirements.

Brick and wood are the main materials used in the layout, giving this very personal garden its unity. The bricks which form the path are laid in areas of contrasting pattern, such as herringbone and soldier course, and separated by strips of wood. The adjoining retaining wall, also built of brick, is wide enough to be used for casual seating and for pots of favourite plants. Vertical timber beams, set in the wall, dramatize the end of the garden. The same beams are used for a hammock support; they also form the screen at the far end and the table set into it

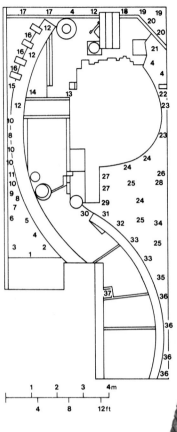

| | | |
|---|---|---|
| 1 | *Rhododendron* 'Corneille' | 13 | *Phyllostachys bambusoides* | 25 | *Ajuga reptans* 'Atropurpurea' |
| 2 | Borage | 14 | *Arundinaria nitida* | 26 | *Rhododendron* 'May Day' |
| 3 | *Dahlia* 'Bishop of Llandaff' | 15 | *Clematis* x *jackmanii* | 27 | *Curcubita pepo ovifera* |
| 4 | *Helianthus annuus* | 16 | *Eucalyptus gunnii* | 28 | *Digitalis purpurea* |
| 5 | *Solidago canadensis* | 17 | *Viburnum tinus* | 29 | *Mahonia aquifolium* |
| 6 | *Forsythia suspensa* | 18 | *Anaphalis triplinervis* | 30 | Avocado |
| 7 | *Potentilla* 'Glory of Nancy' | 19 | *Laurus nobilis* | 31 | *Daphne cneorum* |
| 8 | *Antirrhinum majus* | 20 | *Buddleia davidii* 'White Cloud' | 32 | *Gunnera mannicata* |
| 9 | *Matthiola incana* | 21 | *Cydonia oblongata japonica* | 33 | *Stachys lanata* |
| 10 | Herbs including: thyme, lemon thyme, chives, mint | 22 | *Althaea ficifolia* | 34 | *Hosta lancifolia* |
| 11 | *Iris pallida* | 23 | *Parthenocissus tricuspidata* | 35 | Plum tree |
| 12 | Tomato | 24 | *Aster novi-belgii* | 36 | *Fatsia japonica* |
| | | | | 37 | *Escallonia* 'Donard Seedling' |

The tall wooden beams form a dramatic focal point in the layout (left) by providing a strong vertical accent in an otherwise rather flat garden. At the same time the beams act as a support for the outdoor tomato plants, grown annually. The leaves of *Eucalyptus gunnii* and a *Clematis* x *jackmanii* being trained upwards offset the starkness of the beams

The bricks, in a herringbone pattern, are laid on sand to give an informal feel to the paving. Sawn-off timber discs (above) are used as both decoration and play features; such incidents contribute to the very individual character of this garden

Old floor joists, left over from a house conversion, give the end of the garden a distinct character (above). In irregular lengths, they form a screen just in front of the rear boundary wall, softened by planting in between. A functional table constructed of the same seasoned timber joists is built-in, as it will withstand all weathers. Other salvaged objects, such as the sand-filled tyre, furnish a play area for the young child

# Two water gardens: strong layout and soft planting

These two gardens are the work of the same landscape architect, whose philosophy is to contrast man-made, regular shapes with natural ones, straight lines with irregular forms. The layouts are designed on strong architectural lines and within them are plants which will grow informally, spilling over the edge of the beds. Subjects that self-seed or look after themselves are preferred.

Enclosed by high hedges of cypress, the garden below is predominantly a water garden, softened by flowering plants. The main pond is L-shaped, with one arm running under a bridge at one end of the garden. A small pond set within the long south-facing border is almost a continuation of the other arm of the 'L'.

The beds in the long border are stepped up towards the background hedge with low-growing subjects, mostly in pale colours, planted on the first level. A paved sitting out area on the opposite side of the garden gives a pleasant view of this lush border. Planting throughout the garden is for leaf shape and contrast as well as summer colour. The whole effect is delightfully rambling and full: quite the most difficult sort of planting to achieve successfully.

The geometric theme is present more strongly in the garden on the opposite page; the single lily pond and almost all the individual beds are square, though their sizes vary. The culmination of the small paved site is a pergola-covered arbour, backed by flowering cherry and crab apple trees, formed in the angle of cast concrete block walls. It is furnished with a timber bench seat, placed to overlook the nearby pond. Beds progress from the pool in an abstract pattern. The soft planting of most of them is contrasted with a large bordering hedge of cotoneaster and areas of box hedging.

Both these gardens have been established for some years and time enhances rather than diminishes the charm of such plans.

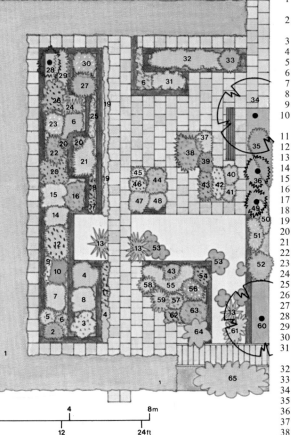

4   8m

12   24ft

1   *Chamaecyparis lawsoniana* 'Ellwoodii'
2   *Cotoneaster melanocarpus laxiflorus*
3   *Dianthus deltoides*
4   *Aubrieta deltoidea*
5   *Lavatera olbia*
6   *Gypsophila paniculata*
7   *Iris germanica* 'Joanna'
8   *Phlox subulata*
9   *Geranium psilostemon*
10  *Juniperus communis* 'Hornibrookii'
11  *Gentiana lagodechiana*
12  *Salvia turkestanica*
13  *Typha latifolia*
14  *Bergenia stracheyi* 'Silberlicht'
15  *Anemone vitifolia*
16  *Helianthemum nummularium*
17  *Campanula portenschlagiana*
18  *Festuca glauca*
19  *Sedum spectabile*
20  *Centranthus ruber*
21  *Stokesia laevis* 'Blue Star'
22  *Rosa* 'Baroness Rothschild'
23  *Physostegia virginiana*
24  *Yucca flaccida*
25  *Saponaria ocymoides*
26  *Delphinium*
27  *Chelone obliqua*
28  *Buddleia farreri*
29  *Epimedium pinnatum*
30  *Iberis sempervirens*
31  *Geranium pratense* 'Johnson's Blue'
32  *Spiraea japonica alpina*
33  *Echinops banaticus*
34  *Taxus baccata*
35  *Vaccinium corymbosum*
36  *Mahonia pinnata*
37  *Picea abies* 'Echiniformis'
38  *Rosa* 'White Wings'
39  *Bergenia* x 'Morgenröte'
40  *Aconitum arendsii*
41  *Alchemilla mollis*
42  *Primula pulverulenta*
43  *Astilbe* x *arendsii* 'Red Sentinel'
44  *Tradescantia virginiana*
45  *Iris laevigata* 'Monstrosa'
46  *Hemerocallis* 'Black Prince'
47  *Primula florindae*
48  *Pennisetum compressum*
49  *Cornus kousa chinensis*
50  *Jeffersonia diphylla*
51  *Aruncus sylvester*
52  *Rhododendron forrestii repens*
53  *Nymphaea indiana*
54  *Iris kaempferi*
55  *Hemerocallis* 'Bonanza'
56  *Astilbe* x *arendsii* 'Professor van der Wielen'
57  *Rodgersia pinnata*
58  *Primula rosea*
59  *Hosta sieboldiana* 'Elegans'
60  *Betula pendula* 'Youngii'
61  *Lysichiton camtschatcense*
62  *Astilbe* x *arendsii* 'Fanal'
63  *Astilbe* x *arendsii* 'Erica'
64  *Petasites japonicus giganteus*
65  *Petasites hybridus*

Massed foliage planting in the main pool (left) shows up against the long, colourful flower bed. Plants include the giant reedmace, *Typha latifolia*, with a clump of *Pennisetum compressum* to the right and water lilies to the left

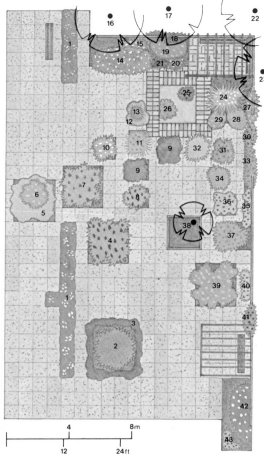

4       8m
12      24ft

| | |
|---|---|
| 1 *Cotoneaster simonsii* | 13 *Miscanthus sinensis* |
| 2 *Rosa* 'Chicago Peace' | 14 *Viburnum opulus* |
| 3 *Ligustrum lucidum* | 'Compactum' |
| 4 *Rosa* 'Champs Elysées' | 15 *Ranunculus aconitifolius* |
| 5 *Salvia virgata nemorosa* | 16 *Prunus sargentii* |
| 'East Friesland' | 17 *Prunus* x *yedoensis* |
| 6 *Rosa* 'Allgold' | 18 *Lonicera periclymenum* |
| 7 *Rosa* 'Anne-Marie | 'Serotina' |
| Trechslin' | 19 *Verbascum nigrum* |
| 8 *Rosa* 'Baby Baccara' | 20 *Viburnum davidii* |
| 9 *Buxus sempervirens* | 21 *Fuchsia* |
| 10 *Rosa* 'Silver Moon' | *longipedunculata* |
| 11 *Hemerocallis* 'Bonanza' | 22 *Malus floribunda* |
| 12 *Sedum* x 'Ruby Glow' | 23 *Prunus padus* |
| | 24 *Tradescantia virginiana* |
| | 25 *Pontederia cordata* |

The paved surface of this geometric garden is *in situ* brushed concrete divided into squares with hardwood. The squared pattern is repeated in the large cedar tub containing a *Rhus typhina* 'Laciniata'; smaller wooden tubs placed at random and planted with bright petunias offset the regularity of the layout. The pergola in the background looks out over the pond

| |
|---|
| 26 *Nymphaea indiana* |
| 27 *Lonicera henryi* |
| 28 *Sorbaria aitchisonii* |
| 29 *Salix hastata* |
| 'Wehrhahnii' |
| 30 *Rosa* 'Zéphirine |
| Drouhin' |
| 31 *Rosa* 'Michèle Meillard' |
| 32 *Iris sibirica* 'Perry's Blue' |
| 33 *Rosa* 'New Dawn' |
| 34 *Rosa* 'Pink Peace' |
| 35 *Delphinium* |
| 'Völkerfrieden' |
| 36 *Delphinium* |
| 'Berghimmel' |
| 37 *Lavandula spica* |
| 'Munstead' |
| 38 *Rhus typhina* 'Laciniata' |
| 39 *Rosa* 'Papa Meillard' |
| 40 *Delphinium* |
| 'Finsteraarhorn' |
| 41 *Wistaria sinensis* |
| 42 *Macleaya cordata* |
| 43 *Rosa* 'Sangria' |

The square pond is surrounded by widely-spaced rectangular paving stones; their overhang gives a crisp finish. A clump of *Pontederia cordata*, a hardy aquatic perennial, bears attractive purple flowers

# A pattern of herbs

This small herb garden, although part of a larger garden, forms a complete and satisfying entity in itself. Based on a medieval plan, the design is a good example of balanced asymmetry; in other words the sides have the same visual weight without reflecting each other exactly.

The garden is approached through an arch cut in a magnificent old cypress hedge and the pattern of the garden is immediately established by the balance between beds of herbs on one side and a circular brick well head and bench seat on the other side. The central feature of the garden is a geometric pattern of low box hedging, with a single 'Peace' rose as the focal point around which the whole design radiates. To one side of this centrepiece are two large square beds containing paeonies and dill; on the other side are two narrow beds with lilies, lavender and rue growing in front and with rhubarb and lovage behind. In the lower area of the garden a group of eight small beds, overflowing with different herbs, is offset by a large rectangular bed containing blueberry, fennel and woodruff, backed by sorrel in the border behind.

The pattern of hedge and beds is set in brick paving and is contained by huge-leaved *Petasites japonicus giganteus* on one perimeter and by herbs and fruit growing against a fence on the opposite side. The tall hedge at the top of the garden is balanced at the bottom by a lower but wider area of planting.

This is a garden which combines utility with beauty; the herbs—as well as being of culinary use—provide a satisfying composition of shapes and colour and fill the air with a rich variety of scents.

A variety of herbs grow in informal clumps round the geometric centrepiece of box hedge in this asymmetric, but balanced, garden design

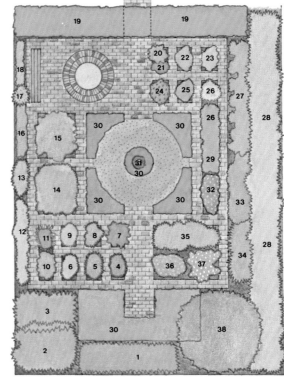

1 *Rosa* 'Dagmar Hastrup'
2 *Rosa eglanteria*
3 *Hosta sieboldiana*
4 Common marjoram
5 Mint
6 Balm
7 Horseradish
8 Burnet
9 Basil
10 Parsley
11 Chives
12 Gooseberry
13 *Rubus trilobus*
14 *Paeonia officinalis*
15 Dill
16 Strawberries
17 *Rubus phoenicolasius*
18 Sweet cicely
19 *Chamaecyparis obtusa* 'Nana Gracilis'
20 *Ilex* 'Veitchii'
21 Summer savory
22 Hyssop
23 Chervil
24 Thyme
25 Sage
26 *Lilium longiflorum*
27 Rhubarb
28 *Petasites japonicus giganteus*
29 *Lavandula spica*
30 *Buxus sempervirens*
31 *Rosa* 'Peace'
32 *Ruta graveolens*
33 Lovage
34 Sorrel
35 *Asperula odorata*
36 Fennel
37 *Vaccinium corymbosum*
38 *Juniperus squamata* 'Meyeri'

# The beauty of a kitchen garden

Originally the working part of a much larger garden, this sunny, south-facing little corner was derelict when the owners took it over. The greenhouse originally built on the site had been smashed and the area was full of glass and debris and had been so for ten years.

The owners decided to clear a part of the site, originally for growing fresh herbs. It was a daunting task and most of the first year was spent taking pieces of glass out of the soil. However, the herb garden flourished and, encouraged by this, they gradually cleaned up the whole area for growing fruit and vegetables. The surrounding walls were whitewashed and the greenhouse improved and fitted with new

All the available space has been used in the most interesting way possible in this productive kitchen garden. A young peach tree is fan-trained on canes while strawberry runners from a terracotta jar are rooted in small pots (right)

Large wooden barrels (below) contain vegetables which are ornamental in themselves, such as sweet corn and a cucumber plant

Trees, climbers and wall-trained fruit will eventually cover the boundaries of this vegetable plot (left). The fronds of a 'tree of heaven' (*Ailanthus glandulosa*) show up well against the white-washed walls, and a blackberry rambles against the adjoining wall

1 Tomatoes
2 Quince
3 Potatoes
4 Sweet corn
5 Cucumber
6 Gourds
7 Courgettes
8 Marrows
9 Herbs, including: basil, dill, sorrel, cayenne, marjoram, parsley, camomile, caraway, lovage, fennel, sage, rosemary, thyme, chervil, bay, garlic, juniper, chives, bergamot, winter savory, Russian tarragon, French tarragon, sweet cicely, *Artemisia arbrotanum* and *Artemisia absinthium*
10 Chicory
11 *Rhododendron* 'Elizabeth'
12 *Lonicera japonica*
13 Mint
14 *Ficus carica*
15 Rhubarb
16 Parsnips
17 Carrots
18 *Tropaeolum majus*
19 *Camellia* x *williamsii*
20 *Rosa* 'Mme Alfred Carriere' (climber)
21 *Hedera helix* 'Goldheart'
22 Lettuces
23 Peppers
24 *Fuchsia* 'Brilliant'
25 *Olearia gunniana*
26 Sprouts
27 Strawberries
28 Radishes
29 Beetroot
30 Leeks
31 Broccoli
32 Horseradish
33 Lemon balm
34 Angelica
35 Camphor

glass. Creepers, like ivy, and climbers, such as clematis, wistaria and a vine, have been introduced against the walls.

The raised brick beds, originally the bases to glass frames, make the layout of the garden quite strict and regular. An enormous range of vegetables and herbs are grown in the beds; summer and winter varieties are planted and the arrangement of raised beds makes crop rotation simple. Fruit bushes are planted near the walls for extra protection; these include a fig and fan-trained peach and apricot trees and as well as the more hardy gooseberry, blackberry and redcurrant bushes. Colourful flowers such as asters and nasturtiums are planted along the edges and in the beds themselves to brighten up the green foliage. Containers and barrels help to furnish the area; at the same time they too are used for production. As the garden borders the river certain materials, including barrels

and an old park bench, have been salvaged from it.

The enclosed garden gets the sun for most of the day, until late in the afternoon, and the fact that the plot is so sheltered ensures that the area is highly productive. This has encouraged the owners to experiment with more exotic vegetables, fruit and herbs as well as growing dependable root vegetables, brassicas and salad crops. During a good summer outdoor tomatoes thrive and less hardy vegetables such as peppers, aubergines, cucumber and sweet corn can all be grown outside.

The area, naturally, is predominantly green but shrubs, climbers and annual flowers provide splashes of colour to brighten the area. The whole plot clearly illustrates the fact that herbs, fruit and vegetables can be as decorative as any other garden plants, while the treatment of it has made a hard-working kitchen garden a positive pleasure to sit in.

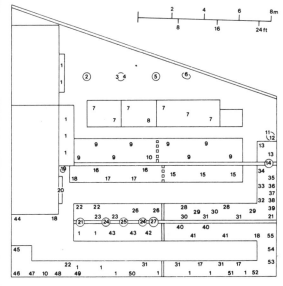

36  Borage
37  Comfrey
38  *Lavandula spica*
39  *Lippia citriodora*
40  *Aster novi-belgii*
41  Beans
42  Globe artichokes
43  Aubergines
44  *Buddleia crispa*
45  Loganberries
46  Gooseberries
47  Redcurrants
48  *Vitis vinifera*
49  *Clematis* x 'Vyvian Pennell'
50  Peach
51  *Ailanthus glandulosa*
52  Apricot
53  *Wistaria sinensis*
54  *Heliotropium* x *hybridum*
55  Blackberry

The raised brick beds impose a certain regularity on the layout of this vegetable garden (right). This strictness is offset, however, by the contrasting foliage of overhanging plants. The dramatic spiky leaves in the foreground are young globe artichokes, with aubergines growing behind them and outdoor tomatoes at the back. The concrete paving is softened in appearance by the clump of nasturtiums which flop over it and roses are trained to grow over the walls of the building

# Vegetables for

The increasing cost of fresh produce, combined with a general interest in a return to organic gardening, has brought about an upsurge in growing vegetables at home—however small the garden.

The vegetable plot often used to be relegated to the bottom of the garden, partially screened by a tottering trellis. Today, however, limited space dictates that vegetables are integrated within the main layout. This conspicuous positioning means that they should be grown to look as neat and attractive as possible. The choice of particular vegetables has to be made with almost as much consideration of their

Space is used to the full in this vegetable plot within a garden. Narrow concrete paths divide up the area, giving it form and providing access to the beds. Flowers such as poppies and sea lavender are grown alongside the vegetables and herbs, making the display more colourful. Beans trained up tall canes exploit the available height

These six vegetable beds (left) are slightly raised and edged with old railway sleepers and preservative-treated pine boards. Gravel paths connect the areas for easy and dry access at all times, with a grass path leading to the centre of the garden. Although never colourful in a flowery sense, the bright shades of green foliage and the varied leaf shapes of the massed vegetables have a charm of their own. Vegetables are carefully selected for the locale and soil and include brassicas, different varieties of lettuce, beet and spinach. There is an asparagus bed and another bed for sweet corn. Companion planting of nasturtiums, marigolds and rue discourage pests. In the corners of the beds large herbs are planted: lovage, sage, rosemary and fennel

# a small space

visual appearance as of their productivity. A combination of herbs and decorative vegetables can provide interest throughout the year.

In the formal walled vegetable gardens of the past, beds were usually edged with low box hedging or espalier fruit trees; today's layouts on a more limited scale may be composed of raised vegetable beds, for example. It is obviously important to use the limited space in the best possible way, and to exploit the height and any odd corners within the garden. Many vegetables and herbs can be grown in containers, which will also provide spots of interest in the general layout.

The whole of this small plot (above), measuring only 10 m by 17 m (30 ft by 50 ft), has been turned into a kitchen garden. It is managed by one person and produces fresh fruit and vegetables all year round. The neat, attractive plot is laid out in a cruciform shape with a sundial in the centre. Rows running away from the house give added perspective to the layout. The beds are edged with alpine strawberries, lavender and parsley. The vegetables—beans, lettuce, spinach,

carrots and broccoli—are rotated annually and the ground heavily mulched to discourage weed growth. Insect-repelling plants, such as marigolds, nasturtiums and chives are also included in the layout. Fruit such as rhubarb and gooseberries are grown, with lilies and campanula, in the bed by the fence and there are two standard currant bushes by the kitchen door. A second planting of vegetables in mid-summer ensures fresh food crops in the autumn

Vegetables and herbs are planted along one side of this garden (above). The beds are raised and treated pine boards are used to contain the compost. This type of cultivation allows a selection of vegetables to be grown at a convenient height for picking.

Container-growing is a particularly suitable method for tomatoes: they do not need too much space and have a decorative value, with their dense foliage and brightly-coloured fruit. Herbs such as comfrey, sorrel and basil fill up the beds

The distinctive spiky foliage of globe artichokes (left) makes a spectacular display in a vegetable border. On the path a terracotta strawberry pot has numerous runners coming out of the sides and rooting in a series of smaller pots. Beyond are brassica seedlings

A corner of a roof garden (left) has been set aside for growing plants of culinary use. Where space is so restricted, it is more important than ever that the containers used should look decorative. An old chimney stack contains a strong-growing rosemary bush while the discarded sink in the foreground has been given a new use as a plant trough. Parsley, lettuce seedlings and mint are all growing well

177

# Growing fruit

Home-grown fruit is a luxury to which many owners of small gardens feel they cannot aspire. If one considers the decorative aspect of fruit, however, it becomes obvious that a fruit tree or bush, or a vine, can serve the same role as any other tree, shrub or climber and be productive too.

In limited garden space it makes sense to grow fruit either as a climber, like a vine, in bush form like gooseberries or redcurrants or against a wall or fence as fan-trained specimen trees. Currants and gooseberries can also be grown fan-wise on walls, while soft fruits like raspberries or cultivated black-

Cherry trees grown in square beds are incorporated within a formal layout (above). The trees themselves are underplanted with dense ground cover and between the trees are rectangular rose beds.

In the foreground a long bed contains alternate rows of heavily fruiting strawberries and garlic (*Allium sativum*)

Grape vines (*Vitis*) can be grown through a pergola (right) to provide an attractive overhead view. This method of cultivation provides a shady canopy under which to sit and makes it easy to thin out the vine and harvest the crop. Vines can also be grown to enhance an attractive old wall and they make excellent screening for ugly water pipes or fences

A chain link fence gives strong support to cultivated blackberries (below), which in time will make a splendid and productive screen. Make sure that the fence or trellis is sufficiently strong, otherwise the plant's woody stem may warp it in time

Where space is very limited a dwarf bush apple tree (right) is the ideal solution. This is the lowest form of free-growing tree, as it has no trunk, but it will produce fruit quite abundantly nonetheless

# in a small space

berries can be trained along fences, with the added advantage of providing effective screening. Apple and pear trees can be grown against a wall in either espalier, fan or cordon form, or trained on wires and used in this way as garden dividers.

The advantage of the trained tree principle is that it encourages greater cropping: the tree's energies are kept firmly in control and directed to fruiting rather than vegetative growth. The espalier differs from the cordon in retaining lateral growth branches at 90° off a central vertical lead, while the cordon retains one lead, grown at an angle with only side fruiting spurs.

Fruit trees can provide interest for many months of the year; not only do they produce fruit in late summer but they are extremely decorative in spring, when they are covered in blossom. This can even be extended by growing a climbing plant up the stem—a rambler rose or perhaps a clematis. The standard apple tree (above) is the largest form, with a height and spread of up to 6m (20ft). It is best grown at the side or in a corner of a small garden, so that it can overhang the boundary if necessary

An old fan-trained pear tree (above) produces a heavy crop of fruit. A sturdy frame and strong wires are necessary for support but cropping from both sides of a tree trained to grow out horizontally is easier than from a tall, free-standing one

A fruit tree needing a warm climate, such as peach (below), can be fan-trained against a south-facing brick wall: the brick absorbs and re-radiates heat. Each winter, prior to leafing, last year's shoots are tied into the wires to extend the fan

# designing with plants

*Though selecting plants may be the final stage in planning a garden, it is in many ways the most important. The right choice of plants can complement and at the same time soften the lines of a layout and will ultimately bring your garden to life in an individual way. Height, shape and texture all need to be considered when using plants as elements in a design; colour is another significant factor, especially important when planning for year-round interest. The illustrated lists are divided into categories to help you make a personal plant selection. They suggest favourite plants for particular purposes and situations, many of which appear in the individual gardens already featured.*

# Planting design

A garden should be more than a collection of individual plants, however successful or interesting the plants may be in themselves. It is plants, more than anything else, which will transform a two-dimensional garden plan into three-dimensional reality. Consider them, therefore, as a means of moulding the available space into pleasing shapes and choose particular plants to reinforce the general conception of your garden layout. Integrating them into an overall design, with the shape, colour and leaf form of neighbouring plants carefully considered in relationship to one another, distinguishes your plant collection from that of the horticulturist.

While individual plants should always be selected as part of a total plan, planting design can be approached in a variety of different ways, depending on how much emphasis is placed on controlled design, and how much on the natural development of the plants. At one extreme, it is possible to select plants without either the landscaper's concern for design or the horticulturist's interest in growing characteristics, to pull out a species if it fails to develop successfully while allowing it to grow freely and multiply by self-seeding if it flourishes in the particular environment; in other words, a system of natural trial and error. This can be a lengthy process and it may be difficult to reconcile with functional requirements, such as planned areas of shade or deliberate screening from neighbours. Since the final appearance of the garden will also be unpredictable, not many people will want to plant the whole of their small garden in this way, though you could try it out in a small corner.

### The wild garden
The creation of a wild garden involves a less extreme approach than the trial and error system but with the emphasis still on natural planting. The natural garden in fact requires considerable planned effort, but the planning should not be in evidence if the 'wild' illusion is to succeed.

Observation of natural plant distribution, of what species grow together in different places, is particularly important if you want to create a credible wild garden. Just as an area has a distinctive type of building, due to the availability of natural materials such as wood and stone, and a characteristic topography of the general landscape, so there will be a particular range of plants. And building style, topography and plants all relate back to the soil and underlying rock of a region.

This natural grouping of indigenous plants, ranging from the smallest shoot to the tallest tree, is known as a plant association. You can see such an association when a piece of land has been left uncropped by animals and uncultivated for any length of time. Over a period of hundreds of years, certain low species have emerged first and other plants have then grown through these, killing off the first ones unless they adapted themselves to shade conditions. The shrub layer is superseded by low trees, and so on with vegetation of increasing height. In a wood the dominant species, known as the climax vegetation, will be the major tree type, though on an open moor it might be a low plant such as heather.

In addition to the dominant species, each association has its subdominant, its occasionally distributed plants and its rare plants. For example, in dense beech woods on chalk soil, where the ground is well manured by the humus formed from fallen leaves, abundant bluebells (*Endymion nonscriptus*) often grow at the edge. Distributed occasionally through these woods will be the bird's nest orchid (*Neottia nidusavis*), a saprophytic plant (one which lives off dead organic matter) which does not suffer from the dense shade; green herbs, which cannot thrive in the shade, will be rare.

By examining natural plant associations, especially those in your own locality if you live in the country, you can get some idea of what combinations would look credible in a wild garden. Whereas the planting plan for most gardens usually starts with the larger species and works down to the smallest, it may help when creating a wild garden to echo nature's evolutionary process and think of the plants as built up in layers, from bulbs and carpet-forming ground cover to shrubs and trees.

If the effect is to be natural, it is usually best to limit your plant selection to a few varieties at each level, as a wide range of plants seldom grows within a small area in the wild. When you observe local plant associations, note not only what grows where but also how densely it is distributed. For instance, bluebells or wild garlic (*Allium ursinum*) are usually found massed in dense carpets, whereas orchids or snake's head fritillaries (*Fritillaria meleagris*) normally grow individually or in small groups.

The contrast between the use of plants to create a wild garden and a more design-orientated approach should not be exaggerated. The most precise and contrived design must still succeed naturally, while it is always useful, for aesthetic and practical reasons, to observe how plants associate in the wild. Plants will seed themselves however rigorously you look after your garden, and it is the happy accident of self-seeding which can make old gardens seem so mellow. They may also provide the incidental focal points that bring a developing garden to life, and can succeed even within the concept of a controlled and functional design.

### Choosing plants for a small garden
If the design of a garden is to be wholly successful, the planting has to be worked out as carefully as the basic structural layout. It is helpful to consider the planting design on three levels. The first is the sculptural level, which forms part of the garden's basic framework, establishing the broad shapes and outlines. The second level provides the bulk of the garden planting, against which the third, decorative element is set. A common error is to concentrate mainly on the decorative, flowering plants, throw in the occasional sculptural-shaped shrub and allow the bulk of the planting to emerge in an unplanned, piecemeal fashion.

The natural trial and error approach to planting design was put into practice in this shady corner: plants which thrive in shady conditions, such as *Rheum palmatum*, *Senecio clivorum* and *Astilbe*, have spread to dominate the area

This rock garden is planted with low-growing species, such as heathers, and carpet-forming plants to create an illusion of nature, although the different plants have in fact been carefully positioned for the overall visual effect

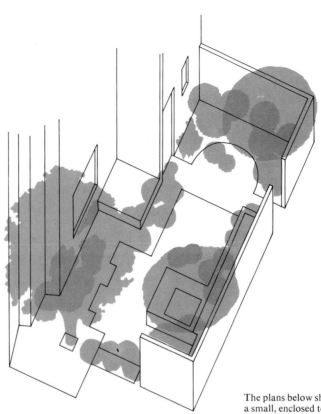

The plans below show how the planting design of a small, enclosed town garden can be built up in stages. The aim behind the planting was to achieve a jungly effect swiftly, to afford privacy in a site which was overlooked by other apartments and to create a retreat from the urban environment.
The three-dimensional drawing sketches in the approximate shape and density of the final planted areas. The first plan (below left) shows details of the basic planting—to establish the framework and fill in the spaces—while the second (below right) adds the decorative elements

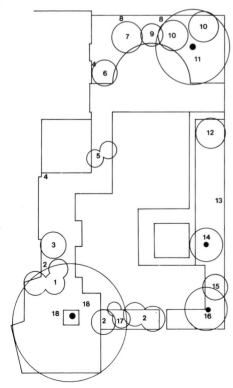

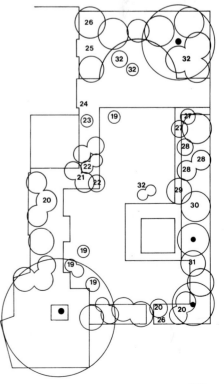

**Framework planting (left)**

1   *Hebe anomala*
2   *Pyracantha crenulata rogersiana* 'Flava'
3   *Romneya coulteri* (Californian tree poppy)
4   *Hedera helix* 'Goldheart'
5   *Yucca flaccida*
6   *Euphorbia wulfenii*
7   *Choisya ternata* (Mexican orange blossom)
8   *Lonicera halliana* (honeysuckle)
9   *Daphne odora* 'Aureomarginata'
10  *Fatsia japonica*
11  *Catalpa bignonioides* 'Aurea' (golden Indian bean tree)
12  *Pittosporum tenuifolium* 'Silver Queen'
13  *Hedera canariensis* 'Gloire de Marengo'
14  *Taxus baccata* 'Fastigiata' (Irish yew)
15  *Camellia japonica* 'White Swan'
16  *Rhus typhina* (stag's horn sumach)
17  *Viburnum davidii*
18  *Betula papyrifera* (paper birch)

**Decorative planting (right)**

19  *Alchemilla mollis* (lady's mantle)
20  *Hydrangea macrophylla*
21  *Caryopteris* x *clandonensis*
22  *Potentilla fruticosa*
23  *Acanthus mollis*
24  *Rosa* 'Mermaid' (climber)
25  *Nicotiana* (tobacco plant) in summer; tulips in winter
26  *Jasminum nudiflorum* (winter jasmine)
27  *Salvia officinalis* 'Purpurascens' (purple sage)
28  *Rosa* 'Iceberg' (floribunda)
29  *Rosa hugonis*
30  *Cortaderia selloana* (pampas grass)
31  *Clematis* 'Madame le Coultre'
32  Herbs

*Framework and bulk planting*

The first stage of planting should, as it were, establish the bones of the planted areas. Here we are referring mainly to trees and large shrubs, especially those which are tall, particularly decorative or of a sculptural outline. A weeping willow (*Salix alba* 'Tristus'), a cedar tree (*Cedrus*) or a flowering cherry (*Prunus*) for instance, all have a distinctive shape which means that they tend to dominate the areas in which they grow.

The shape of a tree can also create certain mood. For example, a group of upright growing trees (*Fastigiata*) have considerably more visual vigour than a group of weeping trees. Many trees, in common with other plants, have some form of association which gives them a particular character. Yew trees (*Taxus baccata*) remind many people of graveyards, where they were in fact often planted in medieval times. The weeping willow is always considered romantic and the less well-known weeping beech (*Fagus sylvatica* 'Pendula') creates a similar atmosphere.

Although trees are the most obviously sculptural elements, other plants, when they are grouped together, can be used in a similar way in your garden design. A well positioned group of yuccas, for example, can be effective, while the acanthus has been admired for its sculptural qualities ever since the Greeks used its leaf pattern on the capital of the Corinthian column.

Planting at the second level has the most functional role to fulfil; it must fill in the spaces, creating bulk in the planted areas as well as providing wind shelter and screening where necessary. It will form a backdrop for the smaller, decorative plants, but should of course also be visually pleasing in itself. Indeed, since it is all that will be seen in winter once the more colourful annual or herbaceous elements have gone, it is important that it should be effective in its own right and many of these plants, particularly the shrubs, will need to be evergreen to do their job successfully.

The smaller plants in this category should probably be grouped in twos or threes in order to keep the whole arrangement steady. If the garden is composed only of single species it will become simply a horticultural collection. The overall silhouette of planted areas should be consciously composed, bearing in mind the angle from which a group of plants will be seen most often. Try to create a contrast between the character of one group of plants and another, rounded ones and vertical ones for instance. In general you can expect the overall shape of a group of the same species to take on the particular shape of the single plant. The characteristic outline of taller subjects, especially trees, comes immediately to mind but many shrubs have equally distinctive shapes. For example, 'Jessup's Upright' is a striking vertical variety of rosemary (*Ros-*

Plant species with interesting sculptural or architectural shapes can be as valuable in establishing framework planting as many shrubs and trees. The yucca is one such plant: the variety *Yucca filamentosa* (Adam's needle) has a dramatic upright shape and grows up to 0.8 m (2 ft 6 in) high (above). The striking grey-green spikes of *Euphorbia wulfenii* (top right) stand out as equally strong architectural features against the luxuriant green background of conifers and ivies.

*Gunnera manicata* (below right) is a supremely sculptural foliage plant. The opening spring-time leaves, which create an interesting pattern of light and shade, eventually grow to as much as 2 m (6 ft 6 in) across, while the plants can be as high as they are wide

A well designed border (left), while it can include plants chosen for their individual characteristics, should be planned as a whole in terms of height, colour, leaf shape and texture, and the overall pattern and silhouette.

Low growing plants, including different species of heather and heath (*Erica* and *Calluna*), grouped together near the front of a bed or border (below) can form an attractive series of soft mounds. Ground cover plants such as ivy can be allowed to spill out on to the path. Once again, the individual plants have been chosen for their contribution to the overall effect

*marinus*) while *Viburnum tomentosum* 'Mariesii' has a strong horizontal form; many hebes are rounded and New Zealand flax (*Phormium tenax*) has a dramatic spiky silhouette.

### Scale and growth rate

When selecting the most suitable trees and shrubs for your own garden, it is important to consider at the outset their speed of growth and the dimensions they eventually reach. Bear in mind that a tree which grows to a considerable size in its natural habitat can look sad and cramped if heavily pruned down to the suburban scale. The incongruity of a large garden planted entirely with miniatures is obvious but, by contrast, a fairly small garden can succeed by being densely planted with large plants. The jungly effect can be achieved quite quickly, though this type of planting needs constant maintenance if it is not to get out of hand.

The unique quality of planting design, as opposed to any other type of design, is that your design materials will radically change their shape and size over the years. It is now possible to buy larger plants and semi-mature trees, but their cost and the guying, after-care and general maintenance necessary makes them an unlikely choice for most people. The desire for an instantly mature garden is, in any case, not an approach conducive to successful gardening; observing each stage in the growing process should prove interesting and enjoyable in itself.

There are situations, however, where a screen will be necessary, and this can be achieved by plants with a particularly fast rate of growth. But remember that growth will not suddenly stop once the screening has reached the right height, as the 'hedge' plantings of Lombardy poplars (*Populus nigra* 'Italica'), 18 m (60 ft) high or more, bear witness.

### Deciduous or evergreen?

The choice will depend on the character and composition of your design, but most planting needs a good proportion of evergreen to make the conception work through the winter; otherwise you may find yourself looking out on to a collection of twigs for half the year. Evergreens will obviously also give far better screening from neighbours and more effective shelter from the wind. In general, evergreen plants tend to be slower growing than deciduous species, so interplanting with fast-growing deciduous trees or shrubs, which usually have a shorter lifespan, is often sound policy. The fast-growing plants can always be taken out when they begin to impede the growth of slower species.

Depending on your local climate and how much wind your garden gets, certain deciduous shrubs can, in fact, be semi-evergreen during a mild winter. Buddleias and several cotoneasters come into this category. There are also plants such as broom (*Cytisus, Genista* or *Spartium*) which, although not actually evergreen, have minute leaves which give an interesting evergreen effect during winter, if correctly

Leaf shape and colour are important elements when you come to consider the particular characteristics of plants and begin to work out in detail which species will combine successfully together. The combinations can work either by virtue of contrast or by complementing one another, as shown in these photographs. In one group (above) variegated *Hosta albomarginata* are set off by the colour and different shaped leaves of *Senecio clivorum* behind them. Plants of similar colour but contrasting shape, such as the lavender and purple sage (right) can work well together. In another group (below) the upward-growing leaves of *Bergenia* or 'elephant ears' are contrasted with *Epimedium* which has drooping leaves

pruned. Many vegetables are evergreen and can have a decorative value used in a winter border. Examples include crinkly-leaved kale, sprouting broccoli, red pickling cabbages, celery and also many herbs.

### Leaf and stem interest

Trees and shrubs selected for the framework and the bulk planting should not be grown primarily for their flower colour. The shape and colour of the leaves comes higher in the list of priorities, for few plants flower over an extended period, and certainly not for as long as the time they are in leaf. If the plant is evergreen, its coloured leaves are invaluable in winter, both to look at and for picking. In general, leaf colour is more subdued than flower colour but makes an ideal background contrast to it. Many of the leafier deciduous shrubs do, however, turn very brilliant colours in autumn.

The shape of leaves is the feature which

attracts millions of buyers to house plants every year and is also an obsession with the Japanese gardener. The leaf shape and featheriness of the false acacia (*Robinia*) and the tropical effect of dracaena leaves, for instance, can set the mood of an area of planting. In smaller plant species, the texture of leaves is probably more important. Plants with very textured leaves tend to come from warmer climates, such as the grey furry species from New Zealand. The common whitebeam (*Sorbus aria*) is unusual for a tree from the temperate zones, in that it has downy grey-white leaves when young which later become dark green and smooth on top while remaining grey-white and hairy on the underside. The contrast between different leaf textures should be exploited when you are planning what plants to juxtapose. It can be seen by comparing the whitebeam leaves with, for example, the smooth glossy leaf of a *Magnolia grandiflora*.

Although you should consider in broad

Contrasts in leaf texture can enhance the appearance of an area of planting as much as the more obvious characteristics of shape and colour, as these three details of garden planting demonstrate. The delicate, feathery leaves of _Robinia pseudoacacia_ (above) are effectively juxtaposed with the shiny, tougher foliage of _Choisya ternata_. The combined textures of ferns, hydrangeas and a mass of ground-covering _Helxine_ create a varied effect in this damp and shady corner (right). The smooth, spotted leaves of _Pulmonaria officinalis_ (Jerusalem cowslip) interweave gracefully with the rougher, ribbed leaves of hydrangeas (below)

terms what flowers combine well when they are adjacent and bloom at the same time you only need to plan colour in detail towards the front of a planted area. However, the odd lilac (_Syringa_) or forsythia for cutting, or a few buddleias to attract butterflies and bees, can be successfully incorporated within the mass of planting.

Many trees and shrubs have berries or fruit which are their main attraction. A good proportion of these appear in late autumn or early winter, when any bright colour in the garden is at a premium. Firethorn (_Pyracantha_) and several cotoneasters have magnificent clusters of berries, while ordinary apple and flowering crab apple (_Malus_) are good examples of ornamental fruit trees.

Plants with decorative stems are also of great value in winter. With maturity, certain tree trunks have interesting peeling characteristics. Most silver birches have attractive trunks, but the paper birch tree (_Betula_

_papyrifera_) peels in addition, as does the red-barked _Prunus serrula tibetica_. London planes (_Platanus acerifolia_) develop patterned bark markings as areas of the old bark fall off to leave a marbled effect. The strawberry tree (_Arbutus_) has a delightful cinnamon-red bark and the snake-barked maples (_Acer grosseri hersii, Acer henryi_ and _Acer pennsylvanicum_) all have striped barks. Certain shrubs, particularly dogwood (_Cornus alba_), and some willows have brilliant orange, red or yellow stems, provided they are pollarded back regularly, since it is the youngest wood which colours best. _Rubus cockburnianus_ has arching purple stems overlaid with a thick white bloom and the stag's horn sumach (_Rhus typhina_) has hairy stems resembling antlers in both shape and texture, which have given it its common name.

Plants with strong individual characteristics should be placed where they can be admired at their best. Though they may only

Plants can be chosen primarily for their stem interest: these teazles (_Eryngium_), with their long stalks and distinctive spiky heads, create interest in the garden when flowering species have died

feature in a minor way in the summer brilliance of a garden, they will be striking in winter when the rivals for attention may be few and far between.

### Decorative planting

When choosing the last category of plants for their decorative qualities, consider all aspects mentioned above, but the emphasis here will be on the individual interest of the plant. Flower colour will probably be paramount, though shape and texture remain important. This category may include woody stemmed shrubs like the tree peony or shrub rose, bulbs and herbaceous plants: perennials (which have soft stems and which die down in winter to re-emerge the following spring) such as phlox or lupins; biennials like wallflowers (*Cheiranthus*) or sweet william (*Dianthus barbatus*)

which you plant one year and which flower the next; and annuals which have their total life cycle contained in one growing season.

The selection and arrangement of this decorative element will do much to determine the character of your garden. When choosing plants for their flowers, it is a good idea to start by concentrating on particular colour ranges, so that you can at least eliminate some of the many plants listed in any catalogue's blinding display; this will also help you to maintain some unity within your arrangement. The blues and pinks of, say, asters and dianthus, with some purple and white (such as sage and white lilies), make a cool summery collection; yellows, reds and whites, of heleniums, sunflowers (*Hellianthus annuus*) and red hot pokers (*Kniphofia*), for example, make a striking

display. The all-white garden is fashionable, though not to everyone's taste, and a combination of cream and green coloured flowers is unusual and interesting using, perhaps, alchemilla and green nicotiana.

If you are too rigid in planning these combinations, there is some danger of producing an excessively mannered effect by imposing the flower arranger's precision on nature. It is, however, far better to work to rules of scale, form and colour contrast to begin with, and then learn to break these rules, than to flout all the strictures and end up with a mess. Not everything in nature goes well together, and the simplest and most natural looking results are often the most difficult to achieve and require as much planning as the most complex and formal designs.

It is a good idea, when designing the planting of your garden, to use colour themes as a starting point, as they give a certain unity. Colour combinations in beds and borders are usually best kept relatively simple. A straightforward mixture of blues and whites can be effective (above); the dominant plants shown here are *Sisyrinchium striatum*, with its numerous star-shaped flowers, and a low growing form of *Veronica*.

Greys and pinks have an attractive range of soft pastel combinations and give an opportunity to make the most of soft, grey-leaved plants. In this colour scheme (above right) the predominant pink flowers are phlox, roses and *Monarda didyma*. Rosemary and rue have green-grey foliage and *Stachys lanata* and *Artemisia* are the grey-leaved plants in the foreground

A large number of different species and colours can be combined in a wide mixed border, provided the planting works well together visually. In this bed (right) the upright shape of most of the species gives the planting its unity, allowing bands of grey/white and purple/blue coloured flowers, with touches of yellow and red, to interweave successfully within the predominant green mass

The value of looking at natural plant associations is not only that you find out about successful growing conditions, but also that you pick up hints about colour design from nature. In temperate climates, colour outside is naturally fairly subdued; even in a meadow, the great variety of colours, when seen close to, merges with the greenery at a distance. The hotter, stronger colours we have introduced into our gardens tend to be either imports from countries of clearer light or the result of plant breeding and hybridization. Although dramatic colour can be effective, it is easy to overdo the use of bright, garish shades.

### Arranging your flower border

If you are choosing plants for a mixed border and you are combining colours, it is normally good practice to keep the hotter colours in the foreground, with the cooler ones at the back. If you reverse this order, the distance becomes obvious and you reduce the visual width of the border. In addition to colour, consider all the other characteristics of plants and blend the individual plants into a composition. The different species used can be interwoven or planted in regular groups; grouping plants in a regular pattern is a technique often used in public arrangements and lacks the subtlety of the interspersed approach.

Begin at the back of the border and repeat in miniature the overall planting stages. Place the tallest upright plants first, the evergreen shrubs and sculptural-shaped plant species, and then arrange the infill planting, from the larger plants down to the smallest at the front. This is the place for your evergreen or grey species which will be prominent in winter. Next come the deciduous plants, again ranging from large shrubs to small ones and from the taller herbaceous plants, such as delphiniums and hollyhocks, to the short ones. Bulbs come last, including lilies and summer bulbs like summer hyacinth (*Galtonia*), as well as the spring flowering ones. Roses may also be introduced, using the old fashioned shrub ones and the floribundas; the miniatures and the Hybrid Teas are less suitable.

The whole conception should both work in itself and relate to the overall plan of the garden. The border will probably not be perfect the first year, or the second or indeed ever, for both you and your plants change, and half the pleasure of a garden is derived from moving your plants about, as you might re-arrange the furniture in a room from time to time.

As each of these examples shows, the apparent visual depth of a border is increased by placing the warmer colours at the front. The brightness of the orange flowers of *Corocosimia masonorum* (top) is accentuated by being adjacent to plants as cool and subtle in colour as the blue-grey *Perovskia atriplicifolia* and against a predominantly evergreen background.

Red hot pokers, or torch lilies (*Kniphofia*) also stand out when placed at the front of a border (above), making dramatic focal points in any area of planting by virtue of their stunning colour and spiky vertical shape.

Autumn is a time of year for particularly rich colours of fruit or berries. The orange lanterns which surround the fruit of the *Physalis franchetii* (left), seen with the brilliant leaf colour of rue (*Ruta*, 'Jackman's Blue' variety), provide rich patches of colour in this area of planting

The lists on the following pages are designed to help you choose the most suitable plants for your own garden. The selection represents plants which are most appropriate for the small garden and in general the hardier species are chosen. The plants are listed alphabetically under their botanical names and each description, whether of the whole genus, a particular species or a specific variety or hybrid, covers essential details of shape, type of leaf and flower, favourable growing conditions and height. Several species are particularly versatile and are included in more than one list, in which case a cross reference is given to avoid repetition of the detailed description.

The illustrations show selected plants at an average height after several years' growth and all are drawn in scale with one another. Additional features such as flowers or berries are usually displayed to help with identification, but a composite illustration does not indicate how an area of planting appears at any one time of year.

# Plants to establish a framework

## TREES

### Betula (birch)
A graceful ornamental tree with a whitish bark when established, golden yellow foliage in autumn and catkins in spring. Being shallow rooted, and providing a very light shade, it is an admirable tree for informal use in the small garden. However, its roots are greedy and the soil below often dry and starved, so plants underneath it can be expected to grow poorly. Most species are extremely hardy and will grow in either damp or dry soil.
*B. pendula,* the common silver birch, with various forms. See PLANTS FOR DAMP SITES, page 220

### Eucalyptus (gum tree)
A fast-growing evergreen tree with rounded blue foliage when young and grey-green, sickle-shaped leaves when mature. After four or five years the outer bark is shed annually, leaving a striking patterned effect. Different species vary considerably in height and in hardiness, though most will withstand wind and maritime conditions. *E. gunnii* is one of the hardiest species.

### Malus (crab apple)
These small to medium sized trees offer magnificent floral displays in spring and the added attraction of apple-like fruit which ripen in autumn. Some fruit are edible and can be used for making preserves. *Malus* are tough and will thrive in all fertile soils. Favourite species include: *M.* 'Aldenhamensis', *M.* 'Lemoinei' and *M.* 'Profusion'.

### Prunus
This large genus includes the ornamental almond, peach, plum, sloe and cherry tree. The ornamental cherries are particularly useful small trees to help establish the design framework of a small garden. They are deciduous, need an open, preferably sunny, position and do well in most soils including chalk ones.

The white-flowered species are particularly attractive.
*P.* 'Shirotae'. A vigorous tree with bronze-green leaves when young and white flowers appearing mid-spring; height: 5.5–7.5m (18–25ft).
*P. subhirtella* 'Autumnalis'. This tree grows 6–9m (20–30ft) high and produces single white flowers intermittently from autumn through to spring.
*P.* x *yedoensis* 'Ivensii'. A weeping tree with drooping branchlets, bearing white blooms in spring. Height: 3–4.5m (10–15ft); spread: 3–5.5m (10–18ft).

### Pyrus (ornamental pear)
This group of small to medium sized deep-rooted trees has green to silvery grey leaves and white flowers appearing in spring. They will succeed in all types of soil and are tolerant of the cold, drought, damp and atmospheric pollution.
*P. salicifolia.* Probably the most decorative of pear trees, this slow-growing 'willow-leaved' species has narrow silvery leaves and creamy white flowers; in outline it is a weeping tree. Height: 6–7.5m (18–25ft).

### Sorbus
An excellent genus of medium sized deciduous trees, useful for background planting. Although most species have attractive white flowers, the interest of autumn foliage and berries is usually greater. They are hardy and will grow in any well-drained soil.
*S. aucuparia* (mountain ash). This is one of the most common species, with small pinnate leaves and red berries in autumn.
*S. aria* (whitebeam). This has simple, toothed leaves and does well in chalky soils but the species may be considered too large and too dense for a small garden.
*S. hupehensis.* A suitable species for the small garden; its blue-green leaves turn red or orange in autumn and are accompanied by bunches of white berries.
*S. aucuparia*: see FAST-GROWING PLANTS FOR SCREENING, page 220

## SHRUBS

### Buxus sempervirens (box)
Box can be used effectively as a framework shrub though it is often considered only for clipped specimens or hedges. Evergreen, hardy and happy in most soils, including chalk, it tolerates sun or shade. Height: 3–4.5m (10–15ft).

### Choisya ternata (Mexican orange blossom)
A rounded bush, growing 1.5–2m (5–6ft) high and spreading 1.8–2.5m (6–8ft), which is useful for giving shape to a border. It bears fragrant white flowers. See SCENTED FLOWERS AND FOLIAGE, page 218

### Cotoneaster
A large genus of hardy evergreen and deciduous shrubs which range from prostrate creepers to small trees; invaluable as bulk planting for any garden, they will succeed even in cold, sunless positions. Masses of pink and white flowers are produced in spring and berries in autumn.
*C. horizontalis.* A low-growing deciduous shrub with branches arranged in a herringbone shape. The small, oval leaves are glossy and dark green but they turn red in autumn; pink flowers appear in summer, followed by scattered red berries. Height: 0.5m (2ft); spread: 1.5–2m (6–7ft).
*C. lacteus.* A robust species with deep green oval leaves, showy milky flowers in summer and orange-red berries in winter.
*C.* 'Rothschildianus'. A large shrub with a distinctive wide-spreading habit and clusters of creamy yellow berries in summer.
*C. salicifolius flocossus.* A graceful variety of arching habit. Its glossy green leaves are woolly white underneath; it produces masses of small scarlet berries.

### Cytisus (broom)
A fast-growing (but short-lived) shrub which can be planted among slower-growing elements of a border; it is free-flowering during

spring in a range of colour. While most species are deciduous, their twigs nonetheless provide interest in the winter. Generally hardy, brooms require full sun and, though fairly adaptable, prefer a sandy soil. They must be planted from pots and not straight from cuttings.

**4 *C. scoparius*** (common broom). A species of upright habit, with a height and spread of about 2.5m (8ft). The numerous hybrids and varieties include: 'Burkwoodii' with red flowers and 'Golden Sunlight' with rich yellow flowers.

### *Escallonia*
Fast-growing evergreen shrubs with small leathery leaves; red to pink flowers are produced in summer and early autumn. Escallonia grows particularly well near the sea, requiring protection elsewhere; it can be useful for hedges. It thrives in well-drained soils and is lime-tolerant. Height: 2–4.5m (6–15ft).
***E. 'Donard Radiance'.*** A strong species of erect habit, with dark green leaves and pink-red flowers.
***E. rubra.*** A species of loose habit bearing panicles of red flowers in mid- to late summer. It is fast-growing, up to 4.5m (15ft); spread 2m (6ft).
***E. macrantha:*** see FORMAL, INFORMAL AND DWARF HEDGES, page 194

### 5 *Griselinia littoralis*
A large evergreen shrub with apple-green, leathery leaves; the flowers are green and inconspicuous. It will succeed in all types of soil except heavy clay and is particularly good as a hedge

plant in maritime areas (but liable to frost damage in cold inland areas). Height: 3–7m (10–24ft), depending on the mildness of the climate.

### *Hebe*
A large genus of evergreen shrubs previously listed under *Veronica*. Most species have attractive foliage ranging in colour from the brightest green to purple and grey. Hebes are neat and cushion-like, offering a rounded outline in a border; they produce white, lavender, violet or pink flowers from spring through to autumn. They grow in most well-drained soils and are best suited to maritime sites; many species, however, are not very hardy.
**6 *H. speciosa* 'Midsummer Beauty'.** A large-growing hybrid which bears long, lavender-coloured racemes throughout summer. It is moderately hardy. Height: about 1m (3–4ft).
*H. brachysiphon:* see PLANTS FOR A SEASIDE GARDEN, page 225

### *Ilex* (holly)
A large genus of which the most useful and common species are hardy and evergreen. Holly makes an excellent background shrub and comes into its own in midwinter when its red berries provide some colour in the garden (providing both sexes are present for pollination). Many variations of foliage are available. It is tolerant of atmospheric pollution and maritime conditions.
*I. aquifolium:* see FORMAL, INFORMAL AND DWARF HEDGES, page 194

### 7 *Rhododendron ponticum*
One of the fastest growing species, *R. ponticum* makes ideal background planting against which to display more elaborate species. Mauve to lilac-pink flowers are produced in summer. Like all rhododendrons the *ponticum* species prefers an acid, moist but well-drained soil and a shady location; it will grow even under beech trees. Height: 3.5–6m (10–20ft); spread: 4.5–10m (15–35ft).

### *Rhus* (sumach)
Species of *Rhus* are grown mainly for their striking foliage and rich autumn colour.

*R. glabra* (smooth sumach). The smooth, mid-green leaves have glaucous undersides; they turn brilliant red in autumn. 100–150mm (4–6in) long panicles of light red flowers appear in midsummer. It is hardy and easily cultivated, thriving in any fertile soil. 'Laciniata' is a variety which makes a splendid foliage plant. Its deeply incised, fern-like leaves turn orange, yellow and red in autumn. Height: 1.5–2.7m (5–9ft); spread: 1.5–2m (5–6ft).
*R. cotinus:* see *Cotinus coggygria* under PLANTS FOR AUTUMN COLOUR, page 212
*R. typhina:* see ARCHITECTURAL PLANTS, page 219

### *Sambucus* (elder)
A group of deciduous shrubs which achieve an effect quickly. Few elders are particularly decorative in flower, but many have ornamental foliage and fruit. They are hardy and tolerant of most soils and situations.
**8 *S. racemosa*.** It has mid-green ovate leaves of five to seven leaflets and yellow-white flowers borne in spring, followed by red berries in summer. The golden-leaved varieties, such as 'Plumosa Aurea', are slower growing. The species has a height and spread of about 2.5–3m (8–10ft).
*S. nigra* 'Aurea': see GOLDEN AND YELLOW FOLIAGE PLANTS, page 215

### *Viburnum*
A large genus of deciduous and evergreen shrubs, conveniently divided into spring-flowering varieties, which have globular heads of white to pink flowers; autumn-colouring and berrying species; and winter-flowering species. The deciduous plants of this latter category should have an evergreen background to show up the flowers to best advantage.
**9 *V. tomentosum* 'Mariesii'.** A deciduous shrub of tiered spreading habit with large white flowers. The leaves turn dark red in autumn. Height: 2.5–3m (8–10ft).
*V. opulus* (Guelder rose): see PLANTS FOR COLD AND EXPOSED SITES, page 222
The best evergreen varieties include: *V.* x *burkwoodii*, *V. tinus* (see EVERGREEN SHRUBS, page 192) and *V. rhytidophyllus* (see ARCHITECTURAL PLANTS, page 219)

# Deciduous shrubs

### *Amelanchier canadensis* (snowy mespilus)
Drooping racemes of white flowers in spring may be followed by berries in June. The autumn foliage is rich red or yellow. It is hardy, thrives in moist, well-drained soils and grows up to 3m (10ft).

### *Berberis* (barberry)
The deciduous species of this large genus, such as *B. thunbergii* and *B. wilsonae,* are grown chiefly for their attractive foliage in autumn and winter and their display of berries. Generally hardy, they thrive in sun or shade in almost any garden soil that is not waterlogged.
*B. thunbergii* 'Atropurpurea': see RED AND PURPLE FOLIAGE PLANTS, page 215
*B. thunbergii* 'Atropurpurea Nana': see FORMAL, INFORMAL AND DWARF HEDGES, page 194
*B. thunbergii* 'Aurea': see GOLDEN AND YELLOW FOLIAGE PLANTS, page 214
*B. thunbergii* 'Rose Glow': see VARIEGATED FOLIAGE PLANTS, page 216

### 10 *Buddleia davidii* (butterfly bush)
A fast-growing shrub, often reaching 2m (6ft) in the first year. In mid-summer it bears long racemes of flowers, ranging from white through lilac and mauve to deepest purple: these are fragrant and attractive to butterflies.
*B. davidii* is hardy, likes full sun and most soils; it does well near the sea and in towns, where it naturalizes itself readily. It is semi-evergreen when grown in a sheltered position.

### *Chaenomeles* (Japanese quince)
A genus of early spring-flowering shrubs, with saucer-shaped flowers of red, orange or white and bearing yellow quince fruits. The shrubs are hardy and tolerant of most soils and situations. Height: 1.2–2m (4–7ft).
*C. japonica,* with mid-green, downy leaves and *C. speciosa,* with glossy dark green leaves, both have bright red flowers.

191

**Cornus** (dogwood)

The species in this genus range from creeping shrubs to trees; they have ornamental stems and leaves as well as flowers. Most are easy to cultivate, growing in any good garden soil but preferring either sun or light shade. The listed species are hardy.

*C. mas* and *C. alba*: see PLANTS OF WINTER INTEREST, page 213

*C. alba* 'Elegantissima' and *C.a.* 'Spaethii': see VARIEGATED FOLIAGE PLANTS, page 216

**Deutzia**

An easily-cultivated shrub, with graceful clusters of white, pink or purple flowers appearing in summer. It is hardy and easily cultivated in all fertile soils.

11 **D. x elegantissima.** An upright bushy species, with light green pointed leaves and fragrant star-shaped, rose-pink flowers. Height and spread: 1.2–1.5m (4–5ft).

**Forsythia**

A popular shrub with bell-shaped yellow flowers which wreathe the branches in spring. It is very hardy and easy to grow and will survive exposed situations, though its growth may be inhibited.

12 **F. x intermedia 'Spectabilis'.** A vigorous, compact and upright species with a mass of bright yellow flowers. Height: 2.5m (8ft); spread: 2–2.5m (7–8ft).

**F. suspensa atrocaulis.** A species of looser, more open habit with black-purple young shoots and lemon-coloured flowers. Height: 3m (10ft), though it can be higher when grown against a wall.

**Fuchsia**

A shrub chiefly grown for its graceful bell-shaped flowers, which appear in summer and autumn. It is variable in hardiness, but the more tender types often still come up strongly in spring when cut to ground level by frost during the winter; normally, however, old fuchsia shoots should not be removed until spring. Fuchsias thrive in either sun or shade and have no objection to a well-drained limy soil.

13 **F. 'Mission Bells'.** A vigorous bushy hybrid with red sepals and rich purple petals.

**F. magellanica**: see PLANTS FOR A SEASIDE GARDEN, page 225

**Genista**

A genus closely related to *Cytisus* (broom). The shrubs are almost leafless but have wiry branches wreathed with masses of scented yellow flowers through the summer. *Genista* are hardy, easily grown and ideal for dry sunny sites; they prefer a light soil.

**G. aetnensis** (Mount Etna broom). An elegant tall shrub of open pendulous habit with golden yellow flowers. Height: 5m (16ft).

14 **G. cinerea.** A slender, arched shrub with a profusion of yellow flowers in early summer. Height: 3m (10ft); spread: 1.5–2.5m (5–8ft).

**G. hispanica**: see GROUND COVER PLANTS, page 204

**Hydrangea**

Most species are deciduous and produce dome-shaped heads of flowers in summer or autumn. Though moderately hardy and easy to cultivate, they require moisture at the roots. Some shade is also essential for the larger-leaved species.

15 **H. paniculata 'Grandiflora'.** A hardy, showy species, producing white flowers—fading to pink—up to 450mm (1½ft) long. Height and spread: 1–2m (3–7ft).

**H. macrophylla**: see PLANTS RESISTANT TO POLLUTION, page 223

**H. sargentiana**: see ARCHITECTURAL PLANTS, page 219

**Philadelphus** (mock orange)

A hardy deciduous shrub with fragrant white flowers.

**P. 'Virginal'** has double white flowers and grows 3m (10ft) high.

*P. coronarius* 'Aureus': see GOLDEN AND YELLOW FOLIAGE PLANTS, page 214

*P.* 'Belle Etoile': see SCENTED FLOWERS AND FOLIAGE, page 218

**Rosa**

No garden should be without its shrub roses. More subtle in effect than the many Hybrid Tea and Floribunda varieties, they range from low ground coverers to large shrubs and tall climbers. The foliage of roses varies from coarse to delicate and fern-like: their flowers are mainly white, pink or magenta, with a few yellows and reds. Some species are scented and many bear hips (fruit) in autumn.

Generally hardy and easy to cultivate, shrub roses are happy in most soils except those which are very wet or acid; they flower better when planted in full sun.

**R. x alba.** A handsome shrub rose with grey-green foliage and slightly scented single or semi-double white flowers in early summer and bright red hips in autumn. Height and spread: 1.8m (6ft) or more.

**R. 'Nevada'.** An excellent variety of modern shrub rose of arching habit. The profuse flowers which it bears throughout the summer are single, up to 125mm (5in) across, and white, sometimes flushed with pink in hot weather. When the flowers are fully open, the yellow stamens are seen. Height and spread: 2–2.5m (7–8ft).

**R.** 'Frühlingsgold': see FAST-GROWING PLANTS FOR SCREENING, page 220

**R. rubrifolia**: see SILVER AND GREY FOLIAGE PLANTS, page 216

**Spiraea**

A hardy deciduous flowering shrub which does best in deep soil in an open, sunny position.

*S. x arguta*: see PLANTS FOR COLD AND EXPOSED SITES, page 222

*S. aitchisonii*: see *Sorbaria aitchisonii*, under FAST-GROWING PLANTS FOR SCREENING, page 220

**Syringa** (lilac)

Lilacs are useful either as specimen shrubs or to grow in borders; they are popular for the scent of their late spring to early summer flowers. Hardy and happy in most soils, especially chalk ones, lilac do best in full sun.

16 **S. vulgaris** (common lilac). An upright shrub with pyramidal panicles of scented, single or double, flowers. The leaves are ovate or heart-shaped. Height: 2.5–3.5m (8–12ft); spread: 1.5–3m (5–10ft).

17 **Weigela florida**

A reliable shrub with clusters of trumpet-like, mainly pink flowers —though carmine red in the shade —which appear in early summer. It has large, veined green leaves and thrives in any situation as long as the shallow roots are well fed. It has a height and spread of about 1.5m (5ft).

**Viburnum x bodnantense**

An upright species of *Viburnum*, with dull green, toothed leaves. It is one of the most frost-resistant winter-flowering shrubs, producing clusters of rose-tinged white flowers on the naked wood. Height and spread: 2.8–3.5m (9–12ft).

# Evergreen shrubs

**Aucuba**
A genus of hardy and versatile shrubs, forming rounded bushes. There are both green and varie-gated leaved varieties, which berry well if both sexes are present. They thrive in any soil and will tolerate a smoky atmosphere and dense shade. Height: 2–3m (6½–10ft).
*A. japonica* 'Maculata': see VARIE-GATED FOLIAGE PLANTS, page 216

**Berberis** (barberry)
There are many evergreen forms of *Berberis*: most are grown for their foliage but some, such as *B. darwinii*, also bear abundant yellow flowers. They are hardy and can be grown in any fertile soil.
8 **B. darwinii.** A shrub of bushy habit with dark green, holly-like leaves. Clusters of yellow flowers appear in spring, followed by blue berries. Height and spread: 2.5–3m (8–10ft).
*B. stenophylla*: see FORMAL, IN-FORMAL AND DWARF HEDGES, page 194

**Camellia**
A beautiful evergreen shrub flower-ing in late winter and spring. It must be sheltered from wind but is hardier than generally supposed and can be excellent on a north-facing wall. Camellias dislike lime or chalky soils and prefer ones rich in humus.
9 **C. japonica.** This species has dark green leathery leaves and single or double flowers varying from white through pink to red. It is generally hardy, but since flowers may appear early in the year, it is easily damaged by frost. Height and spread: 1.8–3.5m (6–12ft).
Favourite varieties include 'Adolphe Audusson', which has semi-double, deep red flowers with conspicuous yellow stamens; 'Elegans', with rose-pink flowers; 'Lady Vansittart', which has semi-double white flowers with pink stripes; and 'White Swan', with pure white single flowers and golden stamens.

**Cistus** (sun rose)
As the name suggests, this shrub thrives in full sun, doing well on dry banks even in a chalk soil. Saucer-shaped flowers appear in mid-summer. Though not fully hardy, it is resistant to wind.
Species over 1.2m (4ft) tall in-clude: *C. x corbariensis,* with white flowers blotched with mauve and sage-green foliage giving off a resinous smell, and *C. purpureus,* with purple-red flowers and scented foliage.
20 *C.* **x 'Sunset'.** An attractive hybrid, with dark green leaves and pink, yellow-centred, flowers. Height: 2m (6½ ft), or more.

**Cotoneaster**
See PLANTS TO ESTABLISH A FRAME-WORK, page 190
*Cotoneaster conspicuus.* A small-leaved evergreen shrub with arch-ing branches. A mass of white flowers appear in summer followed by dense clusters of bright red berries. Height: 1.8–2m (6–7ft); spread: 1.5–1.8m (5–6ft).

**Erica** (heath, heather)
A large genus which grows best in acid soil and full sun, though it is tolerant of semi-shade. There is a wide range of foliage types and flower colours, so that it is possible to have a different species in flower for each month of the year. Apart from the older species, many new cultivars are constantly becoming available.
Important species include: *E. carnea,* many varieties of which are lime tolerant and usually low-growing; *E. x darleyensis,* which grows up to 600mm (2ft); and *E. arborea,* with white flowers in spring, height 3m (10ft).
21 *E. mediterranea* (syn. *E. erigena*). A large heather of upright growth, covered by red-pink flowers in early spring. It is lime-tolerant. Height: 3m (10ft).

**Escallonia**
Most of the commonly grown species of this genus are evergreen. See PLANTS TO ESTABLISH A FRAME-WORK, page 190

22 **Euonymus japonicus** (spindle tree)
A bushy upright shrub, with glossy dark green leaves, incon-spicuous flowers and winged fruits which persist in winter. It can be used for hedging. It is necessary to plant several shrubs together to obtain cross pollination. Height: 2–4.5m (7–15ft).
*Euonymus japonicus* is very hardy and will grow in any soil, including chalk. It is also tolerant of maritime and polluted conditions.

23 **Fatsia japonica**
An interesting medium sized ever-green whose dramatically large dark leaves give a strong architectural effect, offsetting the globular creamy white flowers which appear in late autumn. It is moderately hardy but requires wall protection in colder areas; it thrives in most soils but prefers semi-shade. Height and spread: 2.5–4.5m (8–15ft).

**Hebe**
See PLANTS TO ESTABLISH A FRAME-WORK, page 190

**Ilex** (holly)
See PLANTS TO ESTABLISH A FRAME-WORK, page 190

24 **Lavandula** (lavender)
Lavender is a shrub valued for its fragrance, its grey foliage and the long flowering period of its spiky blue blooms. It succeeds best in a light soil, preferably in full sun.

25 **Ligustrum japonicum** (Japanese privet)
A very dense and compact hardy evergreen, with shiny olive-green foliage and panicles of white flowers in mid- to late summer. It is useful for hedging and screen-ing but should be cut with seca-teurs rather than shears as cutting turns the edges of the leaves brown. It likes most soils and is shade-tolerant. It grows to a height of 1.8–2.5m (6–8ft).
*L. ovalifolium* 'Aureum' (gold privet): see FORMAL, INFORMAL AND DWARF HEDGES, page 194

**Mahonia**
A hardy evergreen shrub grown for its attractive foliage, yellow flowers and blue-black berries.
*M. aquifolium.* A species with dark green glossy leaves and dense clusters of yellow flowers in early spring. These are followed by blue-black berries. It is suitable for ground cover. Height: 1–1.5m (5–6ft).
*M. x* 'Charity': see ARCHITECTURAL PLANTS, page 219

26 **Olearia x haastii** (daisy bush)
A tough evergreen bush with small, oval leaves which are green on top and grey underneath. It bears masses of white daisy-like flowers in summer. It needs full sun. Height: 1.2–2.5m (4–8ft); spread: 1.8–3m (6–10ft).

**Viburnum**
The evergreen types of this large genus are easily cultivated and produce flat heads of white flowers in different seasons. They grow in most soils but prefer a well-drained deep loam.
*V. x burkwoodii.* A medium sized shrub flowering in spring. Its ovate leaves are dark shiny green above and brown-felted beneath. Height: up to 2.5m (8ft); spread: 2.5–3.5m (9–12ft).
*V. davidii.* A small compact species forming an effective ground cover. Its early summer flowers are followed by autumn berries. Height: 0.5–1m (2–3ft); spread: 1.2–1.5m (4–5ft).
*V. tinus.* A winter-flowering species of dense, bushy habit. It is hardy in all but the coldest areas and tole-rates shade and maritime con-ditions. Height: 2–3m (7–10ft); spread: up to 2m (7ft).

# Formal, informal and dwarf hedges

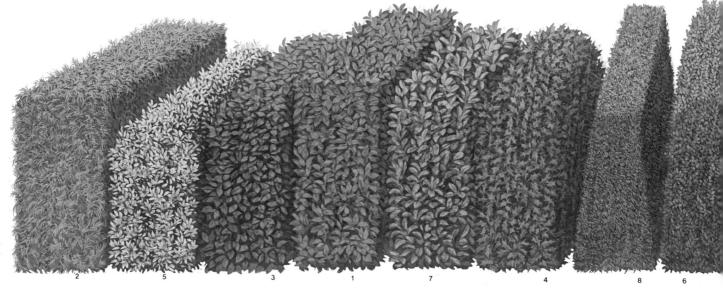

Hedges, large or small, clipped or informal, are an important element in many gardens. They are used to define boundaries, give privacy and provide shelter from the wind; in a larger garden they can be planted to sub-divide the space or even to create wings, as at the sides of a stage, to act as a background to other plants. Another possibility is to adapt the complicated geometric patterns of low box hedging used in the French *parterre* or the English knot garden, for a more abstract design.

Owners of new properties often demand a fast-growing hedge. Hence we have seen the mass planting over the last twenty years of the ubiquitous *Cupressocyparis leylandii* (Leyland cypress) which quickly forms a hedge 2–3m (6½–10ft) high; without considerable restriction, however, its growth will not miraculously stop at the required height. Indeed many hedging plants develop into trees if left unclipped.

Clipping does not restrict the root run of a plant, but close planting does and it is for this reason that hedging plants beyond a certain age—particularly coniferous ones—often begin to die off, either through lack of nourishment or through drought. It is therefore vital to feed and look after a hedge, keeping all the plants alive, since it is very difficult to fill in gaps to the necessary height.

You need to consider a hedge's ultimate breadth as well as height and to plan access for clipping and clearance—so do not grow your favourite plants too close to the hedge itself. The growing requirements of nearby plants is another factor. Privet has a bad reputation in this respect, in that its roots are hungry feeders and take the nourishment from a large surrounding area of soil.

The density of a hedge will depend on the way in which it is clipped or pruned. To encourage thickness it is often necessary to cut a hedge down quite savagely in its early stages, which will also encourage fast growth. In areas of heavy snowfall it is advisable to pick a tough species which maintains its shape and to clip the top of the hedge like a sloping roof, since a heavy weight of snow may destroy the shape of a hedge. If a hedge is to be kept severely clipped it is often best to choose a small-leaved shrub, since these are easier to trim into a neat shape.

If a hedge is to do its job the whole year round it will probably need to be evergreen, or at least to retain its leaves through most of the winter, as *Fagus* (beech) and *Carpinus* (hornbeam) do.

In a rural situation a mixed hedge can look effective, combining, for example, holly with thorn or yew with beech; such hedges can still retain a uniform shape. Looser hedges, simulating hedgerows found in the countryside, can be made by combining roses with thorn. Honeysuckle can be grown through or over informal hedges; clematis looks marvellous through yew, as indeed do any of the annual climbers.

## FORMAL HEDGES

**1 *Carpinus betulus*** (hornbeam)
A robust deciduous shrub which forms an effectively dense windbreak or screen, as it retains its autumn leaves until the following spring. However it cannot be used to make a narrow hedge, being at least 1m (3ft) wide at the base. Catkins appear in late spring and, if the hedge is unclipped, they are followed by clusters of winged nutlets. It prefers sun or light shade.

Plant hornbeams 450mm (1½ft) apart; trim annually in late summer. Height: 1m (3ft) after three years, 1.5–2.5m (5–8ft) after six years.

**2 *Cupressocyparis leylandii***
(Leyland cypress)
An extremely fast-growing and vigorous columnar conifer, excellent for tall hedges. It has grey-green foliage and produces cones 12–20mm (½–¾in) across. It may be grown in sun or light shade.

Plant them 0.5–1m (2–3ft) apart; trim in late spring. Height: 3m (10ft) and over after six years.

**3 *Fagus sylvatica*** (common beech)
Though deciduous, beech is effective as a windbreak since it retains its autumn leaves throughout winter. The young foliage is bright green, turning mid- to deep green as it matures; the leaves turn yellow and russet in autumn. It grows well in all but wet, heavy soils and is particularly good on chalk; it prefers sun or light shade.

Plant the trees 450mm (1½ft) apart; cut off the upper quarter of the shoots after planting and trim annually in late summer. Beech is very slow to establish itself. Height: 1.2m (4ft) after six years, 1.5–2.5m (5–8ft) after ten years.

**4 *Ilex aquifolium*** (holly)
This is the common holly, found wild in hedgerows, with glossy, dark green spiky leaves. Its thick growth makes a dense, effective hedge. Red berries appear on female plants in autumn and winter, normally only when a male tree is nearby. It grows in conditions of sun or part shade.

Plant hollies 0.5m (2ft) apart; trim in mid-summer. Height: 1–1.2m (3–4ft) after six years, 1.8–2.5m (6–8ft) after ten years.

***Ligustrum*** (privet)
A genus of hardy, fast-growing evergreen and deciduous shrubs, which produce cream-white flowers. They are much used for hedging, in particular *L. ovalifolium*, the oval-leaved species. Privet will grow in any well-drained soil and most species tolerate shade.

Plant privet 450mm (1½ft) apart; trim established hedges two or three times annually. Height: 1m (3ft) after two years, 1.2–1.8m (4–6ft) after three years.

**5 *L. ovalifolium* 'Aureum'** (golden privet)
This popular variety forms a compact shrub with rich golden leaves. It is evergreen except in very severe winters and prefers a sunny position.

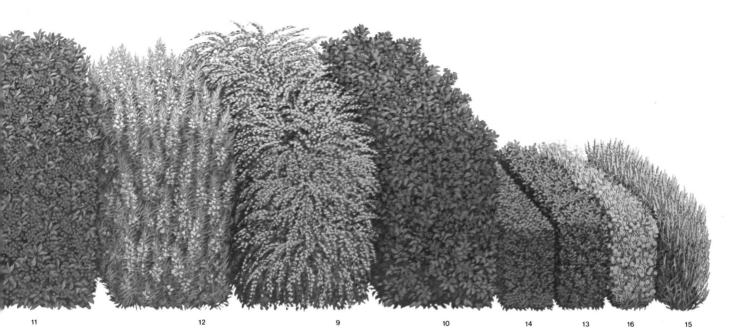

**6 *Lonicera nitida***
(Chinese honeysuckle)
An evergreen honeysuckle, which forms a dense hedge; it has small, glossy, dark green leaves and inconspicuous yellow-green flowers. If allowed to grow over 1.2m (4ft) high, there is a danger that the hedge may break open in the middle; growing it with a chain link fence in the centre will prevent this and will also keep the hedge narrow. It likes sun or half shade.
Plant the shrubs 250–300mm (9–12in) apart; trim in spring and early autumn. Height: 1m (3ft) after three years.

**7 *Prunus laurocerasus*** (laurel)
A useful evergreen hedging shrub, with large pointed leaves and white flowers which appear in spring. It is tolerant of shade.
Plant the laurels 0.7m (2½ft) apart; trim in spring by pruning with secateurs, to prevent dead edges to the leaves. Height: 1.2m (4ft) after three years, 1.8–2.5m (6–8ft) after six years.

**8 *Taxus baccata*** (common yew)
Yew is a slow-growing conifer, but it forms a broad evergreen hedge. Most varieties have dark green leaves (though some golden-leaved forms are in cultivation). It is a very hardy shrub, tolerant of most soils and growing conditions.
Plant yew 0.5m (2ft) apart; clip in summer. The leading shoots should be pinched out to encourage dense growth. Height: 1m (3ft) after six years, 1.8m (6ft) after twenty years.

**INFORMAL HEDGES**

**9 *Berberis* x *stenophylla***
This species of *Berberis* forms an attractive wide evergreen hedge (at least 1.8m (6ft) wide). Its arching branches bear clusters of golden flowers in spring and purple berries in autumn. It grows in sun or light shade.
Plant the shrubs 525mm (1¾ft) apart; clip once a year. Height: 1–1.2m (3–4ft) after three years, 1.8–2.5m (6–8ft) after six years.

**10 *Escallonia macrantha***
An evergreen shrub with glossy, deep green leaves and bright red flowers in summer. Though only half-hardy, it is highly resistant to saline winds. It prefers a position in full sun.
Plant the shrubs 0.7m (2½ft) apart; trim in spring and again after flowering. Eventual height: 1.8–3m (6–10ft).

***Pyracantha*** (firethorn)
A genus of berrying evergreens which are useful both as wall shrubs and as hedges. When clipped to shape, however, they bear few berries. A sunny position is desirable.
Plant them 0.5m (2ft) apart; trim once a year in spring or summer. Height: 1.2m (4ft) after two years, 1.8–2.5m (6–8ft) after four years.

**11 *P. crenulata*.** This species makes a compact evergreen hedge, with white flowers appearing in early summer followed by red-orange berries.

**12 *Rosmarinus officinalis***
(rosemary)
'Fastigiatus' and 'Miss Jessup's Upright' are varieties of rosemary well suited to hedges. They are vigorous evergreens of upright habit, though not fully hardy. Mauve flowers appear in early spring and may continue through the summer. They need full sun.
Plant the shrubs 450mm (1½ft) apart; trim in spring. Height: 1m (3ft) after three years and ultimately 1.2–1.5m (4–5ft).

**DWARF HEDGES**

**13 *Berberis thunbergii***
'Atropurpurea Nana'
The leaves of this variety of *Berberis* turn a rich red-purple in autumn. The shrub prefers full sun. Plant the shrubs 300–600mm (1–2ft) apart. Height: 450mm (1½ft).

**14 *Buxus sempervirens***
'Suffruticosa'
A dwarf form of the common box, ideal for edging paths, lawns or borders. It likes conditions of sun or half shade.
Plant the shrubs 300mm (1ft) apart. Height: 600mm (2ft).

***Erica*** (heather)
Several species and varieties of heather make ideal dwarf hedges, 300mm to 1m (1–3ft) high. Most require an acid soil.
Plant them 250–450mm (9–18in) apart; trim in early spring.

**15 *Lavandula spica*** (lavender)
Lavender makes an excellent loose dwarf hedge, though it is not long-lived. It has silver-grey leaves and fragrant mauve flowers in summer. It prefers a sunny position.
Plant lavender 300mm (1ft) apart; trim in spring and after flowering. Height: 450mm (1½ft) after three years, 0.7m (2⅓ft) after six years.

***Philadelphus* x 'Manteau d'Hermine'**
This dwarf variety of mock orange makes a compact deciduous hedge. It bears clusters of fragrant cream-white flowers in early to mid-summer. It is a hardy shrub, easily grown in all conditions.
Plant the shrubs 0.5m (2ft) apart; trim once a year after flowering, removing the flowered shoots. Height: 1–1.2m (3–4ft).

***Santolina*** (cotton lavender)
A genus of hardy evergreen dwarf sub-shrubs which can be grown as low hedges. They have fern-like aromatic foliage and bear button-shaped flowers on tall stalks. They require a sunny position and well-drained soil.
Plant them 225mm (9in) apart; trim in spring and after flowering. However, *Santolina* will not live long if clipped hard. Height: 300–450mm (1–1½ft).

**16 *S. chamaecyparissus*.** This species has woolly silvery leaves and bright yellow flowers borne in summer. It forms a dense mound and is particularly suitable as a hedging subject.

# Climbers and shrubs for walls

## FOR SOUTH-FACING AND WEST-FACING WALLS

**1 *Abutilon megapotamicum***
This elegant shrub has beautifully marked, light green, slender pointed leaves and exotic red and yellow bell-like flowers borne from late spring and throughout the summer. The species is half-hardy; it needs the protection of a wall, full sun and a light soil. Height and spread: 1.8–2.5m (6–8ft).

***Actinidia kolomikta***
The colour and shape of the leaves makes this an unusually striking climber. The pointed ends of the dark green, heart-shaped leaves are coloured creamy white flushed pink, looking almost as if paint had been splashed over them. (This characteristic may not appear in the young plant.) The flowers are white and slightly fragrant; they appear in early summer. The species thrives in most soils except those that are chalky. The variegation on the leaves will be most impressive if the plant is grown in full sun against a south- or west-facing wall. Height: 1.8–4m (6–12ft).

***Akebia quinata***
This semi-evergreen climber has leaves composed of five oblong, notched leaflets and bears fragrant red-purple flowers in spring. Unusual plump and oval-shaped fruits, which turn a dark purple colour, are produced if a mild spring is followed by a long hot summer. It is hardy, and succeeds in most soils in sun or shade. It can grow up to 9–12m (30–40ft).

***Aristolochia macrophylla***
(Dutchman's pipe)
Given support for its twining stems, this vigorous deciduous climber will provide a good wall covering. It has large, heart shaped, mid-green leaves and yellow, brown and green flowers shaped like an old Dutch pipe; these are borne in early summer. The species is hardy and can be grown in sun or shade in any normal soil. Height: 6m (20ft) or more.

**2 *Campsis radicans***
The trumpet vine is a vigorous self-clinging climber with light green leaves similar to those of wistaria. Its vermilion, trumpet-shaped flowers appear in late summer. The plant is half-hardy and requires a sheltered situation in full sun; given a warm site, it will grow up to 12m (40ft).

***Ceanothus azureus***
This deciduous shrub, which needs the protection of a sunny sheltered wall, has mid-green leaves and long fluffy panicles of small, deep blue flowers that appear in late summer. It is half-hardy and may be planted in any light garden soil in sun or partial shade. Height: up to 4m (12ft).

***Clematis***
The climbing species of this large family support themselves by curling their leaf stalks around whatever is available. The large-flowered garden hybrids can be divided into two main groups. The Florida, Lanuginosa and Patens types flower in late spring and early summer and the only pruning required is to trim the old flowering growths immediately after flowering. 'Nelly Moser' is a variety of the Lanuginosa group and bears beautiful pale mauve-pink flowers with a carmine stripe down the centre of each sepal. It usually flowers in late spring and again in late summer.
The Jackmanii, Texensis and Viticella types comprise the other main group. These usually flower in late summer and autumn and need to be pruned to within 300mm (1ft) of the ground in late winter. 'Ville de Lyon' is a variety of the Viticella group and has bright red flowers with golden stamens. Most clematis are relatively hardy and will grow in well-drained garden soils. They flower most profusely in sunny positions, but the roots should be shaded by larger shrubs; the paler blooms may bleach if exposed continuously to very hot sun.

**3 *Eccremocarpus scaber***
This rambly evergreen supports itself in the same way as the clematis. It is a fast-growing climber with fern-like leaves and clusters of orange-red flowers in summer and autumn. The species is not fully hardy and can be grown as an annual; it grows in any well-drained soil. Height: 2–3m (8–10ft).

***Humulus lupulus*** (common hop)
A fast-growing herbaceous climber with long, twining stems which can grow up to 6m (20ft) in one season. The leaves are three- to five-lobed and toothed. The female flowers are yellowish green and borne in cone-like clusters in late summer; they enlarge to form the fruit which is the major flavouring for beer.
*H. l.* 'Aureus': see GOLDEN AND YELLOW FOLIAGE PLANTS, page 214

**4 *Passiflora caerulea*** (passion flower)
A remarkably beautiful flower smothers this rampant climber from mid- to late summer. The flowers, which are up to 75mm (3in) wide, have white, greenish or bluish petals and a corona of slender purple filaments. In a hot summer the species may produce egg-like yellow fruit. The species requires a sunny or semi-shaded sheltered position. Frost may sometimes kill the top growth but new shoots often grow from the base. 'Constance Elliott' is an unusual variety with pure white flowers.

**5 *Polygonum baldschuanicum***
(Russian vine)
'Mile a minute' is the common name for this extremely fast-growing deciduous climber. It has mid-green oval leaves and a mass of white flowers which appear from mid-summer. This species is hardy and will flower in any normal garden soil. It can grow 3–4.5m (10–15ft) in a year and may reach an eventual height of 12m (40ft).

***Rosa***
There are many varieties of hardy, deciduous, climbing or rambling roses suitable for growing against walls. Those described have glossy or matt mid-green leaves and bear flowers in summer.
*R.* **'Mermaid'.** This is an extremely vigorous, almost evergreen climber which requires a sheltered position but which does well even on a north-facing wall. The flowers are cream-yellow, single and scented. Height: up to 8–9m (25–30ft).

**6** *R.* **'Mme Alfred Carriere'.** This climber does well if grown in full sun. The flowers are white flushed slightly pink, double and fragrant. Height: 4.5–6m (15–20ft).
*R.* **'New Dawn'.** This bushy variety can be successfully grown as a pillar rose or trailing through a hedge as well as up a wall. A disadvantage is that it sometimes suffers from mildew. The small, scented, silvery-pink double flowers are borne almost continuously. Height: 3m (9ft).

**7** *Solanum crispum* **'Glasnevin'**
This variety of the Chilean potato-tree is hardier than the species. It is a semi-evergreen of untidy shape with leaves that are dark green above and paler green underneath. Rich purple-coloured flowers are borne throughout the summer. It is tolerant of most soils including chalk and grows 4.5–6m (15–20ft).

**8** *Wistaria sinensis*
This is possibly the finest and most popular of a genus of hardy deciduous climbers. The light to mid-green leaves consist of eleven leaflets. Long drooping racemes of scented mauve flowers are borne in early summer before the foliage

is fully developed. The main stem becomes trunk-like and the main branches very woody with age. The species prefers a sunny position and will grow in any soil that is not excessively poor and thin. It can grow as high as 30m (100ft).
*W.s.* **'Alba'.** This is a variety with white flowers.
*W.s.* **'Plena'.** This variety has double mauve flowers.

## FOR NORTH-FACING AND EAST-FACING WALLS

**9** *Chaenomeles speciosa*
This is the best known species of flowering quince. The leaves are dark green, oval and glossy. The flowers of the species, and of most of the garden varieties derived from it, are bowl-shaped; in various shades of red, they are borne in clusters of two to four blooms in early spring. Fragrant, apple-shaped, golden yellow fruits, which are used for jam making, appear in the autumn. The shrub is hardy and thrives in any normal garden soil. It grows to over 2m (6ft).

**10** *Clematis montana*
A vigorous deciduous species which is one of the easiest climbers to cultivate. It usually grows straight up at first and then branches out at the top. The leaves are dark green; the delicate flowers are white and they are produced in large clusters in late spring. The species is hardy and does well in most soils. Height: up to 12m (40ft); spread: 4.5–6m (15–20ft).
'Elizabeth', a good garden variety derived from the species, has slightly fragrant soft pink flowers.

*Euonymus fortunei*
A trailing evergreen shrub which can be used either as ground cover

or to grow up a wall, where it is self-clinging. The leaves are oval, toothed, dark green and glossy. The green-white flowers are relatively insignificant; the fruits consist of orange seeds enclosed in a pink capsule. The shrub is hardy and tolerates most soils and a considerable degree of shade. It grows 3m (10ft) against a wall.

**11** *Garrya elliptica*
A bushy, quick-growing shrub with leathery dark green leaves. Long grey-white catkins, appearing early in the new year, are the distinctive feature of the male plant. The female catkins are less interesting but are followed by attractive purple-brown fruits. Plants of both sexes are necessary for fruits to be produced.
This climber is generally hardy although it requires the protection of a wall in cold or exposed areas. It reaches 2–4.5m (8–15ft) in any well-drained garden soil.

*Hedera* (ivy)
Ivy is probably the toughest and most adaptable of all evergreen climbers. It is self-clinging, reaches great heights, is hardy and thrives in almost any soil or situation.
*H. canariensis.* A species with large leaves up to 200mm (8in) across. These are bright green in summer, turning to a deep bronze with green veins during winter, especially if grown in a dry situation. The leaves of the climbing shoots are kidney-shaped while those of the flowering shoots are rounded.
*H.canariensis* 'Gloire de Marengo': see VARIEGATED FOLIAGE PLANTS, page 216
*H. colchica.* The Persian ivy has dark green leaves which are as large as those of *Hedera canariensis*. 'Dentata' is a magnificent variety with leaves even bigger than the type.
*H. helix.* The common ivy thrives in situations where little else will grow. The type has glossy dark

green leaves but there are also many named varieties with coloured or variegated foliage.
*H. helix* 'Buttercup': see GOLDEN AND YELLOW FOLIAGE PLANTS, page 214
*H. helix* 'Goldheart': see VARIEGATED FOLIAGE PLANTS, page 216

**12** *Hydrangea petiolaris*
(climbing hydrangea)
This strong-growing, self-clinging climber positively prefers the shade of a north-facing wall. The leaves are oval-shaped with a pointed apex and slightly serrated edges; they are pale green underneath and dark green on top. Flat heads of white flowers cover the plant in early to mid-summer. The species is hardy, tolerates almost any soil and can reach a height of 18m (60ft) or more.

**13** *Jasminum nudiflorum*
The winter-flowering jasmine is a superb deciduous plant for enlivening a sunless north wall during dull winter days. It is sprawling in habit and may need trellis support against a wall. Bright yellow flowers appear on the naked green branches throughout the winter. The leaves are trifoliate and dark green. The flowers can be susceptible to cold winds but the plant is generally hardy and tolerant of almost all soils and locations. Height: up to 3m (10ft).

**14** *Parthenocissus quinquefolia*
The true Virginia creeper is a vigorous self-clinging species of branching habit. With insignificant flowers and berries, this is an attractive and popular climber on account of its magnificent leaves; these consist of three or five serrated leaflets which turn brilliant crimson in autumn. This hardy species can be planted in any soil; it will grow to 21m (70ft) or more.

# Dependable perennials

**1 *Achillea filipendulina* (yarrow)**
This is a handsome architectural plant for growing in borders. The stems are clothed with feathery mid-green leaves; clusters of golden or lemon-yellow flowers are borne from mid-summer into the autumn. It thrives in most soils in a sunny position and grows to 1–1.5m (3–5ft) high.

**Agapanthus (African lily)**
A distinctive family of perennials with strap-shaped leaves and heads of magnificent flowers, which appear in mid-summer, borne on top of tall stems. They should be planted in a sunny position, in any fertile soil.
**2 *A. campanulatus*.** This almost hardy deciduous species has powder blue flowers in a circular array, supported by leaves 0.5–1m (2–3ft) tall. 'Headbourne Hybrid' is a hardy garden hybrid.

**3 *Anemone* x *hybrida*
(Japanese anemone)**
Suitable for growing in herbaceous borders, these hardy perennials have groups of mid-green three- or five-lobed leaves around the base, and branching stems which carry pink or white cup-shaped flowers in late summer and early autumn. They usually take two growing seasons to become established but are then free-flowering; These anemones prefer moist soil and partial shade. Height: 0.5–1.2m (2–4ft).

**4 *Anthemis tinctoria*
(ox-eye chamomile)**
One of a genus which includes several carpet-forming ground-covering plants. The leaves are attractively cut; the flowers, borne throughout the summer, are yellow or white and daisy-like. This hardy perennial should be planted in a sunny position; it is tolerant of any well-drained soil. This is a relatively tall species growing to 0.8m (2½ft).

**Bergenia**
This is the ideal hardy evergreen perennial to provide bold foliage contrast at the front of a mixed border. A creeping root sends up rounded, green, leathery and glossy leaves. Many assume burnished tones in winter. Heads of bell-shaped pink, red and white flowers appear in early to mid-spring, carried on top of red stems. The plant grows to about 300mm (1ft) in any soil in sun or shade; it should be regularly divided.
**5 *B. cordifolia*.** This variety has large rounded leaves and rose-pink flowers.

**6 *Campanula lactiflora***
Invaluable for grouping together in a bed, this hardy species has mid-green, oval-shaped leaves and bears pale lavender-blue, bell-shaped flowers in early and mid-summer. It will thrive in sun or shade in most soils but requires staking in windy weather and locations since it grows to 3m (10ft).

**7 *Delphinium***
The hardy perennial delphinium hybrids make excellent large border plants. Their dark, fern-like leaves are particularly attractive. The flowers of most varieties are in varying shades of blue but excellent pale yellow, white and pink delphiniums have also been developed. They prefer a well-drained, deeply dug and manured soil, in full sun. Some types only grow 1m (3ft) high, others reach up to 2m (7ft).

**8 *Digitalis purpurea* (foxglove)**
The common foxglove can be grown either as a biennial or as a perennial in ideal conditions. They seed themselves and are often seen in cottage gardens. The attractive spikes of bell-shaped flowers are produced in early and mid-summer. These are purple or mauve in the wild, but cultivated strains in primrose, apricot and white have been developed. The plant will grow in most soils and situations, although it is usually associated with woodland planting. Height: 1–1.5m (3–5ft).

**Euphorbia**
The perennial species of this large genus are an asset in any border, forming tall, dramatic clumps. They will grow even in a poor soil, but prefer a sunny position.
**9 *E. griffithii*.** A hardy species with long, thin, mid-green leaves which have pale pink midribs. The bracts, or flower-like modified leaves, are a brilliant flame colour; they appear in late spring or early summer. 'Fireglow' is a variety with particularly striking orange bracts. Height: 0.5–1.2m (2–4ft).

**Geranium**
This family of hardy herbaceous perennials should not be confused with *Pelargonium*, many of which are commonly known as geraniums. Most species are low-growing, with flowers in deep hues of blue, purple and pink. Geraniums are very easy to grow; they like most soils and thrive in sun or half-shade.
**10 *G. ibericum*.** This species has five- to seven-lobed mid-green leaves and violet-blue flowers in mid-summer. It grows about 0.5m (1½–2ft) high.

**11 *Gypsophila paniculata***
This perennial species produces large rounded hummocks of grey-green grass-like leaves covered with a shimmering mass of tiny white flowers during the summer. It is invaluable for floral arrangements. It thrives in any well-drained garden soil in a sunny position. Height: 1m (3ft).

**12 *Hemerocallis* (day lily)**
These hardy, almost indestructible, herbaceous perennials form clumps of strap-shaped, pale to mid-green leaves. In summer they bear trumpet-shaped, lily-like flowers in a wide range of yellow, red or pink colours; these are short-lived but there is a succession of them and they are extremely attractive. Day lilies thrive in sun or partial shade in all except very dry soils. Height: 1m (3ft).

**Hosta (plantain lily)**
Grown for their distinctive architectural ribbed foliage, hostas slowly form dense clumps which, once established, can be left unattended for years. They require a moisture-retentive soil enriched with humus. Hardy and adaptable, they can be positioned in deep shade or full sun; those with variegated leaves retain their colouring better in partial shade.

**13 *H. crispula*.** This species has splendid dark green leaves with distinctive white edges. Its lilac-purple flowers are borne in late summer. Height: up to 0.5m (2ft). ***H. sieboldiana*.** This popular species has strongly veined, glossy mid-green leaves and bears off-white flowers in late summer. Height: up to 0.5m (2ft).

### *Iris*

The plants of this large family offer valuable lance-shaped grassy foliage which acts as a foil in a border to the more common rounded type of leaf. All irises bear exquisite flowers, some of which are fragrant. Irises are divided into two groups: those with hairs—known as beards—on the outer petals, and those without. There are hundreds of varieties in each group. They are generally easy to grow, preferring well-drained soil in a sunny position.

**14 *I.* 'Harbour Blue'.** One of the tall bearded irises. It is fully hardy, flowers in late spring to early summer and grows to a height of 0.8–1.5m (2½–5ft).

### *Kniphofia*
(torch lily, red hot poker)
These hardy or slightly tender herbaceous perennials have a bold outline, with tall stems rising erect above grass- or reed-like foliage. They carry poker-like spikes of tubular flowers, usually orange-red in colour. They grow best in a sunny position in a good fertile loam which is well-drained in winter but not liable to dry out in summer.

**15 *K.* 'Springtime'.** This species has yellow-white flowers, tipped red. It grows 0.5–1m (2–3½ft) high and flowers in early to mid-summer.

### *Lupinus polyphyllus* (lupin)
This species, and the Russel hybrids derived from it, are the best hardy herbaceous lupins. Long spikes of flowers rise out of the attractive digitate, mid-green foliage. The plants prefer a sunny position and a well-drained loamy, preferably lime-free, soil. The height range is 1–1.5m (3–5ft).

**16 *L.p.* 'Elsie Waters'.** An attractive pink and white variety, flowering in early to mid-summer.

### *Paeonia* (peony)
A genus of hardy herbaceous perennials and shrubs grown chiefly for their handsome globular flowers which appear in early summer. The flowers, which are excellent for cutting, may be single or double and come in many shades of pink and red; there are white and yellow varieties too. The foliage is also very attractive, often richly tinted in spring and autumn. Peonies prefer a good fertile loam and a position in the sun or half-shade; they loathe being moved and may take many years to establish themselves.

**17 *P. mlokosewitschii*.** This perennial species has soft grey-green downy foliage which deepens in colour with age and sometimes turns yellow-brown in autumn. Great cool chalices of single, lemon-yellow flowers with masses of golden yellow stamens appear in the spring; the seed pods produced in the autumn are particularly striking. Height 0.5–0.6m (1½–2ft).

### *Papaver orientale*
(oriental poppy)
This hardy spreading border perennial forms clumps of deeply cut, hairy, mid- to dark green leaves. It has brilliantly coloured, giant paper-like red flowers with a black spot at the base of each petal; these appear in late spring to early summer. It grows in any well-drained soil and prefers a sunny position. Height 0.5–1m (2–3ft).

**18 *P.o.* 'Mrs Perry'.** A variety which has delicate salmon-pink flowers.

### *Primula*
A large genus of hardy and half-hardy perennials with primrose-like flowers.

**19 *P. denticulata*** (drumstick primrose). One of many hardy border primulas, this species has pale green leaves and dense globes of pink to lilac flowers in early spring. It prefers light shade and moist soil. Height: 0.3m (1ft).

# Annual and biennial flowers

The flowering plants in this list are those which provide bright and attractive colour in the garden throughout the summer months. In addition to annuals, which have their whole growth cycle contained in one year, and biennials, which are sown one year to bloom the next, it includes those half-hardy perennial or shrubby species commonly used for summer bedding in small gardens.

These flowering plants, which are mostly tropical or sub-tropical in origin, are too tender to survive the average winter: they are therefore raised in greenhouses or bought as small seedlings in spring and planted out in borders or containers as soon as the soil is warm enough. Once mature they bloom profusely to provide a colourful display throughout the summer. Several plants, such as pelargoniums, will survive successive winters if they are brought indoors.

### *Alyssum*
A popular hardy annual with racemes of small cross-shaped flowers. It looks best planted in large drifts.

1 *A. maritimum.* A familiar low edging plant, often grown between paving or on walls. It is a bushy annual with grey-green leaves, covered with rounded racemes of white, lilac or purple flowers throughout the summer. Height: 75–150mm (3–6in); spread: 200–300mm (8–12in).

2 *Antirrhinum majus* (snapdragon) Garden varieties of this annual come in many sizes and a wide range of mainly hot colours. The flowers are fragrant. 'Apple Blossom' is a favourite pink variety. A sunny position and a well-drained, light to medium soil enriched with manure will give best results. Height: 1–1.2m (3–4ft).

3 *Bellis perennis* 'Monstrosa' (daisy)
These perennial plants are best treated as biennials; they are basically an enlarged and double-flowered form of the common daisy, available in white, pink and crimson colours. They are useful for planting alongside spring bulbs, but they will seed into lawns unless the faded flowers are removed. They are hardy and adaptable to most soils and situations, and will flower all summer. Height: 124–150mm (5–6in).

4 *Calendula officinalis* (pot marigold)
A hardy annual of bushy habit with narrow, light green leaves and large daisy-like flowers in bright orange or yellow. The flowers are borne from late spring until the first autumn frosts if the dead flowers are removed; they make a strong focal point. Marigolds will grow and flower even in the worst situations and soils. Height: 600mm (2ft).

5 *Campanula media* (Canterbury bell)
A vigorous upright biennial species. The leaves are bright green and long, with toothed edges. The flowers are bell-shaped and are borne singly on long spikes from late spring to mid-summer. They come in delicate shades of blue, pink, purple and white. Particularly popular is the 'cup and saucer' variety (Calycanthema), so-called because of the shape of its flowers. Canterbury bells grow in any fertile soil in sun or light shade. Height: 0.5–1m (2–3ft).

6 *Cheiranthus cheiri* (wallflower)
A spring-flowering hardy biennial useful for planting alongside bulbs. Wide flowers, in various shades of yellow, red and purple, are carried in dense spikes; they are scented. Wallflowers grow in any well-drained soil in a sunny position. Taller varieties reach 375–600mm (1¼–2ft). Dwarf varieties grow 225–300mm (9–12in).

### *Dianthus*
This large genus includes pinks, carnations and sweet william.

7 *D. barbatus* (sweet william). A short-lived perennial which is grown as a biennial. It bears densely-packed flat heads of flowers in early and mid-summer. These are usually of mixed colours, with red, white and purple predominant. It is a useful border plant, providing strong colour in the garden after the spring bulbs have finished and before most summer annuals have started to flower. Sweet william thrives in most soils, doing best in the sun. Height: 300–600mm (1–2ft).

8 *D.* 'Perfect Clove' (border carnation). Border carnations are hardy perennials but are often grown as biennials. They are short-lived and best replaced after two years. They have grey-green leaves, and flower once in mid- to late summer; the flowers are often scented. 'Perfect Clove' is a deep crimson, scented variety. Height: 0.5–1m (2–3ft).

9 *Gazania splendens*
This is a tender perennial which must be grown as an annual in most areas. The leaves are dark green on top and silver-white underneath; the daisy-shaped flowers are bright orange and they bloom from mid- to late summer. Several hybrids have been developed from this species. It needs a dryish soil and a sunny position. Height: 225mm (9in).

10 *Heliotropium* x *hybridum* (cherry pie)
The deliciously scented flowers of this tender shrub vary in colour from white through lavender to deep purple; they appear throughout the summer. The leaves are finely wrinkled and mid- to dark green in colour. The plants are best grown as annuals and bedded out for the summer; they need a fertile, well-drained soil and prefer full sun. Height: 0.5m (2ft) or more.

11 *Iberis umbellata* (candytuft)
This hardy annual species is easy to grow, doing well even in relatively poor soils; it is also resistant to pollution. The cross-shaped flowers, in white and pale pink, are borne throughout the summer. Height: 150–375mm (6–15in).

### *Impatiens*
A large genus including annual species which are suitable for bedding out in some areas.
*I. biflora.* A hardy annual, suitable for a moist position in the shade. Its oval, mid-green leaves have toothed edges; orange flowers, spotted with red and brown, appear from late summer to autumn. Height: 1m (3ft).

12 *I. holstii* (busy lizzie). The bright green leaves and five-petalled flowers are borne on pale green, almost translucent, stems. The flower colours range from white through pink to purple and scarlet, and appear from late spring to early autumn. Busy lizzies are suitable for bedding out in mixed borders, pots or tubs. *I. sultanii* is now considered a form of *I. holstii*, which it closely resembles. Height: 0.5m (2ft).

*Lathyrus odoratus* (sweet pea)
A favourite 'old-fashioned' annual grown for the delicate pastel colours and evocative scent of its flowers. The tall climbing forms are self-supporting by means of tendrils and can be grown through other climbers up walls; the dwarf types can be used in boxes and tubs. They are relatively easy to grow; any fertile garden soil will be adequate, though a slightly alkaline, well-drained, medium loam is best.

The Spencer varieties are the most popular climbers. They flower throughout the summer in shades of red, pink, blue, purple and white. Height: 1.8–3m (6–10ft).

13 *L.o.* 'Bijou'. This dwarf variety grows only about 300–375mm (1–1¼ft) high and bears a mass of flowers all summer long. Varieties come in a wide range of colours; the individual stems are long enough for cutting and carry three or four flowers.

*Lunaria annua* (honesty)
A quick-growing biennial with jagged-edged, heart-shaped leaves of mid-green colour and cross-shaped fragrant purple blooms in spring and summer. Some forms have white flowers; 'Variegata' has crimson flowers and variegated leaves. However, the plant is usually grown for the mass of exquisite papery silver-white pods which can be used for indoor decoration in winter. Honesty is easy to cultivate in sun or shade and prefers light soil. Height: 0.5m (2ft).

*Matthiola* (stock)
A useful family of annuals and biennials, grown primarily for the colour and scent of their flowers.

14 *M. bicornis* (night-scented stock). A hardy, bushy annual. Inconspicuous, pale lilac coloured flowers appear in mid- and late summer carried on tall spikes; they open up at night, giving an attractive heavy scent, especially in warm weather. They can be combined with other annuals such as mignonette to provide fragrance day and night. Height: 375mm (1¼ft).

15 *Mesembryanthemum criniflorum* (Livingstone daisy)
A low-growing, carpet-forming annual, with narrow, glistening, light green leaves and brightly coloured flowers. Throughout summer a mass of daisy-like flowers are produced which open up in full sun; they range in colour from white to pink, crimson and orange-gold. *Mesembryanthemum* thrives in a light, dry, sandy soil. Height: 150mm (6in).

*Nicotiana* (tobacco plant)
One species of this genus provides the leaves for tobacco. Most of the other species are colourful garden flowers, usually grown as annuals in borders or pots; the flowers open up at night and have a heavy fragrance.
*N. affinis.* In mild areas this species can be grown as a herbaceous perennial but, since it is only half-hardy, is best grown as an annual in colder regions. It has a tall stem, upright branches and large mid-

green leaves. Thin white tubular flowers, opening out at the mouth, appear throughout summer; they are fragrant at night. It prefers a moist, partly shaded position. Height: 0.5–1m (2–3ft).

**16** *N.a.* **'Lime Green'** has subtle yellowy green flowers.

*N.a.* **'Sensation Mixed'** is another garden variety; it bears white, pink, red and yellow flowers.

### Oenothera biennis
(common evening primrose)
A hardy biennial which will flower from seed in the first year. The leaves are narrow and mid-green; both leaves and stem are hairy. Pale yellow flowers appear through the summer, opening in late afternoon and staying open during the evening. It may become an overgrown weed if allowed to seed itself without restriction. *Oenothera* prefers a sunny, open site and will grow in any well-drained soil. Height: 1m (3ft).

*O. trichocalyx.* A hardy biennial which can be treated as an annual. It has greyish leaves and fragrant white flowers in early summer. Height: 450mm (1½ft).

### Pelargonium
The zonal pelargoniums are commonly known as geraniums, but they should not be confused with the genus *Geranium.* They are a group of sub-shrubs but, being mainly tender, are usually brought inside during the winter and bedded out in the summer. The zonal pelargoniums have rounded, mid-green leaves with a ring of bronze or maroon. The most popular varieties have red flowers, but pink and white are also available. The ivy-leaved trailing varieties are particularly suitable for hanging baskets and containers.

This is one of the few plants that flowers better on poor soil with a shortage of water; it likes full sun. Height: 0.5–1m (1½–3ft).

**17** *P.* **'Paul Crampel'.** A bright red-flowering cultivar with large heads of bloom.

### Petunia
An excellent genus of annuals to grow in a hot, open situation in the ground or in window boxes or containers. The double or single trumpet-shaped flowers appear throughout summer in a wide range of colours; some varieties have striped flowers. They grow in a light, well-drained soil in a sunny position. Over-rich soil or too much shade results in vigorous leaf growth but fewer flowers.

**18** *P. hybrida* **'Brass Band'.** This variety is one of the multiflora group of garden hybrid petunias. These are bushy plants bearing a large number of flowers 50mm (2in) wide. 'Brass Band' has creamy yellow flowers. Height: 150–300mm (6–12in). There are also hybrid groups of dwarf and long trailing habit.

**19** *Reseda odorata* (mignonette)
A branching, upright annual with smooth, mid-green leaves. It is hardy and useful for planting in an annual border or for cutting. Heads of flowers, each of four to seven yellow-white stamens, appear throughout the summer. The fragrance of the flowers attracts bees.

A well-drained, rich, alkaline soil in a sunny position is best, but any fertile soil will be adequate. Height: 0.3–0.7m (1–2½ft).

### Verbascum bombyciferum
A hardy biennial species which seeds itself liberally. It is magnificent in mid-summer when tall spikes are studded with cool yellow flowers. The large ovate leaves are covered with a silvery down. The leaves are evergreen during the previous winter, making a valuable addition to a border.

*Verbascum* prefer a light soil in full sun and need no staking. Height: 1.5–2m (4–6ft).

# Bulbs, corms and tubers

**1 *Allium giganteum***
The rich lilac-coloured, star-shaped flowers are grouped in 100mm (4in) wide globes on the end of tall stems; they appear during early summer. The flowers are ideal for cutting, since they last well and can also be dried. The bulbs are hardy and easy to grow in almost any soil but they need sun. Height: 1.2m (4ft).

***Chionodoxa*** (glory of the snow)
These bulbs produce blue, white or dull pink flowers soon after the disappearance of snow, so earning their name. They look best when planted in bold drifts in rough grass. They are hardy and will grow in any well-drained soil.
**2 *C. luciliae*.** The light blue, white-centred flowers are borne in late winter to early spring. Height: 150mm (6in).

***Colchicum*** (autumn crocus)
These are among the most showy of autumn-flowering bulbs or corms; the white or pink flower heads are thrown up straight from the ground before the bulky, rather untidy foliage appears the following spring. They are hardy and tolerate any well-drained soil.
**3 *C. speciosum* 'Album'.** This variety has fine white flowers 150mm (6in) high.

***Crinum*** (Cape coast lily)
A handsome plant with large, funnel-shaped flowers over strap-like foliage. It flowers in late summer. *Crinum* is not fully hardy and should be planted at the base of a sunny wall in any well-turned fertile soil.
**4 *C.* x *powellii*.** The most commonly grown hybrid, with pink and white flowers. Height: 450mm (1½ft).

***Crocus***
A beautiful, gently-scented spring flower suitable for naturalizing in grass. The species types tend to be more subtle and delicate than the larger and late-flowering Dutch crocuses. Crocus are hardy in most situations and tolerant of all well-drained soils.
**5 *C. vernus*.** One of the parents of the numerous large Dutch varieties, with yellow-orange or purple flowers. Height: 75–125mm (3–5in).

***Cyclamen***
A genus of tuberous plants with very distinctive shuttlecock-shaped flowers. They require perfect drainage and do particularly well at the foot of trees or of old north-facing walls. Only some varieties are hardy.
**6 *C. neapolitanum*.** A hardy, autumn-flowering species. The leaves are deep green with silvery markings on top and red beneath. The colours of the flowers vary from pale pink to mauve. Height: 100mm (4in).

**7 *Eranthis hyemalis*** (winter aconite)
A hardy perennial with yellow, buttercup-like flowers resting in emerald green cushions of leaves. Once established, it spreads rapidly by self-seeding and forms thick blankets of colour early in the year. The small tubers establish themselves most readily in a heavy loam. Height: 100mm (4in).

***Eremurus*** (foxtail lily)
Though not strictly a bulb or tuber, this tall plant, with light green strap-shaped leaves, usually appears in bulb catalogues and grows from a star-shaped tuberous root. It produces spectacular candles of flowers, usually pink, in late spring. It prefers sunshine and a well-drained soil.
Foxtail lily is hardy, but should not be planted in exposed situations. Height: up to 2.7m (9ft).
**8 *E. elwesii* 'Albus'.** This is a pure white variety.

**9 *Fritillaris imperialis*** (crown imperial)
An imposing plant bearing a circle of large pendulous flowers surmounted by a crown of green leaves; both flowers and leaf crown sit on top of stems up to 1m (3ft) high. The flowers range from yellow-orange to red and appear in spring. They are hardy and should be planted in a shady position, in any fertile, well-drained soil.

**10 *Galanthus nivalis*** (common snowdrop)
The familiar snowdrop has tiny drooping white flowers that look best in bold drifts and appear very early in the year. *Galanthus* are variable in height, from 75–200mm (3–8in), growing tallest in a rich soil in partial shade.

**11 *Galtonia candicans*** (summer hyacinth)
This species of hyacinth produces tall spires of slightly scented white flowers in late summer. *Galtonia* are moderately hardy but require a well-drained soil at the base of a warm wall. Height: up to 1.2m (4ft).

***Gladiolus***
The genus includes many species and garden hybrids in a large colour range. It is variable in hardiness and needs support in windy situations; it prefers a rich soil.
**12 *G.* x 'Scarlet Knight'.** Primulinus hybrids are free-flowering, in mid- to late summer, though less vigorous than the larger-flowered hybrids. Height: 0.5–1m (1½–3ft).

***Hyacinthus*** (hyacinth)
While often regarded as primarily a house plant, this sweetly scented bulb can do equally well outside in pots, window boxes or flower beds.
**13 *H. orientalis* 'Jan Bos'.** Hybrids of

this species, commonly known as Dutch hyacinths, produce 100–150mm (4–6in) spikes of flowers in late winter and spring. 'Jan Bos' is a deep pink variety. Height: 150–225mm (6–9in).

**4 *Leucojum* (snowflake)**
The species of this bulbous genus are similar to snowdrops, but generally taller; they flower later, with more rounded flowers. The plants are hardy and will naturalize in any soil or position. Height: 200mm (8in).

***Lilium* (lily)**
Lilies fall into one of the following categories: Asiatic, martagon, longiflorum, trumpet, Oriental, hybrid or species. All need careful planting with plenty of humus, leaf mould or peat to retain moisture.

**5 *L. monadelphum*.** A hardy species lily, with fragrant yellow flowers which open in early to mid-summer. It is lime-tolerant and best grown in half shade. Height: up to 1m (3ft).

**6 *Muscari* (grape hyacinth)**
An excellent genus of small spring-flowering bulbs, with lance-shaped leaves. The tightly packed flowers are bunched in pyramids on top of upright stems. The typical blooms are bright blue. *Muscari* are easy to grow and are hardy, naturalizing freely. Height: 150–200mm (6–8in).

*Narcissus*
A vast family which includes the familiar daffodil. Most species are adaptable to less than perfect growing conditions; however, some thrive better than others in deep shade. The most common varieties naturalize most successfully and the smaller heads of the species forms do best in windy situations.

**17 *N.* 'February Gold'.** One of the many popular garden varieties whose flowers have yellow petals and a slightly darker yellow cap. Height: 200–275mm (8–15in).

**18 *Nerine bowdenii***
One of the hardier species of a somewhat tender family of bulbs. It produces clusters of spidery, bright pink flowers in early winter. Plant the bulbs preferably at the base of a warm wall. Height: up to 600mm (2ft).

***Tulipa* (tulip)**
Except for a few simple varieties, tulips tend to look best either in containers or in areas of formal planting. There is an almost un-limited choice of colours. Tulips prefer an alkaline soil.

**19 *T.* 'Charles Needham'.** The Darwin group contains probably the most popular tulips for bedding. They produce slightly rounded flowers, 100–125mm (4–5in) across, in late spring. 'Charles Needham' is a scarlet variety. Height: 0.5–0.7m (2–2½ft).

# Ground cover plants

### Ajuga reptans
A herbaceous perennial which forms a good evergreen ground cover. It has dark green oval leaves and bright blue spikes of flowers produced in early summer. It needs a moist, partly shaded situation. Height: 100–300mm (4–12in).

**A.r. 'Multicolor'.** The foliage of this variety is variegated bronze, yellow and red.

**A.r. 'Variegata'.** A more vigorous though lower-growing plant with light grey-green and cream variegated leaves.

A.r. 'Atropurpurea': see RED AND PURPLE FOLIAGE PLANTS, page 215

### Alchemilla mollis (lady's mantle)
This hardy herbaceous perennial makes an effective weed-smothering carpet. The distinctive light green, hairy, leaves are concave and palmate with serrated edges. The panicles of small, star-shaped, lime green flowers appear 0.5m (2ft) tall in late spring and early summer. The foliage is an effective addition to flower arrangements.

The species thrives in sun or partial shade in any moist but well-drained soil. It seeds itself readily, often adding a charming unplanned touch to a garden, by growing up between the cracks in paving for instance.

### 1 Cotoneaster dammeri
This fast-growing evergreen shrub is excellent for carpeting the ground beneath taller shrubs and trees since it has a spreading, completely prostrate habit and thrives in shade. It has glossy dark green leaves, white flowers which appear in early summer and masses of red berries in autumn.

The species is hardy and will tolerate most soils including those which are heavy and limy. It grows only about 50–75mm (2–3in) high but rapidly spreads to 1.5–2m (5–7ft).

### Epimedium
These evergreen or semi-evergreen perennials are useful ground-coverers and are worth growing for both their flowers and their foliage. Slow creeping roots put up a dense covering of long-stalked leaves composed of elonged heart-shaped leaflets. These are attractive throughout the year. In spring, the young leaves are light green, tinted with red or pink; in summer they turn a deeper green and are prominently veined and in autumn they take on rich red and yellow colours. The flowers appear in spring and are a delicate saucer shape, in a range of colours.

*Epimedium* are fairly adaptable to soils and situations but do best in partial shade in sandy moist loam. The old leaves should be removed in early spring before the flower spikes appear.

**2 E. x rubrum** has crimson flowers and grows about 0.3m (1ft) high.

**E. x youngianum** has pink flowers and grows 150–200mm (6–8in) high. 'Niveum' has white flowers.

### Erica carnea
This hardy heather makes excellent ground cover. Usually the leaves are light green, though in some varieties they are bronze or yellowy. The pink or white flowers appear from late autumn through to late spring. The plants are either completely prostrate or may reach up to about 0.3m (1ft); the spread averages about 0.5m (2ft). Although most heathers are lime haters and do best on sandy soil, *E. carnea* is tolerant of lime. It does best in full sun but survives quite happily in semi-shade.

**E.c. 'Aurea'** is a variety with golden yellow foliage and pink flowers.

**E.c. 'Loughrigg'** has dark green leaves which turn bronze and pink flower buds which open to a pink-purple colour.

**3 E.c. 'Springwood'** is of spreading habit; it bears a mass of white flowers.

### Genista hispanica (Spanish gorse)
This is a low cushion-like shrub with spiny branches up to 1m (3ft) long. Deep green growths shoot upright from these laterally spreading branches. A dazzling display of golden yellow flowers is produced in early and mid-summer.

The species is not fully hardy and prefers dry hot soil in full sun. It grows about 1m (3ft) high with a spread of 2.5m (8ft).

### Hebe pinguifolia 'Pagei'
Hebes are extremely hardy evergreen shrubs, invaluable for seaside and industrial planting. This variety makes an excellent shrubby ground cover, attractive throughout the year. It forms wide mats of rounded glaucous foliage, composed of small grey leaves, and produces spikes of pearly white flowers in early summer. It grows in any well-drained garden soil. Height: 150–300mm (6–12in).

### 4 Hypericum calycinum (rose of Sharon)
This is a vigorous evergreen sub-shrub which rapidly spreads to form a carpet by means of stolons, or prostrate creeping stems which give rise to further plantlets. The leaves are bright to mid-green and in the shape of an elongated oval. Throughout the summer cup-shaped golden yellow flowers are borne, usually singly but sometimes in pairs, at the ends of the shoots.

The species is hardy and will grow in most well-drained soils, although it does best in light sandy soil. It tolerates shade but flowers most profusely in positions of full sun. Height: 0.3–0.4m (1–1½ft); spread: indefinite.

### Juniperus sabina tamariscifolia
Several creeping junipers can be successfully used as ground cover. This variety is compact and low-growing with bright green tapering leaves.

Junipers thrive in most well-drained soils in full sun or light shade. This type is tough and hardy and grows about 0.5m (2ft) high with a spread of 1.5m (5ft) or more.

**J. chinensis 'Pfitzerana'** is another low-growing variety of spreading habit. See ARCHITECTURAL PLANTS, page 219

### Lamium galeobdolon 'Variegatum'
This form of ornamental 'dead' nettle is a useful, rampant, evergreen ground-cover plant; the only problem is that it may soon become invasive and take over areas allotted to other plants. It has attractive silver-streaked leaves which take on bronze tones in winter. Spikes of tubular hooded yellow flowers are produced in early and mid-summer.

The species is a hardy perennial and is tolerant of most soils and situations, being particularly suitable for poor soils in shady sites. It grows about 0.3m (1ft) high.

### 5 Pachysandra terminalis
Suitable for shady sites where little else will grow, this hardy creeping evergreen rapidly spreads to form a green carpet. In the centre of rosettes of dark green lobed leaves, small yellowy green to white flowers appear in spring. 'Variegata' has white-margined leaves and is slightly less fast-growing than the type.

The plant will grow in any fertile soil in partial or deep shade. It has a height of 0.3m (1ft) and a spread of 0.4m (1½ft) or more.

### Prunus laurocerasus 'Zabeliana'
This variety of the common laurel has low horizontal branches and elegant, narrow, willow-like leaves. It produces small white flowers in spring.

The plant makes an excellent ground cover and is tolerant of wet shady positions under trees.

### Sedum spectabile
This hardy perennial has small, fleshy, white-green leaves and bears broad heads of slightly mauvish pink flowers which more or less cover the plant in autumn. These flowers are very attractive to insects, particularly to butterflies.

Several garden varieties exist with generally brighter coloured flowers. 'Brilliant' has striking deep rose-pink flowers and 'Meteor' has deep carmine-red flowers. The species will thrive in most well-drained soils in full sun. It is relatively resistant to drought. It grows 0.3–0.4m (1–1½ft) high.

### 6 Stachys lanata (lamb's tongue)
This distinctive foliage plant can either be grown as ground cover or incorporated within a mixed border. It forms dense mats of woolly grey leaves. Spike-like grey stems bear small purple flowers during mid-summer. 'Olympica' is a variety with whiter leaves and pink flowers. 'Silver Carpet' is a non-flowering variety.

Grow in any well-drained soil. An open, sunny position is preferable but half-shade is also acceptable. The flower spikes reach about 0.4m (1½ft) with the foliage growing about half that height.

### Vinca
These hardy invasive plants make excellent evergreen ground cover. They can be grown in any fertile soil in shade or half-shade.

**V. major** (greater periwinkle). A vigorous spreading sub-shrub with glossy, dark green, oval-shaped leaves and attractive purple-blue flowers, consisting of five flat petals; these appear in spring and sometimes re-appear in the autumn. *V.* 'Elegantissima' is a somewhat less vigorous variety; it has light green and white variegated leaves and pale purple-blue flowers. It has a height of 150–300mm (6–12in) and a spread of 1–1.2m (3–4ft).

**7 V. minor** (lesser periwinkle) has glossy dark green leaves and small blue flowers which appear in early spring and then continue intermittently through to the autumn. It has a height of 50–100mm (2–4in) and a spread of 1–1.2m (3–4ft).

Garden varieties include: 'Alboplena' with double white flowers; 'Aureo-variegata' with yellow variegated foliage and blue flowers; 'Burgundy' with red flowers; and 'Multiplex' with double red-purple flowers.

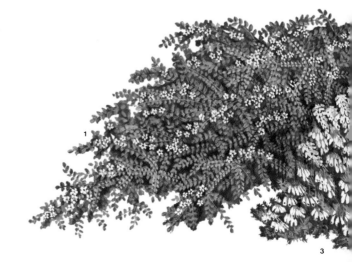

3

# Grass for lawns

Although seldom the most spectacular feature of a garden, a lawn is usually one of the most important, as a result of the space it occupies and the constant use to which it is put. As such, it requires as much thought in planning and care in maintenance as the more eye-catching elements of the design.

The basis of a successful lawn is adequate preparation of the site before sowing or turfing—ensuring that the soil is well-drained, fertile and free of most stones and weeds. Once the grass is established, regular mowing is not just a matter of keeping up the day-to-day neat appearance of the lawn and providing a regular form of therapy for the gardener; it is also an operation, similar in function to pruning, which is vitally necessary if the health and vigour of the grass is to be maintained. The effect of mowing, especially in late spring when growth is strongest, is to ensure the development of thick, firm turf which will be resistant to invasion by weeds and the ravages of drought. At the very least, an infrequently mown lawn will, over the years, come to be entirely dominated by the coarser grasses.

To ensure a healthy lawn in dry periods, see that adequate peat is topdressed into the sward annually; regular watering after the sun has gone off the garden is, of course, also important. In addition, proper lawn maintenance may require: the removal of isolated weeds; the even spreading of an appropriate fertilizer during the spring; a thorough raking at the end of the summer to clear debris and dead grass, plus a lighter brush-over in the spring; and finally, the aeration of the turf in early autumn, using a garden fork or a mechanical spiker. This latter process will be especially necessary either if the grass is growing on naturally heavy soil where drainage is poor, or if the soil has become compacted through heavy use.

However well you intend to look after it, the success of a lawn will also depend on selecting a type of grass appropriate to the growing conditions and functions of your particular lawn. The first decision facing you is whether to grow from seed or to buy and lay turf. There is no generally applicable easy answer to this question; it is really a matter of balancing cost against time and convenience. Turf is more expensive but requires less preparation of the ground and marginally less after-care and it forms a usable surface far more rapidly—often a decisive factor in circumstances where it is difficult to keep children or animals off a seeded lawn over a long period of time.

Whether grown from seed or turf, it is important to choose the right sort of grass for the purpose. If the lawn is primarily a visual feature which is unlikely to be subjected to hard wear, then the fine-leaved grasses which tend to be the most attractive in appearance and texture, will be possible. If the lawn is liable to constant or heavy use, by children playing games and so on, then the coarser, broad-leaved grasses should predominate; such grasses will tolerate a greater degree of neglect as well as harder wear. The following list indicates the characteristics and growing conditions of most of the grasses found in seed mixtures.

## Fine grasses
**Browntop bent** (*Agrostis tenuis*) has a creeping growing habit; it is spread by runners. In the wild it thrives on acid soils, but it tolerates most garden soils, including fairly dry ones.

**Chewing's fescue** (*Festuca rubracommutata*) is a grass of tufted habit, which will grow on both alkaline and acid soils even in dry conditions.

## Coarser, tougher grasses
**Crested dog's tail** (*Cynosurus cristatus*) spreads by sending out rooting tendrils along the surface. It is not particular as to soil; some types of this grass should not be closely mown.

**Rye grass** (*Lolium perene*) is a tufted grass; some strains are better than others, in that they are more leafy and compact in habit. The species is tolerant of most soils but thrives on the heavier ones.

205

# Ornamental grasses

Smooth-stalked meadow grass (*Poapratensis*) is a tufted species; it spreads rapidly via underground stems, tolerates shade and does best on medium or light soils.

Rough-stalked meadow grass (*Poatrivialis*) is the best choice for shade; it thrives in wet, heavy soils.

To establish a hard-wearing lawn quickly, the following combination would be appropriate for most fertile garden soils: 10 per cent rough-stalked meadow grass, 20 per cent crested dog's tail, 30 per cent of a good strain of rye grass and 40 per cent Chewing's fescue. It is probably best, however, to rely on seed mixtures made up by the manufacturers; choose one to fit your requirements and growing conditions.

## Choosing turf
When selecting turf, make sure it does not contain many weeds as, even if these can be easily removed, the grass that is left will be thin and weak. Meadowland turf is often offered for sale at relatively cheap prices, but it is likely to consist of too high a percentage of the coarser grasses. Sea marsh (Cumberland) turf which is used on bowling greens for example, is magnificent but is probably too fine and in need of too much expert maintenance for average garden purposes. Old parkland turf or downland turf are ideal for creating a lawn which is of finer grass than is usually found in fields but which is reasonably hard-wearing and easy to maintain.

## Lawns without grass
There are several very low-growing ground covers which can be used for a small lawn; a lawn mower, adjusted sufficiently high, can even be used on some of them.

### *Anthemis nobilis* (chamomile)
A mat-forming perennial species which can be used instead of grass to form a small, fragrant lawn which is not subject to heavy wear. Its aromatic feathery foliage makes it resemble moss. It may need careful mowing once or twice a year to remove long stems. Chamomile needs a well-drained soil and an open position. Height: 150mm (6in).
'Treneague' is a very suitable variety for lawns, as it is non-flowering and needs little mowing.

### *Trifolium repens* (white clover)
Clover can be used to form a loose-textured lawn on its own, but is more commonly combined with a coarse or medium grass to form an attractive mixed turf. The lobed leaves are composed of three leaflets and round white, or sometimes pink, flowers are produced in mid- to late summer. It spreads vigorously by means of runners. Clover grows best in full sun in a well-drained soil but it tolerates shade.
'Purpurascens quadriphyllum' is an ornamental variety with purple-tinged leaves of three to six leaflets. Height: 50–100mm (2–4in).

### *Arrhenatherum elatius* 'Bulbosum Variegatum'
Despite its name, this is an attractive low-growing ornamental grass. The leaves are striped green and white. It is a tuberous plant; the clumps have to be divided to spread the area it covers. The plant is very hardy and tolerant of most soils and situations. It grows about 300mm (1ft) high.

### *Arundo*
This is a family of tall, hardy perennial grasses which do well in a sunny position, preferably in somewhat moist soil.
1 *A. donax* is the best of the genus. It has stems growing up to 2.5m (8ft) high and these bear long drooping blue-green leaves. It seldom flowers. Cut the plant down to the ground each spring.
*A.d.* 'Variegatus' has leaves striped with white and is much shorter than the type; it grows about 1m (3ft) high.

2 *Avena candida*
This species consists of dense clumps of intense steel blue grass, growing about 300–500mm (1–1½ft) high and graceful stems bearing oat-like heads, reaching up to 1m (4ft) high. It is hardy and will grow in sun or shade in any well-drained garden soil.

### *Carex* (blue grass, sedge)
This is a hardy or slightly tender herbaceous perennial with grass-like leaves and spikes of flowers. *Carex* should be grown in moist soil and does especially well on the margin of a pool. It is tolerant of sunny and shady positions.
*C. morrowii* 'Variegata' forms a clump of leaves edged with gold. It creates a fine show of flowering heads during the spring. It grows about 500mm (1½ft) high.
*C.m.* 'Alba' is slower-growing than the parent plant but has brighter leaves.
*C. riparia* 'Variegata' has leaves striped with white.

3 *Cortaderia selloana* (pampas grass)
Long silvery flowering plumes are the most striking features of this ornamental grass These plumes are carried on top of 2–3m (6–10ft) high stems. A dense mass of slender arching leaves surrounds the base of the stems. The species is reasonably hardy but is best planted in a sheltered sunny site in any well-drained fertile soil.
*C.s.* 'Pumila' is a more compact form than the type, reaching about 1–2m (3–6ft) high.
*C.s.* 'Sunningdale Silver' is an attractive variety with plumes which are somewhat larger and looser than the type.

4 *Festuca ovina* 'Glauca' (sheep's fescue)
This species forms an attractive mound of very narrow blue-grey leaves. In summer, flower heads are carried on stalks somewhat taller than the leaves.

This perennial grass is hardy; it should be grown in a sunny position, preferably in a light, well-drained soil.

### *Miscanthus*
This is one of the most widely-grown ornamental grasses. It is excellent as a specimen planted in a lawn or in a mixed border and can also be grouped to form an unsupported windbreak. The dried leaves can be effective in flower arrangements.
*Miscanthus* do best in sunny positions in moist soil.
*M. sacchariflorus*. This hardy species grows 3m (10ft) high and makes a useful windbreak or sun screen. The mid-green leaves are narrow and of arching habit. 'Variegatus' has white stripes on the leaves.
*M. sinensis* is a vigorous hardy species growing 1–1.5m (3–5ft) high. The narrow leaves are blue-green with a white midrib. 'Gracillimus' is a smaller variety growing 0.3–1m (1–3ft) high and with particularly elegant very thin grey-green leaves.
5 *M.s.* 'Variegatus' has green and yellow variegated leaves.
6 *M.s.* 'Zebrinus' has lateral golden yellow stripes crossing the leaves at intervals.

### *Pennisetum setaceum*
(fountain grass)
The graceful arching habit of this half-hardy perennial grass gives rise to its common name. It looks good in mixed borders and forms an attractive indoor decoration when dried. The foliage consists of tufts of rough-textured, narrow, mid-green leaves. Thin stems curve out from the leaves, bearing 300mm (1ft) long feathery heads made up of masses of silky spikes; these flower heads are a white-green colour tinged with purple and are produced from mid-summer through to the autumn.

The species should be planted in a sunny sheltered position, in any well-drained soil. It grows 0.5–1m (2–4ft) high.

### 7 *Phalaris arundinacea* 'Picta'
(gardener's garters)
This is a hardy perennial grass which shoots from a creeping rhizome. It spreads very rapidly and should therefore be grown in a location where it can be easily confined. The leaves are distinctive, consisting of narrow arching blades variegated with longitudinal stripes of bright green and cream. The green or purple flowers which appear in early and mid-summer are relatively insignificant.

The species should be planted in a sunny or lightly shaded position in any normal, well-drained soil. It grows about 0.5m (2ft) high.

### *Stipa* (feather grass)
A genus of attractive perennial grasses with magnificent feathery plumes. The plants make good specimens set within an expanse of lawn; the plumes can be cut and dried for use as indoor decoration.

These grasses should be planted in full sun, in a light, fertile soil.
*S. calamagrostis* is a species which forms dense tufts of grey-green leaves out of which long stems arise. These stems support silvery buff-coloured plumes, about 300mm (1ft) long, which appear throughout the summer. It is hardy and grows 1m (3–4ft) high.
*S. gigantea* consists of dense, low clumps of grey-green grass and 1.5m (5ft) long stems bearing purple and yellow oat-like flower heads in early and mid-summer. These flower heads are not unlike those of pampas grass.

# Decorative vegetables

**Asparagus** (*Asparagus officinalis*)
A herbaceous perennial member of the lily family, asparagus has been cultivated since ancient times for the sake of its delicious immature shoots. These shoots, or spears, are green or purplish, and white near the base. They bear small leaves, like scales, which are very close together and abundant at the tip. If not picked the shoots branch out and develop into beautiful feathery asparagus ferns, growing up to 1.5m (5ft) high. Asparagus is hardy in all but the coldest areas, but it likes a sunny site, sheltered from north-east winds. Plants are best grown on a well-drained soil, enriched with plenty of organic matter. A bed of asparagus takes three years to become sufficiently established for spears to be picked; but after that it will go on for years, providing it is manured. 'Connover's colossal' is an early variety. 'Argenteuil' is a well-flavoured, later type.

**8 Beetroot** (*Beta vulgaris*)
This hardy biennial (treated as an annual) is grown primarily for its

# Space-saving vegetables

**1 Asparagus pea** (*Lotus tetrangonolobus*)
This vegetable originated in southern Europe and grows best in a sunny situation. The plant, a half-hardy annual, grows into a loosely-formed bush about 300mm (1ft) high. The stems are hairy, the leaves are grey-green and the flowers are a shade of red-brown. The pods are green and cylindrical with four wavy 'wings'. Pods should be picked when only about 25mm (1in) long, then cooked and served whole. Asparagus peas will grow on any good, well-drained soil, enriched with organic matter.

**2 Dwarf cos lettuce**
Lettuce (*Lactuca sativa*) is a very easy vegetable to grow in almost all soils, enriched with compost or manure. It does, however, need a lot of water. There are three main types of this popular salad plant: cabbage varieties, which can be either soft or crisp in texture; those non-hearting varieties which form loose-leaf plants; and—probably best of all—crisp cos lettuces. There are several compact dwarf varieties of cos lettuce.

**3 Dwarf French kidney beans** (*Phaseolus vulgaris*)
This type of bean is low-growing and therefore needs only the support of twiggy sticks. The leaves are mid-green and the sweet-pea-like flowers come in a range of colours, depending upon variety. The pods are usually pale or mid-green, fairly flat, and grow up to about 125mm (5in) long. There are, however, varieties which produce yellow pods, and at least one which bears green and violet ones. French beans grow best in well-drained, light, but rich soil and in a sunny position.

**4 Radish** (*Raphanus sativus*)
It is not often realized how many forms of this useful little salad vegetable there are. The round-rooted ones, either red or red and white, are the most popular, although there are also cylindrical radishes available.

This hardy biennial, grown as an annual for its root, does best in a well-drained, fertile soil, and needs plenty of moisture. A row of radishes can be fitted into a space temporarily vacant in the vegetable plot as they take only about four weeks to be ready for eating. Winter radishes have firmer, more solid, roots which are larger than the usual types. They are left longer in the ground before lifting in autumn and storing for winter use.

**5 Soya bean** (*Glycine max*)
This comparatively new annual vegetable on the Western scene has been known for centuries in other parts of the world. It has far more nutritious protein value than most other vegetables, and is very high in vitamins. Young pods can be cooked and eaten whole; older ones are shelled and only the beans used.

Soya usually forms an upright, bushy plant about 300mm (1ft) high; its stems are covered with brown hairs, as are the leaves and pods. The plant, a member of the pea family, is an attractive one which has pretty white or purple flowers. To produce a good crop it needs plenty of warmth.

**Spring onion**
Spring or salad onions are grown from seed and harvested when young. 'White Lisbon' is a good popular variety; it is quick-growing and has a clear white skin. Seeds should be sown fairly thickly in 12mm ($\frac{1}{2}$in) deep drills, during late spring and summer or as soon as the ground is ready to work after the winter. No thinning is needed.

Any good well-drained soil which has been manured will suffice; an area which has been treated with garden compost for a different crop the year before would be ideal. When harvesting the onions, carefully pull each plant out individually to avoid damaging the roots of plants that remain.

**6 Tomato** (*Lycopersicon esculentum*)
Although still principally a greenhouse crop in temperate regions, with the development of new, hardier, fast-maturing varieties, it is now possible to grow tomatoes outdoors. They need the maximum amount of sun and a soil enriched with organic matter. The dwarf bush type is best when space is limited. There are varieties available which grow to only 750mm (2$\frac{1}{2}$ft) tall, but bear a profuse crop of small, tasty fruit. These can even be fitted into a window box if necessary.

**7 Tree onion** (*Allium cepa* 'Prolifera')
This is one of the most decorative forms of the onion family. The tree onion grows its bulbs both underground and clustered together on the end of hollow stems, in place of seeds. The plants are hardy and easy to grow in a sunny site and on well-drained, manured soil. Plants may reach 1.5m (5ft) in height within two or three years when the onion heads bend over gracefully and drop the bulbs on the ground. The onions themselves are small but useful for pickling or other culinary uses; they are also very strongly flavoured.

root, used in soups and salads. The most popular varieties today have globular roots. The plant has attractive leaves, usually dark green, veined with deep red. Beetroot needs a friable fertile soil, though not too rich in manure; one which has been manured for a previous crop is best.

## 9 Courgette (or Zucchini)

These are in fact marrows which have been bred to produce many small fruit rather than one or two monsters. They are picked when about 150mm (6in) long. The stems and leaves are mid-green and hairy. The plant is decorative in both its typical, yellow, marrow flowers, and its green, golden or green-striped cylindrical fruit. Courgettes, which form a trailing, but bushy, plant, are annuals which may be grown most successfully flat on the ground, or, with greater difficulty, up a fence or trellis. A rich soil is necessary for cultivation as well as full sun and plenty of watering.

## Endive (*Cichorium endivia*)

There are two principal types of endive. The most attractive have very curly, divided leaves, and are for late-summer use. The other type, called Batavians, have undivided, wavy leaves, more like those of a lettuce; these are ready in autumn and winter. Both types are used in salads but, because the leaves are bitter when green, they are blanched by covering for one to three weeks before picking.

Endive, which is a half-hardy annual, prefers a light soil which is well-drained. 'Moss curled' endive is a good variety of the curly, or staghorn type.

## 11 Globe artichoke (*Cynara scolymus*)

This superb plant is as suitable for the flower garden as the vegetable plot. It is a herbaceous perennial and grows up to 1.5m (5ft) high. The plant needs a well-drained soil, rich in humus, and a sheltered, sunny site. (Young plants like some shade.) The globe artichoke is not particularly hardy and winter protection is necessary.

The edible immature flower heads are not usually produced in quantity until the second or third year. It is the fleshy base of the scales and the bottom, or heart, which are eaten; not the hairy choke in the centre. If left to mature the choke grows up through the head and appears as blue-purple florets, not unlike a thistle. The leaves are deeply serrated, greyish, and may reach 0.5m (2ft) in length.

'Gros vert de Laon' is one of the best eating varieites.

## Kale (*Brassica oleracea* 'Acephala')

This biennial, grown as an annual, is a descendant of wild cabbage and one of the hardiest greens. It fills the 'hungry gap' in winter when little else is available. The most decorative types of kale have large, very curly leaves. These are usually dark green but there are varieties which have leaves variegated with silver or purple. Kale likes a heavy or medium loam which has been manured for a former crop.

## Leek (*Allium porrum*)

This relation of the onion has long grey-green, strap-shaped leaves which provide interest, by their leaf colour and form, through the difficult winter period. The bases of these leaves are tightly wrapped round one another in concentric circles to make up the elongated bulb of the plant. This is the part of the leek used in cooking. It has a delicate oniony flavour and is usually blanched before harvesting by binding with paper or black polythene and then earthing up. Leeks can be grown even in a cold climate. All that is needed is a well-drained soil to which some rotted compost or manure has been added.

## 12 Purple sprouting broccoli (*Brassica oleracea botrytis cymosa*)

This vegetable is cultivated for its flowering shoots, which are usually boiled. It is closely related to the cauliflower, but the flower heads are much smaller and loosely-formed of purple, non-opening flowers. Sprouting broccoli produces stems bearing a flower head at the top and other smaller ones in the leaf axils. Plants need a rich loam for best results and a sunny site.

Calabrese (*Brassica oleracea* 'Italica') is similar to broccoli but less hardy. The heads are green; the first one produced is rather like a cauliflower but when this is cut, tasty small heads grow up on side shoots. Sometimes called green sprouting broccoli, calabrese has a better flavour than the white or purple types.

## 13 Red cabbage

Although grown usually for pickling, red cabbage is delicious when cooked with apple and served as an accompaniment for game. Like other cabbages, the red type will grow on most well-drained soil to which some rotted compost or manure, and lime, have been added. Its rich colour makes it a truly decorative vegetable.

## 14 Rhubarb (*Rheum rhaponticum*)

This hardy perennial has large, wavy, dark green leaves which are carried on thick, usually red, stems. These fleshy stems are used for desserts and in wine making; the leaves are poisonous and should never be eaten. Rhubarb prefers to grow in light shade on a rich soil.

## 15 Runner bean (*Phaseolus multiflorus*)

This climber can be used to create a variety of screening and other ornamental effects, as well as being a delicious vegetable. The runner bean is a tender perennial, most often grown as an annual, which may reach 3m (10ft) or more in a season. It can be grown on tripods, up netting or twined around individual vertical, or sloping, poles. The more common varieties have scarlet flowers and green pods, but white-flowered varieties are available, as well as one with purple flowers and pods. Runner beans prefer a rich, well-prepared soil, plenty of water, and a site out of the wind.

## Sweet corn (*Zea mays*)

This is an extremely handsome, tall grassy plant which reaches a height of up to about 2.5m (8ft). The long, mid-green leaves are spaced at intervals up the stem, and from the leaf axils female flowers grow which develop into the familiar cob encased in light green leaves. At the top of each stem is a plume of male flowers. The plant, a half-hardy annual, demands maximum sunshine and a richly-manured soil. It should be planted in blocks rather than rows since it is wind pollinated. Plenty of watering is also essential.

## Swiss chard, or seakale beet (*Beta vulgaris* 'Cicla')

The leaves of this versatile plant can be cooked like spinach, or the stems can be served like asparagus. This is an extremely attractive vegetable which grows to about 1m (4ft) high and has wide stems up to 75mm (3in) across. There are two varieties: one with green leaves and white stems, called Silver beet; the other, which is prettier, is red Ruby chard. A relation of spinach beet, Swiss chard is not fussy about its site or soil; it does, however, need lime.

# Useful and attractive herbs

**1 Basil** (*Ocimum basilicum*)
An essential ingredient in many Italian dishes, basil has a sweet, yet spicy flavour. The ovate leaves are bright green above with green-grey undersides. Whorls of whitish flowers are borne in racemes in late summer.

In temperate climates basil is a half-hardy annual. A well-drained, light soil and a warm, sheltered situation are essential. Alternatively, it can be grown in a pot on a sunny window sill. Basil forms an erect plant, growing to about 600mm (2ft), but regular pinching out will keep it more bushy.
**Bush basil** (*O. minimum*). This species has smaller leaves and grows to a height of only 150–300mm (6–12in).

**Chamomile** (*Anthemis nobilis*)
This is an aromatic perennial ground cover plant. See GRASS FOR LAWNS, page 191

**Chive** (*Allium schoenoprasum*)
Like onions and leeks, chives belong to a genus noted for their flavour and odour. The plant is bright green, grassy and clump-forming in habit with a burst of mauve-pink flowers in summer. The leaves, which have a mild onion flavour, are used dried or fresh in many recipes. This useful hardy perennial makes an excellent edging plant. It prefers sun or light shade and a fertile soil.

**2 Dill** (*Anethum graveolens*)
This decorative plant which originated in the North Mediterranean regions is now widely used and distributed throughout Northern Europe. Its flavour, similar to caraway but milder, is very popular with fish. Both the seeds and the leaves are used for seasoning. The tall plant has blue-green, feathery leaves carried on upright stems. Umbels of yellow flowers are produced throughout the summer, followed by seeds.

Dill is a hardy annual or biennial. It prefers a sunny position and a light soil which should never be allowed to become completely dry. Height: 0.5–1m (2–3ft).

**3 Fennel** (*Foeniculum vulgare*)
This perennial herb grows in many temperate regions. It is similar to dill in appearance but grows taller—up to 1.2m (4ft). The foliage can be chopped and served in a salad or other dish; the seeds, which have an aniseed-like flavour, have both culinary and medicinal uses. It is a relation of Florence fennel, of which the root is cooked. Most types of soil are suitable, but a sunny position is necessary for successful growth.

**Marjoram** (*Origanum*)
There are three cultivated types of majoram, making it a most useful herb. All have similar spicy-sweet flavours good in meat dishes and soups.
**4 Wild marjoram** (*O. vulgare*). This species has an upright habit. The leaves are mid-green and ovate and during mid- and late summer small spikes of pink-purple flowers are produced. This hardy perennial will grow on any poor or chalky soil in a temperate climate. It grows to about 450–600mm (1½–2ft) tall.
**Sweet marjoram** (*O. majorana*). This is a Mediterranean native and as it needs protection from frost is best grown as an annual in temperate regions. The leaves are greyish and hairy and the flowers, produced from early summer to early autumn, may be white, or in shades of purple and pink. Sun and good soil are necessary to grow sweet marjoram satisfactorily. It grows to a bushy sub-shrub, up to about 450mm (1½ft) tall.
**Pot marjoram** (*O. onites*). This type is best grown as an annual. The leaves are bright green and the plant has a carpeting habit, but tall white flowers are borne in mid- and late summer. It prefers a light, dry soil and sun.

**Mint** (*Mentha*)
There are around forty varieties of mint, of which about eight are in common use. Mint is a creeping perennial, increasing itself rapidly by runners. Its invasiveness can be checked by keeping it contained in a pot. It prefers some shade and a moist rich soil, although it will grow in most situations. Some of the more widely-grown, edible varieties are listed here.
**5 Spearmint**(*M. spicata*). The common green mint has mid-green, aromatic leaves and bears purplish flowers from mid-summer to early autumn. It is used for making mint sauce and for flavouring young vegetables. Height: about 0.5m (2ft).
**Bowles mint** (*M. rotundifolia* 'Bowles'). This variety is taller than spearmint, and has a flavour which is preferred by many people.
**Peppermint** (*M.* x *piperita*). Peppermint oil produced from this plant is used to flavour confectionery. It reaches 300–600mm (1–2ft) in height.
**Pennyroyal** (*M. pulegium*). This type is not much used today as a flavouring for meat because of its rather strong flavour. It does, however, make a very fragrant lawn as it is a small creeping variety which grows to no more than 150mm (6in) high. It bears purple flowers in autumn.

**6 Parsley** (*Carum petroselinum*)
High in vitamins A and C and in iron, parsley is one of the most useful of all herbs. Alone or with other herbs, its distinctive flavour and attractive bright green colour complement a wide variety of fish, meat and vegetable dishes. The crisply-curling, mid-green leaves are carried on branching stalks 300–600mm (1–2ft) tall. Parsley is a most decorative subject for edging and as a foil for other plants.

Parsley now thrives in temperate areas, often growing wild. It is a biennial—in its first year it produces leaves only and in its second flowers as well. In colder climates and for culinary uses it is usually grown as an annual. It needs a sunny or part-shaded site and a well-manured soil.

**7 Sage** (*Salvia officinalis*)
This small evergreen sub-shrub is invaluable as a garden plant and as a culinary one; for centuries its leaves, fresh or dried, have been used to counterbalance the effects of some rich meats. The soft stems become woody with age; the ovate leaves are grey-green and in summer bluish mauve flowers are produced. It grows up to 0.5m (2ft) high.
**Broad-leaf sage** (*S. officinalis*). This non-flowering variety is often considered the best for cooking.
**Purple-leaf sage** (*S. officinalis* 'Purpurascens'). This variety has purplish leaves; it can be grown for its decorative value alone.

**8 Sorrel** (*Rumex acetosa*)
This erect perennial has mid-green, arrow-shaped, acid leaves which are used as a vegetable or in salads and sauces. The flowers are a greenish red. Sorrel will thrive in partial shade and likes a fertile, well-drained soil. It grows wild in many places and can be a very small plant or grow up to 1m (3ft) tall.

**9 Tarragon**
(*Artemisia dracunculus*)
This bushy perennial, sometimes called French or Russian tarragon, has narrow olive green leaves and in late summer bears small whitish green flowers. The leaves, besides being used in the famous tarragon vinegar, are a flavouring for fish, meat and some pickles. Use this herb with respect for, mild as it seems, it is easy to overdo the characteristic flavour. It likes a light soil and a dry, sunny position.

**Thyme** (*Thymus*)
There are many thyme species but the two described here are representative of the two major types.
**Common thyme** (*T. vulgaris*). This species forms a low evergreen bush. Its small leaves are dark green, narrow and strongly scented. In early summer it produces clusters of pinky mauve flowers. A favourite herb in a *bouquet garni*, thyme is a native of the Mediterranean area and consequently prefers a sunny spot and well-drained soil.
**Lemon thyme** (*L.* x *citriodorus*). This aromatic hybrid has larger leaves than common thyme and is an excellent subject for a rockery; it also attracts bees.

# Garden fruit

**10 Apple**
This is probably the most popular fruit planted. Nearly all apples, both cooking and eating, need another variety close by which flowers at the same time so they will cross-pollinate. It is, therefore, advisable to plant at least two trees whose flowering seasons coincide or overlap. Should your area be subject to frost, choose varieties which flower late. The selection of trees will also depend, to an extent, on when you want to use the fruit—whether in autumn, winter or the following spring. Your fruit grower will advise on these points.

The shape of tree or bush which you buy will also be influenced by the space available. Standards, up to 6m (20ft) tall, and half-standard trees, up to 4.5m (15ft) tall, may be too large for many small gardens. A better choice is bush or, for a very small site, dwarf trees, which need as little as 2.5–3m (8–10ft).

Management and harvesting are a simple matter with both types. Today trees are formed by joining the variety to a different root system, or 'stock', which determines the size of the resultant tree. For example, M9 rootstock produces the most dwarf tree, M26 more vigorous ones and MM106 semi-dwarf specimens.

Both decorative and space-saving are trees trained as cordons and espaliers. Buy maiden (one-year-old) trees if you wish to train them yourselves into one of these artificial shapes. Alternatively, ready-trained trees, two or three years old, are available from fruit growers. The shape is relatively simple to maintain and you will achieve the effect you want more quickly.

A cordon consists of a single stem bearing fruiting spurs. The tree is planted at an angle to restrict growth and encourage early fruiting and an even production of buds. A row of cordons can be grown against a fence or used as a screen between one part of the garden and another. Espaliers can be used for the same purpose. With this type of tree the branches are trained, on a framework, at regular intervals at right angles to the trunk. Eventually the branches of adjacent trees intertwine in a very attractive way.

Apples need a sunny, sheltered site which is frost-free at blossom time. A well-drained, slightly acid medium loam is the best type of soil.

### Blackberry

This autumn fruit is used for pies and preserves and can also be eaten raw. Blackberries need support; they may be grown on wires against a fence or wall. Chain-link fencing is sometimes used for the purpose.

The canes, which are usually thorny, grow best in a good soil which has been prepared by deep digging. The earth should be well-drained but retain some moisture. A sunny site is best. The flowers appear late, so frost protection is unnecessary.

There are several varieties available; choose one of the less rampant types for a small space. Stems grow up to 2.5m (8ft) tall and each plant has a spread of up to 3m (10ft).

11 **'Oregon thornless'.** This ornamental variety of blackberry has finely divided, parsley-like foliage as well as delicious fruit.

### Currants (*Ribes*)

Black, white and red currants are hardy deciduous shrubs grown chiefly for their small fruit, borne in mid-summer. The fruit are excellent for jam-making.

**Black currants** (*Ribes nigrum*). Black currants have a long life and established bushes will give a high yield. They produce the best fruit on one-year-old wood and should be pruned to encourage a good crop. Plant black currants about 1.5m (5ft) apart, with 2m (6ft) between the rows, and prune the long shoots to about 75mm (3in) after planting. They prefer a sunny position but will tolerate partial shade. A well-drained, moisture-retentive soil is needed; black currants respond well to heavy manuring, especially on a light soil.

**Red and white currants** (*R. sativium* and *R. petraeum*). These varieties succeed better in shade than black currants and in fact need a fairly sheltered situation. They can be trained as cordons or fans against a north-facing wall or a fence, or can be grown as standards (about 1.2m (4ft) high), allowing another low vegetable or salad crop to be planted underneath. They need a good soil and repay both feeding and watering in a dry season.

All currant bushes have a height of about 2.5m (8ft) and a spread of 1.2m (4ft).

### Fig (*Ficus carica*)

A handsome deciduous shrub or small tree with palmate leaves which for many centuries has been cultivated for its fruit. Figs can be eaten fresh or dried. It is most likely that the fig came originally from Western Asia so it grows best in areas where there is plenty of warm sun. In a moist temperate climate figs grow too vigorously to fruit well so, if you want a tree which is productive as well as decorative, some provision should be made to restrict root growth. Make a hole about 1m (3ft) square and the same depth; lay a hard floor of closely-packed lumps of brick, and box in the sides with concrete or brick to divert the surface water. Alternatively, sink a large pot or concrete tub into the earth or paving.

Grow the fig tree in loam to which some bonemeal has been added. Cold winds will kill young shoots, so planting against a sunny wall is a good idea. However, where conditions permit, a fig makes a splendid free-standing tree.

### 12 Gooseberry

A hardy, deciduous shrub, which is very thorny. The fruit is valuable for bottling, cooking and dessert uses. To obtain top-quality berries, thinning is necessary when the fruit is half-grown. The small thinned green berries may be used up for cooking.

Gooseberries can be grown in

most situations and are successful in many temperate and cool regions. They prefer a well-drained, moist soil with plenty of humus. Gooseberries grow up to 1.5m (5ft); they can also be grown as cordons.

### Grape vine (*Vitis*)

A long-lived and deeply-rooted deciduous climber. It is hardy in winter frosts but easily spoiled by late spring frost after growth has started. Vines for wine-making and dessert purposes are grown in many temperate regions, although they need continuous warmth over a long period to ripen the fruit. This means that in many areas vines may be grown under glass for successful results. They can, however, be grown against a wall or over a pergola for the beauty of their large leaves.

*Vitis coignetiae*: see PLANTS FOR AUTUMN COLOUR, page 212

### 13 Plum

This fruit is best grown in a climate of hard winters, short springs and hot summer. An early spring brings the blossom before the air is warm and dry; the best crops follow a late spring. Plums prefer a fairly light, well-drained soil; they do not like one which is acid. The site should be sheltered from prevailing winds and high enough to escape valley frosts.

Plums vary in fertility, some setting a good crop with their own pollen, but many need a cross-pollinator planted nearby. The smallest type of tree available is grown on a semi-dwarfing root-stock, producing a tree up to 3–3.5m (10–12ft) tall and needing the same amount of space. Plums can also be grown successfully as fans against a warm wall.

### 14 Raspberry

This luscious fruit is produced on tall canes which are grown 450mm (1½ft) apart in rows and supported on a system of poles and wires. By growing both summer- and autumn-fruiting varieties it is possible to have a supply of fresh raspberries for a fairly long season.

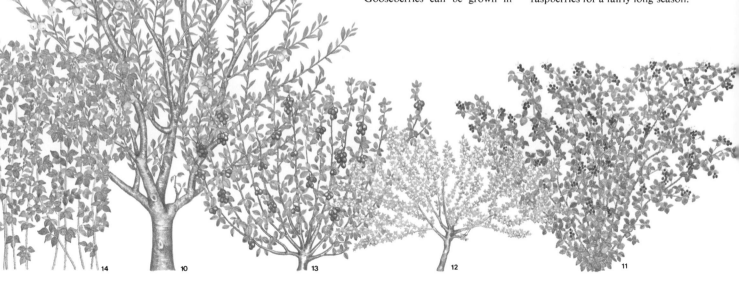

# Plants for autumn colour

## TREES

*Acer* (maple)
Ornamental leaves which assume brilliant colours in autumn are the outstanding feature of this genus of generally deciduous trees. The species described are hardy and thrive in any well-drained but moist and cool soil in sun or half-shade. They should be sheltered from prevailing autumn winds.

1 *A. japonicum.* This bushy, slow-growing species has seven- to eleven-lobed palmate leaves, which turn rich crimson in autumn. There are many attractive varieties. Height: up to 6m (20ft); spread: 2.5–3m (8–10ft).
*A. tataricum.* This species is slow growing and bushy, with broadly oval-shaped, pale leaves which turn yellow in autumn. Height: 4.5m (15ft); spread: 2.5m (8ft).

*Crataegus* (ornamental thorn)
Thorns are reliable, hardy trees and shrubs which will survive in adverse situations such as areas of extreme pollution or exposure. Following the pink, red or white flowers, bunches of colourful fruit or haws appear in autumn.
*C. coccinea* (scarlet haw). The dark green leaves of this species turn red in autumn. The white flowers, in clusters, appear in early summer, followed by red haws. Height and spread: 4.5–6m (15–20ft).

2 *Liquidambar styraciflua* (sweet gum)
This hardy deciduous tree has five-pointed, shiny dark green leaves which turn brilliant orange and scarlet in autumn. Old trees develop corky outgrowths. The common name derives from the amber-coloured resin which the tree exudes. A sheltered position in full or partial sun and a well-drained but moist loam soil are preferable. Height: 10–12m (30–40ft); spread: 4–6m (14–20ft).

3 *Parrotia persica*
This is a slow-growing deciduous tree of wide spreading habit. The mid-green leaves take on superb crimson, amber and gold tints in autumn. The flowers are inconspicuous. In old trees it is worth removing the lower branches as the bark flakes away from the trunk leaving an attractive pattern. The species is hardy, lime-tolerant and should be planted in sun or light shade. Height: 3–5.5m (10–18ft); spread 3–4.5m (10–15ft).

4 *Quercus borealis* (red oak)
Of narrow habit when young, this hardy oak soon develops a spreading shape. In autumn the leaves turn to a deep red-brown colour. Like most oaks, it will grow in any normal, well-drained soil; while tolerating partial shade, the tree will take on a better shape if planted in an open, sunny position. Height: 7.5–9m (25–30ft); spread: 4.5–6m (15–20ft).

## SHRUBS

*Azalea* (Ghent hybrids)
Many of this group of deciduous azalea cultivars, which are distinguished by their long-tubed, honeysuckle-like flowers, exhibit richly-coloured autumn foliage. The flowers appear in late spring to early summer. As with other azaleas and rhododendrons, chalk or lime soils, dryness at the roots and direct sunlight should be avoided. The average height of the group is 2–2.5m (6–8ft).
*Rhododendron* 'Corneille'. This Ghent azalea has especially good autumn leaf colour and double flowers, pink in bud and cream, flushed pink, when open.

*Calluna vulgaris* (ling, heather)
Several named varieties of this hardy evergreen shrub flower throughout the autumn. These include 'Serlei' and 'White Crown', which have long racemes of white flowers; 'Durfordii', which has rather dark foliage and pale pink flowers; 'H.E. Beale', which has long racemes of double, bright rose-pink flowers; and 'Hibernica' which has masses of mauve flowers hiding the leaves.
Heather will grow in all except extremely limy soils. Though tolerant of shade, it flowers most freely in full sun.

5 *Cotinus coggygria* (smoke tree)
The leaves of this rounded deciduous shrub take on a brilliant orange colour in autumn. Feathery panicles of small cream flowers are borne in mid-summer. The species is hardy, best grown in a sunny position in any normal garden soil and grows to about 2.5m (8ft).
Named varieties include 'Atropurpureus', which has pink-purple inflorescences, and 'Foliis Purpureis' and 'Royal Purple' both of which have purple foliage, taking on light red autumn tints.

*Fothergilla*
A genus of hardy, deciduous low-growing shrubs, remarkable for brilliantly coloured autumn foliage.
6 *F. major.* In autumn the oval, glossy, dark green leaves of this species assume orange-yellow or red tints. Cream-white scented flowers made up of spiky stamens appear in late spring, before the leaves. The shrubs should be planted in full sun or light shade, in moist, lime-free soil enriched with peat or humus. Height: 2.5m (8ft).

*Hypericum elatum*
This semi-evergreen shrub has deep green aromatic leaves, yellow flowers from mid- to late summer and attractive red berries in autumn. 'Elstead' is a variety with red-tinged autumn foliage as well as outstanding clusters of pink-red berries.
The species is half-hardy and thrives in any well-drained fertile soil, preferably in a sunny position. Height: about 1m (3–4ft).

7 *Ribes aureum* (golden or buffalo currant)
This deciduous shrub has coarsely toothed pale green leaves which turn yellow, flushed orange, in autumn. Yellow tubular flowers, with a clove-like scent, appear in spring, followed by black fruit.
The species is hardy and thrives in any garden soil in sun or half shade; it grows 2–2.5m (6–8ft) high.

8 *Vitis coignetiae*
(Japanese crimson glory vine)
Perhaps the most spectacular of the ornamental vines, this deciduous species has magnificent large leaves which turn yellow, orange, red and purple in autumn. Panicles of green flowers appear in late spring followed by black berries with a purple bloom. This climber clings by its tendrils and is very suitable for growing over trees or old buildings.
It is hardy, thrives in most situations and should be planted in loam enriched with compost or manure. It may grow as high as 27m (90ft).

# Plants of winter interest

## TREES

**9 *Acer griseum*** (paperbark maple)
This is one of the most beautiful of small, slow-growing deciduous trees. The trifolate, mid-green leaves turn red in autumn. The most interesting feature, however, is the buff-coloured bark of the trunk and branches, which peels off to reveal a rich orange-brown colour.

It is hardy and should be planted in moist but well-drained soil in sun or half-shade. Height: up to 4.5m (15ft); spread: 3m (10ft).

***Betula papyrifera*** (paper birch)
The gleaming white bark of this attractive species peels away in strips on older trees. The leaves are mid-green and triangular. It makes a splendid specimen tree throughout the year.

It is hardy and tolerant of all degrees of sun and shade, and of most normal soils. Height: 6–9m (20–30ft); spread: 3–4.5m (10–15ft).

***Corylus colurna*** (Turkish hazel)
This distinguished tree has an interesting grey corrugated bark. The dark green leaves are oval-shaped. Yellow male catkins appear in early spring, followed by clusters of nuts.

The species is hardy and thrives in most garden soils. It does best in a sunny site protected from east winds. Height: 9m (30ft).

***Prunus***
Several species of this genus of ornamental deciduous trees will provide pleasure through the winter months. The two species of cherry listed here will thrive in most soils and situations.
*P. serrula.* This cherry is chiefly grown for its attractive bark which

peels off in strips to reveal shiny red-brown new bark underneath. The leaves are willow-like and there are clusters of white flowers which appear in spring. The tree grows 6–7.5m (20–25ft) high, with a spread of 4.5–5.5m (15–18ft).
**10** *P. subhirtella* 'Autumnalis Rosea'. This tree produces semi-double pink flowers throughout the winter. Height: up to 7.5m (25ft).

**11 *Salix* x *chrysocoma*** (weeping willow)
This spectacular weeping tree is an attractive feature of any garden, even when there are no leaves on the branches. Bear in mind, however, that it will eventually grow very tall, so may not be suitable for very small gardens. The delicate lance-shaped leaves are pale to mid-green. Long yellow male catkins appear in early spring.

The species is hardy and prefers a moist soil in a sunny position. Height and spread: 6–7.5m (20–25ft) or more.

## SHRUBS

***Cornus*** (dogwood)
This genus contains several widely-differing species; most are hardy, deciduous and grown for their flowers, coloured bark or attractive foliage.
**12** *C. alba* (red-barked dogwood). The upright stems of this species are bright red, providing a splash of colour in the winter garden. The oval-shaped mid-green leaves are grey underneath; they sometimes turn red or orange in autumn. Yellow-white flowers appear in spring, but they are inconspicuous. The variety 'Westonbirt' has particularly brilliant red stems.

The species is hardy; it should

be planted in moist soil in sun or half shade and grows 2.5–3m (8–10ft) high.
**13** *C. mas* (cornelian cherry). This hardy bushy shrub has dark green, oval-shaped leaves. Small yellow flowers are borne in clusters early in the new year, on the naked stems of the previous year's growth. The flowers are sometimes followed by red berries. 'Aurea' has yellow-tinged foliage; 'Elegantissima' is variegated yellow and pink; 'Variegata' has white margins.

*C. mas* should be grown in sun or partial shade, in a moist soil. Height: 4–6m (12–20ft); spread: 3–4m (10–12ft).

**14 *Corylopsis pauciflora***
This densely-branched species of spreading habit has yellow, scented flowers, which appear at the end of winter before the bright green leaves. It is hardy but requires shelter from the wind. A sunny or partially shaded position and an ordinary lime-free soil is best. Height: up to 2m (6ft).

**15 *Daphne mezereum***
Purple-pink flowers appear towards the end of winter on this deciduous bush; they are borne in dense clusters on the upper parts of the previous year's leafless stems. The leaves are dull green above, pale grey-green underneath.

The species will thrive in most garden soils, in sun or partial shade. It is hardy and grows up to 1m (3ft) high.

***Hamamelis* x *intermedia***
(witch hazel)
This vigorous deciduous shrub has mid-green leaves which turn yellow in autumn. The spidery yellow flowers appear in late winter.

Several varieties have copper-red flowers.

The species should be planted in sun or semi-shade, sheltered from cold winds, in moisture-retentive neutral or acid soil. It is hardy and grows 2–3m (6–10ft) high.
*H. mollis* has flowers appearing even earlier: see SCENTED FLOWERS AND FOLIAGE, page 218

***Lonicera fragrantissima***
Hardy and semi-evergreen, this shrubby honeysuckle has oval-shaped mid-green leaves and strongly fragrant cream-white flowers throughout the winter. It will grow in sun or partial shade in any ordinary well-drained soil. Height and spread: 2m (6ft).

***Mahonia***
A family of hardy evergreen shrubs with leathery dark green leaves. They are chiefly grown for their yellow flowers and their distinguished foliage; blue-black berries are also produced.
*M. japonica.* Dark green, spine-toothed leaves and drooping racemes of lemon-yellow scented flowers appearing in the new year are two features which make this a useful and attractive species for the winter garden. It is hardy and can be grown in any normal garden soil in sun or light shade. Height and spread: 2.5–3.5m (8–12ft).
*M.* x 'Charity' is similar but flowers earlier in winter. See ARCHITECTURAL PLANTS, page 219

***Sarcococca*** (Christmas box)
This is a genus of evergreen small or dwarf shrubs with attractive glossy foliage and small fragrant white flowers opening in late winter. They are generally hardy, tolerant of shade and will succeed in most soils, particularly in chalk.

# Golden and yellow foliage plants

## TREES

### 1 *Acer pseudoplatanus* 'Brilliantissimum'
A distinctive small, slow-growing variety of sycamore. Its young leaves are pink, later changing to yellow-green. It is hardy and grows in any soil; this variety dislikes exposure and needs a position in light shade. Height: 3.5m (12ft) after 20 years.

### 2 *Gleditsia triacanthos* 'Sunburst'
This variety of the elegant 'honey locust' tree has golden yellow foliage, especially bright when young. It is hardy, likes any soil and tolerates industrial pollution. It ultimately reaches 5.5–9m (18–30ft); spread: 3.5–4.5m (12–15ft).

### 3 *Robinia pseudoacacia* 'Frisia' (false acacia)
This stunning, small variety of the false acacia has pinnate leaves which open golden yellow in spring and turn green-yellow in summer. It creates a bright patch of colour in a shrub border. Cream-white fragrant flowers are borne in summer.

The false acacia is hardy, grows in any well-drained soil, and is tolerant of pollution. It prefers a sunny position and, as the branches are brittle in the wind, should be given wind shelter. Height: up to 9m (30ft); spread: 3–4.5m (10–15ft).

### *Sorbus*
This large genus has many hardy species, which range in size from dwarf shrubs to large trees. Two varieties have particularly attractive yellow-tinged foliage.

*S. aria* 'Aurea' (whitebeam). The leaves of this whitebeam are tinted soft yellow-green. *S. aria* is a particularly hardy species, tolerating industrial pollution and any soil, including chalk. Height: 4.5–6m (15–20ft); spread: 3–4.5m (10–15ft).

*S. aucuparia* 'Dirkenii' (mountain ash, rowan). This variety of rowan has yellow leaves when young, turning yellow-green when mature. The species bears clusters of red berries in autumn. It is easily grown on all but shallow chalky soils. Height: 4.5–7.5m (12–25ft); spread: 2.5–3.5m (8–12ft).

## SHRUBS, CLIMBERS AND PERENNIALS

### 4 *Berberis thunbergii* 'Aurea'
*B. thunbergii*: see RED AND PURPLE FOLIAGE PLANTS, page 215.

This variety has yellow leaves, turning pale green by late summer.

### 5 *Calluna vulgaris* 'Golden Feather'
A heather with soft yellow foliage, flushed orange, on long feather-like plumes. It is sometimes tinged red or deep orange in winter. The purple flowers are seldom much in evidence. This heather is hardy and can be grown in all but limy soils, preferably in full sun. It also needs good drainage and a dressing of peat or leaf mould. Height: 300–500mm (1–1½ft).

'Gold Haze', with white flowers, and 'Joy Vanstone', with pink flowers, also have golden foliage.

### *Corylus avellana* 'Aurea'
A hardy, deciduous, nut-bearing shrub. It has soft yellow leaves and yellow catkins, which appear in late winter to early spring. *Corylus* do best in open sunny sites protected from east winds, though they will grow in semi-shade. Any well-drained soil should be adequate. Height: up to 6m (20ft); spread: 4.5m (15ft).

### *Erica carnea*
There are several golden or yellow-foliaged varieties of the alpine or winter heath. They are all hardy and thrive in virtually any type of soil, even under adverse conditions. Height: up to 300mm (1ft); spread: about 600mm (2ft).

*E.c.* 'Aurea'. This variety has lime-green to pale yellow foliage in summer turning gold yellow, tinted orange, in winter. Short racemes of deep pink flowers are produced from mid-winter to spring.

*E.c.* 'Foxglove'. This form has light yellow-green foliage turning rich yellow in winter. It assumes a reddish flush during cold weather. The flowers open white, then turn pink in late winter to early spring.

*E.c.* 'Sunshine Rambler'. The foliage of this variety is bright yellow throughout the year. Pink flowers appear in winter to early spring.

### 6 *Hedera helix* 'Buttercup' (ivy)
This variety has small golden leaves, excellent for ground or wall cover. Like other species of this familiar evergreen genus, this one is hardy and thrives in most soils and situations.

### *Humulus lupulus* 'Aureus'
A yellow-leaved variety of the common hop. A vigorous, attractive climber, it is most effective when trained on a pergola. Female flowers are carried in yellow-green clusters in late summer. It is a hardy perennial, best grown in full sun. Its leaves are 75–150mm (3–6in) long and the twining stems 3–6m (10–20ft) long.

### *Ilex aquifolium* 'Flavescens'
Known as 'moonlight holly', this variety has yellow leaves shaded with deep gold. It is especially effective in spring when the young leaves appear and also provides necessary colour on dull winter days.

Hollies can be planted in most garden soils, though a moist loam is preferable. They normally enjoy either sun or shade but *I.a.* 'Flavescens' scorches badly in full sun and therefore needs light shade. Height: 5.5–7.5m (18–25ft); spread: 2.5–3.5m (8–12ft).

### *Ligustrum ovalifolium*
See FORMAL, INFORMAL AND DWARF HEDGES, page 194

### *Lonicera nitida* 'Baggessen's Gold'
A golden variety of this small-leaved, dense evergreen shrub. It grows in most well-drained soils, in sun or partial shade, and is often used for hedging. Height and spread: 1.5–1.8m (5–6ft).

### *Philadelphus coronarius* 'Aureus'
A dense, bushy, deciduous shrub which is particularly suitable for dry soils. The young foliage of this variety is bright yellow, becoming green-yellow in summer. The species is hardy; the variety retains its colour most successfully when grown in the shade. Height: 1.8–2.7m (6–9ft); spread: 1.8–2.5m (6–8ft).

## CONIFERS

### *Chamaecyparis lawsoniana* (Lawson cypress)
There are several golden and yellow varieties of this hardy conifer. They thrive in any well-drained garden soil, in an open position or

# Red and purple foliage plants

moderate shade and are useful both as ornamental specimens or for a hedge or screen.

*C.l.* **'Aurea Densa'**. A slow-growing conical bush of compact habit, with densely-packed short flattened sprays of golden yellow foliage. Height: up to 2m (7ft).

*C.l.* **'Ellwood's Gold'**. A slow-growing compact columnar variety, with feathery sprays of yellow-tinged foliage. Height: 1.8m (6ft); spread 0.5m (1½ft).

### Cupressus macrocarpa
A vigorous conifer, hardy in all but the severest winters, when young trees will be damaged. Several golden and yellow forms exist; they colour best in an open position, turning green in the shade.

*C.m.* **'Coneybeari'**. A wide-spreading conical tree, with drooping yellow or yellowish green foliage. Height: 4.5–9m (15–30ft).

*C.m.* **'Goldcrest'**. A somewhat taller variety of narrow columnar form and dense compact habit. Its juvenile foliage is rich yellow. It thrives in any ordinary soil.

**7** *Juniperus chinensis* **'Aurea'** (golden juniper)
A slow-growing columnar evergreen with golden foliage which tends to burn in full sun. However it is one of the best golden conifers for a town garden. It thrives in any well-drained soil. Height: 3.5m (12ft), after 20 years.

## TREES

**8** *Acer palmatum* **'Atropurpureum'**
One of the most attractive and popular of the ornamental Japanese maples. It is a slow-growing tree of rounded form reaching about 4.5m (15ft). 'Atropurpureum' has bronze-red foliage. It is lime-tolerant and hardy, but requires protection from cold winds.

### Betula pendula 'Purpurea'
(purple leaf birch)
The silver birch is a slow-growing tree of graceful habit though a disadvantage of all birches is the wide spread of their surface roots. This variety has extremely ornamental purple leaves but is sometimes slightly difficult to grow. Although usually found on thin acid or sandy soil in the wild, it is hardy and thrives in most garden soils in sun or shade. Height: 6–9m (20–30ft); spread 2.5–3.5m (8–12ft).

### Malus (crab apple)
There are several red- and purple-leaved species whose flowers, produced in clusters, are usually wine-red in colour. *Malus* are hardy and thrive in any well-drained garden soil. Height: 0.3–1m (1–3ft).

*M.* x **'Lemoinei'**. A hybrid crab apple with oval purple-coloured leaves, tinged bronze in late summer and autumn. The fruit are also purple-bronze. Masses of crimson-

purple single flowers are produced in spring. Height: 4.5–6m (15–20ft); spread 3.5–6m (12–20ft).

*M.* **'Profusion'**. This is an excellent upright hybrid with mid-green leaves, tinged purple. The flowers are deep red in bud and purple-red with a pink centre when open; as the name indicates, they appear in great profusion in late spring. The autumn fruit are small and red. Height: 4.5–6m (15–20ft); spread: 2.5–4.5m (8–15ft).

**9** *Prunus cerasifera* **'Pissardii'** (cherry plum)
This deciduous ornamental plum is an attractive small tree with black-purple leaves and white to pink flowers. It can be effectively used for hedging, particularly as its dense foliage makes it difficult to grow other plants beneath it when it matures. It is hardy and thrives in any normal well-drained soil. Height: up to 6m (20ft).

## SHRUBS

**10** *Berberis thunbergii* **'Atropurpurea'**
This robust hardy species is ideal for a background hedge or in a mixed shrub border. The rounded leaves of the 'Atropurpurea' variety, borne in rosette-like clusters, are bright red-purple when young, maturing to a deep green-purple and turning red in the autumn. Small yellow flowers open in spring and are followed by red berries. It will grow in any ordinary garden soil but prefers a sunny position. Height: 1.8m (6ft).

### Euonymus europaeus 'Atropurpureus'
A hardy deciduous shrub with narrow pointed leaves; they are a dull purple colour, turning bright red in autumn. Inconspicuous green-white flowers are borne in spring. It is easily grown in ordinary garden soil in sun or shade. Height: 2–3m (6–10ft); spread: 1–3m (4–10ft).

### Pittosporum tenuifolium 'Purpureum'
A half-hardy evergreen shrub with pale green leaves which gradually

change to a deep bronze-purple. Purple-brown flowers with a honey-scent appear in spring. It should be in well-drained soil. Height: up to 4.5m (15ft); spread: 1.5m–2m (5–7ft).

### Weigela florida 'Foliis Purpureis'
This genus includes some of the most popular summer-flowering shrubs. The variety *W.f.* 'Foliis Purpureis' is a slow-growing small shrub of compact habit; it has purple-flushed leaves and tubular foxglove-like pink flowers. It is a very easily-cultivated shrub, excellent for town gardens. It thrives in sun or partial shade in a well-drained soil. Height: up to 2.5m (6ft).

## PERENNIALS

**11** *Ajuga reptans* **'Atropurpurea'**
A hardy ground-cover plant with purple oblong-oval leaves and whorls of blue flowers in early and mid-summer. It is especially good for planting between roses. A moist soil and partial shade is best. Height: 10–30mm (4–12in).

**12** *Phormium tenax* **'Purpureum'**
*P. tenax* is a suitable hardy evergreen species to plant in a border. This variety has bronze-purple spiky leaves which are strap-shaped. Dull red flowers are borne in 1m (3ft) long panicles between mid-summer and early autumn. It requires deep moist soil and a sunny position. Height: up to 2.7m (9ft).

**13** *Rodgersia podophylla*
A hardy herbaceous perennial which has large leaves divided into leaflets like that of a horse chestnut. In particular when young, and from mid-summer onwards, these leaves are purplish in colour. It produces sprays of cream flowers in early to mid-summer. The plant requires moisture and should be planted in partial shade, sheltered from strong winds. Height: 1–1.2m (3-4ft).

### Sedum maximum 'Atropurpureum'
An excellent hardy perennial border plant with dark purple stems and lighter purple toothed leaves. Heads of pink flowers appear in autumn. It needs full sun but grows in any well-drained soil. Height: 0.3–1m (1–3ft).

### Senecio clivorum (syn. Ligularia dentata) 'Desdemona' and 'Othello'
Two varieties of this hardy herbaceous perennial which form clumps of heart-shaped leaves. 'Desdemona' has leaves and stems flushed with purple; 'Othello' is similar but more strongly flushed red-purple. Orange-red flowers appear in mid- and late summer. They can both be grown in any normal soil. Height: 1–1.5m (3–5ft).

# Silver and grey foliage plants

*Artemisia*
Both the herbaceous perennial and the shrubby species of this genus are suitable for planting in mixed borders, where their feathery silver-grey foliage can be a great asset. Once established they spread swiftly by means of underground runners.
*A. absinthium* (common wormwood). A hardy deciduous sub-shrubby species with a height and spread of about 1m (3–4ft). The silver-grey leaves are divided into slender filaments. Panicles of globe-shaped yellowish flowers are borne during mid- and late summer.
1 *A. ludoviciana* (white sage). A hardy herbaceous perennial with woolly grey-white foliage. Silvery brown flowers are produced in autumn. Height: 0.5–1m (2–4ft).

*Buddleia*
Several species of this genus of decorative, flowering shrubs have silvery-looking foliage.
*Buddleias* are lime-tolerant and can be planted in any good loamy soil. They require full sun; the half-hardy species do best against a warm, west-facing wall.
*B. alternifolia* '*Argentea*'. A hardy shrub whose leaves are covered with silky hairs, giving the foliage an attractive silvery sheen. Sweet-scented lavender-blue flowers are produced in clusters during early summer. The species grows 3.5–6m (12–20ft) high with a spread of 4.5–6m (15–20ft).
2 *B. crispa* is a bushy, half-hardy deciduous shrub with toothed leaves covered in white felt, giving the species a silvery appearance. The flowers are lilac-pink with an orange centre; they are scented and are produced in plume-shaped clusters during mid-summer. Height: 2–3m (6–10ft); spread: 1–2.5m (4–8ft).

*Chamaecyparis pisifera*
(sawara cypress)
Several named varieties of this hardy evergreen conifer have blue-grey foliage. They can be planted in any normal, well-drained soil and do best in an open position or in light shade.
3 *C.p.* '*Boulevard*' is cone-shaped, with a mainly bright blue-grey colour and a feathery texture. The

colour is best maintained when the plant is grown in light shade. The variety reaches about 4.5m (15ft).
*C.p.* '*Filifera*' is slightly larger and forms a sparse branching bush of a dark grey-green colour.
*C.p.* '*Compacta*' is a low dwarf form with grey-green foliage. Its spread is about 1m (4ft) and its height is 0.5m (2ft).
*C.p.* '*Nana*' is similar, but even smaller, with height and spread of about 0.5m (1¾ft).

4 *Convolvulus cneorum*
This half-hardy evergreen shrub is one of the few silver-foliaged plants which also offers a magnificent display of flowers. It is of bushy, compact habit and has narrow lance-shaped leaves covered with silver grey hairs. The flowers are produced in late spring and often appear again in the autumn; they are pink in bud, opening up to white petals with a yellow eye.
The species will grow in any normal garden soil but requires a sunny, sheltered position. It has a height and spread of about 0.5–1m (2–3ft).

*Dianthus* (pinks)
Garden pinks have grey-green leaves; the flowers, often with fringed edges to the petals, measure about 25–50mm (1–2in) across. These hybrids can be divided into two main groups: old-fashioned pinks and modern pinks.
The old-fashioned pinks grow about 300–400mm (10–15in) high and flower in early summer. Favourite varieties include 'Musgrave's Pink' which has single white flowers with a green eye, 'Emil Paré' with long-lasting double pink flowers, 'Excelsior' with double flowers which are carmine with a darker red eye and 'Isolde' which has very pale pink flowers streaked with purple.
Modern pinks are slightly faster-growing and taller than the old-fashioned types, reaching up to 400mm (15in) high. They are also freer-flowering, usually blooming in early and mid-summer and then again in the autumn. Good varieties include 'Cherryripe' with bright pink double flowers, 'Daphne' which has single pale pink flowers with a crimson eye

and 'Show Pearl' which has pure white double flowers.
Pinks should be planted in sunny positions in fairly rich, well-drained soil.
5 *D.* '*London Poppet*' has very pale almost white flowers with red borders round the petals.

*Potentilla*
Some shrubby species of this genus display silver or grey foliage. They are hardy, requiring a light, well-drained soil and preferably full sun.
*P. arbuscula* '*Beesii*'. A hardy dwarf shrub, this variety forms mounds of silvery foliage and bears yellow flowers during summer.
*P. fruticosa* '*Mandschurica*'. A mat-forming species with silver-grey foliage carried on purple stems. It has pure white flowers in summer. The spread is about 1m (3ft), the height 300mm (1ft).

*Romneya* (tree poppy)
These are attractive herbaceous perennials with grey-green foliage and white, poppy-like flowers. Once established, they spread swiftly by means of underground runners.
6 *R. coulteri* has white flowers with golden yellow stamens appearing from mid-summer to autumn. The species is not fully hardy and should be planted in a sheltered, sunny position. Light, well-drained soil, enriched with peat or leaf-mould, is desirable. It grows 2–2.5m (6–8ft).

7 *Rosa rubrifolia*
This is one of the few roses grown primarily for its foliage rather than its flowers. The stems are a reddish-purple colour; the leaves are purple in a sunny position and grey-green with a mauve tinge when grown in the shade. Small clusters of attractive, but not very striking, pink single flowers are produced in early summer.
The species is hardy and will grow in most soils and situations.

It reaches approximately 2m (8ft) with a spread of 1.5m (5ft).

*Ruta graveolens* (rue)
The leaves of this hardy evergreen sub-shrub were widely used as a culinary herb; they have a bitter taste which makes a good flavouring for salads. Nowadays, the species is grown primarily as a foliage plant. It has divided blue-green leaves with an aromatic scent. Clusters of yellow flowers appear during the summer.
The species will succeed in any well-drained soil in a sunny position and grows 0.5–1m (2–3ft) high. 'Jackman's Blue' is a more compact form, with a height of about 600mm (2ft). The leaves are a brighter blue-grey colour.

8 *Santolina chamaecyparissus*
(cotton lavender)
With its silvery aromatic foliage, this hardy evergreen dwarf shrub makes a useful addition to a mixed border. Bright lemon-yellow flowers are produced in mid-summer. The plants can be trimmed into a neat mini-hedge.
This species thrives in full sun in any normal garden soil. It normally has a height and spread of 500–600mm (1½–2ft).
*S.c.* '*Nana*' is a very compact, even smaller variety, reaching 300–500mm (1–1½ft).

9 *Senecio laxifolius*
This shrubby evergreen species is more consistently hardy than *S. greyi* with which it is often confused. It forms a bushy outline, approximately 1m (4ft) high and rather more in width. The foliage is a light grey-green colour with a felted texture. Loose clusters of small yellow flowers appear in early to mid-summer.
The species thrives in any well-drained soil, preferably in a sunny position. It does well in seaside gardens.
*S. maritima*: see PLANTS FOR A SEASIDE GARDEN, page 225

# Variegated foliage plants

*Acer* (maple)
There are several forms of maple
with attractive variegated leaves.
*A. negundo* **'Variegatum'** (box
elder). A wide-spreading tree
whose pale green leaves of three to
five leaflets are variegated with
white. It is deciduous and hardy
and grows 6–7.5m (20–25ft) high
with a spread of 4.5–6m (15–20ft).
'Elegantissimum' is another variegated form of this species; its
leaves are green and yellow.
*A. platanoides* **'Drummondii'**. A
white-margined variety of the
Norway maple. It is not, however,
entirely stable and the leaf colour
may revert to green.

*Aralia elata* **'Aureovariegata'**
and **'Albomarginata'**
(Japanese angelica tree)
These are two magnificent deciduous variegated shrubs. 'Aureo-
variegata' has yellow and green
foliage; 'Albomarginata' has silver
and green foliage. The leaves are
doubly pinnate and enormous;
they measure about 1m (4ft) by
0.5m (2ft). The shrubs show up
well when grown in front of a dark
background.
   The plants are moderately hardy
and not particularly choosy as to
soil and situation. They will
grow about 2–2.5m (6–8ft) tall.

**0** *Aucuba japonica* **'Maculata'**
(spotted laurel)
This hardy evergreen shrub forms
a bushy outline. The leaves are a
shiny dark green spotted with
yellow. Erect panicles of green
star-shaped flowers are produced
in spring. Bright red, oval-shaped
berries appear on the female plants
in the autumn and often continue
through to the spring.
   *Aucubas* are very easy to grow
in any normal soil, in sun or half-
shade. They will do well in town
and seaside gardens. Height: 2–4m
(6–12ft); spread 1.5m (5–6ft).

**11** *Berberis thunbergii* **'Rose Glow'**
A new cultivar of this species,
'Rose Glow' has unusually variegated foliage. Basically purple
leaves are covered with patches of
pink and white.
   Plant *Berberis* in any normal
soil. A lightly shaded situation will
show up the coloured foliage to
best advantage while avoiding
scorching from excessive sun. This
hardy deciduous variety grows
1–1.5m (3–5ft) high.

**12** *Cornus alba* **'Spaethii'**
This is an excellent golden-
variegated form of dogwood. As
with the species, it is a hardy
deciduous plant, has striking red
stems in winter and can be
planted in any moist soil in sun or
half shade. It grows up to about
3m (10ft) high.
   *C. a.* **'Elegantissima'** is another
variegated form. The green leaves
are margined with white.

**13** *Elaeagnus pungens* **'Maculata'**
A variegated form of this hardy
evergreen, 'Maculata' has dark
green leaves splashed in the centre
with a rich gold colour. It is
somewhat slower-growing than the
species. However, it shares a
craggy spreading shape, a height
and spread of 2.5–4m (8–12ft), and
a tolerance of most soils and
situations.
   *E.p.* **'Dicksonii'** has leaves of
reverse pattern to those of 'Maculata': green in the centre, with a
golden yellow margin.
   *E.p.* **'Variegata'** is a larger and
faster-growing form with cream-
yellow borders to its leaves.

*Hedera* (ivy)
There are several variegated
ivies, all of which are hardy and
tolerate most soils and situations.
*H. canariensis* **'Gloire de Marengo'**.
This is a fast-growing climbing ivy
with broad leathery leaves which

are dark green in the middle,
shading out through silvery grey
to a white margin. It is ideal for
growing up a trellis.

**14** *H. helix* **'Goldheart'**. This form of
the common ivy has small dark
green leaves with gold centres. It is
excellent for growing up a wall or
as a ground cover.
   Other variegated varieties of
*Hedera helix* include: 'Discolor'
which has leaves mottled like
marble with a red-tinted cream
colour, 'Glacier' which has small
leaves streaked with grey and
margined with white and 'Tricolor' which has light green leaves
with a border of white, turning to
a deep red-pink in autumn.

*Hypericum* x *moseranum*
**'Tricolor'**
This is a hybrid evergreen form of
St. John's wort with green and
white variegated leaves edged with
red. It forms a low-spreading bush
which is excellent ground cover.
Yellow flowers are carried in
clusters of one to five at the ends
of the shoots, from mid-summer
into autumn.
   It is not very hardy and must be
grown in a well-drained soil,
preferably in full sun in a protected position. Height and spread:
300mm (1ft).

*Lonicera japonica*
**'Aureoreticulata'**
(Japanese honeysuckle)
A vigorous semi-evergreen twining
plant, this species soon becomes a
tangle of thin growths. The light
green leaves are veined with
yellow. Scented, white to pale
yellow flowers appear from early
summer through into autumn.
   This honeysuckle needs a well-
drained soil enriched with humus.
Ideally the roots should be in the
shade with the top of the plant in
full sun. The previous year's

growth should be moderately
pruned in spring. It grows up to
4–6m (12–18ft) high.

*Pachysandra terminalis*
**'Variegata'**
Hardy and evergreen, this is a
creeping plant grown as ground
cover in shady situations. 'Variegata' has mid- to dark green
leaves edged with white. It is much
less vigorous than the type. Spikes
of small, petal-less flowers appear
in spring; they have prominent
white, purple-tinged stamens.
   The plant grows in any fertile
garden soil in half or full shade.
Height: 300mm (1ft); spread:
500mm (1½ft).

**15** *Phormium tenax* **'Variegatum'**
(New Zealand flax)
This is a generally hardy evergreen perennial with narrow spiky
leaves striped green and yellow.
The unusual shape of the leaves
makes this an excellent species to
provide contrast in a mixed border.
Long, branched panicles of dull
red flowers appear from mid-
summer to early autumn.
   It thrives in deep, moist soil,
preferably in a sunny position and
grows up to about 3m (10ft).

**16** *Populus candicans* **'Aurora'**
A fast-growing and hardy deciduous tree, this variety has heart-
shaped leaves which are cream-
white streaked with pink when
young and which later turn pale
green splashed with pink or white.
These variegated leaves retain their
colour best if the tree is stooled or
pollarded each year during spring,
although this will mean the life of
the plant is shortened.
   As with other poplars, this
variety is tolerant of very wet soil,
of saline winds and of pollution
in the atmosphere. It has an ultimate
height of 5–7m (15–22ft), with a
spread of 3–5m (10–15ft).

# Scented flowers and foliage

**1** *Acacia dealbata* (mimosa)
This is an attractive evergreen tree with silvery green fern-like foliage. Fragrant yellow flowers are borne in panicles 150–225mm (6–9in) long during the winter.

The species requires plenty of sunlight throughout the year and is not hardy. It may, however, be grown successfully in a sheltered position in mild localities. Height: about 7.5m (25ft).

**2** *Chimonanthus praecox*
(winter sweet)
A bushy deciduous shrub which has willow-like leaves and winter flowers with a strong spicy scent; these are a waxy yellow colour, stained purple at the centre, and appear on the leafless branches.

The species, which succeeds in any well-drained soil, is excellent on chalk. It is best planted against a sunny wall where it grows to over 3m (10ft).
*C.p.* 'Grandiflora' has flowers of a deeper yellow colour with a prominent red stain at the centre.
*C.p.* 'Concolor' has yellow flowers which are larger than the type, do not have the red or purple centre and which open somewhat earlier in winter.

**3** *Choisya ternata*
(Mexican orange blossom)
This evergreen shrub has a wide-spreading bushy shape and glossy green leaves which are aromatic when crushed. The white flowers, which first appear in spring and then continue intermittently through to winter, have a sweet scent.

The species thrives in any well-drained soil, preferably—but not necessarily—in a sunny position. Although hardy, it is best grown against a sheltered wall if in an area subject to severe frost. It grows about 2m (6ft) high with a spread of 2–2.5m (6–8ft).

*Cytisus* x 'Porlock'
This semi-evergreen variety of broom is of upright habit. It has light green, trifoliate leaves and bears sweetly-scented yellow flowers in spring. It is half-hardy and requires wall protection in colder areas. A well-drained poor soil and a sunny position are preferable. Height: up to 3m (10ft); spread: 1.2m (4ft).

**4** *Hamamelis mollis*
(Chinese witch hazel)
This is a large hardy deciduous shrub. It has ascending branches with downy rounded mid-green leaves and clusters of spidery, sweetly-scented yellow flowers which appear during the winter. The leaves turn yellow in autumn.

It should be planted in neutral or acid, moisture-retentive soil, in a sheltered position in sun or semi-shade. Height and spread: 2–2.5m (6–8ft).
*H.m.* 'Brevipetala'. An upright variety with leaves that are glaucous underneath and flowers which have shorter petals and a deeper yellow colour than the type.
*H.m.* 'Pallida' has dense clusters of flowers which are paler than the type and which are faintly flushed with red; they have a particularly strong, yet delicate, fragrance.

*Lavandula* (lavender)
Lavender is widely grown for its fragrant flowers and aromatic foliage.
*L. spica*: see EVERGREEN SHRUBS, page 192

*Lippia citriodora*
(lemon-scented verbena)
The pale yellow narrow leaves of this deciduous shrub have a marvellous lemon scent when crushed. Small, pale mauve tubular flowers appear in late summer.

The species should be planted in any well-drained soil, in a sheltered position as it is not fully hardy. It grows about 1.5m (5ft) high.

*Lonicera* (honeysuckle)
There are many hardy species of honeysuckle with beautifully scented flowers. They can be grown in any well-drained soil although this should be enriched with humus for the climbing species. They will thrive in the sun or partial shade; the climbers do best with their tops in sun but their roots in shade.
*L. fragrantissima* is partially evergreen and bears strongly fragrant cream-white flowers in winter and early spring. It has a height and spread of about 1.8m (6ft).
**5** *L. periclymenum* 'Serotina' (woodbine). A vigorous, deciduous climber of trailing or scrambling habit. The upper dark green leaves are stalkless, the lower ones are stalked. The scent of the flowers is rich and pervasive. Height: 4.5–6m (15–20ft).

**6** *Magnolia stellata*
A charming slow-growing, hardy deciduous shrub. This magnolia forms a compact bush, usually wider than it is high, and it is particularly suitable for the smaller garden. The star-shaped white flowers are fragrant and appear in spring. 'Royal Star' has larger flowers than the type, with more petals; 'Rosea' has pinkish flowers.

Plant in a sheltered position in well-drained loam. The species grows 2.5–3m (8–10ft) high with a spread of 2.7–3.5m (9–12ft).

*Philadelphus* (mock orange)
These medium sized deciduous shrubs bear white, cup-shaped, flowers with a strong scent reminiscent of orange-blossom.
**7** *P.* 'Belle Etoile' is a good named hybrid, with single white flowers stained with a faint purple, appearing in early to mid-summer. Height: 2.5–3m (8–10ft); spread: 3–3.5m (10–12ft).

*Philadelphus* are hardy and can be grown in any normal garden soil, in full sun or half-shade.
*P.* 'Virginal': see DECIDUOUS SHRUBS, page 191
*P. coronarius* 'Aurea': see GOLDEN AND YELLOW FOLIAGE PLANTS, page 214

*Prunus*
Many species of ornamental cherry tree have fragrant blossom.

**8** *P.* 'Amanogawa' (Japanese cherry). An erect tree of narrow columnar habit when young and a slightly more spreading shape as it get older; it is ideal for small gardens. The semi-double pink flowers are scented; they appear in spring. Height: 6–7.5m (20–25ft); spread: 2–2.5m (6–8ft).
*P. padus* (bird cherry) has almond-scented white flowers borne in slender racemes during late spring. 'Watereri', more commonly grown than the type, has racemes up to 200mm (8in) long. Height: 6–9m (20–30ft). spread: 4.5–6m (15–20ft).
*P.* 'Shirotae' and *P.* x *yedoensis* are also almond-scented. For these species and for the growing requirements of cherries: see PLANTS TO ESTABLISH A FRAMEWORK, page 190

*Rhododendron*
Several rhododendrons and azaleas have pleasantly scented flowers. Strongly fragrant deciduous azaleas include 'Daviesii' with white and yellow flowers; 'Exquisitum' with pink and orange flowers; 'Magnificum', with white flowers. flushed pink and orange; and 'Superbum' with pink flowers, streaked apricot.
*R. luteum*: see PLANTS RESISTANT TO POLLUTION, page 223

**9** *Skimmia japonica*
This is a slow-growing, hardy evergreen shrub with mid-green, leathery leaves and fragrant cream-white flowers; these are produced in early to mid-spring and are followed by bright red berries when both sexes of the plant are present. 'Fragrans' is a particularly strong-scented variety.

It is tolerant of pollution, can be grown in sun or light shade in any ordinary soil and reaches 1–1.5m (3–5ft) with a spread of 1.5–2m (5–6ft).

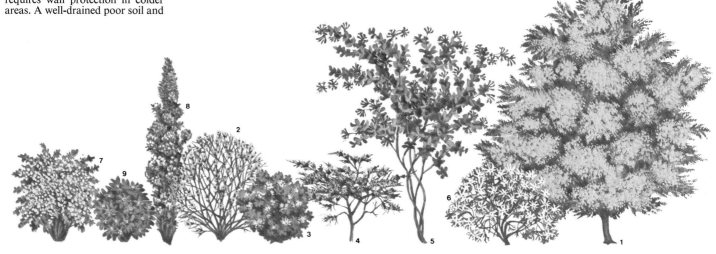

# Architectural plants

### *Arundinaria* (bamboo)
The elegant foliage, the overall architectural shape and the atmospheric associations of bamboo provide an interesting contrast to the type of plant commonly grown in gardens of the temperate zones.

Bamboos require relatively light soil and a position sheltered from cold winds.

*A. variegata* is probably the hardiest bamboo; its leaves are striped with white. It is a low species, growing about 1m (3ft) high.

*A. japonica* and *A. nitida*: see FAST-GROWING PLANTS FOR SCREENING, page 220

### *Carpinus betulus* 'Columnaris'
This is the upright form of the common hornbeam. It is a fast-growing columnar tree of very dense, compact growth, which is deciduous and hardy. The trunk is grey and fluted. The leaves are mid-green and prominently toothed and ribbed. Unlike the parent species, which is most commonly planted as a hedge, this variety is used to best effect as a vertical focal point within the garden.

The tree thrives in any normal soil, in sun or shade; it will normally reach between 6 and 10.5m (20–35ft).

### *Catalpa bignonioides* (Indian bean tree)
This is a hardy, deciduous, small tree grown primarily for its interesting foliage. This consists of bright green, heart-shaped leaves which have a pungent smell when crushed. The species also bears white, foxglove-like flowers streaked with purple and yellow during mid-summer. These are followed by narrow seed pods shaped like beans. There is a yellow-leaved variety, 'Aurea'. Plant in any good soil in a sunny sheltered position. Height and spread: 4.5–6m (15–20ft).

### *Cordyline australis*
A palm-like evergreen, this shrub is grown for its handsome architectural foliage. It has a thick trunk and several ascending branches, each of which is crowned by a dense mass of long, grey-green, sword-like leaves. Mature plants may bear plume-like panicles of scented cream-white flowers in early and mid-summer. These are sometimes followed by white berries. 'Lentiginosa' has leaves flushed with purple.

The shrub is not fully hardy but succeeds in sheltered positions in town gardens in many areas. Grow it in well-drained soil in full sun or partial shade. It can reach up to 7.5m (25ft), with a spread of 2–3m (6–10ft).

### *Eriobotrya japonica* (loquat)
An architectural plant on account of its magnificent firm evergreen leaves, which are leathery and corrugated. After a hot summer, clusters of fragrant hawthorn-like flowers are produced intermittently through the winter.

It is not fully hardy and should be grown in a sheltered, sunny position in a deep, light loam. The species can reach up to 9m (30ft) but is usually seen as a wall shrub around 3–4.5m (10–15ft) high.

### 12 x *Fatshedera lizei*
This unusual hardy evergreen foliage plant normally starts off upright and then flops to become more of a ground-cover. The leaves are a shiny, leathery, deep green in a palmate shape with five lobes. The flowers are inconspicuous.

It grows 1–2.5m (4–8ft) high in any ordinary soil, in sun or shade.

### *Fraxinus excelsior* 'Pendula'
This weeping form of the common ash can be found as a dominating architectural feature of a small garden.

See PLANTS FOR COLD AND EXPOSED SITES, page 222

### *Gunnera manicata*
This is probably the largest-leaved hardy foliage plant which is available to gardeners in the temperate zone. It is fairly bulky and so is unlikely to suit gardens where space is severely limited; but, if room can be found, the dramatic effect of this architectural species is well worth it.

The plant consists of stout, prickly stems supporting single dark green, lobed leaves measuring as much as 3m (10ft) across. These massive leaves are held up by a structure of ribs in the pattern of fan vaulting. Insignificant flowers appear in spring.

*Gunnera manicata* requires a deep, moist soil and does particularly well next to a pool. It can be grown in sun or light shade but the foliage is best preserved in a sheltered position. It reaches 2–3m (6–10ft) high.

### *Hydrangea sargentiana*
A noble shrub of medium size and sparse habit with shoots that are covered all over with stiff bristly hairs. The oval-shaped pointed leaves are deep green above and pale green underneath. The flowers consist of mauve-lilac florets surrounded by sterile white-pink florets; they appear in mid- to late summer.

The species grows about 3m (10ft) high and should be planted in a moisture-retentive soil

enriched with manure, compost or peat; it does well in deep shade.

### *Juniperus*
A large genus of conifers ranging from prostrate creepers to dense shrubs and columnar trees. Many species have a very distinctive shape.

13 *J. chinensis* 'Pfitzerana' (Chinese juniper). This small conifer is of wide spreading habit with arm-like branches drooping at the ends. It is yellowy green in colour and spreads about 2m (7ft) with a height of approximately 1m (3ft).

'Pfitzerana Aurea' is flatter with golden yellow leaves in summer, turning yellow-green in autumn.

These junipers are shade tolerant and are excellent for covering the ground or disguising manhole covers, for instance.

*J. virginiana* 'Skyrocket' is a spectacular variety of very narrow columnar habit. It has blue-grey foliage. Growing 2.5–3m (8–10ft) high with a spread of only 200m (7in), it is a useful design element for providing a vertical contrast in an area of horizontal planting.

These conifers are hardy and will thrive in any well-drained garden soil in sun or light shade.

### *Mahonia* x 'Charity'
This species is a hybrid between *M. japonica* and *M. lomariifolia*. The foliage consists of distinctive spine-toothed dark green leaflets. The yellow flowers appear in the winter and are carried in long tapering racemes.

This hardy evergreen shrub should be grown in light shade, in a moist leafy soil. It grows about 3m (10ft) high with a spread of 2–2.5m (6–8ft).

### *Rhododendron*
This large genus includes many species with magnificent architectural leaves as well as dramatic flowers. The larger-leaved types are, however, subject to wind damage and should be planted under the protection of trees. They need abundant natural moisture in order to thrive. So long as there is a fair amount of shade and no lime present in the soil, rhododendrons will grow in any moist, yet well-drained, soil.

14 *R. calophytum* is a spreading evergreen shrub with leaves of a broad oval shape; these are polished

dark green above and pale green beneath. Waxy, pink-white, bell-shaped flowers open in clusters of about thirty during early to mid-spring. This species grows to about 3m (10ft), with a spread of 3m (10ft) or more.

### 15 *Rhus typhina* (stag's horn sumach)
This is a truly sculptural plant which looks very good in small town gardens of controlled elegant design. A small, hardy, deciduous tree, it bears tiers of pinnate mid-green leaves; these take on magnificent orange-red and yellow tints in autumn. Dense cones of small red flowers are borne in early and mid-summer and are followed by crimson fruit. The tree readily sends up masses of vigorous suckers.

Plant *Rhus* in a sunny position in any normal garden soil. It has a spread of 3–4.5m (10–15ft) and reaches 4.5–6m (15–20ft) high.

### *Viburnum rhytidophyllum*
This is a fast-growing evergreen shrub. The long corrugated leaves are glossy dark green above and greyish beneath. The small cream-white flowers are carried in flat heads 75–100mm (3–4in) across, during late spring and early summer. When several plants are grown together, berries usually appear after the flowers; these start off red and then turn black.

The species has a spreading habit of layered branches. It is hardy and thrives in slightly moist soils, including chalk ones. Grow in full sun if possible. Height and spread: 3–4.5m (10–15ft).

### *Yucca*
These exotic evergreen shrubs have a distinctive shape that is immediately recognizable in any area of planting. They consist of clusters of long strap-shaped leaves with sharp points, out of the centre of which rise erect stems, bearing plumes of bell-shaped flowers. However, the flowers may not appear until after several years.

Yuccas should be planted in full sun in any well-drained soil, including poor sandy ones. The following species both grow to a height of 1–2m (3–6ft).

*Y. gloriosa* has red-pink tinged flowers.

16 *Y. recurvifolia* has pure cream-white flowers.

# Fast-growing plants for screening

**1 *Arundinaria* (bamboo)**
Hardy and evergreen, this genus of bamboos is very fast-growing and forms a distinctive outline. They thrive in moist garden soil, in sun or partial shade.
*A. japonica.* This fast-growing bamboo has sharp-pointed mid- to dark green leaves. It swiftly grows to over 3m (10ft) and forms dense thickets, thus creating a completely opaque screen. The brown foliage should be cut in late spring.
*A. nitida* is another vigorous thicket-forming species. Purple stems carry bright green leaves. It is more shade-tolerant than other bamboos. Height: 2.7–3m (9–10ft).

**Chamaecyparis lawsoniana**
(Lawson cypress)
This hardy evergreen conifer grows up to 0.5m (2ft) in a year. It is useful as a hedge or screen. When growing naturally, it forms a striking column. The leaves are dark green above with grey marks beneath; when crushed they have a parsley-like fragrance. The bark of mature trees peels off in strips. Dark red male flowers appear in spring; during the summer, small woody cones are produced.
The species is hardy and will grow in any fertile soil that does not dry out. An open position or light shade is preferable. It grows about 12m (40ft) high if un-trimmed, with a spread of about 3m (10ft).

**2 *Cotoneaster* x *watereri* 'Cornubia'**
This is a vigorous semi-evergreen with glossy oval leaves. Clusters of small cream flowers appear in late spring followed by abundant red berries. Unless the birds get them these berries will last well into winter. The stems of the plant often become pendulous from the weight of berries.
This shrub is hardy and will grow in any ordinary fertile soil. A sunny position is best. It will reach 5m (15ft) fairly swiftly.

**Ligustrum lucidum**
This is a vigorous evergreen with glossy oval-shaped dark green leaves. It produces tubular cream-white flowers from late summer into autumn. It can be planted in any fertile soil in either sun or shade but may need protection from cold east or north winds. Height: 5–8m (18–30ft); spread: 3–6m (10–20ft).

**Polygonum baldschuanicum**
(Russian vine)
Known as 'mile a minute', this is an extremely fast-growing climber. See CLIMBERS AND SHRUBS FOR WALLS, page 196.

**3 *Rosa* 'Frühlingsgold'**
A modern shrub variety, this hardy deciduous rose quickly forms a bush with a height and spread of about 2m (7ft). During late spring and early summer, the long arching stems bear large, semi-double pale gold flowers which have a rich scent. A well-drained soil and a situation which gets plenty of sunlight are desirable.

**Sorbus**
Several species and varieties of *Sorbus* grow quickly and can be used to screen an unwanted view.
*S. aria* 'Magestica'. This variety of the common whitebeam is faster-growing and more robust than the parent species. It also has larger leaves and fruit.
*S. aria*: see PLANTS TO ESTABLISH A FRAMEWORK, page 190

**4 *S. aucuparia*** (rowan, mountain ash). The mountain ash is a fast-growing small deciduous tree. The pinnate leaves are mid-green on top and slightly grey underneath; they turn orange and yellow in autumn. White flowers appear in late spring to early summer and are followed by large clusters of orange-red berries.
The tree is hardy and tolerant of pollution and can be grown in sun or shade in any except shallow alkaline soils. It grows 4.5–7m (15–25ft) high with a spread of 2.5–3.5m (8–12ft).

**5 *Thuja plicata***
(western red cedar)
Fast-growing long-lived and hardy, this coniferous tree has cinnamon-red peeling bark and spreading branches. It is cone shaped. Although the eventual height of an uncontrolled tree may be 15m (50ft) or more and therefore unsuitable for most gardens, the plants can of course be trimmed, either to form a proper hedge or to create a more informal screen. The scale-like leaves are mid-green above with white marks underneath. A few brown cones are produced on mature trees. *Thuja* thrives in a somewhat moist soil, in full sun.

# Plants for damp sites

**Aronia** (chokeberry)
These deciduous shrubs are related to *Sorbus* and *Pyrus*. White flowers are followed by conspicuous red or black berries. Brilliant autumn foliage appears at the same time as the berries.
*Aronias* prefer sunny positions and are suitable for growing in damp sites.
*A. arbutifolia.* This has white or pale pink flowers in late spring and pear-shaped red fruits in autumn; it grows 1.5–3m (5–10ft).
*A. melanocarpa* has white flowers in late spring followed by black fruits and grows 0.5–1.5m (2–5ft) high.
*A. prunifolia* has similar characteristics but reaches up to 3.5m (12ft).

**Betula** (birch)
Several of this genus of graceful ornamental trees are well adapted to growing in damp soil.
Birches can be grown in sun or shade. They have wide-spreading roots and should not, therefore, be planted near to walls, fences or buildings. It may be difficult to establish other plants near them as they tend to dry out the soil.
*B. nigra* (river birch). As the common name suggests, an excellent species for planting in very damp ground near a river or pond.

It has interesting reddish-brown rough-textured bark and soft green diamond-shaped leaves which are somewhat glaucous on the underside. It is very hardy but does not have a long life.

**6 *B. pendula*** (common silver birch). This graceful tree has a distinguished silver-white trunk which becomes rough-textured in older trees. The leaves are mid-green and diamond-shaped. The species is very hardy and grows to 9m (30ft) or more, with a spread of about 3.5m (12ft).

Several varieties are available. 'Dalecarlica', the Swedish birch, has elegant drooping branches and deeply-cut leaves; 'Fastigiata' is of particularly upright habit; 'Youngii' is a dome-shaped weeping tree; 'Purpurea': see RED AND PURPLE FOLIAGE PLANTS, page 215

**7 *Crataegus oxyacantha* 'Coccinea Plena'** (hawthorn, may)

The species is less widely seen than the common hawthorn, *Crataegus monogyna*, but the cultivars are very popular. They are all suitable for growing in damp sites. The mid-green leaves are rounded and less deeply lobed. 'Coccinea Plena' bears double scarlet flowers in spring and oval crimson haws in autumn.

It is hardy, tolerant of pollution and coastal winds and will withstand drought as well as waterlogging. Although it survives in shade, it prefers an open position. The plant reaches 4.5–6m (15–20ft), with a spread of 4.5–5.5m (15–18ft).

***Mimulus*** (monkey flower)

These hardy annuals and herbaceous perennials thrive in moist, or even boggy soils. They produce attractive open-mouthed flowers, similar to the snapdragon.

**8 *M. luteus*** (monkey musk) has oblong to oval shaped mid-green leaves and flowers produced from late spring through to late summer; these are 25–50mm (1–2in) long and yellow, marked irregularly with red or brown spots. This species will succeed even in standing water up to 75mm (3in) deep and must have a moist soil. Sun or light shade is preferable. It varies considerably in height: sometimes it spreads out in a low mat only 100mm (4in) high, but it can also reach up to 0.5m (2ft) or over.

**9 *Ranunculus acris* 'Flore-pleno'**

This garden variety of the common buttercup makes an excellent border plant. Not surprisingly for a plant whose genus includes several aquatic plants, this hardy perennial does well in a moist soil. The mid-green leaves are in a deeply-cut and lobed palmate shape. Bright yellow flowers are produced throughout the summer.

The variety succeeds in most soils and situations and grows about 0.5m (2ft) high.

***Rheum*** (ornamental rhubarb)

Two species of this genus, which includes the edible rhubarb, are available for growing as ornamental foliage specimens. They are hardy herbaceous perennials.

*Rheum* should be grown in a sunny position. It flowers most

successfully in rich, moist soils.
*R. alexandrae* consists of glossy, oval, mid-green leaves supported by small stalks and large upright spikes of flowers which rise out of the centre of the foliage. The flowers are yellowy-cream coloured and tongue-shaped; they appear in late spring. Height: 0.5–1m (2–3ft).

**10 *R. palmatum*** has magnificent large, deeply-cut leaves of a green-red colour. 0.5–1m (2–3ft) long panicles of deep pink-red flowers appear during early summer. The foliage fades to green after flowering. Height: 1.5–2.5m (5–8ft).

***Sorbaria***

Fast-growing and hardy, this deciduous shrub has attractive pinnate leaves and white flowers.

*Sorbarias* are suitable for damp soils in sun or light shade.

**11 *S. aitchisonii*** has narrow pointed mid-green leaves similar to those of the ash tree. Plumes of small white flowers appear in late summer and early autumn. The species grows 1.8–2.7m (6–9ft) high with a spread of 2.5–2.7m (8–9ft).
*S. arborea* has mid-green toothed leaves in an elongated oval shape. 300mm (1ft) long pyramidal plumes of cream-white flowers are produced in summer. Height and spread: 2.5–4.5m (8–15ft).

***Symphoricarpos*** (snowberry)

These hardy berry-producing deciduous shrubs are suitable for growing in difficult situations which are both damp and shady.

**12 *S. albus*** has slightly grey-tinted mid-green leaves which are small and oval-shaped. Small pink flowers are produced in clusters from mid-summer to early autumn; these are followed by white berries which continue through the winter. 'Laevigatus' is a garden variety with more prominent berries.

The shrub is tolerant of most

soils and situations and grows 2m (6ft) high with a spread 2.5m (8ft).

**13 *Trollius* x *hybridus*** (globe flower)

This hardy herbaceous perennial has globe-shaped flowers, looking like large double buttercups; they appear in late spring or early summer. The mid- to dark green leaves are deeply lobed.

Several garden varieties are available, with flowers in different shades of yellow and orange. The plant may be grown in sun or half-shade and requires plenty of moisture; it is suitable for the margins of a stream or pond. Height: 0.5–1m (2–3ft).

***Vaccinium*** (bilberry, blueberry, cranberry)

This is a large genus of berry-bearing shrubs. Those described are deciduous and hardy.

*Vaccinium* thrives in sun or light shade in peaty or lime-free soils which are moisture-retentive.

**14 *V. corymbosum*** (swamp blueberry). This species has mid-green leaves in the shape of an ellipse with a pointed end; they assume a brilliant red colour in the autumn. Long racemes of pinkish white flowers appear in late spring and early summer. Blue-black berries ripen towards the end of the summer or the start of autumn. The fruit are edible and several named varieties are grown commercially for their fruit. Height: 1.2–1.8m (4–6ft); spread: 1.8–2.5m (6–8ft).

*V. myrtillus* (bilberry, wortleberry) has bright green oval leaves which turn purple and gold in autumn. Individual flowers, which are green-white flushed with pink, appear in late spring; they are followed by blue-black berries. The species grows 150–450mm (6–18in) high with a spread of 300–450mm (1–1½ft).

# Plants for cold and exposed sites

***Crataegus monogyna* 'Stricta'**
This is a particularly robust and hardy variety of the common hawthorn. It has glossy dark-green, lobed and toothed leaves carried on erect branches. White, heavily fragrant flowers cover the plant in late spring and are followed by small red haws. The shrub is tolerant of exposure, drought and waterlogging. Since the root system is weak, it tends to grow at an angle. It grows 7.5–9m (25–30ft) high with a spread of 4.5–6m (15–20ft).

***Cryptomeria japonica***
This hardy conifer, which is itself too large for most small gardens, has given rise to several smaller garden varieties.
*Cryptomeria* are tolerant of most soils and situations but will do best in slightly acid, deep, moist but well-drained soils, in full sun.
***C.j.* 'Elegans'.** This form retains its juvenile foliage and seldom grows more than 4.5m (15ft) high. Its foliage is blue-green in summer and an attractive bronze colour in winter.
***C.j.* 'Globosa Nana'.** A compact dwarf form, growing about 1m (3ft) tall, with pendulous mid-green foliage which turns slightly bluish in winter.
***C.j.* 'Spiralis'.** Known as 'granny's ringlets', this variety has foliage twisted in spirals round the branches. Some plants of this variety revert to the form of the species and grow into full-size trees.

**1 *Fraxinus excelsior***
(common ash)
This species has wide-spreading roots and should not, therefore, be planted too near to walls, fences or buildings. This characteristic, besides the fact that it may eventually reach 30m (100ft) high, means that it will not be suitable in very small gardens. It nonetheless has the advantage of extreme hardiness and will thrive in any normal garden soil in sun or half-shade, doing well in towns or by the sea.
There are several recommended garden varieties in addition to the type. 'Aurea' has golden yellow juvenile shoots and autumn foliage; 'Diversifolia' has unusual leaves, composed of one or three toothed leaflets; 'Pendula' is an attractive weeping tree.

**2 *Kerria japonica*** (Jew's mallow)
A bushy deciduous shrub of considerable hardiness, this species has glossy green, elegant branches and attractive bright green leaves. Rose-like single yellow flowers are carried during spring at the end of the previous year's shoots. The shrub will succeed in sun or partial shade in any garden soil; it has a height and spread of 1–2m (4–7ft).
***K.j.* 'Pleniflora'.** Commonly known as 'bachelor's buttons', this is a popular variety with double fluffy yellow-orange flowers. It is taller and of more upright habit than the type, reaching up to 3.5m (12ft) high.

**3 *Laburnum* x *watereri***
Along with *L. alpinum* and *L. anagyroides,* from which it is derived, this garden hybrid is hardy and resistant to wind and pollution. In late spring to early summer it bears masses of yellow flowers in hanging racemes. It can be grown in most soils and situations and reaches about 4.5m (15ft).
If the garden is used by young children, remember that all parts of this plant, but especially the seed pods, are poisonous.

***Larix decidua*** (European larch)
This is a tough, wind-resistant deciduous coniferous tree. It is narrowly conical in shape for most of its life, although eventually maturing into a large tree with a spreading top and wide low branches. The needle-like foliage starts green in spring and turns golden yellow by the end of autumn. Woody cones, small green or red female flowers and yellow male ones appear each year.
All larches thrive in any normal moist garden soil in an open sunny position.

**4 *Pieris floribunda***
The hardiest of a genus of compact evergreen flowering shrubs, this species has dark green leathery leaves and pyramidal clusters of small white, lily of the valley-like flowers borne in early spring. The variety 'Grandiflora' has particularly large flower clusters.
The shrub should be planted in moist, lime-free loam in partial shade. Height and spread: 1–2m (4–7 ft).

***Populus*** (poplar)
Most poplars survive considerable frost and exposure. They are fast-growing and tolerant of wet soil, pollution and saline winds.
***P.* x *serotina*.** This is one of the most frequently planted types of poplar. It has attractive glossy green, heart-shaped leaves; on the juvenile tree these have a coppery red tint. The species should be planted in an open position, where it is extremely fast-growing and may eventually reach 25m (70ft).
The variety 'Aurea' has leaves which are bright yellow in spring, green-yellow in summer and then brilliant yellow again in autumn.
***P. tremula*** (aspen). The rounded toothed leaves of this species are grey-green in summer and yellow in autumn. They rustle or tremble in the slightest breeze, a characteristic giving rise to its name. The aspen requires a moist soil; it is a less vigorous grower than *P.* x *serotina,* reaching an eventual height of 6–9m (20–30ft).
*P. candicans*: see VARIEGATED FOLIAGE PLANTS, page 216

**5 *Spiraea* x *arguta***
(bridal wreath)
One of the hardiest of a generally hardy genus of deciduous flowering shrubs. Magnificent clusters of small white flowers are borne during spring on slender arching branches. This hybrid should be planted in deep fertile soil in full sun. Height and spread: 2–2.5m (6–8ft).

***Tamarix***
Since it is extremely resistant to cold winds and frost, this deciduous shrub forms a useful windbreak in exposed situations, particularly on the coast. It does best in an open situation, thriving in any well-drained soil.
**6 *T. pentandra*.** This species has small pale green leaves which give the foliage a feathery texture. The slender branches bear small pink flowers in late summer. The variety 'Rubra' has deep red flowers. Height and spread: 3.5–4.5m (12–15ft).

**7 *Viburnum opulus*** (Guelder rose)
This is a bushy, upright, deciduous species of *Viburnum,* one of the hardiest of the genus. It has dark green maple-like leaves. In summer it produces heads of white flowers; these are followed by glistening red fruits in autumn and winter.
It should be grown in a position of full sun, in good moist soil. Height: up to 4.5m (15ft); spread: 3.5–4.5m (12–15ft).

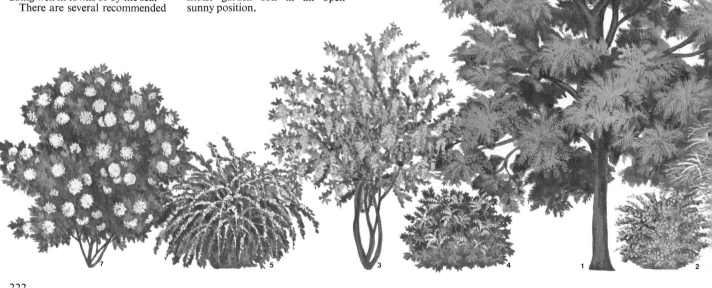

# Plants resistant to pollution

### Ceanothus x *delinianus*
This species, and the cultivars derived from it, do well in areas of industrial or urban pollution. It is a small to medium sized deciduous shrub which produces panicles of soft blue flowers in summer. *Ceanothus* needs full sun and good drainage; a lime-free soil is preferable.

**8** *C.* x **'Gloire de Versailles'.** This hybrid of the *delinianus* group is the most popular deciduous *Ceanothus*. It has splendid panicles of powder-blue flowers, is hardy and grows 2–2.5m (6–8ft) high.

### Chaenomeles x *superba*
This attractive deciduous spring-flowering shrub is vigorous and hardy. Along with other species of the same genus, it is resistant to pollution and does well in the urban environment. The leaves are dark green and glossy. The saucer-shaped flowers are orange, pink or red. Tolerant of most soils, it does best in an open sunny position. Height: up to 2m (7ft); spread: 1–2m (4–7ft).

Varieties include 'Boule de Feu' with red-orange flowers, 'Hever Castle' with pink flowers and 'Knap Hill Scarlet' with scarlet flowers.

*Chaenomeles speciosa*: see CLIMBERS AND SHRUBS FOR WALLS, page 196

### 9 Cistus x *purpureus*
An excellent hybrid rock rose, this is a vigorous, upright bush. It has grey-green, lance-shaped leaves and pink to purple, saucer-shaped flowers which are produced from late spring to mid-summer.

The species is tolerant of exposure to pollution and maritime winds and will grow in most well-drained soils; it is not fully hardy and requires a good deal of sun. Height: 1–1.5m (4–5ft); spread: 1m (4ft).

### 10 Colutea arborescens (bladder senna)
This flowering deciduous shrub is grown chiefly for its interesting seed pods which are a pale green colour heavily flushed with red. The leaves are small and light green; the flowers, which are yellow and similar in shape to those of the sweet pea, appear in summer.

It is hardy and tolerates most soils, doing best in a sunny position. Height and spread: 2.5m (8ft).

### Cotoneaster
The commonly grown species of this hardy shrub are adaptable to industrial and urban pollution.
*C. horizontalis, C. lacteus, C.* 'Rothschildianus' and *C. salicifolius flocossus*: see PLANTS TO ESTABLISH A FRAMEWORK, page 190
*C. conspicuus*: see EVERGREEN SHRUBS, page 192
*C. dammeri*: see GROUND COVER PLANTS, page 204

*C.* x *watereri*: see FAST-GROWING PLANTS FOR SCREENING, page 220

### Elaeagnus x *ebbingei*
This is a fast-growing evergreen hybrid whose large leaves are silvery underneath. Scented silvery flowers appear in autumn; orange fruit are produced in spring. It is an ideal plant for making an informal hedge or screen. It is tolerant of shade and all but shallow chalky soils and is resistant to wind and seaside exposure as well as to pollution. Height and spread: 3–4.5m (10–15ft).

*E. glabra* and *E. pungens* are also suitable for areas of pollution.
*E. pungens* 'Maculata': see VARIEGATED FOLIAGE PLANTS, page 216

### Forsythia
These popular spring-flowering shrubs do well in towns and areas of industrial pollution. See DECIDUOUS SHRUBS, page 191
*F. ovata.* This is a bushy species whose leaves sometimes turn yellow in autumn. The yellow flowers are slightly less abundant than those of other species of the genus, but they appear earlier in the new year. Height and spread: 1.2–1.5m (4–5ft).

### Garrya
These flowering evergreen shrubs, which have leathery leaves and usually prominent catkins, are resistant to both atmospheric pollution and maritime exposure. They will grow in all well-drained soils but require protection in cold districts.
*G. thuretti* has insignificant catkins but is a vigorous grower useful for creating a windbreak in wild localities. Height: 4.5m (15ft).

*G. elliptica*: see CLIMBERS AND SHRUBS FOR WALLS, page 196

### 11 Hydrangea macrophylla
The common hydrangea is an useful medium sized shrub often found in town gardens, where it tends to do well. The ovate leaves are pointed; they are shiny, light green and toothed. The flowers are borne in 150mm (6in) wide flat heads during mid- and late summer. Their colour depends on the soil; in alkaline soil they are pink or red-purple, in acid or neutral soils they tend to blue or purple.

The species should be grown in moisture-retentive loam enriched with compost or peat. Since it is only partially hardy it is best grown under a light canopy of trees or against a wall. Height and spread 1–2.5m (4–8ft).

There are numerous named varieties, in two groups, the Hortensias and the Lacecaps; the latter tend to be smaller than the former.

### Ilex (holly)
This is generally a very tough and adaptable family of evergreens. See PLANTS TO ESTABLISH A FRAMEWORK, page 190
*I. cornuta.* A dense, slow-growing species, it has distinctive rectangular leaves usually with five spines. The female plants produce red berries in winter. Height: 2.5–3m (8–10ft); spread: 1.5–2m (5–7ft).
*I. aquifolium*: see FORMAL, INFORMAL AND DWARF HEDGES, page 194
*I. aquifolium* 'Flavescens': see GOLDEN AND YELLOW FOLIAGE PLANTS, page 214

11    14    12    8    15    9    16    13    10

### Laburnum
This hardy deciduous tree, which thrives in towns, lives up to its common name of 'golden rain tree'. During late spring and early summer, the branches are draped with dramatic masses of bright yellow, slightly scented, flowers borne in pendulous racemes.

The various species are fairly similar, growing between 3m (10ft) and 6m (20ft) high; they will grow in any ordinary, well-drained garden soil in sun or partial shade. All parts of this shrub are poisonous, the seed pods being particularly dangerous; in gardens where children play these should be taken off and burnt.

*L. x watereri*: see PLANTS FOR COLD AND EXPOSED SITES, page 222

### Malus (crab apple)
These small to medium sized trees are all resistant to industrial and urban pollution. See PLANTS TO ESTABLISH A FRAMEWORK, page 190 *M.* 'Profusion' and *M. x lemoinei*: see RED AND PURPLE FOLIAGE PLANTS, page 215

### Philadelphus (mock orange)
All these hardy, deciduous, scented flowering shrubs tolerate polluted conditions.
*P.* 'Belle Etoile': see SCENTED FLOWERS AND FOLIAGE, page 218
*P. coronarius* 'Aurea': see GOLDEN AND YELLOW FOLIAGE PLANTS, page 214
*P.* 'Virginal': see DECIDUOUS SHRUBS, page 191

### 12 Prunus avium (wild cherry)
Vigorous and hardy, this ornamental cherry bears clusters of white cup-shaped flowers in spring. 'Plena' has a mass of splendid double flowers. The leaves of *P. avium* sometimes turn crimson in autumn. It grows up to 12m (40ft) high in any normal soil, preferably—but not necessarily—in a sunny position.

Other types of *Prunus* which are resistant to urban and industrial pollution are *P. amygdalo-persica* 'Pollardii', *P. cerasifera*, *P. dulcis* and *P. padus*.

### Pyracantha (firethorn)
A genus of hardy evergreen shrubs which are very tough and tolerant of polluted conditions. Their flowers appear in mid-summer, to be followed by orange or red berries in autumn. They thrive in any normal garden soil in sun or partial shade.
*P. coccinea.* This hardy species of firethorn has spiny branches and pointed mid-green leaves. The white flowers are followed by bright red berries.
*P. crenulata.* This species is similar to *P. coccinea*. It is usually represented in the garden by the variety 'Rogersiana'.
### 13 P.c. 'Flava'. Another attractive variety, which produces bright yellow berries.

### Rhododendron luteum
This is a popular azalea which is tough, vigorous and adaptable. The winter buds and young shoots are sticky and the leaves take on rich autumn colours. The flowers, appearing in late spring, are a rich yellow colour with a strong fragrance. This species shares with other rhododendrons the need for acid soil. Height: 2–3m (6–10ft); spread: 1–2m (4–6ft).

The Knap Hill azaleas also do well in polluted areas. These varieties have trumpet-shaped, usually scentless, flowers in a wide range of colours opening in late spring. When grown in an open position, the shrubs reach 1–2m (4–6ft).
*R. ponticum*: See PLANTS TO ESTABLISH A FRAMEWORK, page 190

### 14 Ribes sanguineum
This species of flowering currant is deciduous and hardy. The leaves are lobed, mid- to dark green on top and paler underneath. Long pendents of deep red-pink coloured flowers are borne in spring. Blue-black berries may appear in autumn.

The species will do well in any normal soil, in sun or light shade. It grows to 2–3m (7–10ft) and spreads 1.5–2m (5–7ft).

### Sambucus canadensis 'Maxima' (American elder)
This variety of elder has large mid-green leaves up to 450mm (18in) long and bears huge pink-purple flower heads 300mm (1ft) or more across. These flowers, which appear in mid-summer, are followed by purple-black fruits. Hardy and deciduous, this shrub will grow in most soils and situations. It should be pruned each spring to ensure plenty of new shoots. Height: 3–3.5m (10–12ft).
*S. racemosa.* This species is also

resistant to urban and industrial pollution. See PLANTS TO ESTABLISH A FRAMEWORK, page 190

### Syringa (lilac)
Lilac tends to do well in areas of urban and industrial pollution. See DECIDUOUS SHRUBS, page 191

### 15 Ulex europaeus (common gorse)
This tough, hardy, evergreen shrub consists of virtually leafless spiny dark green shoots and golden yellow flowers. These are at their best in spring but continue to appear right through to the winter. 'Plenus' is a compact form with double flowers.

Gorse does well in poor soil in full sun. Height and spread: 1.5–2.5m (5–8ft).

### 16 Ulmus glabra 'Pendula' (weeping wych elm)
Along with many other elms, this species is hardy and resistant to any sort of pollution. With its attractive oval leaves and its wide flat-topped weeping shape, it makes an excellent specimen tree for a lawn.

Elms do best in an open sunny position but tolerate almost any soil. They reach to 6m (20ft) or more.

# Plants for a seaside garden

*Arbutus unedo*
This species of strawberry tree is generally hardy and evergreen. It has rough bark which tends to peel and handsome dark green, glossy leaves. Pendant panicles of white or pink flowers are borne during autumn and early winter at the same time as red-orange, strawberry-like fruits. 'Rubra' is a bushy variety with red flowers.
The tree is lime-tolerant and does best in a relatively sheltered sunny position. It grows about 4.5–6m (15–20ft) high with a spread of 3m (10ft) or more.

*Atriplex* (salt bush)
There are two shrubby species of this family which will thrive in light, sandy, saline soil. Both species are grown for their foliage, the flowers being inconspicuous. They are hardy evergreens, suitable for creating windbreaks.
*A. canescens.* The grey sage bush has narrow light grey leaves and grows about 2m (7ft) high.
*A. halimus.* The Tree Purslane has silvery grey leaves and grows rather taller.

7 *Castanea sativa* (sweet chestnut, Spanish chestnut)
This hardy deciduous tree is fast growing and tolerates saline winds. The leaves are mid-green, prominently veined, toothed and pointed. The bark is ribbed. Yellow-green catkins are borne in mid-summer and are followed by prickly burrs containing nuts.
The species thrives in any good garden soil and prefers an open sunny position. It may eventually grow very tall and so will only be suitable for the larger small garden.

*Crataegus* (ornamental thorn)
Thorn bushes are extremely hardy and adaptable and will do well in windswept coastal districts. For a general description and *C. coccinea*: see PLANTS FOR AUTUMN COLOUR, page 212
*C. monogyna* 'Stricta': see PLANTS FOR COLD AND EXPOSED SITES, page 222
*C. oxyacantha* 'Coccinea Plena': see PLANTS FOR DAMP SITES, page 220

*Elaeagnus umbellata*
This wide-spreading and vigorous, deciduous shrub has leathery green leaves with silvery undersides. Fragrant creamy white flowers appear in late spring and early summer. In autumn, the plant is heavily laden with orange-red berries.
The species will grow even in poor chalk soils. It is best planted in full sun. Height: 3–4.5m (10–15ft); spread: 3–5.5m (10–18ft).

*Escallonia*
Most of this genus of flowering evergreen shrubs thrive in coastal areas. The species average a height of 2.5m (8ft); they usually flower in summer and early autumn. See PLANTS TO ESTABLISH A

FRAMEWORK, page 190, in particular for E. 'Donard Radiance' and E. rubra
*E. macrantha*: see FORMAL, INFORMAL AND DWARF HEDGES, page 194

19 *Fuchsia magellanica* 'Gracilis'
Hardiest of the fuchsias, this species is useful for informal hedging and does well in seaside gardens. The pendant, bell-like flowers consist of a red tube and sepals with purple petals and long protruding stamens; they are borne from mid-summer through into autumn. There are several named varieties. 'Gracilis' is a garden variety with particularly elegant slender flowers.
Fuchsias should be planted in full sun or half shade in any normal soil which has been enriched with additional humus in the form of peat or leaf-mould. The species grows 1–2m (4–6ft) with a spread of 0.5–1m (2–4ft).

*Genista* (broom)
Most of these hardy, deciduous or almost leafless shrubs will do well by the sea. Brooms bear masses of yellow flowers in late spring or early summer. They should be grown in sunny positions. A light soil is preferable but the plants will succeed in most acid or neutral soils and are lime-tolerant.
*G. aetnensis* and *G. cinerea*: see DECIDUOUS SHRUBS, page 191
*G. hispanica*: see GROUND COVER PLANTS, page 204

*Griselinia littoralis*
This large evergreen shrub does well on the coast.
See PLANTS TO ESTABLISH A FRAMEWORK, page 190

*Halimium*
A genus of small evergreen shrubs which are suitable for growing in rock gardens, especially near the sea. The family is related to the sun or rock rose (*Cistus*) and is grown primarily for its attractive yellow flowers which are similar to small single roses. The plants require full sun and will thrive in any light, well-drained soil.
*H. libanotis.* This is a species of erect habit with linear leaves, which are mid-green above and whitish underneath; yellow flowers appear in early summer. It is hardy and grows 0.5–1m (2–3ft); spread: 1–2m (3–6ft).

*Hebe*
All species of this genus are suitable for seaside gardens. For a general description of the family and for *H. speciosa* 'Midsummer Beauty', see PLANTS TO ESTABLISH A FRAMEWORK, page 190
20 *H. brachysiphon.* This is a bushy evergreen shrub with dark green, narrowly ovate leaves. It is not a plant with a very long life, however. Masses of white flowers are borne in early and mid-summer. The species is hardy and grows up to 2m (6ft) high with a spread of 1–2m (4–6ft).

*Helichrysum*
The low-growing shrubby species of this family are chiefly grown for their attractive grey-green woolly foliage. They are half-hardy and do best in a sunny sheltered position in a well-drained soil.
21 *H. splendidum.* This species forms a mound of silvery grey foliage. Small yellow flowers are borne in tightly packed globes during mid- and late summer. Height: 375mm (1¼ft); spread: 1m (3ft).

22 *Hippophae rhamnoides* (sea buckthorn)
This hardy deciduous shrub is grown mainly for its attractive berries. The branches are covered with sharp spines and small, thin silvery leaves. The spring-time flowers are yellow, though relatively inconspicuous. So long as male and female plants are grown together, the latter will bear thick clusters of bright orange berries during autumn and winter.
The plant can be grown in any ordinary garden soil and does particularly well in sandy soils by the sea, where it can be used as an excellent windbreak. It is a bushy shrub which normally stands about 3m (10ft) high, but it can sometimes reach tree proportions of up to 9m (30ft).

*Olearia gunniana*
This evergreen shrub is suitable for coastal gardens in all but the severest winters. It has broad oval-shaped leaves which are glossy mid-green above and grey-white underneath. Masses of white daisy-like flowers appear in clusters during mid- and late summer.
A sunny sheltered position in well-drained loam is the ideal growing situation, but the plant is fairly adaptable to less than ideal conditions. Height: 1–1.5m (4–5ft); spread: 1m (4ft).
Most other species of this genus are also suitable for seaside gardens, though some are considerably less hardy.
*O. haastii*: See EVERGREEN SHRUBS, page 192

*Phlomis*
Of this large genus of shrubs, sub-shrubs and herbaceous perennials only a few are suitable for growing in gardens.
*P. fruticosa* (Jerusalem sage). This is a useful plant for herbaceous borders in a seaside garden, except in very cold areas where it will be susceptible to frost. It is a shrubby evergreen with woolly grey-green, wedge-shaped, leaves; the yellow flowers appear in early and mid-summer. It grows about 1m (4ft) high with a spread of about 2m (6ft). A sunny position and a light, well-drained soil are necessary.
*P. viscosa.* This herbaceous perennial has large, ribbed, mid-green leaves in an elongated heart-shape. The yellow flowers, which appear in early and mid-summer, circle the upright stems in tiers one above the other. The species grows

0.8–1m (2½–4ft) high and will succeed in any garden soil in a sunny position.

*Phormium tenax*
This spiky-leaved evergreen perennial is resistant to saline winds.
*P. t.* 'Purpureum': See RED AND PURPLE FOLIAGE PLANTS, page 215
*P. t.* 'Variegatum': See VARIEGATED FOLIAGE PLANTS, page 216

23 *Pittosporum tenuifolium*
One of the hardiest of a somewhat tender family of evergreen flowering plants, this species is suitable for growing in a seaside garden. It is a useful large shrub or small tree to plant either by itself or for forming a hedge. The pale green leaves with wavy edges are borne on black stems. The flowers are dark purple in colour and are produced in late spring.
The shrub should be planted where it will be sheltered from north and east winds in any fertile garden soil which is well-drained. Height: up to 4.5m (15ft); spread: 1.5–2m (5–7ft).
'Silver Queen', which has leaves suffused silvery grey, is an attractive specimen shrub.
*P. t.* 'Warnham Gold': See RED AND PURPLE FOLIAGE PLANTS, page 215

24 *Senecio maritima* (syn. *Cineraria maritima*)
Although this almost hardy evergreen sub-shrub will survive winters in many areas, it is usually treated as a half-hardy annual. The plant has an attractive silvery appearance due to the grey-white woolly hairs which cover the stems and the deeply lobed leaves. The yellow flowers, which are not particularly spectacular, are produced from mid-summer through to autumn.
The species, which grows about 0.5m (2ft) high, should be grown in a reasonably sunny position in any normal soil. Favourite named varieties include 'Diamond', with almost white, deeply cut leaves, and 'Silver Dust', with fern-like grey-white leaves. Herbaceous perennials and shrubby species of the same genus are also suitable for the seaside garden.
*S. clivorum*: See RED AND PURPLE FOLIAGE PLANTS, page 215
*S. laxifolius*: See SILVER AND GREY FOLIAGE PLANTS, page 216

25 *Spartium junceum* (Spanish broom)
A mass of brilliant golden yellow, sweet-pea-like flowers appear during summer on the slender, almost leafless, branches of this hardy deciduous shrub. It grows best in sandy or alkaline soils in a sunny position. Height: 2.5–3m (8–10ft); spread: 2–2.5m (6–8ft).

*Yucca*
This interesting and unusual flowering evergreen shrub does well near the sea.
See ARCHITECTURAL PLANTS, page 219

# living
## in the
# garden

*There is a strong emphasis on today's garden as an outdoor living area; the contents of the garden create its individual atmosphere and reflect the life of its owners. According to your choice of furniture and decoration, a small garden can become a calm retreat, a children's play area or a place for entertaining your friends.*

# Seating for an outdoor life

The popularity of outdoor living has brought about a range of outdoor furniture as wide and varied as that for indoors. Your choice will similarly depend on usage and the style of the surroundings but one other important consideration should be durability and water resistance.

If the seating is to form part of a dining area it should be located as close to the house as possible, on a terrace if you have one, for carrying food in and out. Remember to allocate more space than the furniture itself takes up; allow enough room round the table for the food to be served and enough space between table and chairs for people to sit round in comfort and for chairs to be pushed back. The area should be private and sheltered from the wind—a pergola with climbing plants grown over it would serve both purposes admirably.

The design of seats and tables should suit the site, where possible, so that they make an attractive point of interest when they are not in use. Chairs themselves fall into two categories of use: the upright ones used for working at and for dining, and the low cushioned ones for resting and dozing. Those for relaxation should be designed for comfort, deep enough to lie back in when you are reading or sunbathing on a hot afternoon. They may have a headrest or be upholstered, though heavy upholstery is not a good idea as it gets dirty quickly and must be covered up or the chair brought inside in wet weather. There are now several elaborate versions of the sun lounger, but traditional deck chairs still have many advantages. They fold up and occupy the minimum storage space, and the canvas can easily be replaced.

If you have trees in the garden, a hammock, again one of the simplest and cheapest traditional forms of seating, is possibly also the most comfortable, though it is probably only suitable for the young and agile. Older people often prefer the more upholstered swing seats with awnings, which are shady and easier to sit in than the low lounger or swinging hammock. In general, plain fabric is preferable to patterned as it is less garish, particularly under bright sunlight.

Upright seating ranges from spindly ironwork chairs, which are often uncomfortable and hardly strong enough for the strain of outdoor use, to sturdy timber benches, often forming a single unit with a table, which even children find indestructible. Choose the style and strength to suit your needs and remember that a few cushions will soften hard surfaces and add variety to the colours. Benches, built-in or free-standing, are always a good idea for family meals outside and they are easy to construct. Built-in garden furniture is not only cheaper and space-saving but it can also strengthen the lines of the garden design. The versatility it gives means that a seating area can be combined with a barbecue corner, for example, or a low retaining wall, especially if it is in a warm, peaceful spot with a good view. Any section of a tree trunk, or slab of stone with a smooth level surface, can be used as a bench or a table top.

Timber is the most commonly used material for outdoor furniture, since it is adaptable to many styles and the hardwoods can be left out all year round without damage, as long as they have non-rust metal fittings. Furniture with a natural wood finish benefits from a seasonal treatment with linseed oil. Painted timber is smarter and more sophisticated in appearance but it needs annual repainting. Timber tables are ideal for garden use; the bigger they are the better, because a garden table in a warm position will be used for everything—preparing food, sewing, playing cards and children's play or homework. A bright tablecloth or some elegant place settings will transform it into an attractive dining area for warm summer evenings.

Portable seating units are an excellent solution for a roof or balcony, and low wooden ones like these could be made at home. They can be softened by large removable cushions, rearranged to suit different needs or stacked up to clear the balcony. They also save space by doubling up as storage units. Moulded plastic furniture is equally at home inside a modern apartment or out of doors in summer

Tubular metal-framed chairs have the simple, uncluttered lines appropriate for a sophisticated outdoor living area. With the plain concrete table, which echoes the paving slabs, they create an intimate corner which is still an integral part of the garden

The canvas-seated wooden 'director's chair' is a more elaborate version of the traditional folding deck chair. Its tilting back makes it comfortable for both relaxing and eating outside. The slatted table is semi-circular, designed to save space on a balcony

Informal garden settings call for simple furniture designs executed in natural materials. Where these can be built round existing features in the garden their placing looks more natural too. Built-in furniture also saves carrying things to and from the house, though these delicate basketweave chairs would need to be brought indoors during bad weather. A slatted top is a good idea for tables constantly exposed to the elements as it allows water to run off

A sturdy old wooden table is versatile enough to serve as a useful work surface or as a dining table for outdoor meals. An occasional coating of wax polish will protect the table top through many years of outdoor life. Traditional rush-seat chairs are ideal for a terrace but would need to be brought inside during the winter

229

A combined wooden table and bench is especially suitable for a family with children. The unit is strongly built and will stand up to fairly rough treatment. Timber furniture which is left out all year must be treated annually with preservative

Concrete is the most indestructible material for outdoor use. Its severe appearance can be tempered by combining it with other materials, like these wooden seats

Oriental woven cane and bamboo furniture has the elegance appropriate for long relaxed summer days; it is now available in a variety of styles, some highly ornate. However it is too delicate to withstand bad weather and cannot take much heavy treatment; it is not a good idea for children

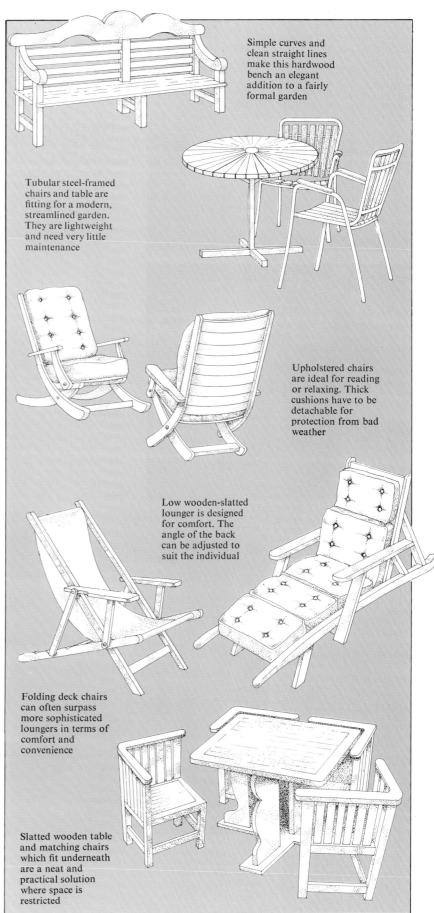

Simple curves and clean straight lines make this hardwood bench an elegant addition to a fairly formal garden

Tubular steel-framed chairs and table are fitting for a modern, streamlined garden. They are lightweight and need very little maintenance

Upholstered chairs are ideal for reading or relaxing. Thick cushions have to be detachable for protection from bad weather

Low wooden-slatted lounger is designed for comfort. The angle of the back can be adjusted to suit the individual

Folding deck chairs can often surpass more sophisticated loungers in terms of comfort and convenience

Slatted wooden table and matching chairs which fit underneath are a neat and practical solution where space is restricted

A sturdy hammock slung between tree trunks can be the perfect place for dozing on a hot afternoon. It is a good solution where space is limited as it does not clutter up the ground and can be taken down easily when not used

Seating which forms part of the overall garden design is often the most successful. It merges into the garden discreetly when not in use, especially if built in a material used elsewhere in the garden

# Cooking in the open air

A barbecue meal is an excellent way of exploiting your garden as a place in which to live and entertain your friends. On a warm night, cooking and eating outdoors is a great pleasure, whether you are entertaining on a lavish scale or merely amusing children with the excitement of cooking sausages over a fire.

The kind of barbecue to suit you will depend very much on how often you mean to use it, the vagaries of the weather in unpredictable climates, and the atmosphere of the garden as a whole. A makeshift structure will be quite adequate if you only cook outside twice a year, for instance. There are endless elaborations, incorporating powered rotisseries, drip trays for fat and electric heaters to light the charcoal or even to cook the food. However, these sophisticated and costly arrangements occupy a large area and would probably dominate a small garden. They are also unsuitable except where the weather permits use of the barbecue all year round. A portable cast iron barbecue, known as a Japanese *hibachi*, such as a brazier with single or double grills, or a circular barbecue on a tripod, may be more suitable.

There are a number of practical considerations in positioning a free-standing barbecue which apply equally of course to designing a built-in one. Remember for safety reasons to keep the barbecue away from overhanging trees; permission from the fire authorities may be necessary in some cases. A barbecue is best placed fairly near the kitchen so that you can carry food in and out easily. The rack for food should be wider than the fire itself if possible, so that you can push cooked food off the direct heat and still keep it hot. The food rack should be at a convenient height so that you need not bend over the heat—600 mm (2 ft) is a good average height.

With a built-in barbecue the other pressing question must be how it harmonizes with the house and garden. The masonry of a barbecue should be chosen to match the paving and walling materials of the garden, though avoid using substances which will be disfigured by the marks of fat and wood smoke.

Elaborate portable barbecues (top) are equipped to allow cooking methods other than grilling and can cater for quite large parties. A trolley base allows the fire to be moved out of the wind, but take care that hot ash does not blow back at you

This roughly built arrangement (above) contains all the essential elements of a barbecue: a fire with air space underneath to create a draught, enclosed in a firebox to hold in the heat, and with a rack above for food

The shape and masonry of a built-in barbecue should play an effective part in the overall design of the garden. The materials and circular shape of this sunken grill tie in with that of the raised pool and concrete step to make a pleasing composition

A sophisticated outdoor kitchen requires plenty of working surfaces, but these need not necessarily be entirely functional

in design; here ceramic tiles surround an elegant table-top barbecue which can be covered when out of use

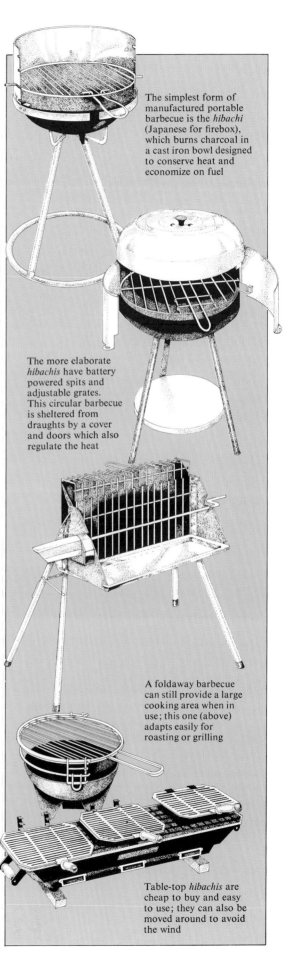

The simplest form of manufactured portable barbecue is the *hibachi* (Japanese for firebox), which burns charcoal in a cast iron bowl designed to conserve heat and economize on fuel

The more elaborate *hibachis* have battery powered spits and adjustable grates. This circular barbecue is sheltered from draughts by a cover and doors which also regulate the heat

A foldaway barbecue can still provide a large cooking area when in use; this one (above) adapts easily for roasting or grilling

Table-top *hibachis* are cheap to buy and easy to use; they can also be moved around to avoid the wind

# Bringing the garden to life at night

Lighting in the garden is either for practical purposes, for guiding visitors safely along paths and drives and illuminating your house number, or can be employed for decoration. Where there is little or no street lighting, several low-lying diffuse lights along the line of the drive and the access paths between the road, the house and the garage, are a virtual necessity to light hidden obstacles and steps. Try out different strengths and positions for the lights before you wire them up permanently. Lighting the living area of the garden makes it pleasant for entertaining or sitting out on warm evenings. A special outdoor lighting system will be necessary if the house lights are not sufficient. Try to strike a balance between flooding the area with blinding white light (the only possible point of this is to keep off burglars) and merely creating a sense of gloom which only emphasizes the surrounding darkness.

The outdoor lighting apparatus available is varied, including low voltage coloured lights intended to light ponds and swimming pools underwater. An element of fantasy can enter your design here, but beware of dominating pools or plants with a garish pattern of unnatural colour. Blossoming trees and shrubs or bare branches under the snow or frost can look magnificent when lit. Lanterns hanging in trees will cast moving patterns of shadow while spotlights from below will show up the intricacy of the foliage, leaving the light source mysteriously concealed.

Setting up a large outdoor electrical system, when the leads must be buried underground, is a professional job, as the electricity authorities must approve the design of the circuit. All fitments and leads should of course be waterproof. Electric lights on the external walls of the house or close to it can be connected directly to the power points inside the house, but again they should be tightly waterproofed.

The easiest way to provide temporary lighting for parties is either to have a string of electric fairy lights which you arrange round the garden, or to use one of a variety of candles (floating on a pool if you have one), flares and oil lamps. Any form of exposed light should, of course, be well safeguarded, especially when children are about.

Light from a hidden source shining at night on sculpture, pools and plants can form a mysterious and impressive composition to be seen from a terrace or window. It is usually more effective to create a striking contrast between the patch of illuminated ground and the surrounding darkness than to cast a general glow over the whole garden. Here bright light brings a Japanese-style corner of a garden into strong relief

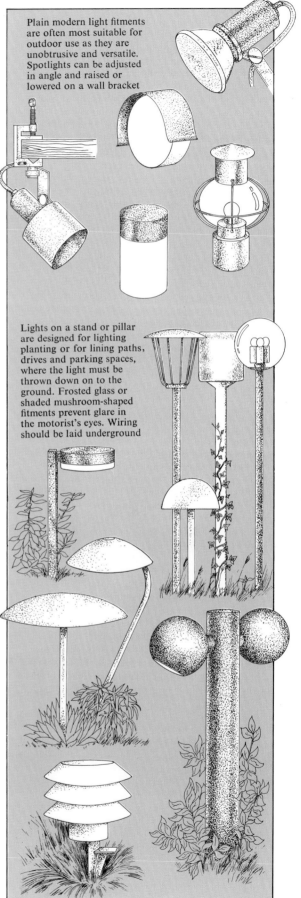

A group of spotlights in a tall tree (above) is easy to install and illuminates intricate foliage patterns from below. It will also shed general ground light downwards, perhaps on to a dining area

Lights on fences and walls (right), or over the front door or garage entrance, are almost indispensable in the country. Street lights can replace them to some extent in urban areas, but they form a welcome guide for visitors nevertheless

Plain modern light fitments are often most suitable for outdoor use as they are unobtrusive and versatile. Spotlights can be adjusted in angle and raised or lowered on a wall bracket

The shape and texture of natural objects, often overlooked in daylight, benefit from a concentrated light which emphasizes their special qualities. The mushroom light (left) casts light down on the lichened rock and contrasting foliage while the fitment itself remains as unobtrusive as possible

Near to the house no special wiring is required for installing outside lamps. Subdued concealed lighting (below) allows the terrace to be used at night

Lights on a stand or pillar are designed for lighting planting or for lining paths, drives and parking spaces, where the light must be thrown down on to the ground. Frosted glass or shaded mushroom-shaped fitments prevent glare in the motorist's eyes. Wiring should be laid underground

# Plain pots, elaborate urns

Flowers in pots, tubs and boxes can create a garden on their own, with little trouble and less space. There is a wide range of containers on the market, but almost any receptacle which has drainage holes in the bottom can be put to use, as long as it is reasonably frost resistant. Good drainage is very important for all containers as the build-up of sour water will rot the roots of the plant or freeze round them in frosty weather. You can make drainage holes in wooden and plastic pots by burning them with a red hot poker.

Achieving harmony between the shape, size and decoration of the pot and the plant which it contains is very important. A rich and showy plant, far from needing an equally elaborate container, is better suited by a simple one which will set it off to the best advantage. Some pots, overhung with foliage, need hardly show at all, while others are a major decorative feature, more impressive than the plant itself. If the plant is on a high ledge, of course, more of the pot will be visible than if the plant is at ground level. Generally speaking, the elaborately decorated urns and classical style pots look best in a fairly formal style of garden, while simpler pots with overhanging foilage and flowers are suited to a modern garden.

Many styles of container are available: antique, facsimile antique, traditional and rustic besides emphatically modern designs in timber, stone, terracotta and concrete, to name only the most obvious. The modern materials such as asbestos, plastic and reconstituted stone have many advantages as well, both as facsimiles of natural material or treated on their own merits. They are lighter, cheaper and often longer lasting than the materials they imitate. Unglazed terracotta, which is popular though becoming increasingly expensive, comes in many shapes and sizes. Timber is probably one of the most commonly used materials, as it is relatively cheap and, with the right treatment, durable.

Asbestos is an appropriate material for containers which are modern and functional in design. It is particularly suitable for large pots as it makes them light and easy to carry when full of earth

A low, shallow container placed on the ground will focus all the attention on the plants growing in it. A plain, modern pot like this concrete saucer-shaped one is best; choose flowering plants to overhang and create a colourful display

Wooden tubs or half barrels are best left plain for a rural situation but painting them black or white makes them appropriate for an urban setting. Painting will also preserve the wood

A terracotta 'parsley pot' allows a variety of plants to spill out at different levels. A mixture of flowering annuals and evergreens creates all-year-round interest

Endless possibilities present themselves for improvised containers. Here an old coal scuttle with holes drilled in the bottom forms an effective foil for the ornamental gourd

The square shape and panelled design of this fibreglass container is reminiscent of the 'Versailles tubs' made in silver for Louis XIV. They suit formal, sophisticated gardens particularly well

Terracotta pots come in a range of traditional Spanish and Italian designs varying from very simple to very ornate. This large, decorated pot is ideal for an upright plant

Always consider the siting of containers. A group of pots and tubs of different materials can make an effective display and emphasize the shapes and textures of the plants

A sink garden must be planted *in situ* as the stone container will be virtually immovable when filled with wet earth. A

low, wide container allows for a considered arrangement of rock, stones, lichen and varied foliage

237

# Sculpture for the garden

Far too many people regard choosing sculpture for the garden as a matter of dotting facsimile classical statues around the available space with little regard for their effect on the overall design. In this situation the eye becomes confused and restless, which is the reverse of the effect that sculpture should have: to guide the eye firmly and set off the particular harmony of the plants and their sculptured shape. A statue should either draw the eye to a single point, the visual focus of the garden, or it should give a pleasant surprise as it suddenly becomes visible half hidden in foliage.

The choice of statuary or a piece of sculpture for your garden is, even more than most things, essentially personal; there are nevertheless several important general points to consider. The piece of sculpture should be large or emphatic enough to be effective when seen at a distance against a broken patterned background of foilage. The atmosphere of the garden can be considerably changed by a single statue and one successful statue is better than several which vie for attention.

Naturally, real antique and modern statuary tends to have very strong character; you might well plan the garden around it, not vice versa. The same definite impact is of course transmitted to facsimile antique statues, which should have a setting suitable to their style. Classical statuary is very often placed overlooking a pool and the surrounding plants, forming a composed corner over which the statue presides. The need for consideration and restraint applies to any kind of sculpture in the garden, whether it is a genuine Henry Moore, or simply a shape carved by you out of driftwood.

The contrasts of shape and texture supplied by a single piece of sculpture in the garden can be suggested by a thoughtful grouping of natural objects such as plants and stones (above)

Where a whole garden is laid out in a particular style, here the Japanese (right), the plants, paving and sculpture all contribute equally to the final considered design

Any statue, sensitively placed, can create a striking impression. Even this small statuette, seen in outline and delicately framed by foliage and masonry, forms a focal point of the garden

Classical statuary can be a commanding focus in a garden but its placing is critical. A line of vision has been planned here, through arches and hedges, to culminate in the statue positioned in a niche

Abstract sculpture must be strong and emphatically designed if it is not to look dwarfed by the larger scale outside. Plants and paving can be used to reinforce it in its garden setting (right)

A small statue, placed at the base of a tree, provides a point of visual interest. Weathered and stained, the white stone figure harmonizes with its environment (below)

Topiary on a grand scale can introduce a touch of humour into the garden, particularly where animals are represented (left). Clipped abstract designs are more dignified and formal

A large pot or urn which is too tall for planting can be treated as a sculptural element. It will have an obvious affinity with the foliage in a garden setting

# Formal and natural pools

Water has been a major element of garden design ever since pre-Christian times, not only as a decorative feature but because it also served a practical purpose in lowering the air temperature and being a cooling element in a hot climate. A pool carefully placed in relation to the contours and atmosphere of the garden is still a very compelling part of the overall design. Water not only brings light and movement into the garden, it is also a very versatile feature; it can be a lively presence, glittering and bubbling in the background, or a tranquil element, a calm shining surface in which plants and buildings are reflected. The sound of playing water is soothing to the ear and can now be valuable to block out the noise of city traffic or neighbours' voices.

If it is conspicuously placed, a pool or fountain is as effective a focal point in a garden as a statue or building. On the other hand, a quiet pond at the end of the garden can be a delightful surprise when discovered. There are a few general rules about siting a pool, which may seem obvious but are in fact often forgotten. Water should be in sunlight at least part of the year, making it come to life and shine and encourage the growth of water plants. It is unwise to site a pond under trees, which will shed their leaves and foul the water. Wind will also blow a high jet fountain about the garden unless it has a wide surround or is in a sheltered position.

Formal pools which are an artificial architectural feature can be at any level and can in fact be raised so that the surround forms a seat. This is also safer if children use the garden as it is beyond their reach. With a formal outline, the edging should be neat, crisp and probably paved. It is possible, though not necessarily appropriate, to grow plants round the edges of a formal, concrete-built pool. The occasional specimen plant, however, looks effective and submerged plants in containers can break up and soften the surface area of the pool.

An informal, natural-looking pond can be made cheaply with plastic sheeting. Care must be taken, however, to conceal the plastic, lining the bottom preferably with gravel and the sides with pebbles or boulders, which will hold down the sheet as well. Having introduced a balanced proportion of submerged, oxygenating plants, you can rely on nature to make the pond harmonize with the landscape. Marsh plants outside the plastic sheet need very little care and it is also possible to introduce a whole population of insects, snails and fish so that it functions as a self-cleaning and self-supporting freshwater pond.

The treatment of informal, natural ponds can present great difficulty. Any decorative additions will entirely dispell the illusion that the pond is natural. A variety of plants grown in the marshy soil at the water's edge helps to create the atmosphere of a natural pond formed from a spring; it also adds to the sense of secrecy and stillness. The marsh plants and rocks around this modest pond contrast with the regular paving along one edge, which links the pond to the rest of the garden

A small, formal pool harmonizes best with the uncluttered shapes and materials of a garden designed on modern lines. The geometric outline of a concrete-built pool should remain crisp and not be obscured by plants at the edge, though submerged, container-grown plants can look attractive within the pool. The flat surface of a formal pool will be softened by the moving water of an overflow and the ripples created. A single jet fountain effectively brings life to a still pool, especially when it catches the sunlight

The effect desired may be a still, mirror-like surface, in which water reflections create the interest. The glass doors and the water surface complement each other here and the reflection of seats and flower pots in the water gives a sense of peace and space for those sitting on the terrace. Paving laid to overhang the water's edge hides the concrete basin of the pool and provides an attractive line of shadow round it

With a large pond, stepping stones may be needed to provide easy access to all of the garden. Where a pool is formal in outline, stepping stones should be square or rectangular, preferably echoing the paving slabs surrounding it. These flat, round stepping stones of concrete are in character with the boulder beach edging to the natural-looking pond and also reflect the circular shape of the lily pads through which they pass

The edging of a pool is one of the most important considerations and the simpler it is kept the more effective the pool will look. The repeated concrete circles here echo the shape of the deep round pool. The seashore pebbles around the edge repeat those at the bottom of the pool, which, as the water moves over them, create a constantly changing surface, patterned with light and shadow

# Where the children play

There is little you can do to prevent young children making the whole garden into their own territory. When they are older, of course, you can replan the garden for a quieter life, converting the sandpit into a formal pool or the climbing frame into a pergola. Until this time, adaptability and inventiveness are the keynotes when designing the children's play area.

A paved terrace is essential near the house, with good drainage so that it dries out as soon as possible after rain. As long as this paving is not raised above ground level, a small child can use a tricycle on it and play games in full view of the house. A sandpit filled with sharp sand can be sunk close by, below the paving level, with perhaps a shelf inside, on which the children can make sand pies. Alternatively, a sandpit raised above the level of the paving will prevent the sandy mess spreading. Later on this might be converted into a paddling pool but if you wish to have both a sandpit and a pool, remember to keep them far apart or there will simply be two pits of mud. The floor of a paddling pool should be of small pebbles or at least have a textured finish, so that it does not become dangerously slippery. It should have a simple plug outlet in the bottom for quick emptying and cleaning.

Trees in the garden are a great boon for children, as they provide a support for swings, rope ladders, climbing structures and tree houses. A swing need be no more than a tough rope with a timber disc held by a knot at the end, and a tree house only a sturdy platform with a makeshift roof, perhaps made of rush matting. Check at frequent intervals that these structures are safe and that ropes are not fraying. All these playthings can of course be bought pre-fabricated but the children will probably prefer the rougher home-made sort which they can extend themselves when they grow older. Metal or timber play structures tend to be expensive and may be so obtrusive that they dominate the garden; they are best hidden away behind bushes. Standard play equipment is rarely necessary in the garden, however; the provision of a basic layout is enough as children will adapt this with astonishing inventiveness.

Children always like the secrecy of hidden play spaces but secret hideouts are rare in small gardens. However, slopes, banks, steps and the slightest suggestion of an enclosed area within the garden will satisfy the young child; overhanging branches or a fallen tree trunk can form a private play space.

An activity which often attracts the older child is gardening, and it is a good idea to provide a smaller space, perhaps even a single planting pot, in which they can grow flowers and possibly vegetables. It is best to choose flowers which bloom quickly, so that the child does not get bored, such as sunflowers (*Helianthus*), Virginia stock (*Malcomia*) and nasturtiums, all of which need an open, sunny position. Children might usefully be encouraged to grow gourds (*Curcurbita*) for decoration, or everlasting flowers (*Helipterum*) for drying.

Children delight in water games but they usually produce mud all over the garden. A home-made system of water channels here confines the mess to a play area

Imagination and inventiveness can turn common household objects into play equipment which is cheap and versatile. This rubber tyre sandpit can simply be abandoned when the child outgrows it

A simple, skilfully designed play structure can be a permanent asset in the garden. This sandpit forms a seat when covered which protects the sand from rain and stray cats

A single sturdy tree with branches conveniently placed for climbing and hanging ropes on will provide endless play opportunities for energetic children. The addition of a tree house creates a secret place, vital in imaginative games of all kinds

Play structures should be
simple in design and strong
enough to bear the heaviest
treatment. They should
stand on soft but resilient
ground to soften landings

The smallest of gardens
will have room for a swing,
hanging from a tree branch,
a house beam or a rough
timber frame. Check the
ropes and structure for
weakness and wear as often
as possible

# The contents of the toolshed

Good quality tools are an investment which should last indefinitely if they are kept in a suitable place and given proper care and cleaning. A dry storage area is essential and the larger it is the better. If you are lucky enough to have a garden shed you will undoubtedly want to expand it as you acquire extra tools, together with the inevitable collection of half-finished bags of fertilizer, piles of seed boxes and plant pots, all typical signs of an active gardener.

Shelves, hanging racks and a work top or table will be necessary; all tools last longer if they are hung up tidily than if piled on the floor. It is a good idea to build a high shelf out of the reach of children on which to store poisonous insecticides and toxic liquids; remember to keep all such substances clearly labelled to avoid accidents. An electric power point is a great asset as you will probably want to use power tools, either in the garden or in the shed itself, which may well be used for hobbies other than gardening—carpentry or welding, perhaps.

The contents of your toolshed will inevitably reflect your particular gardening interests. The basic implements fall into the rough categories of digging tools, cutting tools and cultivating tools which aerate and weed the soil. Most of these are shown in the illustration opposite. There are of course many other tools for specialist tasks and whether or not you need these depends on the nature of your garden. The storage space available will also influence whether or not you have larger items, such as a wheelbarrow. Large lawns, fruit trees and vegetable gardens in particular often call for special equipment—an irrigation system with sprinklers, perhaps, long-handled lopping shears for pruning trees or a pair of edging shears for lawns. An increasing number of these tools are power-driven; electric hedge-clippers and power lawn mowers are among the most common. However, in most small gardens, there will probably not be enough heavy work to justify the purchase of many expensive power tools.

It is worth buying high quality, well-finished tools with stainless steel blades; though they are expensive they will repay their cost with long service if you treat them with care. After use, scrape off the soil then wash and dry them. The metal parts can be wiped over with an oily rag, or even stored away wrapped in rags. In the winter, when you are less busy in the garden, spend some time doing maintenance work on your tools—mending the broken handle of a spade, oiling the spring on a pair of secateurs and sharpening the cutting edges on shears. New wooden handles can be bought ready whittled to fit into the metal heads of digging tools. Digging tools should be sharpened up occasionally too so that they cut through hard packed earth more efficiently.

This spacious garden shed contains all the essential requisites for the keen gardener, and others which are useful though optional. A line (1) for keeping planting rows straight and twine and labels (2) for tying back creepers and marking seedlings are always necessary. Secateurs (3) for pruning should be as large and strong as possible with a safety catch to hold the blades when not in use. A pressure spray gun, with carrying strap (4) is useful for spraying plants with liquid fertilizer or pesticides. Wash it out carefully after every use. Racks (5), for storing and drying fruit and bulbs, are easily constructed by the home carpenter, as are shelves for storing tools. A watering can (6) is vital. Tall canes (7) will support bean plants or drooping climbers. A hand fork and trowel (8, 9) are needed for planting bulbs and for weeding or planting in pots. The comb rake (10) is used for breaking down, clearing and levelling the soil, and making furrows for seeds. The wide-pronged lawn rake (11) will aerate turf and collect fallen leaves and grass mowings. A dibber (12) aids the planting of cuttings and young plants. The draw hoe (13) is a powerful tool for breaking up hard packed soil while the Dutch hoe (14) is pushed along the soil surface to cut down weeds. For digging and breaking up the soil, a spade (15, 16) and a fork (17) are necessary—try out several designs for weight and size before you buy them. You will need a broom of some sort and a twig one (18) is sturdy. A hose pipe (19), preferably of plastic which lasts longer than rubber, is indispensable and can be hung neatly on a rack. The sprinkler attachment (20) saves time and labour. Shears (21) should be kept well oiled and sharpened regularly. A wheelbarrow (22) can be used for building work as well as gardening. Lawn mowers (23) are becoming more sophisticated with rotary action blades and adjustable cutting heights

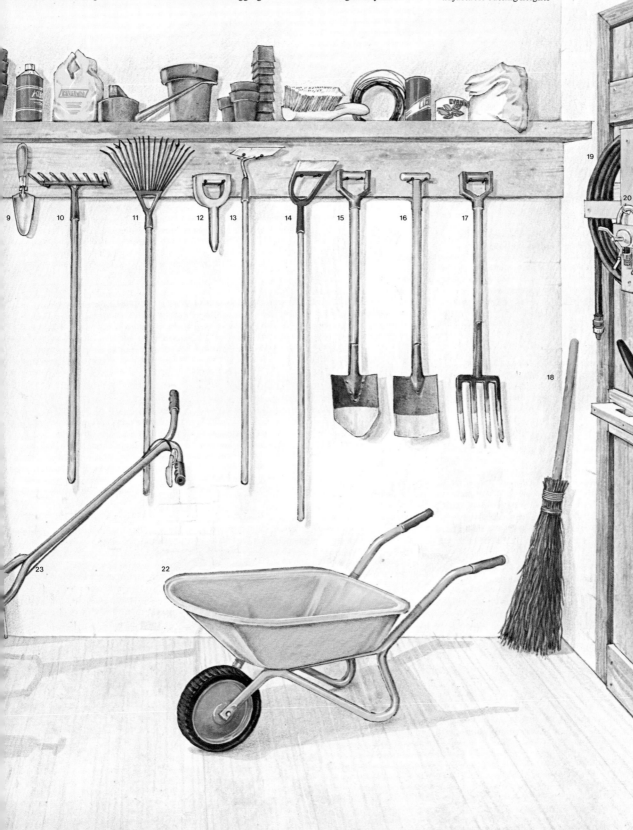

# Useful information

## THE LAW

When planning to create a garden or make improvements on an existing one, it is important to know the regulations and bye-laws, as they affect garden construction. Such laws vary according to the district and those mentioned here relate only to Great Britain.

If the scheme is ambitious and involves building or construction work, it will obviously need official approval. Such approval is two-fold: planning permission is concerned not only with individual plots but with the effect the proposed development might have on neighbouring properties and on the surrounding area; building regulations exist to safeguard standards of design, construction and materials. As individual cases vary it is useful to consult an architect or surveyor for advice on whether your proposal comes within either set of regulations.

Planning permission is required for improvements such as these:

1  A structure which comes in front of any wall of the existing house which fronts on to a public highway (apart from a small porch or hardstanding for a car).
2  Any alteration which involves new or changed access to a trunk or classified road, or to any road near a bend or junction; also any alteration which interferes dangerously with the sight-lines of drivers or pedestrians.
3  An extension to a house which has already been extended since 1 July 1948 or since the date of erection, whichever is the later.
4  An extension which is larger than one tenth the size of the house, larger than 50 cubic metres (65 cubic yards), or higher than the highest part of the existing roof.
5  A garden building more than three metres (ten feet) high, taking up more than half the area of the garden, or to be used for business purposes.

6  An oil storage tank holding 3,500 litres (850 gallons) or more, or one reaching over three metres (ten feet) in height.
7  Fences higher than two metres (six feet), or higher than one metre (three feet) when facing a road used by cars.

If your proposed alterations to house and garden avoid these seven listed categories then planning permission will not usually be required. But remember that the information given here is highly simplified and there are many other complications involved; for example, if your house was built after 1 July 1948 the planning restrictions may be more severe. The full regulations can always be inspected in the planning or development control section of your local council, and unless you feel fully confident that your alterations do not require planning permission, it is probably worth applying anyhow, since a written statement from the council that no approval is needed will settle the matter.

However, planning permission, or a statement that none is required, does not put you in the clear legally over restrictions which may be contained in the deed of purchase, infringements of neighbours' rights, or building regulations. With regard to the latter, detached, single-storey buildings such as summer-houses, tool sheds and greenhouses may be 'partially exempt' from building regulations. But, even in these cases, some form of 'notice' to the council about conditions which are relevant to fire safety, ventilation and similar aspects will usually be required.

The building regulations are complex and it is always a good idea to seek advice from the building control office of the council. If alterations are being made to a front garden, the council rules governing refuse collection may be important. For instance, some councils will not allow the dustmen to walk through a garage to get at the dustbins.

If your proposed structural alterations are ambitious you may well need professional advice from an architect, or a landscape architect, who will prepare the plans for you and guide them through the appropriate authorities. The R.I.B.A. at 66 Portland Place, London W1N 4AD (Royal Institute of British Architects) will be able to provide a list of local architects, and the names of local landscape architects are obtainable from the Landscape Institute (incorporating the Institute of Landscape Architects) which is at 12 Carlton House Terrace, London SW1Y 5AH.

Tree preservation orders are another aspect of the law which concerns the gardener. Sometimes individual trees are covered by preservation orders but often councils make 'blanket' orders on all the trees in a given area regardless of their conditions. If a tree covered by a preservation order is dead, dying or dangerous, it can usually be felled without reference to the council; it must however, be replaced by another tree of the same species in the same place. If you want to replace it by a different species or to change the site, or if you wish to fell a healthy tree covered by a preservation order, then you must apply for permission; each case is dealt with on its merits.

However, in a case where excessively large neighbouring trees or bushes are taking light from a window, there is a legal right to demand their thinning, felling or pruning. When a property is overhung by branches of trees from a neighbouring garden, the owner has the right to remove those which trespass his boundary line. It is usually considered that the maintenance of a party fence or boundary line is the responsibility of the householder on whose side the verticals or structural supports are found. The plan accompanying the deeds of the property will probably indicate such responsibility.

## EMPLOYING A LANDSCAPE ARCHITECT

If you want to employ a professional landscape architect to design or re-design your garden, the Landscape Institute will give you the names and addresses of members in your area. Members of the Institute are governed by a Code of Conduct, which determines any relationship with their clients.

The work of the landscape architect or designer involves studying the requirements of the client and his site, then advising and coming to an agreement with the client on a course of action which meets those requirements and the situation. He will then prepare a design and drawings as necessary. After further consultation with the client, the landscape designer will detail both constructional and planting aspects of the scheme and write a specification, before inviting tenders for the construction of the work. After discussion on the submitted tenders, he will act as the agent of his client in the direction and supervision of the work carried out by the selected contractor. The client himself should not give instructions directly to the contractor. Finally he will settle the financial account between the client and the contractor, acting as arbiter in any area of dispute.

The landscape architect's fee is worked out either on an agreed day rate or a lump sum for the initial work (up to the drawing up of a specification) then, when supervising the contractor's work, on a percentage of the final contract figure. These rates and percentages are on a sliding scale, comparable to other professional rates, and are laid out in detail by the Landscape Institute. Be prepared for the landscape architect or designer to ask for one third of his fee on the placing of a contract, another third after the construction work is done, and the balance when the job is completed.

The client should state from the outset how little or how much of the landscape designer's time or work he wants; it is important to adhere to what is decided, as alterations mean that the working programme is held up and the contractor may be late starting his next job. All decisions should be confirmed in writing.

### Employing a landscape gardener or landscape contractor

Some people prefer to go directly to a landscape contractor or gardener, many of whom offer a good design service as well. However, careful selection is advisable as some landscape gardeners have no design training or experience. If you are asking for design or layout work, check their proposal on a plan and, if you do not understand it, ask for a little elevation or sketch too, then go through it detail by detail on site. Ask for any quotations submitted for the proposed work to be itemized as far as possible, so that you know exactly how your money is being spent. Since the work is outdoors it is probably more economical to agree a lump sum for a particular job, than to pay on a day rate, when weather conditions may make it impossible for work to continue. Be prepared for a small firm to ask for some payment in advance, since even before the work begins they will have to buy paving, sand, cement and so on.

If you do not know of a recommended contractor or are new in the area, if is best to get quotations from several firms; the specification for the work must, of course, be the same for each and for this purpose, a drawing is very useful. Prices quoted on depth of excavation, hardcore, types of fertilizer, grass seed or manure also need careful checking and comparison. The quality of the paving slabs the contractor proposes using must be checked too, as the cheaper ones quickly crack.

It is quite usual, on payment to a contractor, to make a retention of about 10 per cent on his final contract figure, which is kept for one growing season. This ensures that he will rectify any sinkages in newly made up ground, for instance, or alter paving levels to improve surface drainage. Many reputable contractors will guarantee the replacement of any plant specimens which have died after their first season, provided they died through natural causes.

## WHERE TO FIND IT

Many garden centres can now supply nearly all the requirements for the average garden, from containers and statuary to peat and paving slabs, as well as an extremely wide selection of plants of excellent quality—especially those which are container grown. Sometimes, however, a specialist plant or commodity is wanted and some of the larger suppliers are listed below.

### Nurseries

Most general and specialist nurseries operate a mail order service and will send a catalogue on request.

The following general nurseries can be relied on for trees, shrubs, herbaceous plants, roses and fruit trees of high quality:
Clifton Nurseries, Clifton Villas, Warwick Avenue, London W9
Hillier & Sons, Winchester, Hants
Jackmans Nursery Ltd, Woking, Surrey
John Scott & Co, Merriot, Somerset
Notcutts Nursery Ltd, Woodbridge, Suffolk
Sunningdale Nursery Ltd, Windlesham, Surrey

### Unusual plants

Beth Chatto, White House Barn, Elmstead Market, Colchester, Essex
Bressingham Gardens, Diss, Norfolk
The Plantsmen, Buckshaw Gardens, Holwell, Sherborne, Dorset

### Bulbs

Broadleigh Gardens, Barr House, Bishops Hull, Taunton, Somerset
P. De Gaeger & Sons, Marden, Kent
J. A. Mars, Haslemere, Surrey
Peter Nyssen Ltd, Railway Road, Urmston, Manchester
Walter Blom & Son Ltd, Coomblands Nurseries, Leavesden, Watford, Hertfordshire

### Seeds

Samuel Dobie & Son, Upper Dee Mills, Llangollen, Denbigh
Suttons Seeds, London Road, Earley, Reading, Berkshire
Thompson & Morgan, London Road, Ipswich, Suffolk
W. J. Unwin, Histon, Cambridge

### Herbs

E. & A. Evetts, Ashfields Herb Nursery, Hinstock, Market Drayton, Shropshire
Old Rectory Herb Garden, Ightham, Kent
Tumblers Bottom Herb Farm, Kilmersdon, Radstock, Somerset

### Water plants

Perry's Hardy Plant Farm, Enfield, Middlesex
Stapeley Water Gardens, London Road, Stapeley, Nantwich, Cheshire

### Rose specialists

C. Newberry & Son, Bulls Green Nurseries, Knebworth, Hertfordshire
David Austin, Bowling Green Lane, Albrighton, Wolverhampton WV7 3HB
John Mattock Ltd, Nuneham Courtenay, Oxford

### Fruit tree specialists

Ken Muir, Honeypot Farm, Weeley Heath, Clacton-on-sea, Essex
Thomas Rivers & Son Ltd, The Nursery, Sawbridgeworth, Hertfordshire

### Hardy eucalyptus

Blue Gums, The Quarter, Lamberhurst, Tunbridge Wells, Kent

### Garden furniture and equipment

Hozelock Ltd, Haddenham, Aylesbury, Buckinghamshire (hoses, sprinklers etc.)
Room Outside, Goodwood Gardens, Waterbeach, Nr. Chichester, Sussex
Syon House Nurseries, Isleworth, Middlesex (furniture and garden tools)
The General Trading Company, 144 Sloane Street, London SW1 (furniture, tools, books)
Christopher Wray Plant Shop, 600 Kings Road, London SW6 (terracotta pots)

### Garden ornaments and containers

Anthony Mawley Ltd, PO Box 75, London SW1X 0LD
Chilstone Garden Ornaments, Sprivers Estate, Horsmonden, Kent
Haddonstone, The Manor, East Haddon, Northampton NN6 8BU
Seymours, Ewell, Surrey

### Tree surgery

Chichester Tree, The Mill, Beaulieu, Hampshire
K. Weyman, 15 Handel Close, Canon's Drive, Edgware
Southern Tree Surgeons Ltd, Horsham Road, Crawley Downs, Sussex

### Professional bodies and trade associations

The British Association of Landscape Industries, Hon. Sec. J. E. Parnham, North Lane Gardens, Leeds 8
The Cement and Concrete Association, 52 Grosvenor Gardens, London SW1
The Garden History Society, Hon. Sec. Mrs Mavis Batey, 12 Charlbury Road, Oxford
The Horticultural Trades Association, 18 Westcote Road, Reading, Berkshire
John Innes Institute, Colney Lane, Norwich NOR 7OF
The Landscape Institute, 12 Carlton House Terrace, London SW1 5AH
The Royal Horticultural Society, Vincent Square, London SW1P 2PE

# Bibliography

## General

Fish, Margery. *Gardening in the Shade*, David & Charles, Newton
  Abbot, 1972
Hellyer, Arthur. *The Collingridge Encyclopedia of Gardening*,
  Hamlyn, London and New York, 1976
Hellyer, Arthur and Kalmbacher, George. *The Color Guide to
  American Gardening*, Crown, New York, 1974
Hyams, Edward. *A History of Gardens and Gardening*, Dent, London, 1971
Jekyll, Gertrude. *On Gardening*, Studio Vista, London, 1966
Lloyd, Christopher. *The Well-tempered Garden*, Collins, London,
  1970 and Dutton, New York, 1971
Page, Russel. *The Education of a Gardener*, Collins, London, 1971
Reader's Digest. *The Gardening Year*, The Reader's Digest
  Association Ltd, London, 1974
Seddon, George F. and Rdecka, Helena. *Your Kitchen Garden*,
  Mitchell Beazley, London, 1975
Sitwell, Sir George. *On the Making of Gardens*, Duckworth, London,
  and Scribner's, New York, 1951

## Design

Allen, Marjory, Baroness Allen of Hurtwood, and Jellicoe, Susan.
  *The New Small Garden*, Architectural Press, London, 1956
Beazeley, Elizabeth. *Design and Detail of the Space Between
  Buildings*, Architectural Press, London, 1962
Brookes, John. *Room Outside*, Thames and Hudson, London, 1969
—*Improve your Lot*, Heinemann, London, 1977
Church, Thomas D. *Gardens are for People*, Rheinhold Publishing
  Corporation, New York, 1955
—*Your Private World: A Study of Intimate Gardens*, Chronicle
  Books, San Francisco, 1969
Crowe, Sylvia. *Garden Design*, Country Life, London 1958 and
  Hearthside Press, New York, 1959
Jellicoe, Geoffrey. *Studies in Landscape Design*, 3 vols, Oxford
  University Press, London and New York, 1960–70
—and Jellicoe, Susan. *Modern Private Gardens*, Abelard-Schuman,
  London and New York, 1968
Laurie, Michael. *An Introduction to Landscape Architecture*, Elsevier,
  London and New York, 1975
Wood, Dennis. *Terrace and Courtyard Gardens*, David & Charles,
  Newton Abbot, 1970

## Plants

Bean, W. J. *Trees and Shrubs Hardy in the British Isles*, vols 1 and 2,
  John Murray, London, 1970–73, Scribner's, New York, 1974
Colvin, Brenda. *Trees for Town and Country*, Lund Humphries,
London, 1965 and International Publications Service, New York, 1972
Fish, Margery. *Ground Cover Plants*, David & Charles, Newton
  Abbot, 1970
Hillier. *Hilliers' Manual of Trees and Shrubs*, Hillier and Sons, 1973
Lloyd, Christopher. *Foliage Plants*, Collins, London, 1973
Gault, S. Millar. *Dictionary of Shrubs in Colour*, Michael Joseph,
  London, 1976
—*The Color Dictionary of Shrubs*, Crown, New York, 1976
—and Synge, Patrick M. *The Dictionary of Roses in Colour*, Michael
  Joseph/Ebury Press, for the Royal Horticultural Society and the
  Royal National Rose Society, 1971
The Royal Horticultural Society. *Dictionary of Gardening*, 4 vols and
  supplement, Oxford University Press, Oxford, 1956–69
Reader's Digest, *Reader's Digest Encyclopedia of Garden Plants and
  Flowers, The*, Reader's Digest Association Ltd, London, 1975
Thomas, Graham Stuart. *Colour in the Winter Garden*, Dent,
  London and Branford, Newton Center, Mass., 1967
—*Plants for Ground Cover*, Dent, London and Branford, Newton
  Center, Mass., 1970
Wyman, Donald. *Shrubs and Vines for American Gardens*,
  Macmillan, New York, 1969
—*Wyman's Gardening Encyclopedia*, Macmillan, New York and
  London, 1971

# Glossary

## PRACTICAL GLOSSARY

**Ashlar blocks** Stone which is dressed and squared up and used as a facing to a backing wall. Ashlar blocks are laid in courses with thin joints. Tie-stones are incorporated to improve the bond with the backing.
**Battered** Sloping inwards from the perpendicular.
**Bevel** A corner or edge that has been cut or planed (or shaped) at an angle. A chamfer is a bevel at 45°.
**Bolster** A wide-bladed steel chisel used for 'cutting' bricks.
**Bond** An interlocking arrangement of bricks (or stones) laid in courses in mortar to provide strength. There are various standard patterns, such as English bond, Flemish bond, stretcher bond.
**Coping** Weathering to the top of a wall usually made of brick, stone or concrete, and designed to throw off water.
**Coursed rubble** The technique of building walls of stones roughly shaped but laid in courses of 300–450mm (1–1½ft) wide.
**Efflorescence** Soluble salts found in some clay bricks which crystallize on or near the surface as moisture dries out. The salts may reappear for some years (usually in the spring) and wash off naturally and slowly diminish. It can in certain circumstances be serious and affect the stability of a wall, but this is not usually the case.
**Grout** A thin fluid mortar which is used to fill the joints between paving after it has been laid.
**Honeycomb wall** A wall bond (usually stretcher bond) with gaps left between the bricks.
*In situ* 'On site' i.e. not pre-fabricated.
**Loggia** A covered, open-sided arcade or gallery.
**Pointing** Raking out the mortar joints as the work proceeds and then filling in the mortar afterwards.
**Random rubble** The technique of building walls of stones roughly shaped but laid 'uncoursed'.
**Reconstituted stone** Blocks made from crushed stone and concrete. Usually the blocks have a concrete core with a facing of crushed stone.
**Skew-nail** Nailing at an angle to the surface. By skew-nailing in alternate directions a 'positive' fixing is obtained.
**Tie-stones** Stones laid across a wall to improve stability and strength. They may be 'headers', which are over half the thickness of the wall, or 'throughs' which are the full thickness of the wall.
**Unwarped** Condition of timber that has not distorted during seasoning either across the width or in its length.

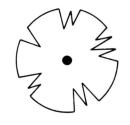

**Tree**

**Tall Shrub**

### The garden plans

In the two-dimensional plans which accompany the gardens featured on pages 110–175 two main symbols (above) are used: tree and tall shrub. These are in outline only, in order that lower-growing plants can be shown underneath.

Other plants, whether shrubs, perennials or climbers, are indicated by areas of solid colour with an outline characteristic of the plant's own shape. Coloured dots indicate flower colour, where the plants were in flower at the time the garden was photographed. Annuals, which do not form part of the permanent planting, are not usually included on the plans.

The numbering, which always starts on the left of the house, or the main entrance to the garden, refers to the accompanying plant list.

# PLANT GLOSSARY

**Acid** (of soils) Peaty and sandy soils are generally acid in character. Acid soils have a measurable pH recording below 6.5.

**Aeration** Breaking up of solidly packed soil which allows air to reach plant roots. In turf aeration is generally done by inserting a fork or spiking machine into the sward, yet not disturbing it.

**Alkaline** Chalk, limy and clay soils are alkaline in character. They have a pH level higher than 6.5.

**Annual** A plant that germinates, grows, matures, flowers, sets and ripens seed, and then dies within one growing season.

**Biennial** A plant that germinates, grows and produces a plant that is capable of surviving an inclement season then flowers, sets and ripens seed in the following year before it dies.

**Bonemeal** The residue of slaughterhouses, being the ground bones of animals that have been slaughtered for meat. The 'meal' is spread lightly on the ground to become a slow-acting fertilizer.

**Bract** A modified leaf, usually found at the base of a flower or flower cluster, often brilliantly coloured, and acting in the same way as a petal.

**Bulb** A plant food storage organ, found at or below ground level, by which certain plants survive inclement seasons. The bulb is formed from modified swollen leaf bases.

**Capsule** A dry seed container, often formed from several fused individual sections.

**Catkin** The male flowers of some wind-pollinated trees.

**Cluster** A grouping of flowers, leaves or fruits.

**Columnar** A plant of slender, narrow habit. This shape is common in coniferous plants.

**Compound** A leaf composed of two or more similar parts.

**Conical** A plant having a cone-like shape.

**Conifer** A plant bearing cones, generally tree-like and wind-pollinated. A primitive flowering plant.

**Cordon** A method of training fruit trees, by planting at an angle. Such trees are small in size, due to their having been grafted on to a dwarfing rootstock and are ideal for the small garden. The fruit buds are initiated more freely by this method of training.

**Corm** An underground storage organ to enable a plant to survive an inclement season. The corm is formed from swollen stem bases.

**Cultivar** A plant variety that has either been specially bred by hybridists, or has occurred spontaneously in a garden.

**Deciduous** A plant (generally a tree or shrub) that loses its leaves in winter.

**Digitate** (of leaves) With the members arising from one point.

**Downy** A plant with soft hairs, generally most noticeable on the foliage.

**Drift** An informal planting where there are no straight lines. The term is often used to describe groups of plants in grass or between shrubs.

**Espalier** A tree with all its branches trained in horizontal lines, and growing against a fence or wall.

**Evergreen** A plant that holds its leaves throughout the year.

**Fertile** (of soils) A well-cultivated soil to which rotting compost, peat, leaves and fertilizers have been added regularly.

**Filament** The stem portion of a stamen, the male organ of the flower, usually long, thin and relatively colourless.

**Form** A wild variant of a plant, that will come true from seed, providing that no cross-pollination with differing variants has taken place.

**Friable** A soil that has been well cultivated, that is neither wet and sticky nor hard and dry, but crumbles up when lightly handled.

**Genus** A sub-division of the plant kingdom in which the general characteristics of a group of plants are all very similar. The first name in the botanic description is the genus or generic name, for example, *Wistaria, Rosa, Jasminum*.

**Globular** A plant of dense habit and rounded shape.

**Glossy** (of leaves) Having a shiny surface.

**Half-standard** A tree growing with a trunk no more than 1m (4ft) high.

**Herbaceous** A plant that dies down to the ground during an inclement season (usually winter) and survives as a perennating rooted bud.

**Humus** Rotting vegetation which, when incorporated into the soil by either natural means or by digging, improves soil fertility.

**Hybrid** A plant produced from the crossing of two separate parents, generally within the genus, certainly within the family.

**Inflorescence** A spike of, or an individual, flower.

**Lanceolate** Lance-shaped, considerably longer than wide.

**Leaflet** Individual part of a compound leaf.

**Leaf-mould** Decaying fallen leaves that have been left for a period of time to break down.

**Leathery** (of foliage) Smooth, hard and slightly glossy.

**Loam** A soil of fine grain, with a high fibrous content.

**Lobe** The natural rounded protruding part of a plant organ.

**Manure** An additive, generally rotted farmyard manure, used to improve soil fertility.

**Maritime** (of plants) Enjoying coastal areas, adapted to strong winds and salt spray.

**Neutral** Soil having a pH level of 6.5. The majority of plants will grow in this soil.

**Ovate** Broadest below the middle (like an egg).

**Palmate** (of leaves) Deeply divided and more or less hand-like, generally 5- or 7-lobed.

**Panicle** A branching raceme.

**Peat** The compressed and slightly rotting remains of a sphagnum moss or sedge bog, or the debris from under a bracken stand. Of the three sphagnum is the best and most expensive. It is sterile, holds a great deal of moisture and rots slowly. Sedge peat is cheaper, but rots more quickly and is slippery. Bracken peat is the cheapest, but has to be sorted for bracken rhizomes. It makes an excellent top dressing to keep weeds down and conserve moisture.

**Perennial** see Herbaceous.

**Petal** An organ forming part of the flower, often brightly coloured, protecting the sexual parts, and helping to attract insects.

**Pinnate** With leaflets arranged either opposite or alternately on a central stalk.

**Plume** A feathery flower head.

**Pollard** An old method of tree pruning, whereby all growths are cut back to a pre-determined point annually.

**Pollen** Dusty secretion from the stamens, generally yellow, orange, white or brown.

**Pollinator** An insect or bird which in the course of collecting nectar transfers pollen from one flower to another.

**Prune** The removal of unwanted growth, usually old, sometimes dead or diseased, or weak, to encourage the production of healthy vigorous flowering shoots.

**Raceme** A long unbranched cluster of flowers, either upright or pendulous.

**Resin** The waste product of many trees, especially conifers, produced to protect a wound.

**Rhizome** A creeping underground stem, often thick and swollen.

**Runner** A slender stem, rooting at intervals.

**Serrated** Edged with forward-pointing teeth.

**Shrub** A woody plant, distinct from trees in having more slender branches, often originating at or below ground level. Shrubs may be evergreen or deciduous.

**Species** A plant type, sub-division of a genus, with constant and distinct characteristics.

**Stamen** The pollen-bearing part of a flower.

**Standard** A tree with a clear trunk of at least 2m (6ft) to the head.

**Stolon** A stem from a plant base, rooting at the tip when it touches the soil.

**Stool** A propagation method whereby shoots or branches are pegged below the soil to root.

**Sub-shrub** A plant with a persistent woody base and soft shoots that tend to die back in winter.

**Sucker** A shoot arising from the underground parts of the plant.

**Tendril** A modified leaf used by the plant for support.

**Thinning** The removal of plant material (shoots, flower buds or fruits) to encourage better size and quality in the remainder.

**Toothed** Having indentations in the margin.

**Trifoliate** Bearing three leaves.

**Tuber** A swollen underground stem, usually with buds, for example, potato.

**Tubular** Tube-like in shape.

**Turfing** Making a lawn by laying evenly flat and square or oblong pieces of grass, usually raised elsewhere.

**Twining** A stem with twisting habit, enabling the plant type to use other plants, canes or poles for support.

**Umbel** A flower head of stalked flowers arising from a single point.

**Variegation** Colouring on foliage, generally yellowish or whitish and usually in lines, spots or splashes.

**Variety** A plant of distinct type or habit, usually a sub-division of a species, but not sufficiently variable for specific rank.

**Whorl** A ring of plant organs all on one level.

# Index

A separate plant index begins on page 252

*Page numbers in **bold** refer to photographs or illustrations*

# Plant index

# Acknowledgments

We should like to thank Clifton Nurseries of London, Michael Dawes, Erica Hunningher, Paul Miles, Ian Mylles, Garry Porter and Geoffrey Smith for their help and advice. Thanks are also due to Chivers Flowers (house plants), Robert Dyas (garden tools), A. Baveystock & Co Ltd (garden furniture) and to all the people who allowed their gardens to be photographed for this book.

Special thanks are due to illustrators Chris Forsey and Michael Woods for their particular contribution

t = top b = bottom l = left r = right c = centre

## ARTISTS

22 Richard Gliddon (l);
Chis Forsey (br)
23 Richard Gliddon (t,bl);
Chris Forsey (t,br)
24 Richard Gliddon (t,bl);
Chris Forsey (t,br)
25 Richard Gliddon (t,bl);
Chris Forsey (t,br)
26 Richard Gliddon
27 Michael Woods
28 Ray Burrows
29 Michael Woods
30–31 Eugene Fleury
32 Peter Morter
33 Kevin Maddison
34 Kevin Maddison
35 Richard Gliddon (tr);
Kevin Maddison
36 Richard Gliddon
38–41 Richard Gliddon
45 Coral Mula
47 Coral Mula
48–51 Michael Woods
54–55 Coral Mula
57 Kevin Maddison
58–59 Michael Woods
63 Trevor Vertigan
65 Coral Mula (bl);
Michael Woods
68–69 Coral Mula
70–71 Michael Woods
73 Richard Gliddon (t);
Norman Barber/Linden
Artists (b)
75 Richard Gliddon
77 Terry Allen Design Ltd
80 Richard Gliddon
82 Chris Forsey
87 Richard Gliddon
88–89 Coral Mula
91 Richard Gliddon
92–93 Michael Woods
110 Chris Forsey (t);
Peter Saag (b)
113 Jim Marks
116 Virginia Nokes/
B. L. Kearley Ltd
118 Chris Forsey (l);
Peter Saag (r)
121–122 Richard Gliddon
127 Chris Forsey (t);
Peter Saag (b)
129 Richard Gliddon
131 Peter Saag
133 Trevor Vertigan (t);
Chris Forsey (b)
137 Peter Saag
139 Virginia Nokes/
B. L. Kearley Ltd
140 Richard Gliddon
143 Peter Saag (l);
Chris Forsey (r)
145–146 Richard Gliddon
149 Peter Saag
151 Chris Forsey (t);
Peter Saag (b)
153 Jim Marks
155 Peter Saag
157 Peter Saag (bl);
Chris Forsey (t)
161 Richard Gliddon
163 Chris Forsey (t);
Richard Gliddon (b)
164 Richard Gliddon
165 Peter Saag
166 Richard Gliddon
168 Chris Forsey (r);
Richard Gliddon (l)
170 Richard Gliddon
171 Peter Saag
172 Richard Gliddon
175 Chris Forsey (t);
Trevor Vertigan (b)
183 Richard Gliddon
190–199 Norman Barber/
Linden Artists
200–201 Ingrid Jacob
202–205 Prue Theobald/
B. L. Kearley Ltd
206–207 Peter Morter
208–211 Ingrid Jacob
212–213 Norman Barber/
Linden Artists
214–215 Prue Theobald
B. L. Kearley Ltd
216–217 Norman Barber/
Linden Artists
218–224 Prue Theobald/
B. L. Kearley Ltd
231–233 Kevin Maddison
235 Paul Kern/
B. L. Kearley Ltd
244–245 Chris Forsey

## PHOTOGRAPHERS

1–3 Steve Bicknell
4–5 Steve Bicknell
Pamla Toler
6–7 Steve Bicknell
8–9 Roger Phillips
10 Michael Holford (t);
Victoria and Albert Museum (b)
11 Michael Holford (l)
Transworld (r)
12 Mauro Pucciarelli
13 Spectrum Colour Library (l);
National Trust (tr);
Edwin Smith (br)
14–15 Architecture and
Landscape Library
15 Elsa M. Megson (t);
Douglas Dickins (b)
16–17 Wolfram Stehling
17 IMS (t); Carla de Benedetti (b)
18 Photo Palot (t);
Syndication International/
Clifford Jones (b)
18–19 Transworld (t);
Wolfram Stehling (b)
19 Wolfram Stehling
20 Elizabeth Whiting/
Jerry Tubby
20/21 Morley Baer/**designer**
Brad Bowman

21 IMS (l); Wolfram Stehling
(tr); Picturepoint (b)
26 Soil Survey of England and
Wales
34 Pamla Toler (l);
Syndication International (r)
35 Susan Griggs/Michael Boys (l)
Steve Bicknell (r)
37 Han Njio
38 Steve Bicknell
38–39 Ianthe Ruthven
39 Susan Griggs/Michael Boys
40–41 Steve Bicknell
42–43 Roger Phillips
44 Michael Warren
46 Peter Stiles (tl);
A–Z Collection (tc); Paul Miles
(tr, cl, c); Elly Arnstein/
Tony Timmington (cr); Steve
Bicknell (bl); Michael Warren
(bc); Bill McLaughlin (br)
49 Michael Warren (r);
Ronald Adams Associates (b)
50–51 A–Z Collection
51 Molly Adams
52 Wolfram Stehling (t, br);
Paul Miles (bl)
53 Michael Warren
54 Steve Bicknell
54–55 Steve Bicknell (t);
Elizabeth Whiting (b)
55 Transworld
56 Tiofoto (t); Wolfram
Stehling (bl); Michael Warren
(br)
56–57 Jerry Tubby
57 Steve Bicknell
58 Carla de Benedetti
59 Cement and Concrete
Association
60 Harry Smith (t);
Paul Miles (b)
61 Walter Bauer (t);
Elly Beintema (b)
62 Roger Perry
62–63 Steve Bicknell (t);
Elizabeth Whiting/Jerry Tubby
(b)
63 Steve Bicknell (l);
Michael Warren (r)
64 Michael Warren
66 Michael Warren (l);
Bill McLaughlin (r);
Steve Bicknell (c)
66–67 Tiofoto
67 Steve Bicknell (l); Zefa (r);
The Picture Library/Nick Holt
(b)
68 Michael Warren (t);
Steve Bicknell (b)
68–69 Steve Bicknell
69 Steve Bicknell (t);
Molly Adams (b)
70 Horst (tl); Steve Bicknell
(r); Transworld (c)
70–71 Molly Adams
71 Wolfram Stehling
72 Wolfram Stehling (l);
Brecht-Einzig (r)
72–73 Cement and Concrete
Association
74 Wolfram Stehling
74–75 Wolfram Stehling
75 Steve Bicknell (t, c);
Keith Winnett (b)
76 Susan Griggs/Michael Boys
(t); Brigitte Baert (b)
77 Elizabeth Whiting/
Steve Colby
78–79 Paul Miles (t);
Steve Bicknell (b)
79 Frank Pettersson (l);
IMS (r); Steve Bicknell (b)

80 Pamla Toler
81 Steve Bicknell (t);
Wolfram Stehling (bl, br)
82 Wolfram Stehling (t);
IMS (b)
82–83 Paul Miles
83 Steve Bicknell (t);
Paul Miles (b)
84 Steve Bicknell (tl, 2nd from
tr, 3rd from tl); Michael
Warren (tr, 2nd from tl);
Susan Griggs/Michael Boys
(bl); Molly Adams/**landscape
architect** Nelva Weber (br)
84–85 Wolfram Stehling
85 Wolfram Stehling (t);
Steve Bicknell (b)
86 Wolfram Stehling
86–87 IMS
87 Ruth Rutter (t);
Camera Press (b)
88–89 Muriel Orans
89 Wolfram Stehling (t);
Steve Bicknell (bl);
Elly Beintema (br)
90 Transworld
91 Paul Miles (t);
Steve Bicknell (2nd from t, b);
Molly Adams (3rd from t)
92 Ruth Rutter
93 Steve Bicknell
94–95 Roger Phillips
96 Daily Telegraph
96–97 Pamla Toler (t);
Brigitte Baert (b)
97 Carla de Benedetti (t);
Elizabeth Whiting/Graham
Henderson/**designer** Nicholas
Hills (c); Wolfram Stehling (b)
98 Steve Bicknell (l);
Susan Griggs/Michael Boys (r)
98–99 Elizabeth Whiting/
Michael Nicholson
99 IMS (t, c); Pamla Toler (b)
100–101 Michael Boys
101 Ruth Rutter (t);
John K. B. Cowley (bl);
Elizabeth Whiting (br)
102 Elizabeth Whiting/
Tim Street-Porter
103 Nico Vink (tl); Tania
Midgley (tr); Richardsons (bl);
Michael Warren (b)
104 Nelson Hargreaves (br, t);
Elizabeth Whiting/Jerry Tubby
(bl)
104–105 Brigitte Baert
105 Steve Bicknell (t);
Helle Borup/**landscape architect** Prof. Th. Sorensen (b)
106 Michael Warren
106–109 Steve Bicknell
110–111 Michael Warren
112–113 Pamla Toler
114–115 IMS
116 Bill McLaughlin
117–121 Steve Bicknell
122 Rolf Muller
123 Jerry Tubby
124–125 Pamla Toler
126 Keith Winnett (t);
Michael Warren (b)
127 Michael Warren
128–135 Steve Bicknell
136–137 Morley Baer
138–140 Steve Bicknell
141 Michael Warren (t);
Nelson Hargreaves (b)
142–143 Michael Warren
144–145 Bill McLaughlin
146 Syndication International
147–149 Steve Bicknell
150–151 Ianthe Ruthven

152 Michael Warren
152–153 E. Beedham
153 E. Beedham
154–155 Han Njio
156–157 Wolfram Stehling
158–159 Ianthe Ruthven
160–161 Frank Pettersson
162–163 Transworld
164 Pamla Toler
165–172 Steve Bicknell
173–175 Ianthe Ruthven
176 Wolfram Stehling (t);
Molly Adams (b)
176–177 Molly Adams
177 Wolfram Stehling (t);
Ianthe Ruthven (c);
Jerry Tubby (b)
178 Camera Press (t); Harry
Smith (c); Pamla Toler (b)
178–179 Spectrum
179 E. Beedham (t);
Brian Furner (c);
A–Z Collection (b)
180–181 Steve Bicknell
182 Michael Warren
182–183 Steven Bicknell
184 Michael Warren
185 Steve Bicknell
186 Michael Warren
186–187 Steve Bicknell
187 Steve Bicknell (l, br);
Michael Warren (tr)
188 Michael Warren (tl, tr);
Steve Bicknell (b)
189 Michael Warren (l, tr);
Nelson Hargreaves (br)
226–227 Roger Phillips
228 Carla de Benedetti
228–229 Elizabeth Whiting
229 Carla de Benedetti (t);
Jerry Tubby (c);
Brigitte Baert (b)
230 Steve Bicknell (tl);
Wolfram Stehling (bl);
Susan Griggs/Michael Boys
(br)
230–231 Susan Griggs/
Michael Boys
231 Michael Warren
232 Le Creuset (t); Zefa (c);
Wolfram Stehling (b)
232–233 Daily Telegraph
234–235 Brecht-Einzig
235 Michael Warren (t);
Steve Bicknell (2nd from t);
IMS (3rd from t); Brecht-
Einzig (b)
236 Key I. Nilsen (t);
Ruth Rutter (bl); Zefa (c);
Steve Bicknell (br)
237 Steve Bicknell (tl, cr);
Ianthe Ruthven (tr);
Michael Warren (bl, br)
238 Steve Bicknell (t, bl);
Susan Griggs/Michael Boys
(br)
238–239 Paul Miles
239 Wolfram Stehling (c);
Syntax Films/Philip Pank (bl);
The John Hillelson Agency/
Tony Ray-Jones (bc); Syndi-
cation International (br)
240 Steve Bicknell
240–241 Wolfram Stehling
241 Carla de Benedetti (tr);
Morley Baer/**designer** Brad
Bowman (cr); Wolfram
Stehling (bl)
242 Wolfram Stehling (tl);
Elizabeth Whiting (tr);
Steve Bicknell (b)
242–243 Roger Perry
243 Wolfram Stehling